Contemporary Issues and Challenges in HRM

Second Edition

Peter Holland
Cathy Sheehan
Ross Donohue
Amanda Pyman
Belinda Allen

Contemporary Issues and Challenges in HRM
2nd edition, 1st printing

Author
Peter Holland, Cathy Sheehan, Ross Donohue, Amanda Pyman & Belinda Allen

Cover designer
Christopher Besley, Besley Design.

ISBN: 978-0-7346-1109-3

Copyright

Text copyright © 2012 by The Tilde Group.
Illustration, layout and design copyright © 2012 by The Tilde Group.

Under Australia's *Copyright Act 1968* (the Act), except for any fair dealing for the purposes of study, research, criticism or review, no part of this book may be reproduced, stored in a retrieval system, or transmitted in any form or by any means without prior written permission from The Tilde Group. All inquiries should be directed in the first instance to the publisher at the address below.

Disclaimer

All reasonable efforts have been made to ensure the quality and accuracy of this publication. Tilde University Press assumes no responsibility for any errors or omissions and no warranties are made with regard to this publication. Neither Tilde University Press nor any authorised distributors shall be held responsible for any direct, incidental or consequential damages resulting from the use of this publication.

Published in Australia by:
Tilde University Press
PO Box 72
Prahran VIC 3181 Australia
www.tup.net.au

ABOUT THE AUTHORS

Associate Professor Peter Holland

Peter Holland is Associate Professor in Human Resource Management and Employee Relations in the Department of Management at Monash University in Melbourne, Australia. Peter has worked in the Australian Finance industry and consulted to the private and public sector in a variety of areas related to human resource management and employee relations. His current research interests include talent management, employee voice and monitoring and surveillance in the workplace. He has co-authored 8 books and over 60 journal articles, monographs and book chapters on a wide range of human resource management and employee relations.

Dr Cathy Sheehan

Cathy Sheehan is a Senior Lecturer within the Department of Management at Monash University and an active member of the Australian Centre for Research in Employment and Work (ACREW). Cathy has taught across the areas of Accounting, Management and more recently HRM and International HRM. Resultant publications have appeared in the *International Journal of Human Resource Management, Personnel Review* and the *Asia Pacific Journal of Human Resources,* plus her recent co-authored text *Contemporary Issues and Challenges in HRM,* as well as numerous media citations.

Dr Ross Donohue

Ross Donohue is a Senior Lecturer in the Department of Management at Monash University. He is a registered psychologist and a member of the Australian Psychological Society. His current research interests relate to personality-environment fit and career change, the influences of emotional intelligence and transformational leadership on career advancement, psychological contracts and organisational justice, and the predictors of organisational commitment. Ross has published in leading international journals such as the *Journal of Vocational Behavior* and the *Journal of Employment Counseling,* and has authored book chapters on careers and employment.

Dr Amanda Pyman

Amanda Pyman is a senior lecturer in Human Resource Management and Employee Relations in the Department of Management at Monash University. Prior to joining Monash, Amanda worked as a lecturer in the Kent Business School, University of Kent in the UK, and also held the roles of

Deputy Director, MBA Programmes and Director, Athens MBA Programme. Amanda has published widely in leading international journals including the *British Journal of Industrial Relations*, *Human Resource Management* and *Economic and Industrial Democracy*, in addition to contributing to several books. Amanda's current research interests include: employee voice, union renewal strategies in a comparative perspective and privacy in the workplace.

Dr Belinda Allen

Belinda Allen is a Lecturer in the Department of Management at Monash University. Prior to that she was a research fellow and lecturer at Melbourne University. She is currently involved in a longitudinal Australian Research Council (ARC) project examining the effects of job changes on wellbeing and occupational drift amongst nurses in the aged care sector. Belinda regularly presents her research findings at prominent international conferences, and has also published articles in several leading international journals including *Work, Employment & Society* and the *British Journal of Industrial Relations*.

Contents

Preface i

Chapter 1: The Brave New World of Virtual Work 1
    Working virtual 1
    Prevalence of teleworking 2
    Modes of teleworking 3
    HRM implications of teleworking 9
    Virtual teams 10
    HRM implications for virtual teams 14
    Conclusions 15
    References 16
    Case study: Lost in translation – The outsourcing of clinical letters 20

Chapter 2: Managing the War for Talent 23
    Attraction and retention – a theoretical perspective 24
    Talent management and the demographic time-bomb 25
    The Australian hegemony 28
    Box 2.1: Talent Trove 31
    Case study: Talent management in practice 36
    Box 2.2: HR checklist 38
    Summary 41
    References 41
    Case study: AgencyCo 47

Chapter 3: Offshoring: Reflections and New Directions 49
    What is offshoring? 50
    The rise of offshoring 50
    The rationales for outsourcing and offshoring 52
    Barriers and implications of offshoring 54
    Emerging issues: Onshoring and near-shoring 61
    Conclusions 64
    References 65
    Case study: Offshoring Coles Myers Credit Card 67

Chapter 4: ICT and Employment: Challenges and Future Directions 70
    eHRM 71
    Box 4.1: Boots - Driving benefits from online recruitment 74
    Box 4.2: The importance of strategic integration - an online application blunder in the UK 75
    Social networking and HRM 77
    e-Unionism 80
    Box 4.3: Innovation with ICT - The Workers Independent News (WIN) 84
    Issues and challenges of e-unionism 85
    Future directions 92
    Conclusions 93
    References 93
    Case study: Electronic Solutions 98

Chapter 5: Psychological Contracts 100
Formation of the psychological contract 101
Types of psychological contracts... 102
Employers' perspective of the psychological contract 104
Psychological contract breach 104
Psychological contract violation... 106
Psychological contract fulfilment 107
Work status and the psychological contract 108
Implications for human resource management 110
Conclusions 114
References.. 115
Case study: Should I stay or should I go?... 119

Chapter 6: Career Management in the 21st Century..................................... 122
Traditional perspectives of career development 122
Environmental and individual changes 123
Contemporary career perspectives 125
Human resource management and career management 128
Conclusions 134
References.. 134
Case study: Becoming protean 139

Chapter 7: HRM and Service Work 142
The rise of service work 142
What is service work? 143
HR challenges and opportunities in the services sector 145
Managing the consequences of services sector work 148
Conclusions 151
References.. 152
Case study: Maintaining service quality in the wedding business 155

Chapter 8: Managing Emotional Labour in the Workplace........................... 157
Emotion and emotional labour... 157
Employee reactions.. 160
What can HR do to manage emotional labour requirements? 162
Conclusions 168
References.. 169
Case study: Emotional stress in call centres 172

Chapter 9: Employee Health and Well-Being in the Workplace 174
Health and well-being 175
Organisational predictors of employee health and well-being............. 177
Individual employee health and well-being consequences................... 179
Organisational health and well-being consequences 180
Employee health and well-being interventions...................................... 181
Conclusion 184
Case study: MV Health 185
Overview case:.. 188
Understanding the work environment 188
Case study: Just managing.. 188
References.. 191

Chapter 10: Trade Unions and the New Workplace 195
Australian unions in decline 196
Australian union strategies in the new workplace 205
Box 10.1: The building blocks of Unions@Work 209
Box 10.2: Future strategies 210
Box 10.3: Future strategies: Australian unions – Working for a better life 212
Union innovation under a hostile legislative environment: 1997-2006 213
Future issues 222
Conclusions 223
References 223
Case study: James Hardie 232

Chapter 11: The Contested Terrain of Monitoring and Surveillance in the Workplace 237
Drug-testing in the workplace 238
eCommunication in the workplace 244
The issue of electronic surveillance at work 245
The issue of control 246
Box 11.1: The Ansett case 247
Monitoring and surveillance in the Australian workplace 248
Policy development and monitoring and surveillance 249
Box 11.2: Federal Privacy Commission guidelines on information technology and internet issues 250
Emerging issues 252
Box 11.3: RFID implant scheme 252
Box 11.4: You bet your life: health insurer's cheap DNA test could prove costly 254
Conclusions 255
References 255
Case study: BHP Pilbara mines 258

Chapter 12: Risk and Crisis Management 263
The process for managing risk 264
Approaches to risk 266
Crisis management 269
Box 12.1: Valuable lessons in adversity 269
Terrorism 274
Pandemics 276
Conclusions 279
References 280
Case study: The Beaconsfield Mine disaster 283

Chapter 13: The Greening of Skills in the 21st Century 286
Defining green skills 286
Developing green skills – a theoretical perspective 287
Developing green skills – a historical perspective 288
Developing green skills – a policy perspective 290
Box 13.1: Setting price will create '34,000 jobs' 291
Developing green skills – an industry perspective 292
Developing green skills – a practical perspective 293
Box 13.2: Growth spurt for green jobs 294

Developing a framework for green skills 296
　　Developing green skills – a case study perspective 297
　　References 298
Chapter 14: Justice at Work 301
　　Justice at work – A theoretical perspective 302
　　The concept of organisational justice 303
　　Contextual factors 305
　　References 306
Index 309

PREFACE

In researching the field of human resource management and employee relations we have become ever-more aware of the complex and rapidly changing nature of these disciplines. For example, when completing the first edition of this book, the concept of social networking was a curious issue developing out of a need for people to keep in touch using increasingly sophisticated technologies. Today, social networking is an important aspect of many people's day-to-day lives and has migrated into the workplace with organisations using these technologies to communicate with current employees and attract new ones. It has also led to employment conflict, with organisations sanctioning and dismissing employees for posting comments about their work and workplace. It is therefore critical for human resource and employee relations specialists to understand the issues associated with the development of work and non-work in cyberspace.

In teaching such contemporary issues to advanced level undergraduates and postgraduate students, we have become aware of the difficulties and challenges in prescribing a book that addresses these topics from a critical perspective as well as providing 'real-world' case study examples that highlight and further explore underlying issues. This gap has been the catalyst for this book. The text sets out to critically analyse contemporary and emerging issues in the workplace, an approach absent in many textbooks that favour a more functional structure. In attempting to capture the dynamics of the workplace, we think this issues-based approach provides students and academics with an understanding of the key contemporary challenges associated with how we work and how the workplace needs to be managed. This book, therefore, aims to fill a gap in the treatment of human resource and employee relations issue in the workplace. In reflecting on the dynamic nature of the changes we have seen in the workplace, this second edition includes four new chapters on crisis and risk management, health and well-being, green skill and organisational justice.

Finally, we would like to acknowledge the publisher, Rick Ryan, who had the foresight to see the potential of this book and the confidence to back the author team in the book's development and delivery.

Peter Holland, Cathy Sheehan
Ross Donohue, Amanda Pyman
Belinda Allen, July 2011

Chapter 1

THE BRAVE NEW WORLD OF VIRTUAL WORK

INTRODUCTION

Over the preceding two decades, business has become increasingly competitive, complex, interdependent and global. During this period there have also been significant advances in information and communication technology (ICT) with the advent of products and services such as email, high-speed broadband internet, intranet networks, mobile phones, virtual chat rooms, video-conferencing, voice-over-internet protocol (VoIP), and wireless networks. These changes have created a paradigm shift in where and when work is undertaken. From global call centres servicing industry – which has grown faster than any other sector to service a 24/7 global economy to virtual teams and individuals teleworking – technology has affected all aspects of the way we work. However, the omnipotence and acceptance of these fundamental changes often happens without more detailed and critical consideration of the actual issues these new work arrangements create. This chapter explores the key aspects of these new work arrangements and uses examples to illustrate issues that managers – and in particular HR managers – need to consider in order to gain effective advantage from these new ways of working.

Working virtual

A number of different terms have emerged to describe virtual work, including: telecommuting, remote working, and distance working. These terms are being used more and more in the literature to describe flexible alternative work arrangements. More recently, the term *teleworking* has become the more generally accepted name for this mode of work. Virtual work is typically denoted by two characteristics: (1) conducting work outside of the traditional workplace; and (2) utilising information technology and telecommunication equipment (Lundber & Lindfors 2002). Thus, teleworkers are employees who work away from their usual place of work during normal business hours with the assistance of some form of communication technology. Often teleworkers allocate their time between office and home, however this mode of work also encompasses working at multiple offices or other remote locations (Golden, Veiga & Simsek 2006). While those engaging in telework differ considerably in terms of their demographic characteristics, typically the profile of a teleworker is a high income, well-educated male working as an independent professional (Bailey & Kurland 2002).

Prevalence of teleworking

While there are problems associated with how telework is operationalised and measured, there is evidence to indicate that its incidence is increasing. In 2005 a study commissioned by the Australian Federal Government (Sensis 2005) found that 30 per cent of Australians who were either employed or operated their own business reported that they had teleworked to some extent. A more recent study (Sensis 2007) indicated that 22 per cent of Australian small- to medium-sized enterprises reported that their employees teleworked in 2007. It would appear that the proliferation of teleworking is a global phenomenon. In the UK it has been estimated that there are currently 3.8 million full-time teleworkers, with 5.5 million people operating remotely for at least a proportion of their working week (Point-Topic 2005). According to Kersley, Alpin, Forth, Bryson, Bewley, Dix and Oxenbridge (2006), approximately 14 per cent of UK employees reported that teleworking was available at their workplace. Similarly, in the US the number of employees who worked from home or remotely at least one day per month rose from approximately 12.4 million in 2006 to 17.2 million in 2008. The rise in the number of teleworking employees represents a two-year increase of 39 per cent and a 74 per cent increase from 2005 when there were approximately 9.9 million employees teleworking in the US. These figures exclude contract teleworkers (i.e. self-employed and business owner teleworkers). Including both employee and contract teleworkers, approximately 33.7 million Americans worked remotely at least one day per month in 2008, increasing by 17 per cent (from 28.7 million) since 2006 (WorldatWork 2009). The findings of a recent survey published by the US Office of Personnel Management (2011) indicated that 113,946 US Federal employees teleworked in 2009, increasing by 11,046 employees when compared to 2008.

However, some researchers have questioned how extensively teleworking is utilised in organisations. For example, Davenport (2005) found that less than 10 percent of teleworkers were engaged in full-time arrangements and that among those employees who did telework, part-time arrangements were the norm. Wells (2001) examined the teleworking practices in Fortune 1000 companies in the US and found that, while most companies offered this type of alternative work arrangement, only 1 to 5 per cent of their employees actually took advantage of it. According to Wells, the under-utilisation of teleworking by employees can largely be explained by the reluctance of management to embrace these new practices – which is often based on issues of trust and control.

Modes of teleworking

In organisations where 'hotdesking' and 'hotelling' are used, employees who are not always physically present are not assigned fixed office space. Rather, these workers share their desks or workspace with other colleagues whose work also requires that they are frequently out of the office. The word 'hotdesking' is believed to be derived from the navel term 'hotracking' where sailors on different watches would share bunks. Some have suggested that it euphemistically refers to the fact that the office chair is still warm from the body heat of the earlier occupant. Companies that use hotdesking include: IBM, Ernst and Young, and Accenture (Cascio 1999). In some organisations where 'hotelling' is used there is a concierge, and teleworkers need to book ahead in order to reserve an office. Prior to the arrival of the teleworker, the concierge changes the nameplate on the office door and replaces the files and personal effects of the previous occupant with those of the arriving teleworker.

Potential advantages of teleworking

Given the skill shortages in many sectors and the 'war for talent' (see *Chapter 2: Managing the War for Talent*) that is currently being waged, where organisations vie to attract the best and brightest employees, flexible working arrangements such as teleworking can provide companies with a competitive advantage. Thus, by providing flexible work arrangements such as teleworking, organisations are able to market themselves as 'employers of choice' and thereby attract and retain employees with high market power who are seeking greater autonomy (Morgan 2004). This view is supported by empirical research examining organisational attractiveness. For example, Heyman and Van Hoye (2005) conducted a study involving 201 Belgian graduate students who were asked to evaluate recruitment advertisements that made no mention of telework as well as recruitment advertisements that listed teleworking as a possibility. The study findings indicated that applicants were more attracted to organisations offering teleworking than those where the opportunity for teleworking was not explicit in the recruitment advertisement.

Telework and other flexible workplace practices such as flexitime and spatial decentralisation have been found to be positively related to firm performance (Sanchez, Perez, de Luis Carnicer & Jimenez 2007). For example, IBM experienced productivity gains of 15 per cent to 40 per cent after introducing telework. Similarly, US West reported that the productivity of some employees who switched to teleworking increased by as much as 40 per cent, and Hewlett-Packard doubled revenue per sales person following a transition to a telecommuting environment (Cascio 1999).

It would also appear that teleworking can engender positive attitudes and behaviours in employees. Golden (2006) examined the organisational commitment and turnover intentions of 393 professional-level teleworkers employed by a company that produced internet solutions for commercial and individual clients. It was found that a higher degree of teleworking was associated with greater commitment to the organisation and reduced intention to leave. Golden concluded that by providing the flexibility of teleworking opportunities, employees perceived that the organisation demonstrated both trust and concern for their welfare. In turn, these employees reciprocated by decreasing their turnover intention and increasing their commitment. Teleworking has also been linked to reduced absenteeism According to the findings of a study undertaken by the International Teleworking Association and Council (ITAC 2007), organisations can reduce the costs associated with absenteeism by 63 per cent per teleworker. The costs – US$2,086 per employee per year – were determined based on the average number of days absent on which teleworkers were still able to work from home.

Another organisational benefit of teleworking is the cost savings that flow from not having to provide office space and parking for all workers. These costs can be quite substantial. Indeed, it has been estimated that firms in the US spend over US$240 billion on office space (Helms & Raiszadeh 2002), and the average cost of providing a workstation in the central business district in Sydney is approximately $7,930 per year (DTZ Research, 2006). Additionally, there is some evidence to suggest that offices within organisations are often under-utilised, with research indicating that up to 50 per cent of workspaces are not in use at any given time during business hours (ITAC 2007).

Undertaking telework has also been found to provide a number of positive outcomes for the individual workers themselves. One of the most important advantages of teleworking is that it provides employees with greater flexibility as it affords them greater opportunity to structure their employment to accommodate other aspects of their life such as family commitments. Indeed, a number of studies have indicated that teleworking provides individuals with the opportunity to balance the competing demands of work and family (Rau & Hyland 2002; Stephens & Szajna 1998). However, teleworking may not be the panacea for achieving work-life balance and in fact it appears to impact differentially. For example, a recent study of 454 professional-level teleworkers (Golden, Veiga & Simsek 2006) found that the more extensively participants engaged in this mode of work, the lower the likelihood of work-to-family conflict (WFC) was. Interestingly though, the more extensively that participants teleworked, the greater was the probability of family-work-conflict (FWC) occurring. Thus, the study indicated that the more that individuals telework, the less work interferes with family (reduced WFC) and the more family interferes with work (FWC). Teleworkers with small children also report that they found it difficult balancing child-rearing with work (Kinsman 1987).

Teleworking may also improve individual productivity. For example, research indicates that teleworkers report experiencing greater control over their workflow as well as fewer unanticipated interruptions or intrusions into their work when compared with traditional workers (Kurland & Eagan 1999; Watson Fritz, Narasimham, & Rhee 1998). Similarly, 87 per cent of employees involved in IBM's alternative workplace program reported that they believed their efficiency and productivity had increased significantly (Apgar 1998). However, the findings of these studies should be interpreted with some caution as they were based on self-reported data rather than objective measures of productivity.

Working remotely may also improve individual well-being and health. For example, Lundberg and Lindfors (2002) examined psychophysical arousal in a group of white-collar professionals while working in different environments. Specifically, they found that stress levels were higher for participants while working at the office than working at home (teleworking). Employees who telework tend to experience more positive work attitudes, are more likely to feel in control of their personal lives, and report higher job performance, motivation, and intention to remain with their organisation than employees who work in traditional offices (Hill, Ferris, & Martinson 2003).

Some studies (McCloskey & Igvaria, 1998) have found that telework is positively related to job satisfaction, however in their review of the literature Bailey and Kurland (2002) questioned this finding. Specifically, they concluded that there was no clear evidence that teleworkers experience greater job satisfaction when compared with their traditional counterparts. These inconsistent findings may be accounted for by recent evidence that suggests that the relationship between telework and job satisfaction is complex and non-linear. For example, Golden (2006) found a curvilinear relationship (an inverted U-shaped relationship) between the degree to which employees engaged in telework and their levels of job satisfaction. This suggests that while minimum to moderate levels of teleworking promotes job satisfaction, when the extent of teleworking becomes extensive, job satisfaction declines. This outcome may be explained by the findings of a previous study (Golden & Veiga 2004) which indicated that when employees engage in moderate levels of telework, they are able to derive the maximum benefit from electronic communication tools. This in turn reduces their sense of isolation and frustration, while simultaneously increasing their feelings of independence and job satisfaction. However, it would appear that intensive utilisation of electronic communication tools, required when extensively teleworking, increases the potential for these employees to feel remote and frustrated, leading to lower job satisfaction. Additionally, Golden (2006) found that while the extent of telework did not negatively impact on the quality of interactions with managers, this was not the case for interactions with co-workers and family. Similar to job satisfaction, curvilinear relationships were found between the degree to which employees engaged in telework and the quality of interactions with colleagues and family (i.e. interactions with co-workers and family were favourable at low to moderate levels of teleworking, however, as teleworking increased, the quality of these interactions decreased).

Disadvantages of teleworking

One of the major disadvantages of teleworking is the social isolation and reduced sense of belonging that comes from working predominantly alone with limited opportunity to interact with co-workers face-to-face. In fact, some teleworkers report feeling as though they are outsiders whenever they enter their organisation to complete on-site tasks (Harpaz 2002). Nonparticipation by teleworkers at their actual worksite can deny these individuals the crucial sense of identity that results from being physically present and interacting with colleagues in a work context (Landy & Conte 2010). Diminished opportunities for face-to-face interactions means that it is more difficult for teleworkers to transmit, maintain and receive instantaneous feedback and affective cues. Often teleworkers indicate that they are perceived by their traditional counterparts as only having part-time status due to the fact they are infrequently in the workplace. Teleworkers are also often left out of office networks and therefore are not privy to the daily informal information flows and discussions within the company. Access to this type of tacit knowledge is essential in terms of guiding one's political behaviour and career advancement. Moreover, the career advancement of teleworkers is further inhibited by the fact that they are often out of sight and therefore are not recognised for their achievement nor given interesting assignments. Research indicates that employee visibility, including engagement in organisational politics, is positively related to managerial advancement (Perin 1991).

A potential negative corollary of the flexibility and autonomy that comes with teleworking is the lack of differentiation between work and leisure time. The blurring of the boundary between these two domains occurs because both work and many non-work activities are co-located in the home. Research suggests that these diffuse boundaries causes teleworkers to experience both guilt over neglecting family responsibilities as well as discomfort over the loss of the feeling that home is a refuge from work (Gurstein 1991). Additionally, this lack of separation may cause a spillover of work into family life leading to the disruption of time patterns in household routines (Habib & Cornford 1996), or a spillover of family life into work with reduced efficiency resulting from family members making constant demands on the teleworker's time (Harpaz 2002).

Another disadvantage of teleworking is the cost associated with setting up a home office compliant with occupational health and safety regulations. Organisations are responsible for the safety and welfare of all of their employees, irrespective of where the work is conducted. A health and safety audit is required in order to determine that the home office is free from hazards and that the workstation is ergonomically sound. Many organisations seek to avoid the costs of complying with occupational health and safety regulations, which has given rise to a variant of teleworkers known as 'teleguerillas'. Teleguerillas are employees who engage in telework informally, with the unofficial sanction of their organisation. There is evidence which also suggests that teleworking may reduce safety costs and workers compensation claims. Kugelmass (1996) reports on modelling undertaken by consultants Arthur D. Little Associates which estimates that if 12 per cent of the US workforce teleworked regularly, work-related accidents would be reduced by 1.6 million cases and there would be 1,000 fewer traffic accidents.

The final negative consequence of teleworking is that it may impinge upon an individual's need for personal space in the workplace For example, in 1994 the advertising firm TBWA Chiat/Day switched to a virtual work environment and introduced non-territorial offices. This involved the creation of a completely open-plan workplace where workstations were obtained on a 'first-come, first-served' basis. This had the unforeseen consequence of causing the employees to feel as if they had no private space within the building and led to a number of unproductive and dysfunctional behaviours. For example, workers would waste time queuing to book out equipment, and people began hiding their personal belongings in corners of the workspace and making personal telephone calls from under desks. One of the first employees to have her desk removed brought a little red wagon into work to hold her files and possessions. In the mornings this employee would drag the wagon around the workspace until she found a vacant workstation (Berger 1999). Eventually, senior management at TBWA Chiat/Day recognised the need for personal space and redesigned the workspace so that each employee had their own private area – referred to as a 'nest' – which housed employees' telephones, laptop computers and personal belongings.

Personality traits and telework

There is some evidence to suggest that not all employees are well suited to telework and that certain personality traits may be predictive of success in this context. The dominant approach in personality research for the last two decades has been Costa and McCrae's (1992) 'Big Five' theory which holds that dispositions can be described in terms of five key dimensions: sociability (i.e. extraversion), agreeableness, conscientiousness, emotional stability and openness to experience.

Individuals who score high on sociability typically seek out social interactions with others and do not enjoy being alone. Consequently, employees who are extraverts may not be well suited to teleworking due to the limited opportunity for face-to-face engagement with their colleagues, and these individuals may be predisposed to feeling isolated. Indeed, research undertaken by Feldman and Gainey (1997) indicated that employees who scored high on sociability were prone to becoming frustrated with telework, and Fireman (1998) found that the desire for social interaction was positively related to withdrawal from teleworking arrangements.

Telework also requires employees to be self-disciplined and reliable, able to organise and prioritise their tasks, and willing to accept personal responsibility for their output. Accordingly, one may expect that individuals who are high on the personality dimension of conscientiousness are more likely to be attracted to telework and perform well as teleworkers. Interestingly, the empirical research evidence examining conscientiousness and telework has yielded mixed findings. For example, a study undertaken by research consultants Pearn Kandola found that teleworkers demonstrated higher levels of personal organisation than non-teleworkers (Conlin 2009). Also, Barrick, Mount and Strauss (1993) found that employees who scored high on conscientiousness were more likely to engage independently in goal–setting behaviours and to work assiduously towards achieving those goals. A recent study undertaken by Renn, Allen and Huning (2011) indicated that low conscientiousness was associated with poor self-management practices, an inability to delay gratification, and procrastination. Additionally, Wayne, Musisca and Fleeson (2004) found that conscientiousness was related to less work-family conflict, and the authors concluded that individuals who scored high on this personality dimension were able to use their superior organisational skills to make more efficient use of their time. However, O'Neill *et al.* (2009) found, contrary to their expectation, that diligence (one component of conscientiousness) was not related to teleworker performance. Moreover, while this study indicated that organisational skills (the second component of conscientiousness) was predictive of teleworker performance, there was no significant difference between the organisational skills of teleworkers and non-teleworkers. Consistent with the finding of O'Neill *et al.*, Da Silva and Virick (2010) found that teleworkers were no more likely to be conscientious than their non-teleworking colleagues.

Telework is a relatively nascent and atypical work arrangement requiring flexibility and innovation from employees working in this mode. As a result, some authors (e.g. Lamond, Daniels & Sanden 2003) have argued that individuals who score high on the personality dimension of openness to experience are better suited to telework than their closed counterparts. These authors base this proposition on the fact that individuals who are open to experience are adventurous, inquisitive when confronted with new situations, adaptable and unconventional. Conversely, those who are closed to experience prefer familiarity, avoid ambiguous situations and are resistant to change. Research undertaken by Gainey and Clenney (2006) provides some support for this proposition, as they found that openness to experience was the only personality dimension among the Big Five that was significantly related to positive attitudes towards teleworking. Specifically, this study indicated that individuals who scored higher on openness to experience were more likely to hold favourable views towards teleworking than those who scored lower on this personality dimension.

Comparatively, less emphasis in the literature has been placed on the personality dimensions of agreeableness and emotional stability in relation to telework. Individuals who score high on agreeableness tend to be cooperative, trusting and generous, while those with low scores tend to be self-focused and sceptical of others' motives. High scores on emotional stability reflect a tendency to be even-tempered and confident, while low scores indicate a tendency to be sensitive and nervous. While limited, research suggests that employees who score high on agreeableness and/or emotional stability may be better suited to telework than employees who score low on either of these dimensions. Offsten, Morwick and Koskinen (2010) found that teleworkers' level of agreeableness was a better predictor of whether telework assignments were likely to succeed or fail than the technical ability of teleworkers. Additionally, Clarke (2007) found that both agreeableness and emotional stability were positively related to favourable attitudes towards telewoking.

HRM implications of teleworking

There are a number of human resource management initiatives that may improve the well-being and productivity of teleworkers. Specifically, HR managers should attempt to address the potential cultural resistance to telework. Many managers still employ a 'line-of-sight' management style, lack training in managing teleworkers, and generally are sceptical of the benefits of flexible work programs. A survey of 600 employees and managers from both Australia and New Zealand found that more than half of employees in the sample believed that their managers were less trusting of flexible workers, and 75 per cent believed that colleagues disapproved when they were sometimes away from the office. In workplaces without flexible work arrangements, 75 per cent of managers indicated they would be unlikely to allow employees to telework (Sweeney Research 2004). This type of resistance to telework should be addressed through education and information programs aimed at providing a rational business case for the practice.

Much of the scepticism and negative views regarding telework are related to the fact that the productivity of these workers is often difficult to measure. Traditional productivity metrics may not apply, and therefore HR managers need to redesign their business processes and rethink their control, measurement, and evaluation processes (Helms & Raiszadeh 2002). For example, given that telework is conducted remotely and the teleworkers' behaviours are not observable, performance should be assessed according to their output rather than time spent on the job. A recent study indicated that managers who are teleworkers themselves and those who supervise teleworkers hold more favourable attitudes towards teleworking than managers who do not telework nor supervise teleworkers. Additionally, this study found that, as managers become more involved in teleworking, they tend to develop increasingly favourable attitudes towards this practice (Telework Exchange and the US Federal Managers Association 2007).

Given that Golden (2006) found curvilinear relationships between the extent of teleworking and outcomes such as job satisfaction and quality of interactions with both co-workers and family, HR managers should limit the degree to which employees telework. Based on his findings, Golden recommended that the optimal extent to which employees should engage in telework is approximately two days per week. This level of teleworking enables employees to capitalise on the benefits of this alternative work practice, while minimising the potential negative impact on job satisfaction and their relationships with colleagues and family.

Research examining the personality characteristics of employees that are predictive of suitability for telework is too scant and the findings too inconsistent to draw definitive recommendations. However, there is some evidence to suggest that, when selecting employees for teleworking roles, choosing those who are high on openness to experience and/or low on sociability may provide more suitable candidates. While research undertaken outside the telework domain (i.e. with general employees) indicates that conscientiousness is the most valid dispositional predictor of job performance (Schmidt & Ryan 1993), the findings in relation to conscientiousness and telework success are equivocal. Additionally, too few studies have been conducted examining both emotional stability and agreeableness in relation to telework to make even tentative recommendations.

Research into the relation between the five-factors model and personnel hiring provides additional evidence that conscientiousness is the most valid predictor of job performance (Schmidt & Ryan, 1993).

Virtual teams

Virtual teams are distributed work groups whose members utilise electronic media in order to communicate and organise their work (Hertel, Geister, & Konradt 2005). Virtual teams apply this mediating communication technology to transcend spatial, temporal and organisational structures. These teams are formed when several teleworkers are combined into a group, with each member reporting to the same manager (Lipnack & Stamp 1997).

With increasing numbers of organisations forming strategic alliances, coupled with the necessity for greater inter-organisational cooperation, virtual teams have become more commonplace. While there are some virtual teams where all members are geographically dispersed and members communicate exclusively via electronic means, most virtual teams engage in at least some level of face-to-face contact.

Advantages of virtual teams

There are a number of benefits that organisations can accrue by implementing virtual teams. One of the major advantages of virtual teams is that they provide organisations with a high degree of flexibility and responsiveness. Virtual teams can be rapidly constituted, organised and then disbanded when a project is completed or when the needs of a dynamic marketplace change (Jarvenpaa & Leider 1999).

Another clear advantage that organisations can derive from the application of virtual teams is that they enable organisations to utilise the most qualified employees for a particular task – irrespective of their location. Additionally, in terms of cost saving, organisations can reduce expenses on travel, accommodation and other costs associated with conducting business face-to-face – whether inter-state or internationally – by utilising virtual teams (Arnison & Miller 2002). Virtual teams also allow cross-functional coordination of activities which lead to synergetic interactions between parties, rather than duplicating activities or working at cross-purposes. Virtual teams similarly facilitate the sharing of knowledge because new information and skills can be disseminated in each member's workgroup, department or organisation.

One company that has utilised virtual teams very successfully is VeriFone, which produces 'swipe' machines and software that reads credit card details. VeriFone employs more than 3,000 workers operating from different locations around the world and has been using virtual teams since the company's inception in 1981. In the data security industry in which VeriFone operates, being 'first to market' with a new product is a primary goal. At VeriFone this is described as 'the culture of urgency', and having distributed teams helps give the company its competitive advantage. This is achieved by utilising a process referred to as 'follow-the-sun technology', which works in the following way. In India, VeriFone's software development group develops new software code, and then at the end of their day the Indian developers send the new code electronically to engineers in Dallas in the US for testing where the workday is just beginning. After the engineers in Dallas have completed the testing at the end of *their* workday, the code is sent to Hawaii – where it is morning – to then be integrated into the software. Thus, by applying this follow-the-sun strategy, VeriFone is able to accomplish within one and a half days a process that would normally require three days to complete.

This follow-the-sun approach is also being utilised by Australian organisations which have been able to capitalise on the fact that normal Australian business hours cover the non-business hours in Europe and the US. For example, Melbourne-based GKN Aerospace Engineering is one of 19 Australian firms that have recently begun collaborating with Lockheed Martin's facility in Texas and Northrop Grumman's plant in California in order to develop the new Joint Strike Fighter for the US Air Force. Using a similar process to that used at VeriFone, employees at GKN Aerospace Engineering work on the common design system of the aircraft during Australian office hours after their counterparts in the US have finished work for the evening. According to Lockheed Martin, the major partner in this consortium, utilising this follow-the-sun approach has resulted in a 22 per cent improvement in manufacturing time for composite components for the aircraft (Jay 2005).

Another potential organisational benefit of virtual teams is knowledge sharing throughout various company sites. Knowledge is a critical resource which allows organisations to gain a competitive advantage. Virtual teams provide an ideal context to share information among geographically dispersed members, who in turn can disseminate this knowledge to their co-located colleagues who are outside the virtual teams. Edwards and Wilson (2004) argue that virtual teams, by their very nature, are required to document information and electronically share it internally for the purposes of collaboration. Consequently, this knowledge can be easily leveraged by sharing it more broadly at each virtual team member's worksite, thereby increasing organisation-wide knowledge.

Virtual teams may also provide a number of benefits to members. Specifically, members of virtual teams often experience high levels of task variety as they are frequently assigned multiple projects involving disparate tasks. This varied experience also leads to the development of new skills which in turn improve their employability. Another advantage of virtual teams, given their often heterogeneous composition, is that they provide employees with the opportunity to work with individuals who may be very different from themselves. Talented people prefer working on challenging assignments with people from diverse backgrounds. A final advantage of virtual teams is that members are not required to relocate in order to be involved in a project (Arnison & Miller 2002). Ties to a particular location may be an important factor in terms of predicting internal mobility, as research examining intra-company transfers found that approximately 65 per cent of the companies surveyed reported employee resistance to geographic moves (Employee Relocation Council 1993).

Disadvantages of virtual teams

One negative consequence of working in virtual teams is that there is a greater likelihood of misunderstanding occurring as a result of communicating via mediated technology such as email. Discussions conducted via email lack the subtle nuances and visual cues that accompany verbal, face-to-face interactions, and research indicates that individuals interpret email statements more harshly and pejoratively than if that same statement were made face-to-face. As virtual teams generally transcend functional, organisational and geographical boundaries, members often have little in common in terms of their work history, cultural background, values and work norms (Maruping & Agarwal 2004). While this diversity may improve creativity, innovation and problem solving, it can also create tension. Research indicates that homogenous teams are more cohesive, and experience significantly less intra-group conflict than teams comprised of diverse members (Staples & Zhao 2006). Virtual team members are more prone than members of co-located teams to forming incorrect judgements about other members' behaviour (Cramton 2002). Additionally, virtual teams may not be as effective in high-context cultures as they are in low-context cultures. In high-context cultures, such as those in Asia, often what is not said is more important than what is said, and much greater emphasis is placed on interpreting verbal cues than in low-context cultures such as those found in Australia and the US (Cascio 1999).

Trust is an important requirement for any team; however, it is particularly important in virtual teams as members do not have regular face-to-face interactions. Face-to-face interactions tend to engender and promote trust because this medium provides a richer information context than electronic communication (Platt 1999). Interestingly, however, a number of studies have found that virtual teams experience high levels of trust soon after group formation. This phenomenon is referred to as 'swift trust' (Meyerson, Weick & Kramer 1996). Swift trust occurs in virtual teams because time pressures reduce the capacity of team members to form expectations based on first hand experience. As a consequence, members of virtual team impute expectations of trust from other familiar contexts. High activity and involvement by members in the early stages of a virtual team's development sustains the trust. However, because the trust is not based on valid, first hand information but rather is imputed, it often is fragile and susceptible to violation (Jarvenpaa & Leider 1999).

Some studies have also suggested that members of virtual teams are more prone to dysfunctional behaviours such as low individual commitment, role overload, role ambiguity, absenteeism and social loafing (O'Hara-Devereaux & Johansen 1994). Another potential disadvantage of virtual teams is that, due to their transitory nature and shifting team membership, customers may perceive that both the team and its product lack permanency, reliability and consistency (Mowshowitz 1997).

Having a distributed workforce also creates new challenges and risks in terms of data and network security. Members of virtual teams frequently need to access information stored on their organisation's private network using public networks such as the internet. The fact that organisations have to provide 'gateways' for off-site workers to gain access compromises the integrity of their private network as it also provides an entry point for individuals with malicious intent such as hackers. Security concerns also extend to the fact that sensitive and proprietary information often resides on virtual employees' storage devices. This remotely-stored information often lacks the same level of security afforded to information stored internally, and is much more vulnerable to inappropriate access resulting from human error. For example, a senior member of the Australian Defence Force investigating the bungled return of Private Jake Kovco's remains from Iraq was censured after leaving a highly sensitive document relating to the case in a Qantas Club computer at Melbourne airport (Nicholson & Schuber 2006).

HRM implications for virtual teams

Organisations can implement a number of HR practices to improve the success of virtual teams. During the selection process for determining the membership of virtual teams, consideration should be given to each candidate's personality profile. Individuals with certain personality characteristics – for example lack of impulse control, poor self-monitoring skills, low emotional intelligence, and poor self-discipline – are often not suited to working in virtual teams. Additionally, given the importance and fragility of trust in virtual teams, HR managers should attempt to assist with intra-group team development interventions designed to improve openness and group cohesion. Additionally, as new members enter the team they should be provided with induction and orientation to the group in order to facilitate their socialisation and assimilation (Bell & Kozlowski 2002).

In terms of performance management, members of virtual teams should not only be assessed in terms of their task performance but also in terms of their contextual performance. Task performance is what is typically assessed in performance appraisals and involves activities that produce the organisation's goods and services as well as activities that service and sustain the technical core (e.g. planning, coordinating, supervising). According to Motowidlo, Borman and Schmit (1997), however, the second component of performance is contextual performance, which involves activities (e.g. organisational citizenship behaviours, supporting colleagues, following the rules) that maintain the organisational networks and climate that *surround* the technical core. Specifically, members should be assessed in terms of how they managed stakeholder relationships, their communication skills, and how they positively contributed to team functioning.

Members of virtual teams require access to knowledge in order to function effectively, and therefore HR managers should also attempt to reduce the barriers to information sharing. This may involve a range of activities such as establishing staff discussion forums on the organisation's intranet, collecting and disseminating information, publicising HR practices and initiatives online, or encouraging virtual team members to provide presentations to colleagues from their departments on 'lessons learned' from the project.

Conclusions

Alternative work arrangements such as teleworking and virtual teams have arisen due to the combined effects of globalisation and advances in ICT. Telework involves work that is undertaken at a remote location with the assistance of ICT. While estimates of the prevalence of teleworking are confounded by definitional and measurement inconsistencies, it would appear that increasingly greater numbers of individuals are working under these arrangements. Teleworking may provide a number of positive organisational benefits such as the attraction and retention of talent, improved firm performance, increased commitment, lower absenteeism costs, and reduced workspace costs. Similarly, teleworking may engender a range of positive benefits for the workers themselves such as greater flexibility, improved work-life balance, increased productivity, and reduced stress levels. However, research also indicates that teleworking may be related to negative outcomes such as increased isolation, more diffuse boundaries between work and leisure, and increased costs associated with setting up a remote office. In terms of the implications of teleworking for human resource management, HR practitioners should attempt to address the possible resistance and scepticism of supervisors who still subscribe to the "if you're not at your desk, you're not working" management style. Additionally, HR managers should ensure that performance management systems are refined to accommodate teleworkers by focusing on measuring outputs rather than completion times.

Virtual teams are workgroups comprised of members who are often not co-located and who use mediating technology to overcome organisational, temporal and geographical barriers. By utilising virtual teams, organisations can improve their flexibility and responsiveness, increase organisational knowledge sharing, save on travel expenses, improve coordination and increase synergetic interactions, and reduce production times. Involvement in virtual teams also provides members with benefits such as increased task variety, skill development, the opportunity to work with diverse colleagues, and reduced likelihood of relocation. Virtual teams, however, also carry risks and potential negative outcomes such as a greater probability for misunderstanding, increased intra-group conflict, incongruence with high-context cultures, the development of swift but fragile trust, increased likelihood of dysfunctional behaviours, and security concerns. In order to improve the effectiveness of virtual teams, HR managers should ensure that the selection involves an assessment of potential team members' personality characteristics. In terms of assessing performance, HR managers should focus not only on the task performance of virtual team members, but also on their context performance as this may impact significantly on team cohesion and conflict. Finally, HR managers should attempt to reduce the impediments to knowledge sharing within the organisation as the 'stock in trade' of virtual teams is information.

References

Apgar, MI 1998, 'The alternative workplace: Changing where and how people work', *Harvard Business Review*, May–June, 121–136.

Bailey, DE & Kurland, NB 2002, 'A review of telework research: Findings, new directions, and lessons for the study of modern work', *Journal of Organizational Behavior*, 23: 383-400.

Barrick, MR, Mount, MK & Strauss, JP 1993, 'Conscientiousness and performance of sales representatives: Test of the mediating effects of goal setting', *Journal of Applied Psychology*, 78: 715-722.

Bell, BS & Kozlowski, SW J 2002, 'A typology of virtual teams: Implications for effective leadership', *Group and Organization Management*, 27: 14-49.

Berger, W 1999, *Lost in space*, Wired, 7, viewed 9 March 2007, <http://www.wired.com/wired/archive/7.02/chiat_pr.html>.

Cascio, WF 1999, 'Virtual workplaces: Implications for organizational behavior', in CL Cooper & DM Rousseau (eds), *Trends in Organizational Behavior*, 6: 1-14.

Clark, LA 2007, Relationships between the Big Five personality dimensions and attitudes toward telecommuting. Unpublished doctoral dissertation, Southern Illinois University.

Conlin, M 2009, 'Chatty workers actually are best telecommuters', *Business Week*, viewed 12 March 2011, http://www.msnbc.msn.com/id/31428341/ ns/business-management_101/.

Costa, PT & McCrae, RR 1992, Revised NEO Personality Inventory (NEO PI-R) and NEO Five-Factor Inventory (NEO-FFI) - professional manual. Lutz, FL: Psychological Assessment Resources.

Cramton, CD 2002, 'Attribution in Distributed Work Groups', in PJ Hinds & S Kiesler (eds), *Distributed Work*, MIT Press, Cambridge, MA, USA.

Da Silva, N & Virick M 2010, *Facilitating telecommuting: Exploring the role of telecommuting intensity and differences between telecommuters and non-telecommuters*, MTI Report No. 09-14, Mineta Transportation Institute College of Business.

Davenport, T 2005, *Rethinking the mobile workforce*, viewed 10 February 2011, http://www.optimizemag.com/article/showArticle.jhtml?printableArticle= true&articleId=166402970.

DTZ Research 2006, *Global office occupancy cost survey*, 9th edn, January 2006.

Edwards, A & Wilson, JR 2004, *Implementing Virtual Teams: A Guide to Organizational and Human Factors*, Grower, Burlington, VT.

Employee Relocation Council 1993, *1993 Relocation Trends Survey*, Employee Relocation Council, Washington, DC.

Feldman, DC, & Gainey, T W 1997, 'Patterns of telecommuting and their consequences: Framing the research agenda' *Human Resource Management Review* 7: 369–389.

Fireman, S 1998, 'Evolution of the telecommuting withdrawal model: A U.S. perspective', in P Jackson and W van der Wielen (eds), *Teleworking – New International Perspectives from Telecommuting to the Virtual Organization*, Routledge: New York, pp. 281–291.

Gainey, TW & Clenney, BF 2006, 'Flextime and telecommuting: Examining individual perceptions. *Southern Business Review*, 32: 13-21.

Golden, TD 2006, 'Avoiding depletion in virtual work: Telework and the intervening impact of work exhaustion on commitment and turnover intentions', *Journal of Vocational Behavior*, 69: 176-187.

Golden, TD & Veiga, JF 2004, 'The impact of extent of telecommuting on job satisfaction: Resolving inconsistent findings', *Journal of Management*, 31: 301–318.

Golden, TD, Veiga, JF & Simsek, Z 2006, 'Telecommuting's differential impact on work-family conflict: Is there no place like home?', *Journal of Applied Psychology*, 91: 1340-1350.

Gurstein, P 1991, 'Working at home and living at home: Emerging scenarios', *The Journal of Architectural and Planning Research*, 8: 164-180.

Habib, L & Cornford, T 2002, 'Computers in the home: Domestication and gender', *Information, Technology and People*, 15: 159-174.

Harpaz, I 2002, 'Advantages and disadvantages of telecommuting for the individual, organization and society', *Work Study*, 51: 74-80.

Helms, MM & Raiszadeh, FME 2002, 'Virtual offices: Understanding and managing what you cannot see', *Work Study*, 51: 240-247.

Hertel, G, Geister, S & Konradt, U 2005, 'Managing virtual teams: A review of current empirical research', *Human Resource Management Review*, 15: 69-95.

Heymans, M & Van Hoye, G 2005, 'Telework and organizational attractiveness: A person-organisation fit perspective', *Gedrag en Organisatie*, 18: 199-209.

Hill, EJ, Ferris, M & Martinson, V 2003, 'Does it matter where you work? A comparison of how three work venues (traditional office, virtual office and home office) influence aspects of work and personal/family life', *Journal of Vocational Behavior* 63: 220–241.

International Teleworking Association and Council 2007, website, viewed 3 March 2007, <http://www.workingfromanywhere.org/index.html>.

Jarvenpaa, SL & Leider, DE 1999, 'Communication and trust in global virtual teams', *Organization Science*, 10: 791-815.

Jay, C 2005, 'Sun never sets on the design of jet fighter', *Australian Financial Review*, September 23, p. 64.

Kersley, BC, Alpin, J, Forth, A, Bryson, H, Bewley, G, Dix, J & Oxenbridge, S 2006, *Inside the Workplace: Findings from the 2004 Workplace Employment Relations Survey*, Routledge, London.

Kinsman, F 1987, 'The homeworker's tale', in F Kinsman (ed.), *The Telecommuters*, John Wiley & Sons, New York, pp. 70–93.

Kugelmass, J 1995, *Telecommuting: A Manager's Guide to Flexible Work Arrangements*, Lexington Books, New York.

Kurland, NB & Eagan, TD 1999, 'Telecommuting: Justice and control in the virtual organization', *Organization Science,* 10: 1–31.

Lamond, D, Daniels, K,& Standen, P 2003, 'Teleworking and virtual organizations: The human impact', in D Holman, TD Wall, CW Clegg, P Sparrow,& A Howard (eds.), *The New Workplace: A Guide to the Human Impact of Modern Working Practices,* Wiley: London, pp. 197-218.

Landy, FJ & Conte JM 2010, *Work in the 21st Century: An introduction to industrial and organizational psychology*, Blackwell: New York.

Lipnack, J & Stamps, J 1997, *Virtual Teams: Reaching Across Space, Time, and Organizations with Technology*, John Wiley & Sons, New York.

Lundberg, U & Lindfors, P 2002, 'Psychophysiological reactions to telework in female and male white-collar workers', *Journal of Occupational Health Psychology,* 7: 354-364.

Maruping, LM & Agarwal, R 2004, 'Managing team interpersonal processes through technology: A task-technology fit perspective', *Journal of Applied Psychology,* 89: 975-990.

McCloskey, DW & Igbaria, M 1998 'A review of the empirical research on telecommuting and directions for future research' in M Igbaria & M Tan (eds.), *The Virtual Workplace,* Idea Group: Hershey, PA, pp. 338-358.

Meyerson, DKE, Weick, RM & Kramer, RM 1996, 'Swift trust and temporary groups', in RM Kramer & TR Tyler (eds), *Trust in Organisations: Frontiers of Theory and Research*, Sage, Thousand Oaks, CA.

Morgan, R E 2004, 'Teleworking: An assessment of the benefits and challenges', *European Business Review,* 16: 344-357.

Motowidlo, S, Borman, WC & Schmit, MJ 1997, 'A theory of individual difference in task and context performance', *Human Performance,* 10: 71-83.

Mowshowitz, A 1997, 'Virtual organization', *Communications of the ACM,* 9: 30-37.

Nicholson, B & Schubert, M 2006, 'Hand-picked officer "devastated" by bungle, *The Age*, May 19, p. 1.

Offstein, EH, Morwick, J, & Koskinen, L 2010, 'Making telework work: Leading people and leveraging technology for competitive advantage', *Strategic HR Review,* 9: 32-37.

O'Hara-Devereaux, M & Johansen, B 1994, *Global Work: Bridging Distance, Culture and Time*, Jossey-Bass, San Francisco.

O'Neill, TA, Hambley, LA, Greidanus, NS, MacDonald, R & Kline, TJB 2009, 'Predicting teleworker success: an exploration of personality, motivational, situational and job characteristics', *New Technology, Work and Employment,* 24: 144-162.

Perin, C 1991, 'The moral fabric of the office: Panoptican discourse and schedule flexibilities', *The Sociology of Organizations,* 8: 241-268.

Piccoli, G, Powell, A & Ives, B 2004, *Information Technology and People,* 17: 359-379.

Platt, L 1999, 'Virtual teaming: Where is everyone?', *The Journal for Quality and Participation,* 22: 41-43

Point-Topic 2005, *Broadband User Survey,* 7 September 2005, DCITA subscription.

Rau, BL & Hyland, MM 2002, 'Role conflict and flexible work arrangements: The effects on applicant attraction', *Personnel Psychology,* 55: 111–136.

Renn, RW, Allen, DG & Huning, TM 2011, 'Empirical examination of the individual-level personality-based theory of self-management failure', *Journal of Organizational Behavior,* 32: 25-43.

Sanchez, AM, Perez, MP, de Luis Carnicer, P & Jimenez, MJV 2007, 'Teleworking and workplace flexibility: A study of impact on firm performance', *Personnel Review,* 36: 42-64.

Schmidt, MJ, & Ryan, AM 1993, 'The Big Five in personnel selection: Factor structure in applicant and nonapplicant populations', *Journal of Applied Psychology,* 78, 966-974.

Sensis 2005, *Sensis Insights Report: Teleworking,* Australian Government Printer.

Sensis 2007, *Special Report: Teleworking,* Australian Government Printer.

Staples, DS, & Zhao, L 2006, 'The effects of cultural diversity in virtual teams versus fact-to-face teams', *Group Decision and Negotiation,* 15: 389-406.

Stephens, GK, & Szajna, B 1998, 'Perceptions and expectations: Why people choose a telecommuting work style', *International Journal of Electronic Commerce,* 3: 70–85.

Sweeney Research 2004, *Mobility and mistrust,* research report commissioned by Toshiba (Australia) Information Systems Division, viewed 8 March 2007, http://www.isd.toshiba.com.au/sig/downloads/Mobility&Mistrust.pdf.

Telework Exchange and the US Federal Managers Association 2007, *Face-to-face with management reality: A teleworking research report. Telework Exchange,* January, 2007.

United States Office of Personnel Management 2011, *Status of telework in the Federal government: Report to Congress,* Report No. 20415, Washington, DC.

Watson Fritz, MB, Narasimhan, S, & Rhee, HS 1998, 'Communication and coordination in the virtual office', *Journal of Management Information Systems,* 14: 7–28.

Wayne, JH, Musisca, N, & Fleeson, W 2004 'Considering the role of personality in work-family experience: Relationships of the big five to work-family conflict and facilitation', *Journal of Vocational Behavior,* 64: 108-130.

Wells, SJ 2001, 'Making telecommuting work', *HR Magazine,* 46: 34–45.

WorldatWork 2009, *Telework Trendlines 2009,* February 2009.

Case study: Lost in translation – The outsourcing of clinical letters

The advent of high-technology global outsourcing has provided many organisations with the ability to send information, at the end of the working day, across the world to be processed and returned for the next working day. This opportunity particularly appealed to a specialist department within Hospital Co, a large general hospital located in a metropolitan centre in the UK. The hospital moved to outsource the administration of its clinical letters to call centres in India. Technology utilised by specialist doctors in the department allowed them to speak into a Dictaphone, and the information was then uploaded via a web interface and sent to India for transcription by a call centre agent. The ideal and desired turnaround time for the transcribed clinical letters was less than 24 hours. However, the implementation of the process resulted in a slowing down of the production of the letters and increasing quality and service problems with the data, leaving records dangerously incomplete.

A number of issues adversely impacted upon the experiences of the staff. One key problem was the lack of communication and consultation prior to the implementation of the technology. Staff were sold on the idea that the technology was being implemented as a trial rather than as a permanent change to organisational processes. A second issue was the lack of support from the technology sales representative when problems were reported with dictation.

In addition to these concerns, staff experienced a myriad of technical problems with the new system. First and foremost, letters were returned with the misspelling of important medical terms; or alternatively, terms were left blank. This created additional administrative and time costs as dictation had to be revisited to identify any terms that were missing from the letters. Whilst call centre agents tried to list time codes on the dictation to hasten this process, staff reported that often these time codes could not be accessed due to differences in technology between the dictation transcript and the superior technology utilised by call centre agents. This meant secretaries within the department had great difficulties trying to identify any gaps.

A second problem was the consultants themselves. Rather than supplying the basic information required, consultants tended to provide personal and identifiable patient details, thus raising privacy and patient confidentiality issues when the reports were sent to India and transcribed by external call centre agents. Other privacy issues arose because secretaries could access all information from any location, including outside the hospital and department. There were no security requirements governing access to the system. In addition, staff could access all patient details via the web interface, as presumably could the call centre agents.

In relation to concerns of privacy and confidentiality, consultants were reportedly resistant to modifying their behaviour in respect of the provision of patient information. Where consultants did provide only the basic information required to avoid privacy issues, problems arose because the department's internal databases were often inaccurate, meaning time and human resources were wasted on trying to correct patient details. This had a flow-on effect to the referencing and double-checking of the reports sent from India, which took up to three hours in some cases. One suggested solution (by the departmental manager) was to shift the responsibility of checking the reports and letters back to the consultants rather than to the secretaries in an effort to save time. In practice, however, this was often problematic due to the extensive workloads of the consultants.

The third major problem that undermined the technology was the web interface. Staff reported several problems, including that the templates were not suited to the nature of the work that the department undertook. For instance, consultants often left messages within dictations asking for certain issues, facts or details to be cross-checked or followed up. These comments often got 'lost in translation' in the web interface because the template did not have a comments field. In addition, some call centre agents included these comments while others didn't.

In summary, the experience of outsourcing for the specialist department within Hospital Co was an expensive and time consuming one. However, the intangible problem of loss of quality in record keeping for patients was of more concern. As to the service issue, where clinical letters were not substantively checked or cross-referenced, staff were place in a difficult position with regard to queries and patients' problems, and thus service provision was undermined.

Written by: Holland & Pyman.

Case study questions

1. Why has such a potential cost saving and quality enhancement become a major problem?
2. What would you have done to ensure this didn't happen?
3. What would you do now to rectify these problems?

Discussion questions

1. Explain why the implementation of teleworking initiatives often engenders considerable cultural resistance.
2. Discuss the potential disadvantages encountered by employees who telework.
3. What advantages can organisations derive from implementing virtual teams?
4. What is 'swift trust' and how does it develop in virtual teams?
5. How can HR managers improve the functioning of virtual teams?

Chapter 2

MANAGING THE WAR FOR TALENT

INTRODUCTION

In the first decade of the twenty-first century there is a growing recognition of the changing nature of the employment relationship (Cappelli 2005; Critchley 2004; Fullerton & Toosi 2001). The production base of advanced economies is evolving from an industrial focus to a one of service and knowledge. This has contributed to a shift in the nature of work, and an increasing recognition of the individual employee as the primary source of competitiveness (Barney 1991; Boxall 1996; Boxall & Purcell 2003). As a result of this focus on the employee, the HR function has the potential to assume an increasingly critical and dynamic role in generating a sustainable competitive advantage through people by focusing on the development of diverse policies, practices and systems to attract, retain and develop these key resources (Holland, Hecker & Steen 2002).

The recognition of the role of HR has come at a time of major change in the nature of the labour market. Increasing shortages of skills in many advanced economies, combined with a generation of workers focused on employability rather than employment, have been the catalyst for a shift away from the traditional employer-employee relationship, and have caused a major change in the balance of power in this relationship – even *with* the advent of the global financial crisis (GFC) (Losey 2005). In addition, declining birth rates in most countries over the past two decades have exacerbated, and will continue to exacerbate, the growing shortage in labour and skills – a shortage which is only now starting to become apparent. Although, as both Cappelli (2003) and Critchley (2004) argue, this may be more to do with contemporary employment and retirement trends than with demographic issues associated with growing shortages in labour and skills. Despite the differing perspective, it is clear that, in this emerging world of work, if organisations are to remain competitive, the management of talented employees will be a key focus and will be fundamentally different to the latter half of the twentieth century (Thorne & Pellant 2007; Baron & Armstrong 2007). This chapter explores the HRM trends and issues arising from the new perspective associated with acquiring and retaining human resources to build a sustained competitive advantage – also known as 'talent management'.

Attraction and retention – a theoretical perspective

In recent years, the attraction and retention of employees have become increasingly significant aspects of contemporary HRM. A review of the literature reveals two theoretical perspectives, which provide a framework for analysing the strategic approach associated with the long-term development of the organisation's human resources. The first is human capital theory, which links investment in the organisation's key asset, its employees, to increased productivity and sustained competitive advantage (Smit 1998). The strategic aspect is the long-term enhancement of the firm's resource base by linking employees' skill development with retention through training and development, career management, and progression (Garavan *et al.* 2001). This is also consistent with the second theoretical perspective, the resource based view of the firm (RBV) (Penrose 1959). The focus of the RBV is on an organisation retaining and developing these human resources through investments such as human resource development (HRD) strategies. This retention and development will ensure that these assets become valuable, rare and difficult to imitate, enhancing further the organisation's competitive advantage (Barney 1991; Walton 1999; Garavan *et al.* 2001). Many scholars have adopted these theoretical approaches in interpreting the essential elements of building sustained competitive organisational advantage (Boxall & Purcell 2003; Boxall & Steenveld 1999; Delery & Shaw 2001; Wright, Dunford & Snell 2001).

It is possible to link the strategic focus on the management and development of human resources to the deliberate promotion of HRD strategies as a catalyst for the attraction and retention of talented employees. This has led to an increased focus on HRM as a platform for building competitive advantage. A critical element is the strategic development of diverse strategies for staff enhancement and development as important tools for both attraction and retention. Organisations taking the strategic course will seek a long-term and diverse approach to managing and investing in their human resources to ensure that appropriate training and development are available to all employees.

The management of learning and knowledge within organisations is an ever more complex role for HRM in the creation of competitive advantage – a theme which is increasingly reflected in the literature (Garavan *et al.* 2001; Holland & De Cieri 2006; Walton 1999). In a dynamic environment, this means that the organisations must commit resources to develop a diverse and adaptive approach in order to ensure that each area within the organisation has access to appropriate levels of training and development to meet diverse organisational objectives.

Talent management and the demographic time-bomb

Talent management, which involves the cooperation and communication of managers at all levels, has become an imperative in the face of an increasingly complex and dynamic environment. In addition, talent-management processes must be more strategic, connected and broad-based than ever before. Talent-management processes include workforce planning, talent-gap analysis, recruitment, selection, education and development, retention, talent reviews, succession planning, and evaluation. To drive performance, to deal with an increasingly rapid pace of change, and to create sustainable success, an organisation must integrate and align these processes with its business strategies. By assessing available talent and by placing the right people in the right place at the right time, organisations can survive and thrive (McCauley & Wakefield 2006; Oakes 2006; Silverman 2006).

In attempting to quantify talent, Michaels, Handfield-Jones and Axelrod (2001) have argued in its broadest sense: 'Talent is the sum of the person's abilities – his or her intrinsic gifts, skills, knowledge, experience, intelligence, judgement, attitude, character and drive. It also includes his or her ability to learn and grow.'

Talent management has become increasingly important in the more industrialised economies over the past two decades for a variety of reasons. Over the second half of the twentieth century, population trends across most industrialised countries revealed almost static populations and declining birth rates (OECD 2008). This has generated growing concern for the long-term supply of skilled labour in the market as the first wave of baby boomers reaches retirement age. For the foreseeable future, under current strategies for employment, more people will be leaving the workforce than joining it (Critchley 2004).

A global study by the Boston Consulting Group (BCG) (Boston Consulting Group 2003) in 2003 estimated a shortfall in skilled labour worldwide in the order of 60 million by 2020. The US will face a labour shortage of 17 million; Japan, 9 million; China, 10 million; Russia, 6 million; Germany, 3 million; France, 3 million; Spain, 3 million; and the UK, 2 million.

Research by McKinsey & Co – entitled *The war for talent* and involving 77 companies and almost 6,000 managers and executives in the US – highlighted the importance of the coming skill-shortage crisis. The report identified that the principal corporate resource over the next 20 years will be talent, which, due to identified demographic changes, will become increasingly difficult to find and for which it will be costly to battle (Michaels *et al.* 2001). The research recommended a fundamental change in organisations' HR practices, including finding more imaginative ways to attract and retain this talent. The report also identified that 75 per cent of organisations in the survey either did not have enough talent or were chronically short of talent. This shortage was reinforced by another survey undertaken in 2006 by staffing service provider Manpower Inc, the Talent Shortage Survey of nearly 33,000 employers across 23 countries and territories, which predicted major shortages in (Joerres & Turcq 2007):

- sales representatives;
- engineers;
- technicians (primarily production and operations, engineering, and maintenance);
- production operators;
- skilled manual trades (primarily carpenters, welders and plumbers);
- IT staff (primarily programmers and developers);
- administrative and personal assistants;
- drivers;
- accountants; and
- management and executives.

These scenarios, however, have been challenged. Both Cappelli (2003) and Critchley (2004), for example, have acknowledged the changing demographics but argue that the critical flaws in the scenarios suggested above are that they assume employment strategies and relationships will not adapt accordingly. As Cappelli argues:

> Many of the studies that foresee labour strategies in the future assume retirement patterns will be unchanged, and that people will retire at the same age even as life expectancy and the ability to work longer go up.... Surely this is unrealistic for no other reason than financial resources for retirement may not allow it (2005, pp. 7-8).

This is also supported by Critchley (2004), who argues for a fundamental rethink in the nature of employment. He argues that:

- firstly, the retirement concept in advanced economies and the re-engagement of the post-50 age group or sector of the workforce needs to be re-examined; and
- secondly, polices need to be developed to attract and retain a multi-generational workforce.

What the McKinsey report and what others, including Cappelli and Critchley, do agree upon is the need for more creative HR practices to attract and retain talented employees. In this context, the McKinsey report highlighted the changing psychological contract within the employment relationship (see *Chapter 5: Psychological Contracts*), noting that employees will look for employability not employment, and will want to change jobs often.

Critchley (2004) also argues that psychological contracts and engagement profiles will be substantially different for older workers. These trends indicate that organisations that are prepared to focus on attracting and developing talent will be in a stronger position to retain key human resources as the so-called 'war for talent' intensifies. It is also clear that the way organisations seek to retain these highly-skilled resources will have to change. This places human resources at the centre of policy and systems development to achieve outcomes that promote the organisation as an employer of choice for increasingly discerning (potential) employees. The structural changes driving the 'war for talent' are widespread across many of the more industrialised market economies. This creates what Michaels *et al.* (2001) describe as a 'new' business reality, in which management skills and the ability to embrace a new mindset are critical (see Tables 2.1 and 2.2).

Table 2.1 The new reality of talent management

The old reality	The new reality
People need companies	Companies need people
Machines, capital and geography are the competitive advantage	Talented people are the competitive advantage
Better talent makes some difference	Better talent makes a huge difference
Jobs are scarce	Talented people are scarce
Employees are loyal and jobs are secure	People are mobile and their commitment is short term
People accept the standard package they are offered	People demand much more

Source: Michaels *et al.* 2001: 6.

Table 1.2 Differentiated talent strategy

The old way	The new way
HR is responsible for people management	All managers, starting with the CEO, are accountable for strengthening their talent pool
We provide good pay and benefits	We shape our company, our jobs and even our strategy to appeal to talented people
Recruiting is like purchasing	Recruiting is like marketing
We think development happens in training	We fuel development primarily through stretch jobs, coaching and mentoring

Source: Michaels *et al.* 2001: 16.

The Australian hegemony

In the context of this new economic environment, organisations will have to adapt to this new paradigm in a variety of ways. The 'new' psychological contract under which these workers operate will redefine employee benefits. In contrast to the traditional 'relational' contract associated with a conventional (long-term) employment relationship based upon standard terms and conditions of employment, work will be organised to be conducive to the demands of these workers. Management must therefore pay careful attention to both the structural and cultural conditions that exist within the firm (Thomas, Au & Ravlin 2003; Sims 1994), including more diverse and proactive strategies as key retention tools (Newell *et al.* 2002). As Michaels *et al.* (2001) have noted, the way organisations have managed talent in the past will not be sufficient in the future. What will be needed is a new approach to the management of human resources and more particular human resource development strategies linked to employee development and employability.

It is becoming increasingly clear that talent is a critical driver in sustaining corporate performance, and an organisation's ability to attract, develop and retain talent will be a major factor in competitive advantage in the future, requiring organisations to invest more resources in this battle for talent (Michael *et al.* 2001). However, in Australia, this paradigm shift needs to be seen in the context of the traditional approach to training and development. The emergence of the protectionist industry policies in the early 20th century reinforced highly rigid and hierarchical work patterns which were supported by strong trade unions. As a result, training and development in Australia remained largely fragmented and narrowly focused around occupational skills and managerial control (McKeown & Teicher 2006). Reinforcing this approach was the reliance on waves of migration to alleviate the cycles of skill shortages and inter-firm mobility (poaching). These strategies reinforced an insular, complacent and inwardly-focused approach of both industry and of successive federal governments in the development of the Australian workforce (Ford 1990; Lansbury & McDonald 1999; Holland & Deery 2006). Training and development, therefore, became *ad hoc* and crisis driven but remained centred on the apprentice system (McKeown & Teicher 2006). As such, it was not until the dismantling of the trade and protection barriers in the 1970s that issues associated with HRM and HRD as a source of competitive advantage became a major issue for industry and governments alike. Paradoxically, this increased emphasis on human resource management and training and development came at a time of major labour market deregulation. As McKeown and Teicher (2006) note: 'This quickly exacerbated tensions between employer's ability, or even the desire, to invest in employee development for the future and the need to control costs (p.28).' This, despite the consensus between business, trade unions and government in the seminal tripartite report, Australia Reconstructed (1987), that HRD was a major factor in developing and sustaining Australia's economy.

Federal government initiatives through the late 1980s and early 1990s, such as award restructuring where skill and remuneration were linked, only provided limited success, and major programs, such as the Training Guarantee Act (TGA) which was seen as a catalyst for cultural change and required organisations with payrolls in excess of A$200,000 to direct up to 1.5 per cent of payroll to training or be levied an equivalent amount (Smith & Freeland 2002), were seen more as a tax than and a training incentive. The program was suspended in 1994 and abolished in 1996 by the incoming Howard Liberal-National coalition government (Smith 2003). At a management skill level, it was realised that there were significant deficiencies which were identified by the Industry Taskforce on Leadership and Management Skills – or better known by the Chairman's name, the Karpin Report (1995). Key findings from the Karpin Report were the lower education and skill levels of Australian managers in comparison to the management in Australia's major trading partners. Other issues, such as limited leadership skills and educational support, were linked to the need for a significant focus on the development of management education (Smith 1998). However, the release of the report within a year of a change in the federal government saw many of the recommendations largely disregarded.

Since the election of the Howard government in 1996, it has been argued that the increased pace of deregulation has resulted in any progress on an HRD agenda being limited (McKeown & Teicher 2006), although Smith (2003) does note that much training goes unnoticed and unmeasured. However, the issue remains that the continued institutional re-structuring of the labour market has made investment policies in HRD increasingly discretionary. This background suggests that Australian organisations' may not be strategically positioning themselves for this era of skill shortages. This leads to the need to explore the nature and focus of Australian organisations' human resource strategies as they come to terms with an era of increasing and ongoing skill shortages.

The seminal work on talent management by Michaels *et al.* (2001), identified five key areas for organisations to act upon if they were going to be make talent a source of competitive advantage. These were:

1. embracing a talent mindset,
2. crafting a winning employee value proposition (EVP),
3. rebuilding their recruitment strategy,
4. weaving development into their organisation, and
5. differentiating and affirming their people.

The following section discusses these key areas more fully.

Embracing a talent mindset

The McKinsey Group defines a talent mindset in holistic terms as follows (Michaels *et al.* 2001):

> *Talent is the sum of the person's abilities – his or her intrinsic gifts, skills, knowledge, experience, intelligence, judgement, attitude, character and drive. It also includes his or her ability to learn and grow (p. xii).*

Whilst most organisations would like to see themselves in this context, many tend to adopt the old style of talent management, as indicated in Table 2.3.

Table 2.3 Primary emphasis of the HR position

	n = 1372
A broad range of human resource issues	45
HRM strategic development	21
Training & development	11
Recruitment & selection	7
Employee relations	7
Remuneration/performance management	3
Occupational health and safety	2
Industrial relations	2
Human resource information systems	1
Wage/salary administration	1

Source: Australian Human Resource Management Online Survey 2005.

A key element in the McKinsey report is that talent management is increasingly becoming an important role – if not the critical role – for the CEO – a role that cannot be delegated. In this context, the report's authors proposed several key actions that leaders must take (Michaels *et al.* 2001):

- get involved in people decisions,
- develop probing talent reviews,
- instil a talent-focused mindset within the organisation,
- invest real money in talent, and
- be accountable for talent management.

As the issue of skill shortages intensifies, is this message starting to reach the top management level of organisations? Research by the Economist Intelligence Unit on this issue appears to show this is increasingly the case (see Box 2.1).

Box 2.1: Talent Trove

During the GFC, the skills shortage appeared to have been swept away and an appearance that employees should be grateful to hold on to their jobs. In such conditions, why should employers care about creating a great workplace?

It's easy to forget that a productive and motivated workforce is a company's greatest asset when the business is fighting for its survival. But it was excessive short-term thinking that got the economy into the GFC mess. Long-term success depends on planning for what is around the corner.

The accounting firm Deloitte is among the top multinationals on the *BRW Great Places to Work* list. The accounting firm's chief executive in Australia, Giam Swiegers, is clear about the value of being an employer of choice in bad times as well as good ... when we go back to the skills shortage, you will be remembered for what you did in these times," he says.

Adapted from: Gina McColl: 'Talent Trove', BRW, p. 28, April 30-June 3 2009.

Crafting a winning employee value proposition (EVP)

An EVP is everything an employee experiences within an organisation, including intrinsic and extrinsic satisfaction, values, ethics and culture. It is also about how well the organisation fulfils the employees' needs, expectations and aspirations (Michaels *et al.* 2001).

In their study, the McKinsey Group set out to determine what employees look for when making an employment decision. As Table 2.4 illustrates, the items with a strong causal relationship with satisfaction were exciting work, development, great company, and wealth and rewards.

It is evident from the results in Table 2.4 that intrinsic factors, such as having interesting, challenging work that one is passionate about, are rated highly by high-skilled employees such as managers when they consider their place of employment. These factors are followed closely by good culture, commitment, support and career advancement. It is interesting to note that pay and wealth creation were in the bottom quartile, suggesting that extrinsic factors are not the main drivers in attracting and retaining talent.

Table 2.4 Key Employment Feature

	%
Interesting and Challenging Work	59
Work I feel passionate about	45
Career Advancement	37
Building Skills to boost career	35
Senior management commitment to me	30
Annual cash component is high	26

Source: Michaels *et al.* 2001, p.45

Rebuilding your recruitment strategy

When managers restructure a recruitment strategy, a critical issue is being able to understand the new workforce. This means that even in downturns in the market, as we have just seen with the GFC, it is imperative that managers maintain a creative recruitment-and-selection strategy, as the skill shortage is a long-term proposition. Only in this way will organisations continue to absorb new talent. In this context, McKinsey differentiates the new from old approaches to recruitment, as Table 2.5 shows.

Table 2.5 Changing perspectives on attraction and retention

Old recruiting strategies	New recruiting strategies
Grow your own talent	Pump talent in at all levels
Recruit for vacant positions	Hunt for talent all the time
Go to a few traditional sources	Tap many diverse pools of talent
Advertise to job hunters	Find ways to reach passive candidates
Specify a compensation range and stay within it	Break the compensation rules to get the candidates you want
Recruiting is about screening	Recruiting is about selling as well as screening
Hire as needed with no overall plan	Develop a recruiting strategy for each type of talent

Source: Michaels, Handfield-Jones & Axelrod 2001, p. 70

In terms of attraction, along with the primary areas of recruitment and selection, values and ethics act as important sources of attraction as employees become increasingly discerning about their employers. Macken (2005), for example, notes the sophisticated use of blogs and websites by potential employees to find out about real organisational culture and values, and points out that even organisations as large as Microsoft have expressed concern about internal bloggers and their effect on the future workforce and on clients.

Research undertaken by the recruitment agency Talent2 reinforces this point. A survey of 527 people on web-related employment revealed that:

- most job hunters (73 per cent) use an internet search engine to find information about the boss and the company;

- most job hunters (72 per cent) stated that the information obtained from searches has a bearing on the interview and a bearing on whether they decide to take the job; and

- a high proportion (86 per cent) of respondents indicated that this investigation allowed them to ask more job-related questions before accepting the position (Talent2 2005).

In fact, some of these features have been noted in articles appearing in the business press. For example (Macken 2004):

> *The advertisement shows a young man with long hair, hippie beads and casual pants at the edge of a beach. He looks ecstatic as he embraces the sea breeze under the heading "Are you looking for a lifestyle change?" Coke's new campaign? A shot from Survivor'? Or is Hugh Jackman enjoying a break back in Australia? Try a recruitment ad for a bank. Evidently being sales development manager for a northern Australian bank is as good as a sea change. Forget work stations, pinstriped suits and teller boxes. This bank wants you to think a day at the office feels like a day at the beach. Is this what it takes to attract good staff today?*

An understanding of how potential employees view or obtain information about the organisation can enhance the match between the person and the organisation, increasing organisation fit and retention. As Dale, as quoted in Keen (2005), notes:

> *The smart organisations are defining what type of person will fit with the organisation's culture. A lot of that is value-driven - not just what they are capable of doing, but what satisfies them. If someone is unmotivated, their skill set will walk out the door.*

Weaving development into your organisation

In this new era, employees are looking for work that provides opportunities and is challenging. However, this is often given lip service in many organisations, in particular those in the Anglo-American region. As Michaels *et al.* (2001) note: 'Talent rarely arrives fully developed ... People possess vast amounts of potential that, when nurtured and challenged, can be brought to full bloom.' In other words, organisations must develop their talent at all levels and weave it into the culture (see Table 2.6). This requirement is closely linked to areas such as job design, job analysis and team building, which contribute to the day-to-day experience on the job, determining what people actually do at work and how effectively they do it. Boxall *et al.* (2003), in a review of the labour turnover and retention in New Zealand, identified that one of the main reasons why respondents left their employers was to pursue more interesting work elsewhere. In an environment characterised by skill shortages and an increasingly discerning workforce, it is imperative for employers to review how they construct jobs and connect jobs.

Another critical factor in the retention of skilled workers is the provision of training and development. Edgar and Geare's (2005) study of aspects of HRM that are important to employees identified training and development to be of 'paramount' importance. Boxall *et al.* (2003) also identified training opportunities as a determining issue in the decision employees made to leave their employers. This identification reinforces the point that HRM and human resource development assume an increasingly significant role in the retention of key employees. Resistance to investment in human resources may reflect the traditional approach of many organisations and industries, particularly those reliant on immigration and poaching to solve skill shortages. In addition, organisational resistance to heavy investment in career development may reflect the changing psychological contract between employers and employees. Employees are choosing to manage their own careers by moving between organisations. Employers may therefore be questioning the value of investing in training and development opportunities for employees who may not stay (Noon & Blyton 2002). Nevertheless, as Edgar and Geare (2005) point out, training and development are still considered to be critical issues in employee retention and organisations would recognise them as important lures in the 'war for talent'. As Table 2.6 indicates Australian organisations appear to be taking these issues on board.

Table 2.6 Major HR programs or systems that have been initiated with the help of external consultants in the previous 2 years

	n = 1372 %*
Training & development	48
Recruitment & selection	34
HR information systems	29
Change management	22
Employee relations	18
Pay administration	15

*Respondents could select more than one response.

Source: Australian Human Resource Management Online Survey 2005.

Differentiating and affirming your people

We can link approaching the workforce as a diverse set of resources to what are called the 'hard' and 'soft' approaches to HRM. In terms of soft HRM, organisations:

- invest heavily in star performers (the A team),
- develop solid employees (the B team) to contribute their best to retain them, and
- help poor performers (the C team) to improve their performance.

If the technique of soft HRM fails to change the performance of the C team, their organisation will use an exit strategy – hard HRM.

Note that this approach can be seen as producing a potential star-focused culture that undermines a team culture. Michaels *et al.*, however, disagree, arguing that it simply involves recognition of an individual's achievement – as long as it is not overt it will not affect the performance of the organisation. Despite this, organisations should carefully consider the issue if they are considering embarking on such policies.

An important factor in differentiating and affirming employees is awareness of their diverse lifestyles and needs. Initially, the areas of work-life balance, family-friendly benefits and diversity may be seen only as attraction strategies. Allowing employees the flexibility to meet personal needs also becomes an important retention factor by adding to an organisation's 'employer of choice' standing (Landsbury & Baird 2004; Liddicoat 2003).

Pocock (2005) also makes the business case for a link between work-life balance and the attraction and retention of workers, and the ultimate competitive survival of a company. The increase in the number of women in the workforce, coupled with an ageing population base that requires part-time work or carers, elevates the need for organisations to support valued employees who have family responsibilities.

The focus on work-life balance has also been highlighted with regard to childcare problems and some parents' decision to return to work. Research by employers such as Toshiba and others has addressed this issue with their development of the Flexible Workplace Special Interest Group Research (2005).

Evidence of change in traditional professions such as law (noted for its long hours) highlights the sea change mentioned in the advertisement we discussed earlier in this chapter. Brown (2005) notes, that Henry Davis York, a law firm based in Sydney Australia, reported that the development of flexible patterns of work, stemming from its internal survey on work-life balance in 2001, has been a key factor in improving retention. Indicators included an increase in return from maternity leave, low turnover, and employee feedback as identifiable criteria. Another key issue in building diversity is the opportunity to attract a wider range of talent. Writers such as Murray and Syed (2005) and Orland (2000) have highlighted the negative effect of not capitalising on workers from a wide range of backgrounds. Companies employing diversely experienced employees are likely to be more creative and thus better able to meet the expectations of a diverse market. Given that organisations are operating in tight markets for labour, such capacities would be highly advantageous. Thorne and Pellant (2007) provide the following typical set of questions an organisation could use to rate its process for talent management.

Case study: Talent management in practice

Workforce advisory: Superior talent=tomorrow's competitive advantage

It is clear that 'talent management' is a key issue in the workplace. Our recent research suggests, and is duly supported by a multitude of studies conducted over the past ten years, that this is driven by a number of factors including: rapid growth and change, demographics, key people being 'poached' by the competition, and a difficulty in retaining talented people. The rise of the economy out of the global financial crisis (GFC) is a further factor that continues to accelerate these challenges.

With these external realities in the employment market, organisations need to carefully examine their choices of how best to respond.

Research indicates that the most desirable option is for organisations to tap into the quality people already in the organisation and to develop this talent so that they can confidently compete in an increasingly competitive environment. Establishing the right mindset, crafting a powerful employee value proposition (EVP), sourcing, developing and retaining talent all makes for an enormous challenge.

Organisations that managed their physical and financial assets with rigor during the GFC have generally not made their people a priority in the same way. Fundamentally, there are three main arguments in support of effective talent management (the better an organisation is at talent management, the better its return for stakeholders):

- recurring costs are reduced,
- economic outputs improve, and
- enterprise value is maximised.

Acquiring new talent

Instilling a new talent mindset and developing a powerful EVP will operate as a compelling advertisement for organisations, but on their own they are simply not enough of an attraction. A robust sourcing strategy is crucial. Attracting, sourcing and selecting the right talent addresses part of the talent imperative.

Clearly this application has greatest impact where two conditions are met:

- talent required does not exist internally, and
- talent required could be acquired at a reasonable premium.

The difficulty in finding IT professionals at the peak of the technology boom illustrates this well. Provided these conditions can be met, focusing on talent attraction, sourcing and selection can derive the best outcomes.

Leveraging existing talent

Leveraging talent is a priority throughout the company. Developing a sound EVP, and ensuring the sourcing strategy is a powerful one, will do much of what is needed to make the organisation's position in the talent market compelling.

There are also a number of specific steps to do with development that organisations should implement to complete their talent program. There is often little clarity about *who* should be developed, let alone *how*. Senior people more often than not believe that moving people around is not worth the disruption; divisions hoard their best staff; and HR executives are often preoccupied with training and other auditable initiatives. The reality is that people learn by being put in situations that require skills they don't have - a truth poorly served when 'who can do this job best right now?' often dominates staffing decisions.

Rebuilding talent banks via natural attrition and replacement is not only likely to cost a lot of money, but it is also going to take a long time - between five and twenty years. The reality for most organisations is that they need to leverage the talent they already have - reactive management.

Retaining talent

Organisations generally recognise that they could improve recruitment and development; few realise, however, that they have a retention problem. Paradoxically, it is the organisations that have done the best job of recruitment and development that may be most at risk from poaching. But every company needs to understand why its high performers are leaving before they can engage in retention strategies. Keeping hold of your talent is not always easy where there are many employment opportunities for high performers.

Organisations' efforts to effectively retain talent need to be explored across a number of characteristics.

Adapted from: <www.hcamag.com/news/workforce-advisory-superior-talent-tomorrowsdate>, 28/07/2010.

Box 2.2: HR checklist
Tony Kubica, 19 February, 2010, Fast Company

To retain top talent managers need to:

1. Give them a reason to stay.
2. Find a way to motivate them.
3. Reward them.

But, if you reward too much, too fast, it can be dangerous for your entire organisation.

In order for companies to retain top talent and stay competitive in today's market, they are engaging in fast tracking. This means they are moving selected employees quickly to, or through, managerial levels in their organisation.

Five reasons why fast tracking is a dangerous strategy for increasing employee retention

1. Skills can be learned quickly; experience takes time. In order to be an effective leader, your managers need to gain experience in:

- correctly identifying and solving problems,
- framing and making good decisions,
- dealing with the myriad of people-related issues that confront every manager in every organisation,
- organisation course correction, and
- role-based leadership.

2. Many times, when your organisation engages in fast tracking, a new manager will set a new initiative in motion and then leave the position before the impact of the initiative is realised. They are missing the day-to-day experience of interpersonal behaviours and interactions that come with any transition – the intangible. It's these subtleties that are often missed. And it's these subtleties and the way you handle them that hones a good leader.

3. Each managerial level brings new challenges, and requires different skills and behaviours. Moving too quickly through an organisation runs the risk of missing critical experiential learning. Experience is accretive, and it is difficult to learn vicariously. What you learn today you use as a framework for how you behave and react tomorrow. Short changing this learning cycle can result in a leader derailing later.

4. When leaders derail because a company engaged in fast tracking in order to retain top talent, it creates a disastrous domino effect for the organisation as a whole. We all know that the number one reason people leave a company is because of their immediate supervisor. We also know that poor decisions and poor problem-solving skills can result in service and profitability deterioration for a company.

5. Fast tracking creates a winner / loser environment within the company. Unless you want to build a highly competitive, stressful environment and internal culture that makes your employees hate Mondays because it is the start of a work week, creating winners and losers is not a good long-term strategy.

Why companies engage in fast tracking even though it's dangerous to the health of their organisation

Companies need to grow talent internally and insure smooth management transitions. The reality is that some industries are disproportionally affected by talent shortages (such as healthcare) and may have no other choice than to promote an employee who is truly not ready to handle the position. (This is a common practice for technical and clinical staff promoted to management.)

So what should you do?

Seven tips for retaining top talent without hurting your new manager, employees and the company

1. Develop a succession plan for your company. This means get committed to a process or structure of internal management and talent development.

2. Identify individuals within the organisation who have the potential to move into leadership positions. You should be identifying multiple candidates for each position. Don't be afraid to take some risks in candidate identification. Not all high potential candidates initially present an outgoing and aggressive demeanour (and remember these qualities do not necessarily ensure a good manager).

3. Provide the identified individuals with opportunities to take on additional projects to demonstrate their skills as well as their ability to learn and grow. The projects should create the opportunity for the candidates to 'live' with the consequences and take responsibility for their actions and decisions.

4. Provide new managers with an internal mentor and an external coach to insure support during the transition process. This support should be for six months to one year. This process is referred to as 'transition integration'.

5. Give all new managers a personality and job performance assessment. This is a valuable tool for identifying emerging leader attributes and potential risk areas. Now you will be able to enable early intervention and prevention, and give the most effective support to the new manager. This is better than the 'sink or swim' approach to learning that new managers are often thrown into.

6. Provide all candidates with self-assessment tools and learning opportunities. Do this both within the organisation in the form of added responsibilities and through outside learning opportunities such as conferences, executive education programs and professional memberships.

7. Monitor your new manager's progress (through the supervisor and mentoring and coaching support) and review your succession plan each year. Evaluate the success of the current program and the individuals in the program. Improve where necessary, and identify and support new leadership candidates.

> Be aware that some candidates simply may not be interested in this more protracted and performance-based approach. They may feel threatened or choose to leave. That's okay too. The risk of promoting too quickly, and the derailment that could occur, is not worth the harm an unprepared manager could bring to the organisation.
>
> Talent is to be developed, not anointed.
>
> *Adapted from*: Talent Management: How to Retain Top Talent Without Derailing the Organization When Fast Tracking, Toby Kubica, 19 February 2010, Fast Company.

Summary

There is a clear indication that the negotiating position of employees in the workplace is increasing for the first time in a generation. This is beginning to have an impact on the employment relationship and subsequently, employment policies and practices as the 'war for talent' becomes increasingly intense. It is clear that the new workforce is discerning and skilled. Potential employees are exploring whether the organisation pays enough attention to them in terms of both opportunities and resources. Despite the rhetoric, it appears that organisations are still coming to terms with the management of talent as a source of competitive advantage. Over the next decade, it will be interesting to see whether there is any real change in focus as labour markets tighten and workers become increasingly discerning.

References

Australian Bureau of Statistics (ABS) 2004, *Labour force Australia*, cat. no. 6291.0.55.001, Canberra, ABS.

ACIRRT 1999, *Australia at Work: Just Managing*, Prentice Hall, Sydney.

Arnold, J 1996, 'The Psychological Contract: A Concept in Need of Closer Scrutiny?', *European Journal of Work and Organizational Psychology*, 5(4): 511-520.

Australian Council of Trade Unions/Trade Development Council (ACTU/TDC) 1987, *Australia Reconstructed*, Australian Government Publishing Service, Canberra, ACT.

Barnes, D 1999, *Perspectives on Total Rewards: Recruitment and Retention*, Towers Perrin.

Barney, J 1991, 'Firm resources and sustained competitive advantage', *Journal of Management* 17: 99-120.

Baron, A & Armstrong, M 2007, *Human capital management: Achieving added value through people*. London: Kogan Page.

Becker, GS 1964, *Human Capital: A Theoretical Analysis with Special Reference to Education,*, Colombia University Press, New York.

Berger, LA & Berger, DR 2004, *The talent management handbook.* New York: McGraw-Hill.

Boudreau JW & Ramstad, PM 2005, 'Talentship, talent segmentation, and sustainability: a new HR decision science paradigm for a new strategy definition'. *Human resource management*, 44(2):129–136, Summer.

Boston Consulting Group 2003, *India's New Opportunity 2020 Report*, February.

Boxall, P 1996, 'The Strategic HRM debate and the resource-based view of the firm', *Human Resource Management Journal*, 6(3): 59-75.

Boxall, P & Steenveld, M 1999, 'Human Resource Strategy and Competitive Advantage: A Longitudinal Study of Engineering Consultancies', *Journal of Management Studies*, 36(4): 443-463.

Boxall, P, Macky, K & Rasmussen, E 2003, 'Labour turnover and retention in New Zealand: The causes and consequences of leaving and staying with employers', *Asia Pacific Journal of Human Resources*, 41(2): 195–214.

Boxall, P & Purcell, J 2003, *Strategy and Human Resource Management*, Palgrave Macmillan, Basingstoke.

Brown , K 2005, 'Putting the Life Back into Work: The Case of Henry Davis York', *Human Resources*, July, pp. 22-23.

Cappelli, P 2003, 'Will There Really be a Labor Shortage', *Organizational Dynamics*, 3: 15-24.

Cappelli, P 2005, 'Will There Really be a Labor Shortage', in M Losey, S Meisinger & D Ulrich (eds), *The Future of Human Resource Management*, pp. 5-14.

Corsello, J 2006, 'The future is now for talent management'. *Workforce management*, 85(12):52–57.

Critchley, R 2004, *Doing Nothing is Not an Option: Facing the Imminent Labor Crisis*, Thomson, South Western, Australia.

Dale, M 2005, 'Hudson Consulting - National Practice Manager for Talent Management – Australia', interview by Suzanne Keen, *HR Monthly*, February, p. 18.

Davenport, TH & Prusak, L 1998, *Working Knowledge: How Organizations Manage What They Know*, Harvard Business School Press, Boston.

Delery, J & Shaw, J 2001, 'The Strategic Management of People in Work Organizations: Review, Synthesis and Extension', *Personnel and Human Resource Management,* 20: 165-197.

Drake, K 1998, 'Firms, knowledge and competitiveness', *OECD Observer*, 31: 24-30.

Dowling, PJ & Fisher, C 1997, 'The Australian HR Professional: A 1995 Profile', *Asia Pacific Journal of Human Resources*, 35(1): 1-20.

Drucker, P 1998, *Knowledge Management*, Harvard Business School Press, Boston.

Edgar, F & Geare, A 2005, 'Employee voice on human resource management', *Asia Pacific Journal of Human Resources*, 43(3): 361 - 380.

Frase, MJ 2007, 'Stocking your talent pool'. *HR magazine*, 52(4):67–74, April.

Flexible Workplace Special Interest Group Research 2005, *Flexible Working: A Guide to Creating and Managing a Flexible Workplace*, Toshiba Australia.

Ford GW 1990, *Rethinking skilling for a restructured workplace*, 10th Occasional Paper, Commission for the Future, Australian Government Publishing Service, Canberra, ACT.

Fullerton, H & Toossi, M 2001, 'Labor Force Projections 2010: Steady Growth and Changing Composition', *Monthly Labor Review,* November, 124 (110): 21-28.

Garavan, T, Moreley, M, Gunnigle, P & Collins, E 2001, 'Human Capital Accumulation: The Role of Human Resource Development', *Journal of European Industrial Training,* 25: 48-68.

Goffee, R & Jones, G 2007, 'Leading clever people'. *Harvard business review*, 85(3):72–79.

Granovetter, MS 1973, 'The strength of weak ties', *American Journal of Sociology*, 78(6): 1360-1381.

Grigoryev, P 2006, 'Hiring by competency models'. *The journal for quality and participation*, 29(4):16–18, Winter.

Grossman, RJ 2006, 'Developing talent'. *HR magazine*, 51(1):40–46, January.

Hibbard, J & Carillo, KM 1998, 'Knowledge revolution: Getting employees to share what they know is no longer a technology challenge it's a corporate culture challenge', *Information Week,* 663.

Hecker, R & Grimmer, M 2006, 'The Evolving Psychological contract', in P Holland & H De Cieri, *Contemporary Issues in Human Resource Development*, pp. 183-210.

Holland, P & De Cieri, H (Eds) 2006, *Human resource development: a contemporary perspective*. Australia: Pearson Education.

Holland, P, Hecker, R & Steen, J 2002, 'Human resource strategies and organisational structures for managing gold-collar workers', *Journal of European Industrial Training,* 26: 72-80.

Homan, G & MacPherson, A 2005, 'E–learning in the corporate university'. *Journal of European industrial training*, 30(1):75–90.

Joerres, J. & TURCQ, D. 2007. Talent value management. Industrial management, March/April:8–13.

Kamoche, K & Mueller, F 1998, 'Human resource management and the appropriation-learning perspective', *Human Relations,* 51: 1033-1061.

Karpin, D (Chair) 1995, *Enterprising nation: Renewing Australia's managers to meet the challenge of the Asia-Pacific century,* report on the Task Force on Leadership and Management Skills, Australian Government Publishing Service, Canberra, ACT.

Keen, S 2005, 'Work in Progress', *HR Monthly*, February, pp. 18-24.

Landes, L 2006, 'Getting the best out of people in the workplace'. *The journal for quality and participation*, 29(4):27–29, Winter.

Lansbury, R & McDonald, D 1999, 'Employment relations and the managerial revolution in the public sector', in R Morris, D Mortimer & P Leece (eds), *Workplace reform and enterprise bargaining issues*, Harcourt Brace, Marrickville, NSW.

Lansbury, R & Baird, M 2004, 'Broadening the horizons of HRM: Lessons for Australia from the US experience', *Asia Pacific Journal of Human Resources*, 42(2): 147-155.

Liddicoat, A 2003, 'Stakeholder perceptions of family-friendly workplaces: An examination of six New Zealand organizations', *Asia Pacific Journal of Human Resources*, 41(3): 354–370.

Lockwood, NR 2006, 'Talent management: driver for organisational success'. *HR magazine*, 51(6):2–11.

Losey, M 2005, 'Anticipating Change: Will there really be a labor shortage?', in M Losey, S Meisinger & D Ulrich (eds), *The Future of Human Resource Management*, pp. 23-37.

Newell, S, Robertson, M, Scarbrough, H & Swan, J 2002, *Managing Knowledge Work*, Palgrave Macmillan, Basingstoke.

McKeown, T & Teicher, J 2006, 'Human Resource Management in a Deregulated Environment', in *Human Resource Development: A Contemporary Perspective*, Pearson Education, Australia, pp. 25-54.

Macdonald, S 1986, 'Headhunting in high technology', *Technovation*, 4: 233–245.

Macken, D 2004, 'A Sense of Entitlement: The New Worker Wants it All', *Weekend Financial Review*, 27-28 November 2004, pp. 17-18, Fairfax Press, Melbourne.

Macken, D 2005, 'Twentysomethings will vote with their feet', *The Weekend Financial Review*, 19-20 November, The Fairfax Group, pp. 27.

Mathews, J 1994, *Catching the Wave: Workplace Reform in Australia*, Sydney, Allen & Unwin.

McCauley, C & Wakenfield, M 2006, 'Talent management in the 21st century: help your company find, develop and keep its strongest workers'. *The journal for quality and participation*, 29(4):4, Winter.

Meisinger, S 2006, 'Talent management in a knowledge-based economy'. *HR magazine*, 51(5):10.

Michaels, E, Handfield-Jones, H & Axelrod, E 2001, *The War for Talent*, Havard Business School Press, Mass. USA.

Murray, P & Syed, J 2005, 'Succession management: Trends and current practice', *Asia Pacific Journal of Human Resources*, 43(2): 210–224.

Nonaka, I, Toyama, R & Byosiere, P 2001, 'A theory of organizational knowledge creation: Understanding the dynamic process of creating knowledge', in M Dierkes, AB Antal, J Child, & I Nonaka (eds), *Handbook of Organizational Learning and Knowledge*, Oxford University Press, Oxford.

Noon, M & Blyton, P 2002, *The Realities of Work*, 2nd edn, Palgrave Macmillan, Basingstoke.

Oakes, K 2006, 'The emergence of talent management'. *Training & development*, 60(4):21–24.

OECD 2008, Labour Force Statistics, OECD, Paris. For non-OECD countries, Department of Economic and Social Affairs, United Nations.

Orland, R 2000, 'Racial diversity, business strategy and firm performance: A resource-based view', *Academy of Management Journal,* 43(2): 164–177.

Penrose, E 1959, *The Theory of Growth of the Firm*, Blackwell, Oxford.

Pocock, B 2005, 'Work-life 'balance' in Australia: Limited progress, dim prospects', *Asia Pacific Journal of Human Resources,* 43(2): 198–209.

Prince, C & Stewart, J 2002, 'Corporate universities – an analytical framework'. *Journal of management development,* 21(10):794–811.

Ready, DA & Conger, JA 2007, Make your company a talent factory. Harvard business review, 85(6):69–77.

Rousseau, DM 1995, *Psychological Contracts in Organizations: Understanding written and unwritten agreements*, Sage Publications, London and New York.

Russell, G & Bourke, J 1999, 'Where does Australia fit in internationally with work and family issues', *Australian Bulletin of Labour,* 25(3).

Salt, B 2004, *The Big Shift*, 2nd edn, Hardie Grant Books, South Yarra, Australia.

Scarbrough, H 1998, 'BPR and the knowledge-based view of the firm, Knowledge and Process Management', *The Journal of Corporate Transformation,* 5: 1-9.

Scarbrough, H & Swan, J 2003, 'Discourses of knowledge management and the learning organization: Their production and consumption', in M Easterby-Smith & M Lyles (eds), *Handbook of Organizational Learning and Knowledge Management*, Blackwell, Oxford.

Scarbrough, H, Swan, J & Preston, J 1999, *Knowledge Management: A Review of the Literature*, London, Institute of Personnel and Development.

Scholarios, D, Lockyer, C & Johnson, H 2003, 'Anticipatory socialisation: The effect of recruitment and selection experiences on career expectations', *Career Development International*, 8(4): 182–197.

Sheahan, P 2005, 'Generation Y: Thriving and Surviving with Generation Y at Work', Prahran, Hardie Grant Books.

Sheehan, C 2005, 'A Model of HR Change', *Personnel Review*, 34(2): 192-209.

Sheehan, C, Holland, P & De Cieri, H 2006, 'Current Developments in HRM in Australian organisations', *Asia Pacific Journal of Human Resources,* 46(2): 132-152.

Silverman, LL 2006, 'How do you keep the right people on the bus? Try stories'. *Journal for quality and participation*, 29(4):11–15, Winter.

Sims, RR 1994, 'Human Resource Management's Role in Clarifying the New Psychological Contract', *Human Resource Management*, 33(3): 373-382.

Smit, A 1998, *Training and development in Australia*, 2nd edn, Sydney: Butterworth.

Smith, A 1998, *Training and development in Australia*, 2nd edn, Butterworth, Chatswood, NSW.

Smith, A 2003, 'Recent trends in Australian training and development', *Asia Pacific Journal of Human Resources,* 41(2): 231-244.

Smith A & Freeland, B 2002, *Industry training - Causes and Consequences*, National Centre for Vocational Research, Leabrook, SA.

Sparrow, P 1998, 'New Organisational Forms, Processes, Jobs and Psychological contracts: Resolving the HRM Issues', in P Sparrow & M Marchington (eds), *Human Resource Management: The New Agenda*, Financial Times, Pitmans, London, pp. 117-141.

Stewart, J & McGoldrich, J 1996, *Human resource development: perspectives, strategies and practice.* London: Financial Times Pitman Publishing.

Storey, J & Quintas, P 2001, 'Knowledge management and HRM', in J Storey (ed.), *Human Resource Management: A Critical Text*, Thomson Learning, London.

Talent2 (2005) *Employees Snoop on Bosses on Google*, September.

Thomas, DC, Au, K & Ravlin, EC 2003, 'Cultural Variation and Psychological Contract', *Journal of Organizational Behaviour,* 24(4): 451-471.

Thorne, K & Pellant, A 2007, *The essential guide to managing talent: How top companies recruit, train and retain the best employees.* London: Kogan Page.

Tsui, AS & Wu JB 2005, 'The New Employment Relationship versus the Mutual Investment Approach: Implications for Human Resource Management', in M Losey, S Meisinger & D Ulrich, *The Future of Human Resource Management*, Virginia, Wiley & Son, pp. 44-54.

Turnley, WH & Feldman, DC 2000, 'Re-examining the effects of psychological contract violation: unmet expectations and job dissatisfaction as mediators', *Journal of Organizational Behaviour,* 21(1): 25-42.

Walton, J 1999, *Strategic Human Resource Development*, Pearson Education Limited, Great Britain.

Wang, CL & Ahmed, PK 2007, 'Dynamic capabilities: a review and research agenda'. *International journal of management reviews,* 19(1):31–50, March.

Wright, P, Dunford, B & Snell, S 2001, 'Human resources and the resource based view of the firm', *Journal of Management,* 27: 701-721.

Case study: AgencyCo

AgencyCo is the leading supplier of labour hire work, also known as 'on-hire', 'temp' or 'agency' work. Their labour hire staff can be employees who are then on-hired to a client firm (but are not employees of that firm) or self-employed contractors. Initially providing supplementary trades, AgencyCo developed a white-collar sector providing customer contact services, healthcare and general office placement staff in a diverse range of industries.

AgencyCo argues that, to attract and keep talented workers, the work needs to be not only about opportunity and variety but also about quality training, development and career progression, through developing each employee's skill base. The variety of jobs with different client firms is also an important learning feature of working for AgencyCo. Management at AgencyCo identifies working with different clients as a training and development opportunity, and is interpreted this way by labour hire workers who value the new experiences.

AgencyCo aims to become an employer of choice by giving employees and potential employees 'a sense of belonging but not a sense of being owned' by providing a range of benefits and by doing all the things a normal employer would do. AgencyCo treats both their temporary and permanent staff as if they are committed to the organisation, which allows them to demonstrate that, although an assignment is limited or short term, it will not lead to disinterest or second rate treatment on the part of the agency. This people management approach has led to turnover in employees being significantly lower than the industry average.

Becoming an employer of choice in the labour hire industry does raise the issue of talented staff being poached by client organisations. AgencyCo claims to be able to compete with any permanent employer. This is supported by the fact that they do not see themselves as a provider of peripheral workers, but rather as working within a partnership to manage these key employees. AgencyCo sees their competitive advantage as working in areas where they have acknowledged expertise which also corresponds with areas of labour shortage. Since labour hire workers may be subject to conflicting policies and procedures on clients' sites, in many cases there will be an AgencyCo supervisor on site who looks after the AgencyCo employee under every circumstance, even if there is a client supervisor present.

Written by: Rob Hecker and Peter Holland.

Case study questions

1. What characteristics does AgencyCo exhibit with regard to being successful at talent management?
2. Why do you think approach will/won't work in the long term?

Discussion questions

1. Discuss the changing dynamics of the workplace in the twenty-first century facilitating an increased emphasis on talent management.
2. How has the psychological contract between employees and employers been affected by the new era of HRM? Discuss.
3. Discuss the reasons for the perceived increasing shortages of skills.
4. Define the concept of 'talent'.
5. Discuss strategies for dealing with the potential 'war for talent' from a human capital perspective and a resource-based perspective.

Chapter 3

OFFSHORING: REFLECTIONS AND NEW DIRECTIONS

INTRODUCTION

The concept of 'offshoring' has become a major topic of debate in many advanced market economies (AMEs), permeating political, economic and academic discourse. The contentious focus is often the export of skilled – and increasingly white-collar – jobs to more cost-effective regions. This issue has become particularly evident in relation to the export of information technology and service-based operations to countries such as India, Mexico and China, and in more recent years Eastern Europe. The phenomenal rise in this sector is interconnected with the emergence of a digital economy, as it is ideally attuned to a global marketplace where location is incidental to the conduct of work and potentially real-time transactions. Australia is no exception to these changes with a rapid growth in offshoring over the past decade.

Initial explanations of offshoring tended to emphasise tangible economic costs such as labour and location, and to neglect intangibles such as quality, service, security and the human resource management dimensions. A key issue with the emergence of this 'cyberspace' work is that the academic debate has often lagged behind the dynamic changes and evolution of this sector in a rapidly developing global market. This is supported by studies which points to the shortage of hard facts to resolve conflicting points of view on the impact of offshoring (Farrell *et al.* 2005).

As the sector becomes more established, it is important and timely to reflect in more depth on the offshoring debate. The purpose of this chapter, therefore, is to provide an analysis of the offshoring literature and debate through research and case studies which illustrate the changing nature of offshoring and the key emerging characteristics within this debate. This chapter argues that there has been a fundamental shift in the arguments underpinning the rationale for offshoring. This shift has been *away* from a focus on tangible cost-benefit analyses to a balanced approach which looks at intangible issues with equal importance. This broader focus has the potential to affect organisational decisions to offshore, and has implications for developing countries involved in this business – particularly as issues of service quality, security and the management of human resources become key determinants of multinational companies' decisions to offshore.

What is offshoring?

'Outsourcing' is a generic term which implies the use of an external agent providing a service which could be or was being performed by the organisation itself. In the emerging global market, the term offshoring has developed to the point where it now accounts for work that is not constrained by the need for actual customer contact or local knowledge and thus has the potential to be undertaken remotely and therefore globally – and often in low-cost locations (Farrell 2005). This change in categorisation is also a reflection of a longer-term change in the global economy, or 'a global expression of outsourcing' as companies in AMEs are lured by significantly lower labour costs in the developing world (Grant 2005:3).

The rise of offshoring

Whilst the concept of offshoring is seen as a recent phenomenon, it has a history dating back to the 18th century. As Grant points out:

> 'Political offshoring' refers to the exploitation of labour and resources during the centuries of European colonisation. For example, the British East India Company's rule of India between 1757 and 1857 achieved political prestige for Britain and a thriving trade for its empire (2005:6).

In other words, the focus of this first wave of offshoring was the exploitation of natural resources by the nation state. A second wave of offshoring – also referred to as production offshoring – was at the organisational level and emerged in the 1970s with the movement of primarily blue collar work production facilities such as steel and textiles to new industrialising countries, particularly in Southeast Asia (Grant 2005).

The third and most recent wave of offshoring – that is, services offshoring – reflects the evolution of the production base of AMEs from a manufacturing to a knowledge and services focus, and the development of information communication technologies (ICTs), epitomised by the rapid development of the offshore call centre sector. This has taken place in parallel with the internationalisation of the global economy (see Figure 3.1). Whilst the development of service offshoring can be seen as a natural progression in an increasingly service and knowledge-based globally integrated economy, what has created political, economic and employment tension is the increasing *level* of high-skilled jobs that can be offshored. Professions such as medicine,

Chapter 3 – Offshoring: Reflections and New Directions

architecture and financial services have all been affected by this phenomenon. The offshoring of professional white-collar service jobs raises the question: 'Is any professional or high-value job safe?'. As Grant notes:

> *The uniqueness of service offshoring is in who it affects. White-collar workers in developed countries were not meant to be vulnerable to overseas competitors. Governments and economists have argued that the highest value-added jobs will remain in developed nations because they are filled by the best educated. The value-added jobs have been in financial services, telecommunications and computing, the growth areas in the 1990s. The loss of manufacturing jobs, while regrettable, encouraged an educated and innovative workforce, rather than a return to protectionism. However, new technologies, and an increasingly educated workforce, have made poorer nations highly competitive in a range of value added industries, including software engineering and financial services (2005:7-8).*

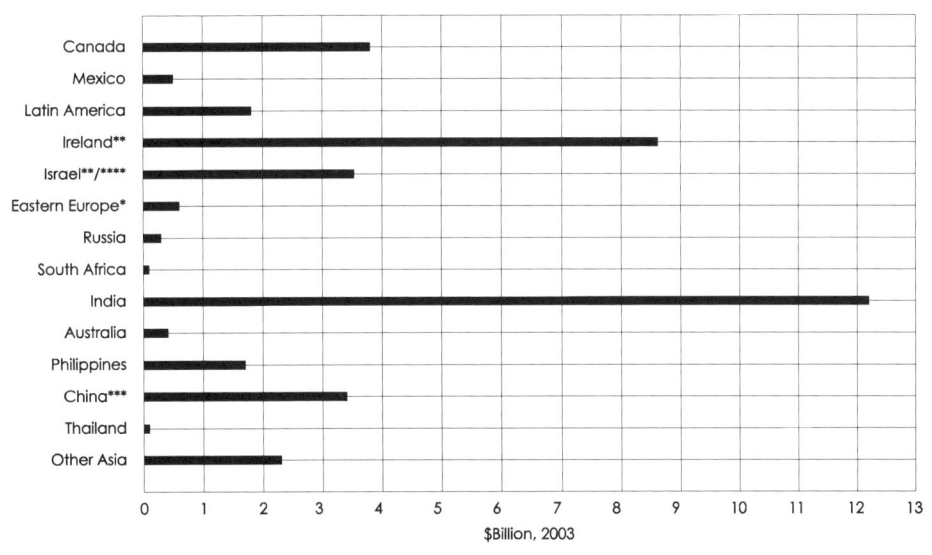

Figure 3.1 Offshored services market size (BPO and IT, captive and outsourced)

* Includes Poland, Romania, Hungary, Ukraine and Czech Republic.
** Primarily composed of MNC captives.
*** Estimate based on total Chinese BPO and IT services revenue (7.*) minus domestic demand for IT services (4.4).
**** Estimate based on 2001 market size of 3.0 and assumed growth rate of 20% pa.

Source: Adapted from McKinsey Global Institute analysis.

The uptake of service offshoring has been rapid, and although this has occurred off a relatively low base, the sector continues to develop in relation to the service sector as a whole. The range of growth varies considerably in estimates from a conservative estimate of 7 per cent growth to 20-25 per cent growth (Grant 2005). Despite this rise, McKinsey estimates in their study of eight sectors that only 11 per cent of worldwide services could in theory be performed remotely; however, within the study there was significant variation (see Figure 3.2), with engineering at over 50 per cent and generalist and support staff at around 9 and 3 per cent respectively. However, as the report notes:

> *Because of the high share of total employment in every sector represented by the two categories (generalist and support), they in fact contain the highest number of jobs that could be filled by remote talent – a combined total of 26 million (2005:23).*

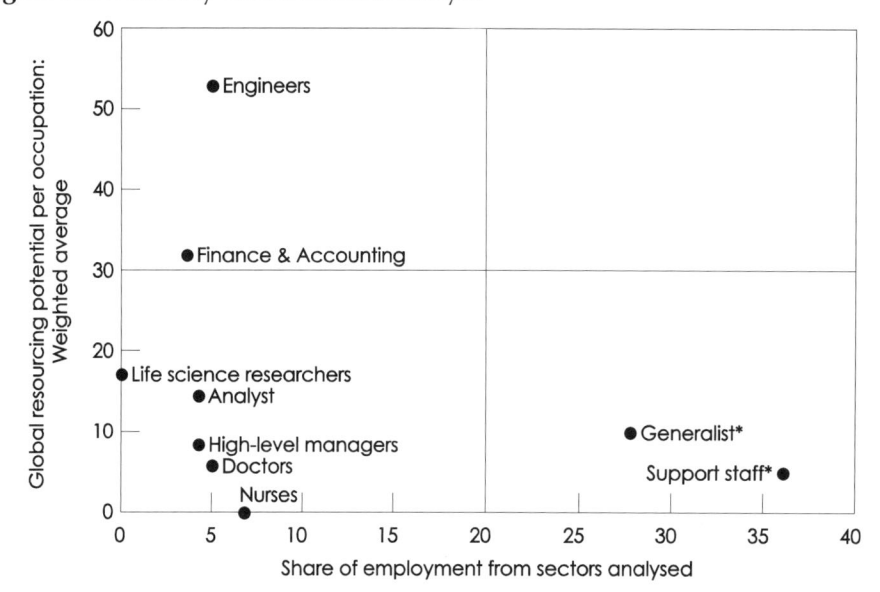

Figure 3.2 McKinsey Global Institute analysis

[Scatter plot: x-axis "Share of employment from sectors analysed" (0–40); y-axis "Global resourcing potential per occupation: Weighted average" (0–60). Data points: Engineers (~7, 52); Finance & Accounting (~8, 30); Life science researchers (~4, 15); Analyst (~6, 13); High-level managers (~7, 9); Doctors (~7, 7); Nurses (~7, 2); Generalist* (~28, 9); Support staff* (~33, 7).]

* Generalist accounts for 36% and support staff accounts for 39% of employment in sectors analysed.

Source: Adapted from McKinsey Global Institute analysis.

A Deloitte research paper found that, in the US, financial institutions had increased offshoring jobs by 400 per cent, with projection showing that 20 per cent of the US financial cost base will be offshored by 2010. In the UK, a survey of 100 large organisations in 2005 found that 81 per cent intended to increase their offshoring activities over the subsequent two years, while four per cent intended to decrease their offshoring activities (TPI 2005). The savings estimates appear considerable.

The rationales for outsourcing and offshoring

The underlying emphasis on efficiency and effectiveness in organisational processes has been the initial catalyst for outsourcing and offshoring non-core – and increasingly core – activities (Hartmann & Patrickson 2000; Nash, Holland & Pyman 2004). In the economic literature, the key benefit of offshoring is the movement of direct labour costs from high-wage labour markets to low-wage labour markets. Estimates of direct cost savings vary between 40 and 70 per cent in labour cost savings for 10 to 12 per cent of overhead costs.

Further, a US study by McKinsey (2003) estimates that the economic benefit to a US organisation on each dollar spent on outsourcing to India is about 14 per cent, mainly through reduced costs. Add to this other labour market factors in India such as 700,000 new university graduates a year – of which the offshoring sector attracts a large amount. Also, the cultural influence of British settlement which has provided India with English as its language for business furthers its attractiveness to Anglo-American countries, especially the UK, Australia and the US, which have led the outsourcing of service and knowledge work. In addition, the accident of geography means that normal working hours in India coincide with the appropriate times for outbound calls – often evening – to the UK and US, and the processing of data overnight (BPO) which is then available for the following day's business in these countries. These factors have led many to suggest that the development of offshoring in India alone appears limitless (Nancarrow 2004:8).

Outsourcing and offshoring are also portrayed as a means of enabling organisations to focus their resources on their *core* business, while facilitating new forms of work in other business areas. By matching organisational resources more closely with customer or product demand, organisations should be able to reduce fixed labour costs and increase efficiency and competitiveness (Domberger 1994). The ability to change the structure of the workforce or work patterns has been described as a key to efficient and effective utilisation of human resources (Emmott & Hutchinson 1998). Offshoring in an era of increasing skill shortages also provides organisations with expertise not available in-house (Young 2000). In addition, Quiggin (1996) also points out that the mainstream economic rationale is that outsourcing/offshoring provides a means of transferring significant or unpredictable risks associated with running a business – particularly financial risks – to contractors, while enabling the principal to retain control over the service. This argument has also been cast in an industrial relations context where using contractors in countries where unionisation is less developed reduces potential exposure to disruptive labour disputes (Perry 1997). In other words, the use of offshoring can enable organisations to transfer the responsibility for employee relations to a third party, thereby also avoiding strong unions and/or side-stepping provisions or agreements in high-cost labour countries. Thus, outsourcing and offshoring can be used strategically by employers, particularly in cases where they 'have not been able to implement cost reductions and/or more flexibility or casual work arrangements, and have therefore contracted the work to a new group of workers who are not covered by legislative protections' (ACIRRT 1999:142).

Barriers and implications of offshoring

As the market for offshoring continues to expand and mature, this is an opportune time to reflect on more complex issues that have the potential to temper or create significant barriers to organisations looking at this option. These issues need to be fully understood by organisations and should form part of their cost-benefit analysis to ensure that the decisions they make regarding offshoring are sound.

Operational issues

McKinsey research identified issues within an organisation's control rather than regulatory factors as being more important barriers to offshoring.

> ***For example*** *... The incompatibility of systems was an important aspect linked to mergers and amalgamations where systems were too complex, too elaborate and/or too idiosyncratic to easily disaggregate and offshore (Farrell 2005).*

Management attitudes and a lack of experience in dealing with the complexities that offshoring can throw up were also important operational issues. A third factor was simply that the small scale of an organisation's activities did not produce the required cost-benefits to proceed. This point is supported by an Australian study by Booz Allen Hamilton which notes that 66 per cent of Australian businesses employs fewer than 100 workers, and that it is this small business sector where most employment growth in Australia is taking place (2004:8).

A further set of issues identified in the McKinsey research was linked to issues of maturity in the new offshoring market, in particular the shortage of middle-management due to the rapid rise of the offshoring sector as well as issues associated with geographical dispersion and local competition. In India and China, university graduates are widely dispersed away from the major cities with international airline connections – important criteria identified in the study of multinationals seeking offshoring (Farrell *et al.* 2005). A secondary issue to this is that many potential offshore workers are unwilling to relocate. This then brings into play the domestic companies and joint ventures which can attract this potential offshore workforce, further reducing the talent pool. As Farrell *et al.* note, from an operational perspective and with a more in-depth analysis of the potential labour supply, only a fraction of the potential job candidates could successfully work at a foreign company (2005:25). As the report notes:

> *2.8 to 3.9 million – or 8 to 12% – of the young professionals in low-wage jobs are available for hire by export-orientated service offshoring companies. This compares to 8.8 million in our sample of high wage countries (Farrell 2005:34).*

Quality and service

The McKinsey research also notes that only a maximum of 19 per cent of the potential, i.e. degree level, talent in low-wage nations is suitable to work for multinational companies. This relatively low level can be linked to the increasing importance of quality and service requirement by customers in AMEs, as the debate on the costs and benefits of offshoring matures and broadens (Grant 2005; Holland, 2005; Nash *et al.* 2004). Key factors in this lack of suitability included: language skill; the low quality of the educational system which limited practical skills including interpersonal skills; and attitudes towards teamwork and cultural fit (Farrell *et al.* 2005). This was also supported by Access Economic which identified that the attraction of tangible savings would be lost if sustained quality and service were not maintained.

This leads to the issue of monitoring quality and service – another subsidiary or hidden cost – which may include visiting sites to ensure that work is being undertaken to the appropriate level and that changes are being implemented smoothly as the relationship matures. As Shiu (2004) acknowledges, at best the issues of culture, language, service integration and maintenance will require adjustment time for client and customers. This may also require onsite staff from the outsourcing company to ensure a smooth transition – and this all requires more time and money. However, time may not be on the organisation's side. As Coles–Myer found, these problems were important considerations in the relocation of its credit card services back to Australia (see CML case study at the end of this chapter). Dell Computers also re-routed technical support for its corporate customers from its centre in Bangalore India back to the US for similar reasons. Interestingly, the reason given by General Electric for moving jobs back to its Phoenix Arizona facility was that US workers could handle a greater volume of calls than their counterparts in India. The issue of financial loss from these examples is one thing, but the long-term loss of current and potential customers due to a lack of confidence in the organisation's ability to provide quality and service also needs to be taken into account.

Security, privacy and legal issues

Growing security and legal issues have been highlighted as increasing volumes of critical or sensitive data and information across international borders. Examples of these concerns have been noted in several reports. In the finance sector, reports of up to 130,000 Australian credit card holders – of approximately 40 million worldwide – being informed that their confidential information had been 'compromised' in an Indian call centre highlights this issue (Norrington & Gluyas 2005). The report identified that India, where most of this data processing is performed, does not have legislative protection of confidential information (Norrington & Gluyas 2005). Other high profile cases, such as an undercover investigation by a British newspaper buying confidential data stolen from call centres in India

(Norrington & Gluyas 2005) and FBI entrapment of ex-employees offering source codes for software packages belonging to Indian outsourcing company (Shiu 2004) reinforce this growing concern. In the health sector where 10% of US medical transcriptions are undertaken offshore, there were reports of a Pakistani clerk threatening to reveal medical information online unless the University of California paid her the wages owed by a subcontractor (Lazarus 2003; 2004). Similarly, the importance of security in this sector is highlighted further by the account of an Indian workers at Heartland Information Services, a US company that offshores medical record work, threatening to release confidential information unless they received a payoff from the company (Public Citizen 2004a).

A position taken by major organisations in response to these issues in Australia, including American Express and AXA, is that they work under Australian law; but this needs to be closely considered. As Grant (2005) points out with regard to intellectual property issues:

> *Agencies will need to be conscious of intellectual property issues. Ownership of intellectual property rights, such as copyright, normally depends on the residence of the creating entity. For example, software developed in India is subject to India's copyright laws (p. 32).*

These issues have dissuaded interest by the Australian Tax Office (ATO) to offshore some of its workload. The ramifications for the ATO where Australian tax files were not fully controlled, managed and secured for the Australian Federal Government needs little expanding upon. In contrast, over 200,000 US tax returns are processed electronically in India. In the US, the Federal Deposit Insurance Corporation (FDIC) released a report in 2004 which listed countries with no general data protection laws where offshoring was a growth industry, including: India, China, the Philippines, Singapore and Malaysia. As Shiu notes:

> *There is no substitute for sufficient due diligence on the legal framework in the offshore service provider's home jurisdiction to determine the scope and practicalities of enforcing legal rights or protecting intellectual property (IP) which may constitute a critical component of the offshoring activity.... Although contractual remedies will often be relied on, it is worthwhile ascertaining the ability to undertake non-contractual enforcement of IP rights. Actual implementation and enforcement of IP rights under domestic law is heavily influenced by cultural and resources factors which are often at a level below the expectations of many Western countries (2004:4-5).*

In addition, various investigations continue to reveal a black market for the personal information of Australian customers from call centre databases. In contrast, the European Union (EU) has developed more extensive protection mechanisms. Under EU law, personal data can only be offshored to countries deemed to have at least equivalent standards of protection and enforceability in privacy laws (EU Data Directive 1995).

Many of the operational issues discussed, including quality, service, security, privacy and legislative support, are linked to the issue of professional standards. As noted above, this regulatory gap is significant at a variety of levels with considerable consumer, economic and professional implications. In a case in a London hospital, medical dictation was offshored to India. Because of the highly technical nature of the work and the low language skills of the transcribers, it was identified that misspelling and gaps – left where words were not understood – caused medical records to be dangerously inaccurate and in many cases rendered the notes worthless (Pyman & Holland 2006). However, it is important to note from a resource perspective the difficulty and the costs involved in monitoring and enforcing standards in such a booming sector. As the US non-government organisation Public Citizen has pointed out in this respect:

> *Enforcement of professional standards and requirements with respect to offshoring is a serious problem. State regulatory agencies do not have the resources to fully monitor and enforce professional standards abroad and consumers cannot realistically be expected to conduct their own investigations before doing business with the growing number of providers that are sending specialised financial, medical and engineering work overseas. The ability to issue and revoke licences has been critical in helping US authorities maintain professional standards among domestic providers. The lack of licensing control and enforcement capability overseas invites abuse in a setting in which consumers have virtually no legal recourse after an injury or loss has occurred. The only current regulatory system is a silent assumption that professional qualifications are assured by the private company that is offshoring the work – which does not have a strong incentive to spend a lot of time or money on enforcement (2004a:1).*

Aware of these problems, the American Association for Medical Transcriptions (AAMT) has been advocating full disclosure of offshoring in an industry worth $US 20 billion. As concern over these issues increases, the trend may result in a move to more 'inshoring' or 'home shoring'. As the Public Citizen report notes:

> *The case can be made that US companies have been too quick to jump on the offshoring bandwagon; a few companies have concluded that sending jobs overseas is not worth their while. Although wages may be one-tenth of those for similar jobs in the United States, by the time administrative and other costs are factored in, first year savings may not exceed 20%. And these are expected to dwindle as costs begin to rise in these labour markets – wage surveys in India have already found 15-30% annual increases. In the United Kingdom, internal research by the Royal Bank of Scotland PLC concluded that using domestic labor would be better for staff, shareholders and customers. The bank is known for having a lower cost-income ratio than any of its major competitors (2004a:26).*

The key point that organisations can draw in respect of security and privacy issues is that responsibility for these critical areas cannot be outsourced.

Social, moral and political issues

The loss of jobs and skills has been used as a social, moral and political tool in the offshoring debate. Campaigns by unions and politicians, combined with criticism by customers and in the media, have had an impact on decisions to offshore. In Australia, the classic example, of this was the reversal of Coles-Myer's decision to offshore their credit card processing after a combination of public opinion, union campaigning, customer dissatisfaction and intense media attention on an Australian retail icon which was portrayed as 'selling' Australian jobs overseas (Nash, Holland & Pyman 2004). In the US, eFund of Scotsdale Arizona moved to return their welfare hotline from India following public attention generated by a bill introduced to the US Senate by New Jersey Senator Turner on the issue (Hopkins 2003). Paradoxically, the unfavourable publicity has also created opportunities for domestic organisations. As the Public Citizen report on the subject noted:

> *In the wake of the backlash against offshoring, some US-based companies have advertised the fact that they do not outsource work offshore. These include TaxBrain, an online tax-preparation outfit that assures customers that all their work is in the United States, and E-LOAN, a home equity lender that offshores some work to India but lets customers choose where their work is done (2004:26).*

It is worth noting that when E-LOAN gave the customer the choice of whether to have their loan processed in India or the US (noting that it would take longer if processed in the US), 86 per cent of customers chose the Indian route (Drucker 2004).

The size and continued job losses in the US during a recession in the early 2000s and the recent GFC have also generated continued debate around offshoring. As the non-governmental organisation (NGO) Public Citizen (2004b) shows, estimates of job relocation in the US include six million jobs moving offshore in the next decade (Goldman-Sachs 2003); 86 per cent of organisations expecting to move more technology jobs offshore; and 25 per cent of IT jobs relocated from the developed to the developing world by 2010 (Gartner Group 2004). The ease and ability of organisations to offshore operations such as business processes and customer services in a matter of hours reinforce the increasing insecurity (Grant 2005; Holland, Nelson & Sheehan 2000). This has created significant tension in AMEs, as not only are many governments supporting free trade and themselves looking to reduce costs, at the same time they are conscious of the backlash of 'jobs going overseas'.

For example ... In the US the Voinovich-Thomas amendment limits federal government agencies awarding certain contracts to organisations that will outsource the work overseas.

At a state level in the US, an increase in constraint is also evident. In December 2002, the New Jersey State Government outlawed the outsourcing of State government work – whether software or call centre work – to non-US citizens. In 2004 the State of Missouri followed this lead, and the Governor of Arizona issued a directive banning state work being sent offshore (Grant 2005). Offshoring also became a topic for the 2004 presidential debate where Presidents Bush's push for free trade was portrayed by his opponents as a green light to offshoring US jobs (Grant 2005). As a result, offshoring became one of the top three political issues. In Australia, despite the tactic support for free trade and, by default, offshoring by both major political parties, the decision of IBM to offshore approximately 400 Telstra IT-related jobs prior to the Federal election in 2004 created a political football. However, since the election the issue has not again become political (Crowe 2004:22). The decision by the Federal Government to not use its previous majority shareholder status within Telstra to change their decision to offshore via IBM Global Services indicated their tacit support for offshoring and the benefits it can bring to Australia. For iconic Australian firm such as the Commonwealth Bank (CBA), decisions to offshore have been referred to as a public relations minefield (Johnston 2005), as report after report reinforces the expectation that Australian jobs will continue to move offshore (see Table 3.1 and Table 3.2). In the finance sector this could be as high as 30 per cent (Johnston 2005).

Table 3.1 Examples of past, current and potential offshoring ventures of Australian organisations

Organisations	Work	Jobs	Location
ANZ	IT/Software	530	India
AXA	IT	65	India
CML/GE Capital	Credit Card	150	India-Melbourne*
Citigroup	Call Centre	150	Philippines
Hewlett Packard	Call Centre Support	128	India
Hutchinson	Customer/Business Support	200	India
NAB	Accounts Processing	20	India
Optus	Call Centre	150	India
Telstra/EDS	IT	580	India
Telstra/Infosys	IT	180	India
Telstra/IBM	IT	450	India
Qantas	Data Processing/Flight attendants	500	England
Westpac/BT	Back office processing	400	India

* See CML case study on page 67.

Sources: Grant 2005; Kremmer 2006.

Table 3.2 Offshoring – a cross-section of Australian jobs at risk

Industries	No employed (000) May 2004	OECD estimates of potential jobs offshore (%)	Number of jobs that could move offshore
Finance	193.6	86.2	166.9
Insurance	59.2	71.4	42.3
Services to Finance and Insurance	89.2	79.4	70.8
Business Services	941.6	51.7	486.8
Defence	22.7	39.2	8.9
Government Admin	438.1	32.0	140.2
Electricity & Gas Supply	53.3	30.0	16.0
Film, Radio & TV Services	48.7	29.4	14.3

Industries	No employed (000) May 2004	OECD estimates of potential jobs offshore (%)	Number of jobs that could move offshore
Printing Pub & Recorded Media	111.1	29.2	32.4
Communication Services	177.5	26.3	46.7
Libraries, Museums & the Arts	58.5	25.0	14.6
Total Australian industry	9969.7	19.4	1934.1

Source: Kremmer 2006.

Emerging issues: Onshoring and near-shoring

With the increasing awareness of the potential downside of offshoring, the issue of onshoring and near-shoring are emerging as alternative and complementary strategies. As a Economist Intelligence Unit (EIU) report noted on this matter:

> *The most important development in offshoring is not a race to the bottom, but the emergence of diverse new locations with different competitive advantages and disadvantages, supplying growth demands for offshoring in all shapes and sizes (Met-Cohn et al. 2006:5).*

In continental Europe, which has not embraced the offshoring concept as comprehensively as Anglo-American countries such as the UK, the US and Australia, the emerging market is starting to resemble the demand of the US and UK in the past decade; however, the decision-making processes reflect a different set of values. US-based consultancy TPI estimated that $US 41 billion worth of contracts were undertaken in Europe in 2004 – nearly twice the level of 2002 (Reinhardt 2005). This is set to continue despite the data processing restrictions enforced by the EU as noted earlier. Europeans have had time to reflect on decisions to offshore in a complex and maturing market, and it is clear that near-shoring is developing as a significant option. In this context, the key facets that organisations are looking for are language and understanding, the skills base and time zones – in other words, cultural fit. In addition, recent expansion of the EU has enabled many Central European governments to develop policies to attract foreign investment (Meth-Cohn *et al.* 2006). Taking these factors into consideration, the EIU report identified the countries listed in Table 3.3 as the most suitable for German organisations to relocate operations to.

Table 3.3 Ranking of potential offshore locations from the perspective of a German company

Country	Score	Rank
Czech Republic	2.3	1
Hungary	2.3	2
Poland	2.5	3
India	2.5	4
Germany	2.6	5
Malaysia	2.6	6
China	2.8	7
Ireland	2.8	8
Russia	2.8	9

Note: Weighting Cost 35%; Business Environment, 35%; Risk Profile 20%; Quality of Infrastructure 10%.
Source: EIU 2006.

Two case studies which illustrate the emergence of these locations are Hewlett-Packard (HP) and Oracle. HP, the world's leading outsourcer, has focused its current growth on Central Europe, building two new business processing sites in Poland and two IT support centres in Romania as well as complementary operations in Germany and Spain. In Oracle's case, it has expanded its back office work to India and has restructured its Ireland and US centres to focus on high-skilled control and compliance issues, employing a small staff of highly-skilled bilingual accountants. Oracle has also opened administrative centres in Romania and two specialised centres in Poland and Hungary (Meth-Cohn *et al.* 2006). A third catalyst for the development of near-shoring is the nature of a 24/7 business world continually requiring diverse and complex global networks of support services – a key factor in DHL setting up IT support services in the Czech Republic to complement its Indian and Malaysian centres. As the Managing Director of DHL Global Business Services noted:

> *In Europe, Prague was competing with the UK, Portugal, Spain, Ireland and other Central Eastern locations. To make the decision, DHL drew up its requirements: IT skills, good infrastructure, a business-friendly government and stable political environment, good air links around the region along with competitively-priced labour, office space and hotels (cited in Meth-Cohn et al. 2006:9).*

In contrast, Spain has extensively embraced offshoring, with Barcelona the main hub due to the lure of its lifestyle. The over 2,000 call centres now in Spain attract employees from all over Europe. For Dallas-based Affiliated Computer Service – their 1,000 Barcelona-based staff come from 38 countries and speak 14 languages – this is seen as a key competitive advantage in customer services (Reinhardt 2005). Benchmarking across a variety of factors, the AT Kearney ranking of offshoring destinations came up with the following standing of offshore destinations:

Table 3.4 EIU offshoring environment (2005)

Country	Score	Rank
India	7.76	1
China	7.34	2
Czech Republic	7.26	3
Singapore	7.25	4
Poland	7.24	5
Canada	7.23	6
Hong Kong	7.19	7
Hungary	7.17	8
Philippines	7.17	9
Thailand	7.16	10
Malaysia	7.13	11
Slovakia	7.12	12
Bulgaria	7.09	13
Romania	7.08	14
Chile	7.08	15

Note: Score based on nine separate measures: proximity, political and security risk, macroeconomic stability, regulatory environment, tax regime, labour regulation, labour costs, labour skills and infrastructure.
Source: EIU 2006.

Whilst India and China are ranked first and second respectively, the global 'footprint' model reflecting more complex and diverse business requirement points to the emergence of European countries which now make up six of the top 15 destinations. As the director of Human Resources Europe, Middle East and Africa for HP notes: "The right location depends on your decision criteria and what you want to achieve" (cited in Meth-Cohn *et al.* 2006). Another factors in favour of dispersion as the market matures is that clustering, once seen as a way to build critical mass, can turn into a war for talent as the labour market becomes saturated and attrition rates and labour costs rise. This development has seen countries such as Russia, the Baltic states, and Middle Eastern and African countries with stable political system – and on European time zones – being identified as suitable locations (Meth-Cohn *et al.* 2006).

Interestingly for Australia (which is not in the top group), Canada – a country of similar size, culture, political stability and high technology infrastructure – is ranked sixth, providing a potential model for Australian policy-makers and organisations. This viewpoint is supported by the Australian Computer Society (ACS) in their position report on the industry. The ACS argues that Australia needs to become a global hub – or a 'destination of choice' – for sophisticated knowledge-based information communications and technology (ICT) services for the US, European and Japanese markets (2005:1). This high-quality end of the market is where the ACS identified Australia's competitive advantage, with labour costs between 20 – 40 per cent lower than in the UK, Japan, the US and major European centres. In addition, Australia's transparent legal system and strong corporate governance practices place it favourably with EU requirements in terms of appropriate provisions and safeguards to ensure data protection.

Conclusions

As the debate on offshoring has matured, issues associated with lead time, integration, culture, service quality and security have increasingly become pivotal in the debate and the decision to offshore. Intangible 'costs' such as these can reduce and even negate the perceived benefits of offshoring if not considered fully. As the manager of Customers Operations at Vodafone Egypt, Duncan Howard, was quoted in a EIU Report:

> *Many have now come to realise that pushing for the lowest possible costs can be bad for business. You can't expect customers to pay for premium services and not mind being handled by someone whose accent they can't understand and who has absolutely no knowledge about how things work in their country (cited in Meth-Cohn et al. 2006).*

Whilst many see the issue of offshoring as a growing concern for Australia and other AMEs, organisations such as the Australian Computer Society have identified opportunities for Australia to become a medium-cost hub for high-value sophisticated offshoring work from other AMEs. Grant (2005) also acknowledges that, despite the potential labour cost savings in developing countries, the attraction of quality, reliability, stability, safety and security may yet see Australia develop as an offshoring destination. For many Australian companies, they may come to realise that trading jobs for competitive advantage may in fact be a false economy.

References

Australian Centre for Industrial Relations Research and Training (ACIRRT) 1999, *Australia at Workplace: Just Managing?*, Prentice Hall, Sydney.

Australian Computer Society (ACS) 2005, 'Policy Statement on Onshoring Based Analytics', September.

Bajkowski, J 2005, 'Ruddock Warns On Offshoring Data', *Computerworld*, 18 August, p. 15, <www.arnnet.com.au>.

Booz Allen Hamilton, 2004, 'Business Processing Offshoring: Making the Right Decision', Business White Paper, USA.

Castro, A 2003, 'Dell to Stop Using Tech Support in India', 24 November, <www.theledger.com>.

Crowe, D 2004a, 'India grabs the global advantage', *The Weekend Australian Financial Review – Perspective*, 7-8 February, pp. 22-23.

Domberger, S 1994, 'Public Sector Contracting: Does it Work?', *The Australian Economic Review*, 3rd quarter, pp. 91-96.

Drucker, J 2004, 'Truth is, Outsourcing Works Anywhere', *The Weekend Australian Financial Review,* 13-14 March, p. 32, Fairfax Publications.

Emmott, M & Hutchinson, S 1998, 'Employment flexibility: Threat or promise?', in P Sparrow & M Marchington (eds), *Human Resource Management: The New Agenda London*, Financial Times, Pitmans, pp. 229-244.

The European Commission on Data Protection (EU Data Directive) 1995, 95/46/EC.

Farrell, D, Laboissiere, M, Pascal, R, Rosenfeld, J, de Segundo, C, Sturze, S, & Umezawa, F 2005, 'The Emerging Global Labor Market'. McKinsey Global Institute, McKinsey and Company, June.

Grant, R 2005, 'Offshoring Jobs: US and American Perspectives', Research Brief No.12, Parliament of Australia, Parliamentary Library.

Hartmann, L & Patrickson, M 2000, 'Externalizing the Workforce: Australian Trends and issues for HRM', *International Journal of Manpower*, 21(1): 7-20.

Holland, PJ, Nelson, L & Fisher, C 2000, 'Australian Trade Unions' Responses to Human Resource Management in a Globalised Era', *Asia Pacific Business Review*, 7(2): 46-70.

Holland, PJ 2005, 'Outsourcing: Is it Working? - Commentary cost benefits of call centres offshore', by M Sullivan, *Sydney Morning Herald*, 23 December.

Hopkins, S 2003, 'States' Ship Contract Work to India', *Charlotte Observer*, 10 August.

Johnston, E 2005, 'Jobs Outflow is about to become a Flood' *The Weekend Australian Financial Review*, 15 August, p. 55, Fairfax Publications.

Konard, R 2004, 'Foreign Accountants Do US Tax Returns', *Associated Press*, 22 February.

Kremmer, C 2006, 'India Calling', *The Age*, 21 August.

Lazarus, D 2003, 'Stopping ID Theft by memo', *San Francisco Chronicle*, 28 November.

Lazarus, D 2004, 'Extortion Threat to Patients Records', *San Francisco Chronicle*, 2 April, p. 28.

McKinsey Global Institute 2003, 'Offshoring is a Win-Win Game?', McKinsey & Company.

McKinsey 2004, 'Exploding the Myths of Offshoring', *The McKinsey Quarterly*, McKinsey & Company, July.

McKinsey Global Institute 2005, 'The Emerging Global Market', McKinsey & Company, June.

Met-Cohn, D, Freudmann, A, Shields, K, Kuncinas, P & Ramberger, S 2006, 'The New Face of Offshoring: Closer to Home?', The Economic Intelligence Unit (EIU), London, UK.

Nancarrow, K 2004, 'Out of India', *The Age*, 8-9 February, Fairfax Publications.

Nash, B, Holland, PJ & Pyman, A 2004, 'The Role and influence of Stakeholders in off-shoring: Developing a Framework for Analysis', *International Employment Relations Review*, 10(2): 29-49.

Norrington, B & Gluyas, R 2005, 'Aussies at Risk of Credit Fraud', *The Weekend Australian*, 25-26 June, p. 3, News Limited Publications.

Perry, C 1997, 'Outsourcing and Union Power', *Journal of Labour Research 17*, Fall: 521-534.

Public Citizen 2004a, 'Offshoring and Professional Standards', Washington.

Public Citizen 2004b, 'How Many Jobs are Involved?', Washington.

Pyman, A & Holland, P 2006, 'The Unseen Risks of Offshoring', Unpublished.

Quiggin, J 1996, 'Competitive Tendering and Contracting in the Australian Public Sector', *Australian Journal of Public Administration*, 55(3): 49-57.

Reinhardt, A 2005, 'Spain basks in the *Hola* Effect', *The Weekend Australian Financial Review*, 10-11 September, p. 30, Fairfax Publications.

Shaw, M 2005, 'Privacy Laws may be Tightened', *The Age*, 15 August 15, p. 3, Fairfax Publications.

Shiu, K 2004, 'Outsourcing: Are you sure or offshore? Identifying Legal Risk in Offshoring', *Society for Computers and the Law*, Issue 56, June.

Spikes, S 2004, 'Shifting Financial Services and Jobs Abroad Doesn't Always Pay Off', *Wall Street Journal*, 28 January.

Taylor & Bain 2004, 'Call Centre Offshoring to India: The revenge of History?', *Labour & Industry*, 14(3): 15-38.

Wu, A 2004, 'Looking Offshore', *San Francisco Chronicle*, 6 July.

TPI 2005, 'European Outsourcing on the Rise', <www.personneltoday.com>.

Young, S 2000, 'Outsourcing: Lessons from the Literature', *Labour & Industry*, 10(3): 97-118.

Case study: Offshoring Coles Myers Credit Card

Coles Myer Limited (CML), Australia's largest non-government employer with over 165,000 staff, was undergoing significant restructuring in the late 1990s to regain profits and growth. Coles Myer appointed a new Chief Executive Officer, John Fletcher, in 2001. A key part of the revitalisation strategy adopted was a low-cost operations approach. One aspect of this strategy was the minimisation of duplication, and an obvious area for consolidation was the range of credit card brands. In 2001, management merged all the individual brands into one corporate card - The Coles Myer Card. The offshoring of this operation followed through a specialist call centre operator, GE Capital. The Coles Myer Card was subsequently managed by GE Capital through their call centres, with 50% of customer queries directed to operations in Dehli, India from 2002. This decision would have been expected to deliver substantial cost savings.

It appears that there was little, if any, communication of this decision to stakeholders. In early 2003 it was publicly revealed and addressed by the media that some of the Myer Card call centre staff were based in India. As Nancarrow (2004:9) highlighted: "Callers to talkback radio complained about poor service and communication, and bemoaned the loss of Australian jobs". Initial adverse publicity following the offshoring of CML's call centre operations was followed by an ABC television documentary entitled 'Diverted to Delhi'. This documentary highlighted the outsourcing of call centre and IT jobs to India more broadly. GE Capital and Coles Myer, however, featured prominently, and an interview conducted with a shareholder of Coles Myer indicated that he was unhappy that part of the call centre operations had been outsourced to India because of the loss of Australian jobs. This documentary generated substantial publicity relating to offshoring, and in particular the decision of Coles Myer to (indirectly) follow this route.

The union movement has been at the forefront of the offshoring debate, particularly in relation to the export of jobs and the exploitation of workers in less-regulated countries. In the documentary, they were also prominent. Belinda Tkalcevic from the Australian Council of Trade Unions (ACTU) and Martin Foley from the Australian Services Union (ASU) both discussed a range of themes, but the export of skilled Australian jobs was clearly their major concern. Both Foley and Tkalcevic attacked the Federal government's position, particularly in light of their role as a key stakeholder in Australian organisations. The issue of quality also emerged in the documentary as a major theme, with adverse feedback in relation to poor quality of service and difficulties in communicating with Indian employees.

The pressure from the stakeholders on the export of Australian jobs (customers/shareholder and unions) forced Coles Myer into a re-evaluation of the low-cost offshoring strategy *vis-a-vis* the moral and social concerns of stakeholders; namely, the perception that an Australian 'icon' company which accounted for 40 cents of every retail dollar was exporting home-grown skilled local jobs. As one shareholder on the Diverted to Dehli documentary surmised:

> *I think the part that annoyed me most... I see this like exporting jobs. Myer does not have stores in India....so their customers are not in New Dehli....The customers are here and I think that kind of employment should be here [in Australia] (Aspinall 2003).*

In late 2003, the call centre operations for Coles Myer were relocated to Australia. In the Coles Myer case it was clear that the unifying issue was the export of home country jobs underpinned by continuous services issues. This was magnified by a clear lack of consultation with these stakeholder groups on what turned out to be a very emotive issue.

The focus on the Coles Myer brand and their reputation – and public (customer) opinion on a company seen as an Australian 'icon' – had the potential to damage the company brand name. Then, when the initial issue of the offshoring of Australian jobs is added to the negative customer feedback, the perceptions of poor quality of service, and the adverse media publicity, the overall pressure placed on CML was significant.

Written by: Nash, Holland & Pyman.

Case study questions

1. Why did offshoring become such a public problem for CML?
2. Why did CML react in the way it did in response to the offshoring of its credit card processing?
3. What lessons can be learned by other companies considering the offshoring option?

Discussion questions

1. What have been the catalysts driving the exceptional growth of offshoring in the service sector in recent years?

2. What have been the major issues driving concerns over offshoring in many AMEs?

3. Identify and explain the key issues to take into account when making a decision to offshore.

4. Is the offshoring of increasingly-skilled jobs inevitable?

5. What advantages does Australia have that allows it the potential to become a medium-cost hub for the offshoring industry?

Chapter 4

ICT AND EMPLOYMENT: CHALLENGES AND FUTURE DIRECTIONS

INTRODUCTION

In 1992, computer expert David Gelernter, in his book *Mirror Worlds*, argued that a software revolution would change the way society's business was conducted and also change the intellectual landscape in the process. This argument could not have been more accurate, and the rapid and continuous advancement of information and communication technologies (ICT) throughout the 21st century will continue to radically reshape the world of work. Commonly identified benefits of ICT for organisations include reduced transaction costs and more efficient management and control of employees (e.g. Cascio 1999; Rubery & Grimshaw 2001). In fact, the organisational benefits of exploiting ICT for information provision and management have been widely recognised in the literature from a range of disciplinary perspectives, including organisational behaviour, ecommerce, social informatics and employee relations. This chapter adopts an employee relations perspective of the use of ICT within an organisation, exploring in particular the issues, challenges and future directions pertaining to electronic human resource management (eHRM) and e-unionism.

The chapter begins with a consideration of eHRM and is followed by a discussion of the practice of online recruitment including its advantages, disadvantages and challenges. The emergence of social networking is also considered. This is then followed by a definition of e-unionism and a consideration of the rationale for the use of ICT within trade unions. The issues and challenges for unions in adopting ICT in an increasingly globalised business environment are then examined. The chapter concludes with a discussion of future directions and a summary of the core arguments presented throughout the chapter.

eHRM

eHRM has emerged in a myriad of ways. The late 20th century, for instance, witnessed the rise of online recruiting, online advertisement of jobs, online storage of employees' resumes, and the sophisticated application and development of human resource information systems (HRIS). As Macy (2007:36) noted, traditional HRIS were designed for record automation, regulatory compliance, reporting and workforce analytics. They are now more commonly-known as human capital management systems (HCMS) and their main features are talent management, competencies and performance (Macy 2007). In fact, the use of 'talent pools' – or candidate database systems – is increasing in Australia among private sector employers (Dahl 2006a).

The most commonly identified definition or vision of eHRM is the application of electronic, predominantly web-based technologies, to HRM practices. However, a small yet growing body of literature has taken a deeper, more integrated approach to the study of eHRM, examining the notion of virtual networks and the consequences and challenges for the development, deployment and management of human and social capital (e.g. Alveson 1993; Blacker 1995; Scarborough, Swan & Preston 1999; Boxall & Purcell 2000; Lepak & Snell 1998; Quinn, Anderson & Finkelstein 1996).

Whilst the use of ICT does not generate a competitive advantage in itself for an organisation, the use of electronic and virtual HRM systems to manage people and complex information in an increasingly global workplace can, if done successfully, increase efficiencies and prevent imitation – the foundation of a sustainable competitive advantage according to HRM theory (Miller & Cardy 2000). One such example may be a firm-specific system through which employees share knowledge and are able to solve problems (Boxall & Purcell 2000; Cappelli & Crocker-Hefter 1996; Coff 1999). However, as various academics have noted, the strategic management of human resources becomes even more complex and critical when electronic and virtual networks are used. A deep understanding by the organisation itself, of the employee relations architecture, of HRM practices, and, of organisational structure, is paramount, if organisations are to capitalise on ICT in the new 'virtual' environment (Coff 1999; Hedllund 1994; Scarborough *et al.* 1999). Whilst the literature recognises benefits for organisations from ICT, empirical research examining the contribution of ICT to competitive advantage is relatively isolated and descriptive.

To illustrate the issues associated with eHRM, this chapter focuses on one of the most widespread developments in the field – online recruitment or e-recruitment. The advantages, disadvantages and challenges of online recruitment for organisations are considered, and two separate case examples are presented to illustrate the disparity in outcomes that can result from the utilisation of online recruitment.

Online recruitment

Organisations have increasingly made use of the internet to deploy human capital in order to streamline recruitment processes, increase the speed of recruiting times, and reduce transaction costs. Organisations can use online recruitment in two main ways (Freeman 2002). The first is by advertising job vacancies online via recruitment sites (e.g. in Australia: MyCareer, careerone, Seek and People Online)[1], and/or by advertising jobs on company web pages. The second use of online recruitment occurs when organisations search and access the resumés of potential employees through online recruitment sites. Potential employees can also make use of the internet to search and apply for jobs and to store their CVs online, which may lead to targeted queries from potential employers (Nakamura, Freeman, Pyman & Shaw 2007). Commercial online recruiting sites also often provide additional services and advice for job seekers (Nakamura *et al.* 2007). For instance, MyCareer in Australia provides online advice on: writing CVs and covering letters, conduct in interviews, and career progression.

The phenomenal growth of online recruitment sites is one of the defining features of the information economy in the 21st century. Millions of workers around the world each week search online recruitment and corporate sites for vacancies, and apply for jobs online. A survey of workers in 12 European countries in 2007 revealed that, for 68 per cent of respondents, the internet was one of the leading methods of finding a job, and was ranked higher than alternatives such as employment agencies, direct approaches to employers, newspaper advertisements, and industry contacts and referrals (Dahl 2006b). Statistics for online job advertisements in Australia also reveal an increase in advertisements on commercial job sites. And, the information technology and telecommunications sector is second only to trades and services in terms of the highest proportion of job advertisements by sector (*HR Monthly* 2007). As Autor (2001:26) suggested, the reasons that job boards proliferated are clear. They offer more information, are easier to search and are potentially more up to date than their textual counterpart (i.e. newspaper advertisements). In addition, job boards allow individuals to advertise their skills to employers as well as the reverse.

As Autor (2001) inferred above and Freeman (2002) discussed in more detail, one of the key benefits that is assumed to flow from online recruitment is that the 'talent pool' of potential applicants is dramatically increased because the transaction costs of job searching – both for the employee and for the firm – are simultaneously reduced. Theoretically, this has benefits for both parties, and, as Freeman (2002) argued, should result in better quality job matches in terms of the employee-job match and the employee-organisation match. Quality job matches are in turn assumed to lead to better performance and enhanced employee loyalty and commitment (Freeman 2002). However, the

---

[1] Online job search sites have also been labelled job boards or e-recruitment sites.

proliferation of online job search tools changes the way employers recruit, and this means that assessment techniques for selecting the best applicants must be improved (Bowmer as cited in Dahl 2006b). As Bowmer (2006 as cited in Dahl 2006b:42) stated: 'because it reaches a bigger audience, online advertising often generates a larger volume of responses, but not necessarily better qualified candidates'. Employers need to carefully consider job descriptions and the specific requirements of the positions they advertise (Bowmer 2006 as cited in Dahl 2006b:42). (See the ES case study on page 98).

Examining the potential benefits of online recruitment in greater depth, Freeman (2002), employing an economic perspective, argued that online recruitment offered three potential efficiency gains to the economy: reduced transaction costs; speedier clearance of the job market; and better quality 'job matches' of employees skills, job vacancies and organisational needs (Freeman 2002). That is, online recruitment can greatly reduce the duration of job vacancies and the costs per employee hired by enabling a wider search for job applicants, thereby shortening recruitment and selection processes for organisations and job searching and recruitment times for employees.

For job seekers, time savings are not the only tangible benefit. Online recruitment makes it possible to evaluate job options, undertake background research and better understand an industry before initial contact (Dahl 2006b:42) Online recruitment, provided one has access to the internet, can also offer convenience and cost savings, for example, in relation to phone calls, photocopying and postage, while at the same time rapidly increasing the number of potential jobs one can consider and apply for (Nakamura *et al.* 2007). For example, if a job seeker is willing to be mobile with respect to their labour, online recruitment makes geographical location redundant – whether it is at a regional, national or international level. Newman (2005) however argued that the 'new geography of work' and growth in labour mobility can actually induce complacency among employers. He suggested that corporations end up with little interest in training employees, with the exception of their most elite employees, because advanced job skills are just a mouse click away in another city (Newman 2005:384).

Examining the benefits for employers and organisations in more detail, the costs of advertising online have been shown to be cheaper than in the traditional newspaper and hard copy press media. In addition, convenience, time and cost savings are often realised in the receipt and processing of online applications – particularly for large numbers of applicants – as a result of the technical processing capabilities of online recruitment systems. One example would be automated replies to job applications available through online systems (Nakamura *et al.* 2007). In theory, the more technologically advanced the online recruitment system, the greater the benefits that may accrue to organisations. As Nakamura *et al.* (2007) explained, one example might be where an online recruitment system utilises an application form that is connected to a database, which in turn, enables online screening of applications in real time, that is, as the applicant is answering the questions. For instance, if an applicant was required to have a vehicle for use on the job and they answered 'no' to this question, these applicants could be automatically sent a rejection notice via email. Nakamura *et al.* (2007) argued that the use of automated online tools to match prospective employees and their skills to jobs may result in a move toward a type of 'just-in-time management of human capital'. An illustration of some of the aforementioned benefits that can arise from streamlining recruitment processes through online systems is illustrated in Box 4.1 with regard to Boots: a UK-based retail organisation.

> **Box 4.1: Boots - Driving benefits from online recruitment**
>
> Boots is a leading health and beauty retailer in Britain and sells products in 130 countries. The company traditionally used a paper and email based process for managing job applications but found this to be time consuming. A subsequent review of recruitment processes led to the adoption of an online recruitment system purchased from a corporate e-recruitment retailer. Boots initially used the new online system to source pharmacy students for summer placements. Benefits derived from this new online approach included allowing candidates to list preferences in terms of geographic location rather than applying to multiple stores, and using a mass emailing tool to communicate with successful candidates. In terms of measurable outputs, one clear benefit derived from the online application system was the placement of students, on average, three months earlier compared with the paper based approach.
>
> Based on the success of the online system for placement students, Boots ran a second online recruitment campaign for store managers in the UK and Ireland. The HR design specialist in Boots pointed to a multitude of benefits. For example, a more efficient, cost-effective and consistent recruitment process could be achieved by removing postage costs associated with the mailing of recruitment packs and instead distributing these online, and, by extending the geographic reach for talent by advertising careers on the company's website.
>
> *Source*: Pollitt 2007.

Despite the potential benefits of online recruitment for employers and employees, there are also drawbacks. One potential pitfall of online recruitment systems is a lack of flexibility. A second and related pitfall is the cost associated with developing, implementing and adapting an online recruitment system that is appropriate and consistent with the business needs (see case study at the end of the chapter). Commercial e-recruiters marketing packages to organisations are known to charge very high prices for adapting and modifying a system. However, it is not simply an issue of the cost of modification – it is modification *per se*. Online recruitment systems must not only have internal coherence, there must also be an external fit with organisational needs and strategies. An example of the problems that can result from a lack of strategic integration of online recruitment systems can be seen in the UK with regard to junior doctors' applications for specialist jobs (see Box 4.2).

> **Box 4.2: The importance of strategic integration - an online application blunder in the UK**
>
> The online application blunder in the UK referred to an online questionnaire-based application known as the Medical Training Application Service (MTAS) which was developed by the Department of Health to streamline the placement of junior doctors in specialist jobs (BBC News 2007). The online system was part of a broader package of reforms introduced by the Blair Labour government under the banner of 'Modernising Medical Careers'.
>
> The new online application system was the source of much controversy, angst and complaints, with the system being invariably described as an 'absolute disaster', 'an utter shambles', 'fatally flawed' and 'chaotic' (BBC News 2007; Hall 2007a; Parkinson 2007). Major concerns included:
>
> - inappropriate wording on application forms and a failure to ask pertinent questions;
> - the inability of applicants to be able to set out their relevant qualifications on the application form;
> - the inability of applicants to upload/attach a CV to their application;
> - inadequate development of the system preventing coordination of online applications;
> - applicants' inabilities to access the website to find out if they were successful in obtaining an interview; and
> - Staffing problems on wards due to junior doctors all being interviewed at similar times.
>
> The result of all these complaints, meant that the best candidates were not selected for the right jobs and, by default, highly-skilled, qualified and experienced candidates were not being offered jobs at all (Hall 2007a,b). As a result, some highly-trained junior doctors expressed a willingness to move abroad to find jobs due to the inadequacies of the system (Parkinson 2007). On the other hand, there was some evidence of senior consultants boycotting interview

> panels because they believed the system was unfair and unfit for its intended purpose (Hall 2007a).
>
> The first round of complaints led to government assurances that changes would be made to the system prior to second round interviews for specialist posts. Changes would include allowing applicants to upload their CVs and conducting one-to-one assessments with those who were not selected for interviews (BBC News 2007). However, a continuous barrage of criticism and the threat of a public protest led the Department of Health to concede and delay second round interviews. They agreed to an immediate independent review, and committed to re-running the first round of applications (Hall 2007a). As Hall (2007b) reported, the system was eventually aborted, with the Department of Health agreeing to traditional interviews for hospital posts for approximately 11,000 junior doctors, to ensure everyone received one interview for their first choice of training post.
>
> *Source*: BBC News 2007a; Hall 2007a, 2007b; Parkinson 2007.

Equality of access – or the 'digital divide' – is also a potential drawback of online recruitment systems for both individuals and organisations. In relation to individuals, access to the internet is a basic requirement that allows one to take advantage of the benefits of online recruitment systems. Research has consistently shown however, that not all socio-economic groupings have equal access to the internet, meaning that the potential benefits of searching for jobs online cannot be realised for all (Ball 2007). Unequal access can also be conceptualised in relation to disability. As Ball (2007: 10) reported, a survey by the Disability Rights Commission revealed 81 per cent of websites in the UK failed to satisfy basic web accessibility guidelines, automatically excluding those disabled people of working age applying for jobs online. In the case of organisations, size is an important factor. As Nakamura *et al.* (2007) pointed out the costs imposed on employers by commercial online recruitment sites for advertising jobs may mean that the utilisation of online recruitment systems is prohibitive for small organisations. Indeed, as Wilkinson (1999) identified, the characteristics of employment relations in small firms – such as informality and a lack of HR specialist expertise – may also act as barriers to the utilisation of online recruitment systems.

A third drawback of online recruitment systems is social sorting, that is, the stratification of employment opportunities based on the norms, biases and decision-making processes used by recruiters (Ball 2007). For example, recruiters may exclude certain candidates on the basis of particular keywords or criteria, and, without being checked, these situations could lead to issues of discrimination or inconsistency (Ball 2007).

Despite a growing literature around online recruitment, the phenomenal growth of online recruitment sites, and, the increasing use of online recruitment in practice, there is still a lack of empirical research in this area (e.g. Parry & Tyson 2008; Parry & Wilson 2009). In particular, there is a lack of empirical research that explores whether the cost and time savings generated by online recruitment – both for organisations and employees – are at the expense of quality 'job matches' (Freeman 2002; Galanaki 2002; Smith & Rupp 2004). Indeed, the implications of online hiring decisions by organisations and the broader economic significance of the utilisation of online recruitment systems represent important areas for further academic research (see Nakamura *et al.* 2007). Such implications arguably become even more significant in a global war for talent (see *Chapter 2: Managing the War for Talent*).

Social networking and HRM

The phenomenon of social networking – through sites such as Facebook and Myspace, and more professional sites such as LinkedIn – have become major features of e-communication inside and outside the workplace in the 21st century. As a result, workplaces are now encountering issues which require new policies and procedures so as to be able to manage these new aspects of work. To give some context to this growing phenomena, Twitter recently claimed to generate 50 million 'tweets' a day or 600 a second (Gettler 2010).

The consequences of these new communications tools are manifest in a wide range of workplace issues. From a productivity perspective, the excessive use of social media tools can have a negative effect as employees become diverted from their normal day-to-day activities due to the immediacy of communication on these sites. In addition, organisational reputations can be damaged where employees make inappropriate comments about their employer. Issues of privacy and security have also been raised. However, as Chilvee and Cowan (2008) note, such mediums are increasingly the preferred method of communication for many employees, and organisations are increasingly looking at embracing this technology to engage with employees and potential employees. For example, with the increasing 'war for talent' (see chapter 2), social networking sites can be used as a tool to engage current and future employees and to retain contact with former employees who may return to the organisation. For instance, Dow Chemicals identified that 40 per cent of its workforce would be eligible for retirement within the next five years. As such, Dow has made talent and career management core issues for the organisation. Dow has launched a corporate social network – My Dow Network – which serves retirees as well as former and current employees. Initial evidence for the social network site has found an increase in re-hires (Chilvee & Cowan 2008). The site also achieved widespread publicity with an Employer of Choice award from Workforce Management, Computer World and Business Week. In contrast, US-based software organisation Institu uses a corporate blog to keep employees globally involved in meetings (Arnold 2009). Other major international organisations, such as Ernst & Young and Unilever, have established their own Facebook pages as a way of developing brand awareness and attracting new talent through listing jobs on their webpage (Zeidner 2009). Indeed, Ernst & Young claim to have 15,000 plus members across 140 countries (Brockett 2007) and KPMG uses social networking medium to inform prospective employees of upcoming campus events (Chynoweth 2007). Watham use their corporate page on Facebook and LinkedIn to announce job opportunities whilst medical organisation Innovis Health utilise YouTube to recruit doctors (Arnold 2009).

The training and development implications of social networking are being explored as the complexity and geographical diversity of many organisations increases. Social networking sites can be used as a catalyst to connect new employees, to build a network, and to learn from each other and develop mentoring (Chilvee & Cowan 2008). Such approaches to social networking can allow organisations to develop highly integrated knowledge networks, such as at IBM. From a human resource management practitioner's perspective, a recent study in the UK of 275 HR managers found that 80 per cent of them belong to social networking sites (Hibberd 2009). The study found that the major use of this form of social networking was to develop knowledge networks. The professional Human Resource Management body in the UK – the Chartered Institute of Personnel and Development (CIPD) – has also developed a 'twitter' page to inform HR professionals about latest practices and legal developments.

However, as noted, risks are also starting to be identified in organisations as the boundaries blur between the workplace and employees' private lives. As a Personnel Today/Charles Russell survey in the UK of 226 senior human resource practitioners found, HR managers' major concerns with social networking were time wasting, loss of productivity, security issues and inappropriate activities (Woolnough 2008) To deal with these emerging issues, organisations' electronic communication policies and practices need to be revised and updated accordingly. However, studies identify a lack of urgency in organisations' developing social media and e-communication policies. A study in 2009 by Buck Consultants of nearly 1500 employers worldwide – the *Employee Engagement Survey* – found that only 45 per cent had social media policies (HRFocus 2009a). A Deloitte Survey in 2009 found that whilst 30 per cent of organisations had a media strategy, 55 per cent did not have policies in place to deal with social networking. Another survey by Manpower of 7,710 SMEs in the Asia Pacific region found that 75 per cent of organisations did not have social networking policies in place (Gettler 2009), whilst a survey of compliance and ethics professionals in the UK private sector by the Society of Corporate Compliance and Ethics (SCCE) and the Health Care Compliance Association, found that over 50 per cent did not actively monitor their employees' use of social networking. More significant, the survey found that only 10 per cent had policies specifically addressing social networks (HRFocus 2009b). The *Social Networking Regulation Pulse Survey* of 10,000 employees – as reported by the US-based Institute for Corporate Productivity – found that the primary issue for organisations with social networking was the leaking of confidential information (HRFocus 2009a). This was illustrated by a case against a former Hay Recruitment consultant who transferred confidential information to his LinkedIn site.

Research by Chretien, Greysen and Chretien (2009) of online posting by medical students, based on a survey of 130 medical Deans in the US identified four themes regarding inappropriate online posting:

- a sexual relations context;
- unprofessional comments about schools and their cohorts;
- substance abuse; and
- threats to patient confidentiality.

The study also found that 82 per cent of the medical schools surveyed had no policies explicitly mentioning internet usage. Other cases emerging around social networking issues include: the example of an employee in the UK retail chain Argos who was terminated following misconduct involving comments on Facebook; a situation where VirginBlue sacked a cabin crew employee for posting critical comments about customers and about the organisation's safety standards (Garnham 2009); and, the British Transport Police (BTP) who gave a written warning to a senior staff member who had posted explicit details of his sex life and photos (in uniform) on his Facebook page. This forced BTP to update its organisational policies regarding social networking (Woolnough 2008).

A key issue arising from social networking is how organisations deal with these issues on external communication sites. Employee's personal and private social networking activities and professional lives are increasingly conflicting. Social networking is also an issue from a recruitment perspective. A survey of over 260 recruitment managers in the UK found that 45 per cent of these managers used social networking sites to undertake background checks on potential employees, with a further 11 per cent planning to. This is more than a four-fold increase in three years (HR Focus 2009c). The major issues cited for rejecting candidates after undertaking online background searches included:

- candidates had posted provocative or inappropriate photographs or information (53 per cent);
- candidates had posted contents about drinking or using drugs (44 per cent);
- candidates bad-mouthed their previous employer, co-workers, or clients (35 per cent);

- candidates had shown poor communication skills (29 per cent);
- candidates had made discriminatory comments (26 per cent);
- candidates had lied about qualifications (24 per cent); and,
- candidates had shared confidential information from previous employers (20 per cent).

The increased use of online information for HR purposes highlights the blurring between professional and private lives. As many commentators have argued, employers need to consider the implications of social data mining (or backgrounding), as issues of discrimination could be considered – particularly if these sites include aspects of the candidate's political or sexual orientation, ethnicity and/or personal interests. This reinforces the point made by Dwyer, Hiltz and Passerini (2007) that privacy concerns with regard to social networking sites are not well understood. In Australia, there have been cases where: a prison officer faced disciplinary action after making comments on Facebook about his employer; a corporate bank sacked an employee for using the word 'recession' in a Facebook profile; and a teacher was disciplined over comments she made about being bullied (Moses 2009). These cases illustrate the issues of managing social networking and the relationship between employees' private and professional lives. Workplace lawyer Steven Penning, a partner with Turner Freeman, indicates that employers may be acting unlawfully, as contracts of employment are unlikely to cover staff usage of social networking sites (Moses 2009). As Gettler (2010) notes, it will be of great interest to watch the case law emerge on this subject.

What is clear is that organisational policy guidelines need to be clearer on what is accepted usage of these mediums, and these policies need to include issues such as:

- where social networking includes the organisation's name, it needs approval;
- employers should stipulate that employees include disclaimers with their online postings; and
- clear policies on where non-business use of the internet is not private and is subject to organisational policy (HRFocus 2009a).

e-Unionism

Since the late 1990s, academics and union activists have increasingly recognised the potential of ICT to enhance and extend trade union organising and servicing (e.g. Fiorito 2005; Pinnock 2005), a notion variously labelled e-unionism, open source unionism or cyber-unionism (Freeman & Rogers 2002; Shostak 1999; Shostak 2005). It is clear from the literature, however, that opinion remains divided as to whether ICT offers a new pathway or 'the next big thing' for unions in terms of the organising and servicing of members, or whether ICT is a tool that poses significant problems for unions and their operation (e.g. Aalto-Matturi 2005; Shostak 2005). This section considers the potential benefits and drawbacks of the use of ICT in unions. However, before a cost benefit analysis of e-unionism is conducted, it is important to discuss and analyse the rationale for e-unionism and the ways in which ICT can be deployed in the organising and servicing of members.

Potential uses and the rationale for the use of ICT in trade unions

There are countless ways in which trade unions can use ICT, many of which overlap and could be categorised under the following four areas: communication (internal and external); member education; member participation, activation and mobilisation; and campaigning and community participation, activation and mobilisation (e.g. Aalto-Matturi (2005); Cockfield 2005; Shostak 2005; Stevens & Greer 2005).

Aalto-Matturi (2005) further suggested that ICT links to the following overlapping activities of trade unions: information provision, information storage, interaction, member services, democracy and participation, community, research and information gathering, virtual trade union activity, training, social influencing, member recruitment, and solidarity work. Fiorito (2005:435) advanced a similar argument, suggesting that IT supports a union's ability in organising and recruiting, membership activation, internal democracy, effective personal communications, leadership, and developing appropriate structures and incentives. For instance, IT provides the primary communication mechanism (i.e. email) to: coordinate volunteers; send short campaign-supporting messages to bargaining unit members to divert their attention to important issues; and disseminate pro-joining messages to non-unionists.

Examples of the potential uses of ICT by unions that fall under these categories include the following:

- to establish a website;
- to utilise list servers to email information to members and constituencies, including targeted groups of members;
- to develop online chat rooms, discussion boards and discussion lists to facilitate the sharing of ideas and comments, and to encourage dialogue;
- to use video[2] and audio broadcasts for information dissemination;

---

[2] One innovations in the US in this area is the concept of micromessaging. This refers to the use of digital media by using a handheld computer to show a short union video or slideshow as an organising tool (Pinnock 2005).

- to keep members informed, for example, by sending out legislative and bargaining updates or circulating minutes of meetings, and by producing online publications, flyers and journals;

- to establish web logs[3] to encourage debate and educate workers;

- to activate and mobilise members – including across regional, national and international boundaries – to work together in a global network of activists, particularly in multinational enterprises[4];

- to plan, execute and coordinate organising campaigns, i.e. 'internet-driven activism' (Newman 2005);

- to enhance employee voice;

- to develop and maintain a membership database through spreadsheet and relational databases[5] to track union progress;

- to communicate and share information with members via email and web postings and enhance service provision, e.g. online calendars detailing union events and job postings; information for organisers; meeting dates; campaign information

- to enhance democracy, e.g. by inviting nominations for elections and facilitating information sharing from the bottom up;

- to counteract employer offensives, such as anti-union campaigns or threatened plant closures, and to publicise and protest against anti-labour corporate actions or corporate wrongdoings so as to build support for organising initiatives or to raise the profile and reach of a campaign (Cockfield 2005);

- to mobilise labour coalitions in the community and develop relations with community groups such as non-governmental organisations (NGOs), other unions and/or social movements to leverage solidarity, support and to globalise disputes[6]; and

---

[3] Web logs or 'blogs' are online journals that can contain news, personal observations and links (Pinnock 2005).
[4] One example is the website developed by the Service Employees International Union (SEIU) in the US which unites workers and supporters in the US and UK seeking to raise employment and service standards in the global bus industry (Shostak 2005:416).
[5] Spreadsheets and databases can also be used to file, track and monitor members' grievances and to cross-check information on collective agreements and employers (Cockfield 2005: Shostak 2005). In this way, databases can facilitate the planning of organising activities, the setting of targets and a review and assessment of performance (Cockfield 2005).
[6] Networks can also be built with peak union bodies and global union federations to develop both formal and informal networks (Cockfield 2005). Arguably one of the most successful internet-driven community campaigns/coalitions was the so-called 'Battle of Seattle' in 1999 at the World Trade Organisation meeting (Newman 2005). More than 1,500

- to educate members – for example using online training, online career assessment and planning tools to archive documentary history, or using computer enabled lending libraries – particularly across dispersed geographical areas[7].

Sources: Aalto-Matturi 2005; Cockfield 2005; Fiorito 2005; Ness 2005; Newman 2005; Pinnock 2005; Shostak 2005; Burgess & Waring 2006).

There are three main rationales for the take up of e-unionism identifiable in the literature. The first is simply one of relevance – to counteract employers on their 'own terms' by establishing a presence in the information technology world (e.g. Newman 2005; Pinnock 2005). As Ness (2005) pointed out, technology is increasingly becoming the primary vehicle in the effort to expand corporate profitability and is emerging as the dominant factor in the globalisation of work, or what has been termed 'networked capitalism'. As employers and governments increasingly implement and advocate neo-liberal capitalist production systems and use networked technology to divide workers – often through company intranet systems (McDaniel 2003; Ness 2005; Newman 2005) – unions must respond to the new terrain to counter corporate power. One prime avenue is email – it is quick, cheap and can simultaneously reach many people instantly (McDaniel 2003).

In light of the above, one obvious way that unions can respond to employers and the new world of work is to utilise technology as a medium to build and mobilise oppositional power, to organise and service members, and to resist employer attempts at deunionisation, outsourcing and offshoring (Ness 2005:377). In other words, unions use the internet as a tool in innovative ways to 'close the IT gap between labour and management' and to play employers at their own global corporate power game (Fiorito 2005; Newman 2005). This strategy is particularly important in light of evidence from the US which illustrated employers were using IT to drive a wedge between workers, to break organising campaigns, and, to undermine union strength, and that unions were lagging behind employers in their effective use of IT to mobilise power (Ness 2005; Newman 2005). However, there are also various examples in the US of the successful use of the internet by unions to publicise campaigns against large multinational corporations, including Apple, Oracle and Hewlett Packard, as part of broader corporate campaigns seeking to tarnish the companies' reputations (Newman 2005). (See *Chapter 10: Trade Unions and the New Workplace*.). In fact, by the end of the 1990s, using the internet as a tool to publish corporate wrongdoings had become an increasingly common activity (Newman 2005).

---

organisations signed a petition that was circulated on the internet and sponsored by an alliance of labour, trades, community and environmental groups.

[7] One example from the US is the AFL-CIO's online shop stewards' training course (see Shostak 2005 for a detailed discussion).

The second rationale for e-unionism is related to the first and is based on the notion that there is a bias in the mainstream media, i.e. a devaluing or delegitimation of labour issues (Chaison 2005; Pinnock 2005; Stevens & Greer 2005). Thus, unions – in order to build oppositional power and challenge neo-liberalism and employer propaganda – must use technology such as the internet to cast 'a wider net' and take advantage of the opportunity to spread their message through a more novel, targeted channel (Chaison 2005; Pinnock 2005). (See Box 4.3 for an example of innovative use of the internet to spread the viewpoint of workers and their unions.)

Box 4.3: Innovation with ICT - The Workers Independent News (WIN)

The Workers Independent News (WIN) was one of the first organisations to produce a daily, online labour-related newscast. WIN is an independent, not-for-profit audio news service that produces news focused on issues important to working people and has approximately two million listeners daily via the internet and radio. In relation to the radio, WIN is broadcast on more than one hundred stations around the USA, including college and community stations and commercial stations (Jamieson 2005).

WIN uses the internet to its advantage by broadcasting three minute news headlines every business day. In addition, several feature stories are broadcast each week. WIN sources its stories and headlines by encouraging unions, labour groups and activists worldwide to email news tips and press releases which are often then developed into news broadcasts or stories. This strategy means that diverse information is broadcast from all over the USA and the world, including issues at the local level (Jamieson 2005).

In relation to radio, WIN also makes extensive use of the internet to support their operations. Essentially, WIN staff send out daily emails to unions, and labour and activist groups providing notification when a story related to them has been broadcast or that they may find of interest. WIN then uses the information gathered online to undertake fundraising letters and phone calls. As a result, their activities have been strongly supported by unions, individuals and labour, media and activist groups. In addition, online distribution of news and stories is cheaper and more efficient than traditional distribution methods. And, by broadcasting on the web, WIN news is heard immediately and thus is easily marketable to radio stations (Jamieson 2005).

Source: Jamieson 2005.

See: http://www.laborradio.org/.

The third rationale for e-unionism builds on the first, and simply argues that ICT are now the communications norm and an accepted part of everyday life. Communication is the currency of power in an information-networked society (Shostak 2005; Burgess & Waring 2006). As a result, unions must 'keep up with the times' to remain relevant to members and to satisfy their information and electronic communication requirements in the information technology age (Aalto-Matturi 2005; Ness 2005). A potential organising advantage that flows from this rationale is that unions can attract and successfully reach more diverse employment groups that have historically been under-represented in the labour movement, such as young workers or workers in the service sector (e.g. employees in banking, finance and IT). Chaison (2005) suggested, however, that in the US at least, such professionals were still not approaching unions in large numbers and that unions were not successfully recruiting them either. In Australia, the role of ICT in unions has been recognised at a policy level. The Australian Council of Trade Unions (ACTU) 1999 and 2003 policy documents (*Unions@Work* and *Future Strategies*) identified technology as a core focus to assist in the building of union strength and growth (Cockfield 2005). (See *Chapter 10: Trade Unions and the New Workplace*).

Underpinning all three rationales is an assumption that ICT is one pathway to union renewal that can help unions to address declining membership (Hogan & Greene 2002; Cockfield 2005). Technology creates opportunities for unions in relation to the gathering, organising and processing of information (Cockfield 2005). In this light, Diamond and Freeman (2002) argued that ICT offered unions' new ways of mobilising and engaging with members and non-members, and created opportunities for strengthening unions on an international scale. However, as Cockfield (2005) pointed out, union renewal strategies require unions to change both their structure and their culture – which has implications for the renewal potential of ICT. Martinez-Lucio (2003) also recognised this dilemma, arguing that a union's extant communication strategies and the organisational context influence the way in which the internet is used. On this basis, Cockfield (2005:94) argued that appropriate renewal strategies must be in place before ICT can have a transformative impact on unions since ICT does not constitute a renewal strategy in itself.

Issues and challenges of e-unionism

e-Unionism poses both opportunities and challenges for trade unions. As Aalto-Matturi (2005:470) pointed out, in an e-society, the network is an essential part of the social infrastructure and employee relations architecture, and, at the same time, is a new space which people and communities can use in any way they choose. Unions must attempt to use ICT and networks to enhance their own abilities to function and act. The potential benefits of ICT for unions in this respect are manifold.

First, the internet offers cost efficiency and effectiveness in information provision in real time – a quick means by which to cast a wide net (Aalto-Matturi 2005; Fiorito 2005; Jamieson 2005). In relation to data processing, the internet and email can generate significant time and cost savings by streamlining administrative or processing tasks. For example, sending an email to 10,000 recipients is less costly than sending a letter to them (Aalto-Matturi 2005; Pinnock 2005). Blogs are a second example of the ease and cost efficiency of sharing information with a wide array of people, partly due to the ease of accessibility. Routine union activities can also be undertaken cost-efficiently using email, e.g. replying to member questions, thereby freeing up the time of union officials to dedicate to more time-intensive activities such as organising (Aalto-Matturi 2005).

Second, the internet can increase the transparency of union activities simply by increasing the number of people to which information is available, and by the fact that information is accessible 24/7 (Aalto-Matturi 2005; Shostak 2005). Transparency and open information can in turn increase trust (Aalto-Matturi 2005). And, there is also the potential for the more efficient interaction through technology to strengthen union democracy. Third, the internet can enhance information storage, for example, by listing frequently-asked questions (Aalto-Matturi 2005). Fourth, unions can use the internet to provide historical information in an easily accessible way, again increasing information provision for a wider audience such as students. Fifth, the internet can be used to offer training to members in a more convenient and cost-effective manner (Aalto-Matturi 2005).

Whilst there are many *potential* benefits of e-unionism, it is also important to analyse these benefits empirically. What evidence is there to suggest that IT use has a favourable impact on union activities, union organising and effectiveness? The work of Fiorito, Jarley and Delaney (2002) in the US is instructive in this regard. Examining IT and the relationship with membership growth, their data revealed that differences in IT use across national unions amounted to a 6 per cent difference in membership figures during the 1990s. That is, unions that made innovative use of IT experienced a 6 per cent growth in membership. Differential use of IT by unions was also identified in Pinnock's (2005) research in the US which revealed that local rather than national unions were more willing to experiment and innovate with IT.

Stevens and Greer (2005) also studied the union democracy-IT nexus in US unions. Multiple indicators of union democracy were used to explore this nexus via the analysis of union websites using a survey-based instrument. These indicators were: democratic content, e-voice functionality (e.g. chat rooms/discussion boards), collective bargaining content, confidential information and political activism content. Some interesting findings relative to these five indicators are summarised in Table 4.1.

Table 4.1 A summary of Stevens and Greer's (2005) findings: the union democracy-IT nexus

Democracy indicator (obtained from union websites)	Research findings: examples
Democratic content	<ul><li>A high proportion of websites devoted substantial content to members' issues.</li><li>A low proportion of websites offered calls for members to run for office.</li></ul>
e-Voice functionality	<ul><li>Only a relatively small proportion of websites encouraged members to use technology to provide input on union governance.</li><li>A decline in chat rooms or discussion boards was evident.</li></ul>
Collective bargaining content	<ul><li>A small to moderate decline in the proportion of websites posting collective bargaining outcomes was evident.</li><li>The most frequently-posted collective bargaining content was in relation to benefits.</li></ul>
Confidential information	<ul><li>An increase in the proportion of websites incorporating a confidential 'members only' section was evident.</li><li>Unions were posting more sensitive information on websites.</li></ul>
Political activism	<ul><li>A decline in political content on websites was evident, yet political content remains one of the most common content areas.</li><li>Many websites provided links to politicians to enable members to easily communicate their views.</li></ul>

Stevens and Greer (2005) also used interviews with a small sample of technology and communications professionals to evaluate the impacts of IT across four particular areas of union activity: leadership; governance and structure; service to members; and, collective bargaining and political action. In relation to these four activities, the interviews revealed the following findings:

- The correlation between IT knowledge and gaining a leadership position in a union as a result was not large.
- One of the largest problems facing unions was the amount of unsolicited email received.
- Resources devoted to processing emails within unions had increased.
- There was significant variation across union websites as to whether they reflected a strong desire on the part of union leaders to promote members' voices.
- A majority believed in the efficacy of websites and email in providing employee voice.
- Many positions became outdated as a result of the take up of IT, or were combined and re-engineered into more relevant IT positions.
- 100 per cent of respondents believed that their website had increased members' awareness of union activities.
- Many unions set up multiple mailing lists to streamline administrative processes and inform members (e.g. e-newsletters, updates on negotiations).
- 100 per cent of respondents indicated that their websites and the use of email had resulted in members' being more aware of political and legislative developments.
- 100 per cent of respondents indicated that they believed frequent updates helped to shape members' expectations in negotiations.

Source: Stevens & Greer 2005: 447-453.

Summarising these findings, Stevens and Greer (2002) concluded that there was a strong belief among these professionals from different unions of the efficacy of websites and email in providing members with a voice, and, in disseminating information to members and the public.

Despite the demonstrated benefits of e-unionism, there are also drawbacks and barriers to adoption. One of the key challenges unions face is how to meet the differing expectations and visions of increasingly diverse membership groups in terms of what they desire from their union (Aalto-Matturi 2005; Cockfield 2005). For example, members frequently prefer their union to maintain traditional service channels (e.g. telephone services and workplace visits) and yet, to also provide information and services on the internet in an efficient manner. These preferences may vary dramatically across different membership groups, resulting in important practical and strategic implications for the way in which unions integrate ICT into their activities and operation. Relatedly, membership apathy is by no means diminished or altered simply as a result of the use of ICT. As Fiorito (2005)

Chapter 4 – ICT and Employment: Challenges and Future Directions

pointed out, it is still very easy for members to withdraw or ignore union activities by deleting emails, as sending information electronically does not necessarily mean it is received or processed (Cockfield 2005). There is nothing to suggest, therefore, that the use of IT will enhance membership participation in union affairs.

A second central challenge and problematic aspect of e-unionism is the degree to which ICT can be used for the internal strengthening of the union movement and to reinforce activism. This issue is particularly problematic in light of the 'iron cage' nature of union bureaucracies, that is, a defensive and slow approach to change (e.g. Pocock 1998). Problems could arise for example, where older officials are resistant to IT adoption and a shift away from traditional servicing and organising methods, or where officials lack the know-how and competence to integrate ICT into union activities (Aalto-Matturi 2005; Fiorito 2005). In fact, as Fiorito (2005) noted, previous research in the US highlighted substantial differences across unions in the way in which they viewed the role of ICT as part of their future activities. In support of the aforementioned challenge, he noted both unions who were complacent about IT and viewed it as a passing fad, and unions who were openly hostile to IT.

A third challenge pertaining to the use of IT by unions is the sending out of electronic communications at the workplace on employer-owned infrastructure (Fiorito 2005; McDaniel 2003). As Cockfield (2005) pointed out, access to and control of information and communication channels for distributing and receiving information is a source of power. The use of employer email systems for union communication and organising purposes has proved problematic in both Australia and the US. In Australia, in the case of the *Australian Municipal, Administrative, Clerical and Services Union v Ansett Australia Ltd (2000)*, Justice Merkel of the Federal Court found that the dismissal of an employee (who was a union delegate) by Ansett, on the basis of the employee's use of the company email system to distribute union material, (i.e. a union bulletin) was unlawful (see Ansett case in chapter 11**)**. However, Justice Merkel did carefully point out that this decision should not be regarded as establishing a general principle for trade unions to use employer email services to distribute material or to conduct union business, and that 'authorisation' would be dependent upon individual cases (Norman Warehouse 2000). Indeed, stipulations on the usage of employer email, in relation to both employees and unions are now a common feature of corporate email policies (see McDaniel 2003).

A related concern for unions is the decentralisation of control that often results from the use of IT. Blogs are an illustrative example. There have been genuine concerns among unions regarding inappropriate postings on blogs, such as objectionable language and gender, racial or ethnic slurs (Pinnock 2005; Shostak 2005). One solution is to impose constraints on what an individual can post (Pinnock 2005). However, the use of censoring is a double-edged sword for unions since it is likely to be regarded with suspicion and may be prohibitive of a robust and transparent debate (Pinnock 2005). As Shostak (2005) noted, it is only by allowing divergent views that open discussions of real topics can be achieved.

A fourth challenge related to the discussion above is the actual skills and know-how of members, potential members and officials to use the ICT available to them and to use it in an effective manner (e.g. Aalto-Matturi 2005; Cockfield 2005; Newman 2005). The use of ICT can require increased competence and capabilities. As Robert Fox of the AFL-CIO in the US indicated, '[we] do not want internet discussions to become a tool of control by "the people with the most time on their hands and who can type fast" (cited in Newman 2005). Relatedly, the 'digital divide' means that not all members have equal access to the internet and to ICT, engendering potential inequality or discriminatory issues (Aalto-Matturi 2005).

Chaison (2005) examined the challenges – or what he termed the 'dark side' – of IT for unions in significant depth. While Chaison's (2005) account is US focused, it does have broader significance for other union movements and activists around the world, particularly those in similar advanced market economies (AMEs) like Australia. Chaison (2005: 396) identified three major threats of e-unionism. The first threat was that technology can transform the nature of union work in an adverse manner by distancing unions from their members (Chaison 2005). Essentially, Chaison (2005) argued that unrestrained adoption of IT could result in a dependency on the tool, and thus lead unions away from renewal. A cogent example is using web pages to communicate with members. Chaison (2005) argued forcefully that this could lead to the replacement of personal contact with members, whereby communication via the web became the primary means of information provision and dissemination. The danger is that unions may become entities focused solely on the provision of online services, thereby diminishing organising and servicing activities together with union power (Chaison 2005).

The second threat is that technology can distance workers – physically and psychologically – from unions and thus intensify the already difficult tasks of organising and servicing in a hostile political climate across national and international boundaries (Chaison 2005). Aalto-Matturi (2005) identified a similar challenge, suggesting that networked technology clashes with traditional trade union culture and modes of action since it is individualistic and lacks hierarchy. Alternatively, it could be argued that given the rapid pace of job fragmentation and the decline in the traditional 'job for life', fewer employees meet regularly in groups or with a union representative at their workplace, meaning that the internet is the most effective medium to bring geographically dispersed groups together to exchange their views and experiences (Aalto-Matturi 2005). More efficient interaction across geographical boundaries can also open up opportunities for enhanced member democracy by increasing participation (Aalto-Matturi 2005).

Subsequently, the availability of greater opportunities for members to express opinions can strengthen commitment to a union's decisions and member commitment in general (Aalto-Matturi 2005:474). Conversely, information overload could make members apathetic or could mean information does not reach its target audience.

The third threat recognised by Chaison (2005:397) was that technology can prompt the use of company intranets by employers as a substitute for union voice in an attempt to control workers and isolate members from their unions by promoting identification with company values and by resolving grievances internally. Internal intranets are also problematic for unions in the sense that they encourage *individual* employee voice and representation rather than *collective* voice – the latter being the express purpose of unions. In addition, intranets are controlled by management specialists who may be hostile to union representation in the workplace (Chaison 2005). In the future, Chaison (2005) argued that intranets may be utilised by organisations to provide personalised communication links, in addition to the basics of HRM, such as training materials and information, thus substituting for the role of trade unions.

In light of the potential drawbacks of ICT for unions, there is a need for union officials and activists to weigh up the costs and benefits carefully; lack of resources may act as an obstacle to implementation (Cockfield 2005). First and foremost, unions must use technology as a complement to – and not a substitute for – traditional organising and servicing methods (Fiorito 2005; Ness 2005). Thus, IT must be strategically integrated into union activities to enable and support organising and servicing practices and to enable the use of an array of technological and communications practices (Fiorito 2005; Pinnock 2005). Technology itself is not enough, and it certainly does not replace the core activities of trade unions. Rather, it facilitates and streamlines processes (Jamieson 2005). Pinnock (2005) and Aalto-Matturi (2005) advocated similar arguments, suggesting that the potential of ICT can only be realised through two-way communication as there is a need for functionality, dynamism and interactivity. There are various ways in which two-way communication can be achieved to ensure that IT enables interactivity and interconnectedness for members and that it creates a forum for social interaction, networking, influencing and activism that will simultaneously strengthen union democracy and enhance union power (Aalto-Matturi 2005; Ness 2005).

Second, unions must learn from their experiences and share these lessons. Given that there is evidence both in favour of and against the innovative use of ICT by trade unions, the creative, cutting edge and leading examples of e-unionism should be widely publicised to improve technology deployment in the future (e.g. Aalto-Matturi 2005; Newman 2005). As Shostak (2005) noted, one of the best things unions can do is share internet lists with each other. In the US, this information sharing actually happens among activists (e.g. The

WorkSite.org[8] site). Large unions must be at the forefront of facilitating experiential learning since they have far more resources to devote to experimentation and innovation with ICT (Aalto-Matturi 2005).

Third and related to the sharing of experiences, ICT must be integrated and used as part of a 'package' of organising and servicing tools and methods within unions. Networked technology – no matter how sophisticated or innovative – does not replace the traditional organising, servicing and representation functions of unions. ICT is not indispensable; it must be used in synergy with, and as a complement to, traditional 'bread and butter' union activities (e.g. Aalto-Matturi 2005; Newman 2005; Shostak 2005). The essential and most difficult question is how to link the new and old tools, as integration and alignment of technology with strategy is key to success (Aalto-Matturi 2005; Cockburn 2005). Related to the need for 'synergistic systems' is a need for investment; unions will not reap the cost efficiency rewards from technology unless they invest in the creation of high quality network services (Aalto-Matturi 2005). At a time when union renewal is paramount and density and membership continue to decline in most Western industrialised countries, the degree to which unions have available resources to invest in ICT could also be questioned.

Future directions

This chapter has identified important implications of eHRM and e-unionism which are likely to impact on the role of HR managers in important ways. It is clear that both eHRM and e-unionism warrant excitement and reservation, with both potentially having important advantages and disadvantages. However, the predominant focus of much of the current literature on ICT and HRM, particularly the practical literature, is the 'Web 2.0 Age' (Macy 2007). Web 2.0 represents the latest in cutting edge technology and the shift from hardwired monolithic systems to more open web services and a service-oriented architectural platform that emphasises connectedness and online communities (Knowledge Wharton 2007; Macy 2007:36).

The new age of computing in the form of Web 2.0 will have important implications and influences for HCMS, and are likely to raise issues of governance – including legal and security issues – and risk exposure. Another commonly cited concern of the Web 2.0 age is 'function creep'; that is, the incremental addition of functions and complexity to technology and equipment which can in turn result in risk and reliability issues (Knowledge Wharton 2007). Macy (2007) identifies mash-ups – that is, the integration of multiple applications, usually through a web portal – as one of the most

---

[8] <http://www.theworksite.org>. Other examples in the US include *The Troublemaker's Handbook* which provides advice on how union officials and activists can use the web (Shostak 2005).

significant developments for HRM in relation to the cross-referencing of employee information. Whilst mash-ups have the potential to increase flexibility and responsiveness to change, they will require careful management and strategic integration. The importance of Web 2.0 is not only being addressed in the practical literature. Academics are also engaging with the business implications of the transition to Web 2.0 and the use of its applications in a corporate context (e.g. Anderson 2007; Bughin & Chui 2011; Andriole 2010).

Conclusions

HR managers and unions alike must comprehend the challenges and opportunities that ICT poses for their effective operation and functioning. There are a wide range of potential benefits and drawbacks that can result from the use of ICT, and a strategic and competent consideration of these is paramount. The central theme that stands out from this chapter in relation to both eHRM and e-unionism is the importance of a strategic approach; that is, the use of technology to complement traditional activities, so as to create synergy in activities, functions and practices. The presence and use of ICT alone is not sufficient; ICT must be strategically integrated into any organisation. If organisations successfully integrate and embed ICT into their employee relations architecture, significant benefits can be realised. However, the new information age is characterised by complexity and rapid change, and ongoing developments in technology and communications will continue to have an important impact on organisations, HR managers and trade unions. All constituencies must keep pace with the changes and yet also be strategic, selective and innovative in their future use and deployment of technology and in their combining of technology with human capital management and development.

References

Aalto-Matturi, S 2005, 'The Internet: The New Workers' Hall, The Internet and New Opportunities for The Finnish Trade Union Movement', *WorkingUSA: The Journal of Labor and Society*, 8(4), Summer: 469-481.

Alveson M 1993, 'Organizations as rhetoric: knowledge-intensive firms and the struggle with ambiguity', *Journal of Management Studies*, 30(6): 997-1015.

Anderson, P 2007, 'What is Web 2.0? Ideas, technologies and implications for education', *Joint Information Systems Committee (JISC) Technology and Standards Watch*, February: 1-64.

Andriole, SJ 2010 'Business Impact of Web 2.0 Technologies', *Communications of the ACM*, 53(12): 67-79.

Arnold, J 2009 'Twittering and Facebooking While they Work', *HR Technology*, December, pp.53-55.

Autor, D 2001, 'Wiring the Labor Market', *Journal of Economic Perspectives*, 15(1), Winter: 35-40.

Ball, K 2007, 'Export Report: Workplace', in D Murakami Wood (ed.), *A Report on the Surveillance Society For the Information Commissioner by the Surveillance Studies Network*, September 2006.

BBC News 2007, 'Junior doctors protest over jobs', BBC News, 17 March, 15:19:00 GMT, <http://newsvote.bbc.co.uk/mpapps/pagetools/print/news.bbc.co.uk/1/hi/health/6457901.stm>.

Blacker, F 1995, 'Knowledge work and organizations: an overview and interpretation', *Organizational Studies*, 16(6): 16-36.

Boxall, P & Purcell, J 2000, 'Strategic human resource management: where have we come from and where should we be going?', *International Journal of Management Reviews*, 2(2): 183-203.

Brockett, J 2007 'Face-Face with Social Networking' *People Management*.

Bughin, J & Chui, M 2011, 'How Web 2.0 pays off: The growth dividend enjoyed by networked enterprises', *McKinsey Quarterly*, 2: 17-21.

Burgess, J & Waring, P 2006, 'Developments in Electronic Employment Relations', *International Journal of Employment Studies*, 14(2): 83-102.

Cappelli, P & Crocker-Hefter, A 1996, 'Distinctive human resources are firms core competencies', *Organizational Dynamics*, 24(3): 7-34.

Cascio, W 1999, 'Virtual Workplaces' in CL Cooper & DM Rousseau (eds), *Trends in Organizational Behaviour*, John Wiley and Sons, Chichester.

Chaison, G 2005, 'The Dark Side of Information Technology for Unions', *WorkingUSA: The Journal of Labor and Society*, 8(4), Summer: 395-402.

Chynoweth, C 2007 'War Games', *People Management*.

Chilvee, L. & Cowan, E 2008 'Networking the Way to Success: Online Social Networks for Workplace and Competitive Advantage', *People and Strategy*, 31(4): 40-48

Chretien, K., Greysen, R & Chretien, J, 2009 'Online Posting of Unprofessional Content by Medical Students', *Journal of the American Medical Association*, 302(12): 1309-1315.

Cockfield, S 2005, 'Union renewal, union strategy and technology', *Critical Perspectives on International business*, 1(2/3): 93-108.

Coff, R 1999, 'When competitive advantage doesn't lead to performance: the resource-based view and stakeholder bargaining power?', *Organizational Science* 10(2): 119-133.

Dahl, S 2006a, 'Warming to pools', *HR Monthly*, Australian Human Resources Institute, October: 37.

Dahl, S 2006b, 'Online is fine, but...', *HR Monthly*, Australian Human Resources Institute, October: 42.

Diamond, W & Freeman, RB 2002, 'Will unionism prosper in cyber-space? The promise of the internet for employee organisation', *British Journal of Industrial Relations*, 40(3): 569-596.

Dwyer, C, Hiltz,. S & Passerini, K 2007 'Trust and Privacy Concerns within Social Networking Sites', Proceedings of the 13th Americas Conference on Information Systems, Colorado August.

Fiorito, J 2005, 'Unions and IT: Personal, Research and Practitioner Perspectives', *WorkingUSA: The Journal of Labor and Society*, 8(4), Summer: 423-437.

Fiorito, J, Jarley, P & Delaney, JT 2002, 'Information technology, union organizing and union effectiveness', *British Journal of Industrial Relations*, 40: 627-658.

Freeman, RB 2002, 'The Labour Market in the New Information Economy', *Oxford Review of Economic Policy*, 18(3).

Freeman, RB & Rogers, J 2002, 'Open source unionism: Beyond exclusive collective bargaining', *WorkingUSA: The Journal of Labor and Society*, 5: 8-40.

Galanaki, E 2002, 'The decision to recruit online: A descriptive study', *Career Development International*, 7(4): 243-251.

Garnham, J 2009 'Why only Twits would Ignore the Potential (and Pitfalls) of Twitter', *People Management*, April, p.23.

Gettler, L 2010 'Facing up to Facebook', *The Age*, March, 16. p.6.

Gerlernter, D 1992, *Mirror Worlds or The Day Software Puts the Universe In a Shoebox'…..How it Will Happen and What it Will Mean?*, Oxford University Press, NY.

Hall, C 2007a, 'Climb down over junior doctor fiasco', 7 March, 10:42am GMT, <http://www.telegraph.co.uk/news/main.jhtml?xml=/news/2007/03/07/ndocs07.xml>.

Hall, C 2007b, 'Hewitt apologises for doctors fiasco', 5 April, 2:00am BST, <http://www.telegraph.co.uk/news/main.jhtml?xml=/news/2007/04/03/nhewitt103.xml>.

Hedllund, G 1994, 'A model of knowledge management and the N-form corporation', *Strategic Management Journal*, 15: 73-91.

Hibberd, G 2009, 'Are You In Touch?', 2009, *People Management*. p.15.

Hinton, S 2003, 'The Rhetoric and Reality of E-Recruitment: Has the Internet Really Revolutionised Recruitment' in R Wiesner & B Millett (eds), *Human Resource Management: Challenges and Future Directions*, John Wiley and Sons, Milton, QLD.

Hogan, J & Greene, AM 'E-collectivism: on-line action and on-line mobilisation' in L Holmes, DM Hosking & M Grieco (eds.) *Organising in the Information Age: Distributed Technology, Distributed Leadership, Distributed Identity, Distributed Discourse*, Ashgate: Aldershot.

HRFocus 2009a, 'Twitter is the latest Electronic Tool with Workplace Pros and Cons', August p.8-9.

HRFocus 2009b, 'Employers need more Social Media Rules', December p.2.

HRFocus 2009c, 'Nearly Half of Employers use Social Media to Research Candidates', December p.8.

HR Monthly 2007, 'Online Ads Subdued', *HR Monthly*, Australian Human Resources Institute, March: 6.

Jamieson, R 2005, 'The Workers Independent News – The New Face of Labor Media', *WorkingUSA: The Journal of Labor and Society*, 8(4), Summer: 483-488.

Knowledge Wharton 2007, 'Two Technology Executives, Two Views of the Virtues/Perils of Connectivity', 11 April, <http://knowledge.wharton.upenn.edu/article.cfm?articleid=1705>.

Kumar, S 2003, 'Managing human capital supply chain in the Internet era', *Industrial Management & Data Systems*, 103(4): 227-237.

Lepak, D & Snell, S 1998, 'Virtual HR: Strategic Human Resource Management in the 21st Century', *Human Resource Management Review*, 8(3): 215 – 234.

Macy, J 2007, 'Welcome to the Web 2.0 Age', *HR Monthly*, Australian Human Resource Institute, March: 36-37.

Martinez-Lucio, M 2003, 'New communication systems and trade union politics: A case study of Spanish trade unions and the role of the internet', *Industrial Relations Journal*, 34(4): 334-347.

McDaniel, TL 2003, 'Organizing, the Next Frontier? Labor Unions Seek Access to Company Email Systems', *Compensation & Benefits Review*, 35(5): 60-65.

Miller, J & Cardy, R 2000, 'Technology and managing people: Keeping the "human" in human resources', *Journal of Labour Research*, 21(3): 447-461.

Moses, A 2009 'Facebook Discipline may be Illegal: Expert', *Sydney Morning Herald*, April 3: p. 12.

Muskat MJ, Martinez SB & Mahony MM, LLP 2007, 'Can Employees Use Their Employers' Email Systems for Union Organizing or Union-Related Matters?', Federal Labour Board Requests Briefing', <http://www.m3law.com/ news011307.htm>.

Nakamura, AO, Freeman, RB, Pyman, A & Shaw, K 2007, 'Jobs Online', paper presented at the Labor Market Intermediaries Conference, National Bureau of Economic Research, Cambridge, Massachusetts, USA, 17-18 May.

Ness, I 2005, 'Letter From the Editor: Information Technology and the Future of Unions', *WorkingUSA: The Journal of Labor and Society*, 8(4), Summer: 377-381.

Newman, N 2005, 'Is Labor Missing the Internet Third Wave', *WorkingUSA: The Journal of Labor and Society'*, 8(4), Summer: 383-394.

Norman Warehouse 2000, 'Employment Briefly: Email and Employees – We Told You So!', May, Issue No. 38', <http://www.normans.com.au/news/empl_aug2000.html>.

Parkinson, C 2007, 'Jobs protest planned by doctors', BBC News, 2 March, 11:29:38, <http://newsvote.bbc.co.uk/mpapps/pagetools/print/news. bbc.co.uk/1/hi/health/6411481.stm>.

Parry, E & Tyson, S 2008, 'An analysis of the use and success of online recruitment methods in the UK', *Human Resource Management Journal*, 18(3): 257-274.

Parry, E & Wilson, H 2009, 'Factors influencing the adoption of online recruitment', *Personnel Review*, 38(6): 655-673.

Pinnock, SR 2005, 'Organizing Virtual Environments: National Union Deployment of the Blog and New CyberStrategies', *WorkingUSA: The Journal of Labor and Society*, 8(4), Summer: 457-468.

Pocock, B 1998, 'Institutional Sclerosis: Prospects for Trade Union Transformation', Labour & Industry, 9(1), August: 17-37.

Pollitt, D 2007, 'Boots has the prescription for simpler staff recruitment: Online system copes easily with large number of applications', *Human Resource Management International Digest*, 15(2): 27-29.

Quinn, JB, Anderson, P & Finkelstein, S 1996, 'Managing professional intellect: making the most of the best', *Harvard Business Review*, 74, March-April: 71-80.

Rubery, J & Grimshaw, D 2001, 'ICTs and employment: The problem of job quality', *International Labour Review*, 140(2): 165–192.

Scarborough, H, Swan, J & Preston, J 1999, 'Knowledge Management: A literature review', IPD, London.

Shostak, AB 1999, *CyberUnion: Empowering labor through computer technology*, ME Sharpe, Armonk, NY.

Shostak, A B 2005, 'On the State of Cbyerunionism: An American Progress Report', *WorkingUSA: The Journal of Labor and Society*, 8(4), Summer: 403-421.

Smith, AD & Rupp, WT 2004, 'Managerial challenges of e-recruiting: Extending the life-cycle of new economy employees', *Online Information Review*, 28(1): 61-74.

Snow, C, Lipnak, J & Stamps, J 1999, 'The Virtual Organisations: Promises and Payoffs Large and Small', in CL Cooper & DM Rousseau (eds), *Trends in Organizational Behaviour*, John Wiley and Sons, Chichester, 15-30.

Stevens, CD & Greer, CR 2005, 'E-Voice, The Internet, and Life Within Unions: Riding the Learning Curve', *WorkingUSA: The Journal of Labor and Society*, 8(4), Summer: 439-455.

Wilkinson, A 1999, 'Employment Relations in SMEs', *Employee Relations*, 21(3): 206-217.

Woolnough, R 2008, 'Get Out of my Facebook'. *Employment Law*. May. pp.14-15.

Zeider, R 2009, 'Employers Give Facebook a Poke'. *HR Technology*. p.54.

Case study: Electronic Solutions

Electronic Solutions (ES) is a small recruitment agency based in Victoria, Australia. The agency employs 12 people and specialises in the recruitment and selection of skilled workers for the off-shoring engineering and drilling industry in the Asia-Pacific region. Recruiting for such a diverse industry means that the company must recruit globally, and this can be time consuming and result in considerable costs. Time and costs were the catalysts for the organisation to undertake the development of electronic recruitment (e-recruitment). Once Electronic Solutions had developed the web systems required, it made its clients and customers aware of the new system and how it would decrease time and costs in the recruitment process for the industry. It also advertised widely to ensure maximum impact within the industry as well as to gain an advantage over its competitors.

The first client that used the new system required a foreman for an off-shore oil rig in operation between Australia and East Timor. The job description was sent electronically to ES, and they posted it on their web page. Of the several replies received, a New Zealand candidate emerged as the most suitably qualified candidate for the job. The potential employee was processed electronically and was successful in obtaining the position. On arrival at the rig, the new employee reported to the manager and to the senior foreman who realised straight away there was a problem. The nature of the foreman's job was to supervise across the entire rig, as specified in the job description. The new employee had undertaken similar – but not identical – work in a land-based refinery in New Zealand. It was clear that the person who confronted the manager and senior foreman would be unable to complete the critical aspects of the job since, in order to inspect work on the rig, the person would have to be able to climb into tanks and through piping – which was clearly not possible due to his physique. As a result of this error, the employee had to have his contract paid out, and the whole process had to be restarted. This resulted in a very costly recruitment process and embarrassment for ES, which in turn could potentially impact negatively on its public relations.

Written by: Mayson and Holland.

Case study questions

1. Does this show that electronic recruitment is ineffective? Why or why not?
2. How could the recruitment process have been handled differently?
3. What organisational lessons can be learnt from this experience?

Discussion questions

1. Identify and explain two advantages and disadvantages of online recruitment systems.
2. Identify two workplace issues with regard to social networking.
3. Compare two rationales that underpin the use of ICT by trade unions.
4. e-Unionism has both advantages and disadvantages. Identify and discuss the primary implication that results from this.
5. Identify and discuss a common theme that emerges from the academic literature on eHRM and e-unionism.

Chapter 5

PSYCHOLOGICAL CONTRACTS

INTRODUCTION

As companies attempt to utilise their human resources more effectively in order to improve their performance and achieve sustained competitive advantage, the relationship between organisations and employees has emerged as an issue of interest to human resource management researchers and practitioners. One construct that is central to understanding organisational-employee relationships is the psychological contract. At a general level, there is broad agreement that the psychological contract refers to the beliefs surrounding the terms of exchange between employees and employers. However, as researchers have attempted to refine and specify this construct, different constitutive definitions and operationalisations have emerged. For example, conceptualisations of the psychological contract differ according to the type of beliefs (e.g. obligations, expectations, promises) as well as the level at which the construct occurs (e.g. individual, dyadic, group, organisational, societal). Rousseau (1989), arguably the researcher who has contributed most to advancing our understanding of this construct, has focused on the obligatory and promissory aspects of the beliefs that constitute the psychological contract. She has consistently advocated that the appropriate unit of analysis is the individual level (Roehling & Boswell 2004). Thus, according to Rousseau the psychological contract refers to the informal, tacit and often unspoken and unwritten set of reciprocal obligations and promises held by the employee of the employer (Rousseau 1990; Rousseau 1995). These promises and obligations may involve promotion, responsibility, job security, training or career development.

In contrast to a formal employment contract, the psychological contract is essentially perceptual and, as a consequence, one party's perception of the obligations and entitlements within the contract may not align with the interpretation of the other party (Lester, Claire & Kickul 2001). According to Robinson and Rousseau (1994), the psychological contract is also conceptually distinct from expectations as expectations merely refer to what an employee expects to obtain from the employer. The psychological contract, however, involves the *perceived* mutual obligations that characterise the relationship that an employee has with his or her employer. The psychological contract may involve any item that may be exchanged between the organisation and the employee. However, given that the psychological contract is dynamic, unwritten, informal, and internally constructed, it is difficult to articulate its specific constituents at the time the contract is formed (Hiltrop 1996).

Psychological contracts exist for a number of reasons. First, they reduce the level of uncertainty that employees may experience by establishing agreed-upon conditions of employment. Second, psychological contracts direct employees' behaviour without direct management supervision and surveillance, with the assumption being that employees will self-monitor based on the expectation of rewards. Finally, psychological contracts provide employees with the sense that they can influence their future or destiny within the organisation (McFarlane, Shore & Tetrick 1994).

Formation of the psychological contract

The beliefs that constitute the psychological contract are formed as a result of the employee's interactions with agents or representatives of the organisation – particularly his or her direct superior – as well as the employee's perceptions of the organisational culture. Initially, these beliefs are developed during the recruiting process and through early experiences in the organisation (Turnley & Feldman 1999). However, expectations may arise prior to meeting representatives of the organisation through information gleaned from the media, promotional material, or friends and family who have had dealings with the organisation (McFarlane, Shore & Tetrick 1994). Additionally, expectations may be formed by interpretations of past exchanges that the employee has had with earlier employers, or they may be influenced vicariously by observing others' experiences (Saunders & Thornhill 2005).

Once a psychological contract has been developed, it tends not to change radically over time. However, it should be noted that the formation of the psychological contract is not a 'one-shot' affair; instead, it is revised and reformulated throughout the course of the employee's tenure with his or her organisation (Robinson & Rousseau 1994). Evidence of the fact that the psychological contract changes over time and indeed is asymmetrical was identified by Robinson, Kraatz, and Rousseau (1994) in a longitudinal study involving a sample of MBA alumni. Specifically, they found that employees' perceived obligations to their employers diminished over time, while the obligations that employees attributed to their employers increased temporally. It is also important to note that individuals, not organisations, have psychological contracts, as organisations are inanimate entities incapable of 'perceiving'. According to Rousseau (1989), organisations provide the context for the formation of the psychological contract; however, individual managers – i.e. agents or representatives of the organisation – can personally perceive a psychological contract with their employees.

Types of psychological contracts

While psychological contracts have many commonalities, they may vary according to the type of work undertaken, the motives of employees, and the human resource management strategy applied by organisations (Rousseau 2004). A number of typologies have been developed to explain variations in psychological contract types, however the majority of extant studies have applied the dichotomous relational verses transactional typology proffered by Rousseau (1989).

The traditional (relational) psychological contracts

A relational psychological contract is established on the basis of an exchange of effort and loyalty on the part of the employee in return for job security and career development on the part of the employer. The conceptual development of the relational psychological contract is primarily based on Blau's (1964) social exchange theory. Essentially, social exchange theory holds that when an individual provides resources or benefits to another, there is an expectation that the other party will give something in return. Thus, if an employee obtains support – such as opportunities for training and career development – from the employer, the employee will feel compelled to reciprocate, perhaps by providing high levels of performance or commitment.

Under the terms of the relational psychological contract, the employer adopts a paternalistic role, showing consideration for the well-being of employees and taking much of the responsibility for the management of their careers. Additionally, the employment relationship is seen as broad, long-term, and open ended. Employees who perform their tasks well are essentially guaranteed tenure with the organisation until their retirement. Thus, the motivators of the relational psychological contract for employees are: job security; working in a friendly interpersonal environment; and opportunities for personal, professional, and career development. The employee's obligations under this relationship include: working on tasks that are not delineated in his or her job description; providing mentoring to less experienced colleagues; developing skills that are specific to the organisation; and accepting a transfer to another division or relocating to another region (Tsui, Pearce, Porter & Tripoli 1997). A central feature of relational psychological contracts is loyalty, as both the employee and the employer commit to fulfilling the needs of the other. Employees who are valued by their organisations are more likely to receive relational psychological contracts than employees whose value is judged as marginal.

The new (transactional) psychological contracts

External factors – such as globalisation, deregulation and increased competition – have precipitated a number of organisational changes – such as restructuring, downsizing and the movement towards more flexible employment options. As a corollary, employees have become increasingly mistrustful of their employers, more cynical about the motives underlying the actions of management, and more likely to feel betrayed by the organisation. There is also evidence to suggest that the level of loyalty and organisational commitment on the part of employees that once existed has decreased. For example, Stroh, Bret and Reilly (1997) examined managers' attachment to their organisations retrospectively, and found that respondents' sense of loyalty to their organisation had declined over a five-year period. One result of these changes is the demise of the traditional relational psychological contract and the advent of the new transactional psychological contract.

Transactional psychological contracts are based on clearly-defined, monetisable exchanges that occur between the employee and the employer over a predefined and typically short period of time (Robinson *et al.* 1994). While the relational psychological contract is based on social exchange, the transactional psychological contract is grounded in an economic exchange. The new transactional psychological contract dismisses the obligations assumed in the traditional relational contract. Permanency and the notion of 'a job for life' in exchange for organisational commitment and organisational citizenship are no longer relevant in transactional relationships (Millward & Hopkins 1998). Unlike its relational counterpart, the transactional psychological contract is characterised by limited personal involvement in the job and reduced organisational citizenship behaviour on the part of the employee. While intrinsic factors are the drivers of individuals with relational psychological contracts, employees with transactional psychological contracts are motivated by extrinsic factors such as promotional opportunities, pay and benefits. Additionally, while paternalism on the part of the employer is a hallmark of the relational psychological contract, the new transactional psychological contract is based on the principle of partnership where the new responsibility for employers is to create opportunities for employees to manage their own careers.

It would appear that a number of factors – such as industry type, status and the nature of the work undertaken – influence the likelihood of a transactional versus a relational psychological contract emerging. For example, employees working in highly volatile industries such as information technology or hospitality, employees whose roles are not seen as being part of the core business of the organisation or employees whose function is viewed as not being essential to attaining competitive advantage often have transactional psychological contracts (Rousseau 2004).

Dispositional factors may also predispose individuals towards either a transactional or a relational psychological contract. Raja, Johns and Ntalianis (2004) examined personality differences in terms of psychological contract type and found that employees who were 'equity sensitives' (i.e. those who closely compare their level of input against the outcomes they receive from the organisation) and neurotics (i.e. those who are anxious, emotionally unstable and mistrustful) were significantly more likely to hold transactional psychological contracts. Additionally, conscientiousness and self-esteem were also positively associated with the relational psychological contract type. Additionally, transactional psychological contracts have been found to be positively related to those with careerist orientations (Rousseau 1990) and higher levels of resistance to change (Rousseau & Tijoriwala 1996).

Employers' perspective of the psychological contract

Some commentators (Guest & Conway 2002; Shore & Coyle-Shapiro 2003) have argued that inordinate emphasis in the psychological contract research has been placed on employees' perceptions relative to the perceptions of employers. In one of the few studies to examine psychological contracts from the perspective of employers, Herriot and Pemberton (1997) applied a critical incident methodology and found that the important obligations expected by employers of their employees were: working the hours they were contracted to work, performing tasks adequately in terms of quality and quantity, and being honest in their dealings. Winter and Jackson (2006) explored the psychological contract from the perspectives of employees and senior managers within an Australian credit union. They found that senior managers and employees converged in their belief that the content of the psychological contract was lacking in both relational (i.e. training, recognition and feedback) and transactional (i.e. salary and bonuses) aspects. However, the two groups diverged in their causal explanations for these deficiencies. Specifically, employees tended to develop emotional explanations and attributed the deficiencies to an unfair, indifferent, and detached management, while managers tended to construct rational explanations that focused on resource constraints and financial considerations.

Psychological contract breach

A breach of the psychological contract occurs when the employee perceives that the organisation has not adequately fulfilled promised obligations. Psychological contract breach is a subjective experience as it is based on an individual's perception and not necessarily on the reality that obligations have not been met. It would appear that breach of the psychological contract is not an unusual occurrence, as Robinson and Rousseau (1994) found that 55 per cent of managers in their study perceived that their organisations had not fulfilled one or more promised obligations.

Morrison and Robinson (1997) have theorised that there are two factors that may give rise to psychological contract breach. The first, reneging, occurs when the organisation – or more correctly an agent or agents of the organisation – is conscious that an obligation exists but intentionally fails to meet that obligation. Reneging may occur as a result of the organisation being unable to fulfil an obligation due to factors such as resource constraints. Thus, while the obligation may initially have been made in good faith, changing circumstances may subsequently make the fulfilment of that obligation untenable. Indeed, psychological contract breach may be more likely to occur under conditions in which an organisation's performance has declined (Robinson & Morrison 2000). The second source of breach, incongruence, arises when an agent(s) of the organisation and the employee differ in their views about whether an obligation exists, or are at variance in terms of the nature of that obligation. According to Robinson and Morrison, the strength of the influence of both reneging and incongruence on psychological contract breach is moderated by vigilance. Vigilance refers to the extent to which an employee monitors the organisation in terms of its fulfilment of the psychological contract. Parzefall and Coyle-Shapiro (2011) examined the events that trigger psychological contract breach and found that they could be grouped into four types: *specific obligation* (i.e. breaches arising from an unmet obligation at a single point in time); *connected events* (i.e. breaches triggered by an unfulfilled obligation embedded in a chain of unfulfilled obligations over a long period); *secondary breaches/'knock-on' effects* (i.e. breaches that lead to negative outcomes for the employee); and *everyday breaches* (i.e. the accumulation of low-level unmet expectations over time).

If an employee perceives that the psychological contract has been breached, he or she is likely to feel less valued by the employer. This in turn can give rise to a number of negative outcomes for both the individual and the organisation. For example, in a study of customer service employees working for an Australian telecommunications company, it was found that psychological contract breach was associated with reduced levels of organisational trust which, in turn, was related to perceptions of less cooperative employment relations as well as increased levels of absenteeism (Deery, Iverson & Walsh 2006).

Similarly, Robinson (1996), in a longitudinal study involving newly-hired managers, found that psychological contract breach was negatively related to: performance, civic virtue behaviour (i.e. involvement in and concern for the life of the company), and intentions to remain with the organisation. It would appear that trust plays an important role in reducing the likelihood of breach occurring, as Robinson found that trust in the employer at the time new managers were hired was negatively related to subsequent psychological contract breach and that initial trust in one's employer mediated the relationship between breach and employees' later contributions to the organisation. Dulac, Coyle-Shapiro, Henderson and Wayne (2008) also found that employee trust in their employer contributed to mitigating the negative outcomes of psychological contract breach. The negative consequences of psychological contract breach has been substantiated by a recent meta-analysis (Zhau, Wayne, Glibkowski & Bravo 2007) which identified more than 100 studies linking breach to outcomes such as lower job satisfaction, reduced organisational commitment, lower in-role performance, and reduced likelihood of engaging in organisational citizenship behaviours.

The impact of psychological contract breach on employee attitudes and well-being may also be contingent upon age. For example, a meta-analysis involving 76 studies and more than 28,000 respondents (Bal, de Lange, Jansen & van der Velde 2010) found that age moderated the relationship between psychological contract breach and job attitudes. Specifically, this meta-analysis found that the negative associations between breach and both trust and commitment were stronger for older workers. Conversely, this study indicated that the inverse relationship between breach and job satisfaction was stronger among younger employees.

Psychological contract violation

Psychological contract violation is distinct from psychological contract breach. While breach of the psychological contract is a cognitive response to unmet obligations, violation is "an affective and emotional experience of disappointment, frustration, anger and resentment that may emanate from an employee's interpretation of a contract breach and its accompanying circumstances" (Morrison & Robinson 1997, p. 242). Thus, breach always occurs temporally prior to violation, however perceived psychological contract breach does not always result in feelings of violation. A number of factors may mitigate the likelihood of violation occurring. For example, the magnitude of the breach may be perceived by the employee to be small and/or the psychological contract is sufficiently robust that feelings of violation do not arise. Another factor that influences the likelihood of violation occurring is psychological contract type. Individuals with relational psychological contracts are more likely to feel violation following a breach, given the high emphasis on mutual trust when compared with those with transactional psychological contracts. Additionally, situational variables such as the availability of attractive alternative employment opportunities appear to moderate employees' responses to psychological contract violation (Robinson 1996). Finally, Tekleab, Takeuchi and Taylor (2005) found that high-quality exchange relationships between the organisation and employees reduce the likelihood of employees perceiving that the organisation has violated the psychological contract. They found that perceived organisational support was negatively related to psychological contract violation, which in turn was negatively related to job satisfaction.

However, when violation of the psychological contract does occur, the empirical research indicates that there are a number of negative outcomes that can ensue. For example, Turnley and Feldman (1999), with a sample of over 800 managers, found that violation of the psychological contract leads to higher levels of turnover intention, increased voicing of complaints, greater neglect of in-role duties, and a decreased willingness to defend the organisation against external threats. Similarly, a study of Australian public sector managers found strong negative relationships between psychological contract violation and both job satisfaction and organisational commitment (Knights & Kennedy 2005). Also, Robinson and Morrison (2000) found that employees experience more acute feelings of violation following a perceived breach of the psychological contract in circumstances when the breach is attributed it to deliberate reneging on the part of the organisation rather than to incongruence. Finally, recent research (Cassar & Briner 2011) indicates psychological contract violation mediates the negative relationship between psychological contract breach and organisational commitment.

Psychological contract fulfilment

Psychological contract fulfilment occurs when an employee believes that the employer has kept promises and met expectations. When employers fulfil the psychological contract, they indicate to employees that they are committed to them, that they value their contribution to the organisation, and that they intend to maintain the relationship. According to Coyle-Shapiro and Conway (2005), psychological contract fulfilment consists of two components: perceived employer obligations and inducements. Based on empirical research, Coyle-Shapiro and Conway argue that perceived inducements lead to perceived organisational support, which in turn reduce employees' perceptions of the organisation's obligations towards them.

Lester *et al.* (2001) examined aspects of the psychological contract that employees valued most and how well organisations were able to meet those expectations using a sample of MBA students. They found that those components of the psychological contract that employees placed most value on were, in fact, the obligations that organisations found most problematic to fulfil. Specifically, the provision of open and honest communication from the organisation, being assigned interesting and challenging work, and having competent management were aspects of the psychological contract rated by employees as most important. However, these dimensions were also found to have the greatest discrepancy in terms of fulfilment.

Robinson and Morrison (1995) found that, if employers failed to fulfil their obligations of the psychological contract, employees were significantly less likely to engage in organisational citizenship behaviours (i.e. discretionary, out-of-role behaviours). Similarly, Harwell (2003, cited in Barnett, Gordon, Gareis & Morgan 2004), in a study involving physicians, found that fulfilment of the psychological contract was negatively associated with intention to leave the organisation, intention to change career, burnout, and career dissatisfaction. Similarly, Lester *et al.* (2001) found that fulfilment of the psychological contract was negatively associated with intentions to leave the organisation and positively related to job satisfaction.

Traditionally, it has been assumed that in situations in which an organisation provides inducements that exceed fulfilment of the psychological contract, the employee's level of satisfaction would increase commensurately. Consistent with this view, Lambert, Edwards, and Cable (2003) found that satisfaction did increase as delivered pay, recognition, and relationships exceeded promised levels. Interestingly however, they also found that there was limited marginal utility for inducements such as variety, skill development, and career training and in fact the provision of these inducements beyond fulfilment actually engendered decreased satisfaction.

Rousseau (1989) has argued that, although breach and fulfilment fall along a continuum, once breach has occurred it is difficult to rectify. This suggests that the effects of breach and fulfilment are asymmetrical, with the former having a greater impact on outcomes than the latter. This contention is supported by recent research (Conway, Guest & Trenberth 2011) which indicated that breach and fulfilment impact differentially on individual level outcomes. Specifically, this study found that increasing levels of psychological contract breach was negatively related to job satisfaction, organisational commitment, contentment and enthusiasm. However, increasing levels of psychological contract fulfilment was only significantly associated (in a positive direction) with one of these outcomes (organisational commitment), and that this relationship was substantially weaker than the relationship between breach and organisational commitment.

Work status and the psychological contract

In recent years many organisations have increased their number of temporary, contingent and casual employees as a human resource management strategy aimed at providing greater flexibility. However, some researchers have raised concerns regarding the effect of flexible employment contracts on employees' attitudes and behaviours. Saunders and Thornhill (2006) examined the impact of a change in work status on the psychological contracts of a group of permanent employees who were forced to take up temporary employment within an organisation. In this case study, the psychological contracts of employees within the firm whose work status remained unchanged – i.e. remained on permanent employment contracts – were also assessed. Saunders and Thornhill found that permanent employees tended to continue to hold *relational* psychological contracts with the organisation while those forced to take temporary positions were more likely to hold *transactional* psychological contracts. However, it appears that the nature of the psychological contract is quite complex, as there was considerable variation within each group. For example, some employees who remained on permanent contracts but were unhappy with the change were concerned that their contracts were becoming more transactional in focus. Moreover, those permanent employees with a low preference for temporary work expressed concern that they, too, might be forced onto temporary contracts in the future. Within the forced temporary group there was even greater variation. For example, some of these employees quickly arrived at the realisation that their psychological contract was now transactional, while others became more calculative following an initial period of denial. Additionally, a number in this group still perceived their psychological contract as relational, despite the fact that the organisation's director defined the contract with temporary employees as transactional.

Van Dyne and Ang (1998) examined the psychological contracts of contingent and permanent professional service employees in Singapore, and found that contingent employees had a more circumscribed psychological contract in terms of their perception of what the organisation was obliged to provide for them when compared to their permanent counterparts. Isaksson, De Cuyper, Oettel and De Witte (2010) also found that permanent employees reported a wider range of entitlements in comparison to temporary employees. Interestingly, these authors disaggregated entitlements according to whether they were relational or transactional, and found that permanent employees reported a similar number of transactional entitlements but a higher number of relational entitlements.

Chambel and Castanheira (2006) compared temporary firm workers (i.e. temporary workers with employment contracts of a maximum duration of three years) with core workers, and compared direct-hire temporary employees (i.e. temporary workers with employment contracts of an indefinite duration) with core workers in two separate samples. They found that temporary workers perceived that the organisation offered them fewer inducements (e.g. promotional opportunities, training and career development) and that their psychological contracts were more transactional (i.e. placed less importance on socio-emotional factors and more importance on economic factors) than core workers. Interestingly, Chambel and Castanheira also found that temporary workers who had enduring relationships with the organisation and the possibility of converting to permanent employment contracts – i.e. direct-hire temporary workers – tended to develop more relational psychological contracts that were similar to those of core workers.

There is also evidence to suggest that non-standard employees may be more sensitive to psychological contract violation than their fulltime counterparts. Barnett *et al.* (2004) compared fulltime and reduced work-hours employees in terms of their reactions to psychological contract violation. The findings of this study indicated that, when violation of the psychological contract occurred, employees whose work hours were reduced were significantly more reactive to violations – expressed in terms of their intention to leave the organisation – than their fulltime colleagues.

Implications for human resource management

Human resource management policies and practices significantly influence the psychological contract by signalling to employees the expectations of the organisation as well as what employees can expect in return (Rousseau 1995). Therefore, an important challenge for human resource managers is to ensure that the rhetoric of HRM matches the reality as perceived by employees. According to Grant (1999), when the espoused benefits of HRM appeal to employees and align with their perceptions of the policies and practices in operation, congruent psychological contracts are likely to emerge. Under this condition, high-trust relationships between management and employees are likely to develop, leading to stronger commitment and motivation from employees and to improved firm performance. However, if the rhetoric of HRM fails to appeal to employees and is incongruent with their perceptions of reality, mismatched psychological contracts are likely to arise – engendering cynicism, poor performance and reduced motivation. Additionally, while it has been established that the alignment of human resource functions is required for strategic success (Miles & Snow 1984), most HRM activities undertaken in organisations continue to operate independently. As HRM functions such as performance management, remuneration and training actively shape the psychological contract, this lack of integration is problematic as it creates inconsistent messages regarding the terms of the psychological contract. Moreover, when HRM practices are fragmented, the possibility that different organisational agents or representatives will transmit inconsistent messages is greatly increased (Rousseau & Greller 1994). Thus, human resource managers need to carefully review their practices in terms of alignment to ensure that the signals they provide to employees regarding the nature of the psychological contract are consistent.

Research conducted by Guest and Clinton (2010) found that, in contrast to individual level variables (e.g. age, gender, education, etc.), work-related factors had the greatest impact on employees' perceptions of the psychological contract. Moreover, among the work-related factors, the most important was the number of HR practices in place within the organisation. Employees who indicated a high number of HR practices in their organisation experienced broader psychological contracts (i.e. expanded content) and more positive psychological contracts (i.e. greater fulfilment, less violation, higher levels of trust, etc.) than those who reported fewer HR practices.

Human resource managers and line managers should make a concerted effort to view the psychological contract from the employees' perspective by attempting to determine what employees perceive as the obligations that the organisation should fulfil. By being cognisant of these perceived organisational obligations, human resource managers are afforded the opportunity to ensure that they are met, or to identify if there has been miscommunication or misperception (Robinson & Morrison 1995). Employers and employees need to continually manage, modify and renegotiate the terms of the psychological contract in order to accommodate changing circumstances.

The importance of monitoring employee psychological contracts and endeavouring to fulfil perceived obligations is underscored by recent research linking breach to increased counterproductive work behaviours (CWB). Counterproductive work behaviours are voluntary acts by employees (e.g. abuse, production deviance, theft, discretionary absenteeism, sabotage and withdrawal) that are detrimental to the organisation's interests. Research (Bordia, Restubog & Tang 2008; Restubog, Bordia & Tang 2007) has found that breach of both relational and transactional psychological contracts is positively related to CWB. Typically, organisations put in place accountability and monitoring policies to reduce CWB, and it has been assumed that these polices moderate the relationship between breach and CWB (i.e. when policies are in place, the strength of the relationship between breach and CWB is reduced). However, recent research (Jensen, Opland & Ryan 2010) indicates that organisational polices used to control and direct employees had minimal impact on their likelihood to engage in CWB when employment expectations were breached.

Given that psychological contracts are often initially formed during recruitment and selection – coupled with the fact that the turnover of newly-hired employees frequently occurs because the job fails to meet their expectations (Vandenberg & Scarpello 1990) – human resource managers should ensure that they provide applicants with realistic job previews. Rather than 'marketing' the position and focusing inordinately on favourable aspects, human resource managers should provide an honest and down-to-earth preview of the job. This can be achieved by presenting accurate information in the job advertisement, or through work sample tests that allow candidates to experience the actual conditions and tasks, or by allowing them to discuss the job with incumbents in similar positions (Sims 1994).

Another factor that can reduce the likelihood of perceived breach or violation of the psychological contract is the early socialisation of new recruits. Formal socialisation processes such as induction and orientation programs provide a process through which new employees can be indoctrinated with the beliefs, expectations, assumptions and obligations that are appropriate for the organisation. If the induction and orientation is sufficiently structured and comprehensive, new recruits are likely to develop beliefs and assumptions that are analogous to those held by the senior management (Robinson & Morrison 2000). Additionally, socialisation processes such as induction and orientation allow new employees to develop and modify their cognitions in accordance with the available information, and it provides them with the opportunity to seek clarification in a proactive manner (Thomas & Anderson 1998). Empirical support for the benefits of induction and orientation can be found in a study by Robinson and Morrison which indicates that perceived contract breach is significantly less likely to occur if employees experience a formal socialisation process.

Perceived organisational support militates against psychological contract violation. In order to foster perceived organisational support, human resource managers should explore options such as merit pay systems, work-life balance programs, and superior working conditions. Human resource development initiatives – such training and career development activities – also engender perceived organisational support (Winter & Jackson 2005). Often, however, the expectations of those responsible for delivering the training and the expectations of trainees are not aligned. As a consequence, human resource managers need to spend time discussing the objectives of the programs with trainees, assessing participants' training needs, and clearly articulating how the programs will address those needs. By making the training aspect of the psychological contract explicit, human resource managers are able to ensure that the organisation's expectations of the training programs and those of the participants are congruent (Sims 1994). Moreover, in light of the findings of Lambert *et al.* (2003) – that providing skills and career development which exceed obligations leads to dissatisfaction – human resource managers should carefully monitor employees' competency levels and training expectations to ensure that employees are not provided with training that is superfluous.

Another mechanism through which human resource managers can positively influence the psychological contract is the design and implementation of an effective performance management process. Supervisory staff within organisations should receive training on how to provide their subordinates with feedback on their performance. In performance management meetings, supervisors can assess employee expectations and assumptions that converge with the organisation's objectives, clarify performance standards, highlight future rewards that are contingent on performance, and identify employee developmental needs (Lester *et al.* 2001). In order to be effective in terms of improving the psychological contract, performance appraisals should be conducted regularly (to accommodate the dynamic nature of the psychological contract) and accurate (due to social desirability, there is a positive bias in raters' assessments) (Rousseau & Greller 1994).

Human resource managers are often the conduit between employees and senior management, and therefore they can play a critical role in ensuring that each group is aware of the other's perceived obligations. The obligations that senior management believe employees should meet can be communicated through well-designed performance management processes as well as through information sessions that clearly indicate to employees what is expected of them in terms of performance standards and behaviour. Conversely, the obligations that employees expect the organisation to meet can be communicated to senior management through informal discussion groups as well as by regularly assessing employee attitudes via climate, culture and satisfaction surveys. However, Guzzo and Noonan (1994) argue that the forced-choice Likert scale response format used in most staff attitude surveys is too limiting to assess aspects of the psychological contract and HRM practices. Instead, they advocate the use of open-ended survey questions that allow employees to express their idiosyncratic expectations and to describe their interpretations of HRM practices.

Human resource managers should also pay particular attention to the psychological contracts of line managers and supervisors, as research indicates that perceptions of breach by senior employees can have a 'trickle down' effect on lower-level employees and ultimately on customer relationships. For example, Bordia, Restubog, Bordia and Tang (2010) found that supervisors who perceived that their organisation had breached their psychological contract were less likely to engage in organisational citizenship behaviours directed towards their subordinates. This resulted in subordinate perceptions that the supervisor had breached their psychological contract which, in turn, caused subordinates to reduce the quality of service they offered to customers.

The rewards systems utilised by organisations are also important in shaping the terms of the psychological contract. For example, compensation systems that account for tenure with the organisation (loyalty) indicate to new hires that the employment relationship is long term. Alternatively, a system based on commission without a retainer is likely to signal to new recruits that the relationship is transactional and short term. Organisations that attempt to introduce cuts in terms and conditions – whether in response to an economic downturn or as a way to increase profits – are likely to violate the psychological contracts of their employees. Consequently, it is better to withhold bonuses and market loadings during periods of recession, as employees are more likely to accept a withheld gain than incur a loss (Rousseau & Greller 1994). In prospect theory (Tversky & Kahneman 1991) this asymmetry is explained by loss aversion, which refers to the tendency for people to prefer avoiding losses to acquiring gains.

The manner in which organisations terminate employment contracts also influences psychological contracts. Indeed, the perceived fairness of involuntary terminations not only affects the psychological contract of the victims, but also the performance and psychological contracts of employees who are retained (Brockner 1988). Specifically, Rousseau and Aquino (1993) found that the obligation to retain an employee when making involuntary termination decisions can be ameliorated through procedural justice mechanisms such as giving advance warning of the termination and providing reasonable severance packages. Interestingly, two management practices – participation and justification – which are often espoused to promote procedural justice had no influence.

Given that psychological contracts are becoming increasingly transactional in nature, coupled with the prevalence of organisational change and delayering, it may be impractical for organisational leaders to expect the traditional conceptions of loyalty and commitment from their employees. Instead, some authors (Cavanaugh & Noe 1999; Hakim 1996) have advocated that employers and human resource managers need to focus on ways of building 'conscious loyalty'. The notion of conscious loyalty is consistent with the new transactional psychological contract, however it provides insights into how to foster high levels of commitment – which is typically associated with relational psychological contracts. Employees who are consciously loyal understand the necessity of developing their own independence, while simultaneously appreciating that they need to work interdependently with their organisation. Specifically, human resource managers need to provide employees with growth opportunities through personal development initiatives and the provision of challenging assignments, as well as clearly demonstrating via education, information and performance management how their career success contributes to organisational performance and vice versa.

Conclusions

Few concepts in recent years have generated the level of interest – in both human resource management researchers and practitioners – as the psychological contract. It refers to an informal set of reciprocal obligations and promises held by the employee of the employer, and it is initially formed based on factors such as early socialisation, the interpretation of past experiences, the media and vicarious observation. The traditional (relational) psychological contract – established on the basis of an exchange of effort and loyalty from the employee in return for job security and career development from the employer – is being replaced by the new (transactional) psychological contract – based on clearly defined, monetisable exchanges that occur between the employee and the employer over a short, predefined period.

There are a number of negative consequences that can arise from breach and violation of the psychological contract, such as reduced performance, loyalty, trust, organisational citizenship behaviour, organisational commitment and job satisfaction as well as increased discretionary absenteeism, counterproductive work behaviours and turnover intentions – which all negatively impact upon the organisation's competitiveness. Conversely, fulfilment of the psychological contract appears to promote positive outcomes such as reductions in intention to leave the organisation, intention to change career, burnout and career dissatisfaction.

In terms of practical implications, human resource managers need to ensure: that their rhetoric matches the perceived reality; that their policies are consistent; and that obligations are made explicit. Additionally, human resource managers should make certain that they present realistic job previews to new hires, conduct formal induction and orientation programs, provide support to employees, develop effective performance management processes, monitor supervisor psychological contracts, institute reward systems that facilitate fulfilment, and apply termination procedures that promote fairness. Effective management of psychological contracts is influential in terms of attracting, retaining, developing and motivating employees, and therefore it is an important weapon in the human resource manager's armourmentarium in the war for talent.

References

Bal, PM, de Lange, AH, Jansen, PGW & van der Velde, MEG 2010, 'Age, the psychological contract, and job attitudes: A meta-analysis' *Gedrag en Organisattie, 23*, 44-72.

Blau, P M 1964, *Exchange and power in social life*, Wiley, New York.

Bordia, P, Restubog, SLD & Tang, RL 2008, 'When employees strike back: Investigating mediating mechanisms between psychological contract breach and workplace deviance', *Journal of Applied Psychology*, 93, 1104–1117.

Bordia, P, Restubog, SLD, Bordia, S & Tang RL 2010, 'Breach begets breach: Trickle-down effects of psychological contract breach on customer service', *Journal of Management*, 36, 1578-1607.

Brockner, J 1988, 'The effects of work layoffs on survivors: Research, theory and practice', in BM Staw & LL Cummings (eds), *Research in Organizational Behavior*, 10, pp. 213-255, CT: JAI, Greenwich.

Cassar, V & Briner, RB 2011, 'The relationship between psychological contract breach and organizational commitment: Exchange imbalance as a moderator of the mediating role of violation', *Journal of Vocational Behavior, 78, 283-289.*

Cavanaugh, MA & Noe, RA 1999, 'Antecedents and consequences of relational components of the new psychological contract', *Journal of Organizational Behavior*, 20, 323-340.

Chambel, M J & Castanheira, F 2006, 'Different temporary work status, different behaviors in organizations', *Journal of Business and Psychology*, 20, 351-357.

Conway, N, Guest, D & Trenberth, L 2011, 'Testing the differential effects of changes in psychological contract breach and fulfilment', *Journal of Vocational Behavior,* dio:10.1016/j.jvb.2011.01.003.

Coyle-Shapiro, JA-M & Conway, N 2005, 'Exchange relationships: Examining psychological contracts and perceived organizational support', *Journal of Applied Psychology*, 90, 774-781.

Coyle-Shapiro, JA-M & Kessler, I 2000, 'Consequences of the psychological contract for the employment relationship: A large scale survey', *Journal of Management Studies*, 37, 903-930.

Deery SJ, Iverson, RD, & Walsh JT 2006, 'Towards a better understanding of psychological contract breach: A study of customer service employees', *Journal of Applied Psychology*, 91, 166-175.

De Cuyper, N & De Witte, H 2006, 'The impact of job insecurity and contract type on attitudes, well-being and behavioural reports: A psychological contract perspective', *Journal of Occupational and Organizational Psychology*, 79, 395-409.

Dulac, T, Coyle-Shapiro, JA-M, Henderson, DJ & Wayne, S 2008, 'Not all responses to breach are the same: the interconnection of social exchange and psychological contract processes in organizations', *Academy of Management Journal*, 51, 1079-98.

Grant, D 1999, 'HRM, rhetoric and the psychological contract: A case of easier said than done', *International Journal of Human Resource Management*, 10, 327-350.

Guest, D & Conway, N 2002, 'Communication the psychological contract: An employer perspective', *Human Resource Management Journal*, 12, 22-38.

Guest, D & Clinton, M 2010, 'Causes and consequences of the psychological contract', in D Guest, K Isaksson & H De Witte (eds.), *Employment contracts, psychological contracts, and employee well-being*, Oxford University Press, Oxford, pp. 121-160.

Guzzo, RA & Noonan, KA 1994, 'Human resource practices as communications and the psychological contract', *Human Resource Management*, 33, 447-462.

Hakim, C 1996, 'Building conscious loyalty', in B Hackett (ed.), *The new deal in employment relationships*, Report Number 1162-96-CR, The Conference Board, Inc., New York, NY, pp. 19-21.

Harwell, JK 2003, 'Making reduced-hours work: The role of psychological contract fulfilment on reduced-hour physicians' intent to leave their positions', Unpublished dissertation, Boston College.

Hiltrop, JM 1996, 'Managing the changing psychological contract', *Employee Relations*, 18, 36-49.

Isaksson, K, De Cuyper, N, Oettel, CB & De Witte, HD 2010, 'The role of the formal employment contract in the range and fulfilment of the psychological contract: Testing a layered model', *European Journal of Work and Organizational Psychology*, 19, 696-716.

Jensen, JM, Opland, RA & Ryan, AM 2010, 'Psychological contracts and counterproductive work behaviours: Employee responses to transactional and relational breach', *Journal of Business Psychology*, 25, 555-568.

Knights, JA & Kennedy, BJ 2005, 'Psychological contract violation: Impacts on job satisfaction and organizational commitment among Australian senior public servants', *Applied H.R.M. Research*, 10, 57-72.

Lambert, LS, Edwards, JR, & Cable, DM 2003, 'Breach and fulfilment of the psychological contract: A comparison of traditional and expanded views', *Personnel Psychology*, 56, 895-934.

Lester, SW, Claire, E & Kickul, J 2001, 'Psychological contracts in the 21st Century: What employees value most and how well organizations are responding to theses expectations', *Human Resource Planning*, 24, 10-21.

Miles, RE & Snow, CC 1984, 'Designing strategic human resource systems', *Organizational Dynamics*, 13, 36-52.

Millward, LJ & Hopkins, LJ 1998, 'Psychological contracts, organizational and job commitment', *Journal of Applied Social Psychology*, 28, 1530-1556.

Morrison, EW & Robinson, SL 1997, 'When employees feel betrayed: a model of how psychological contract violation develops', *Academy of Management Review*, 22, 226-256.

Parzefall, MR & Coyle-Shaprio, JA-M 2011, 'Making sense of psychological contract breach', *Journal of Management Psychology*, 26, 12-27.

Raja, U, Johns, G & Ntalianis, F 2004, 'The impact of personality on psychological contracts', *Academy of Management Journal*, 47, 350-367.

Restubog, SLD, Bordia, P & Tang, RL 2007, 'Behavioural outcomes of psychological contract breach in a non-Western culture: The moderating role of equity sensitivity', *British Journal of Management,* 18, 326–386.

Robinson, SL 1996, 'Trust and breach of the psychological contract', *Administrative Science Quarterly*, 41, 574-599.

Robinson, SL, Kraatz, MS & Rousseau, DM 1994, 'Changing obligations and the psychological contract', *Academy of Management Journal*, 37, 137-152.

Robinson, SL & Rousseau, DM 1994, 'Violating the psychological contract: not the exception but the norm', *Journal of Organizational Behavior*, 15, 245-259.

Robinson, SL & Morrison, EW 1995, 'Psychological contracts and organizational citizenship behavior', *Journal of Organizational Behavior*, 16, 289-298.

Robinson, SL & Morrison, EW 2000, 'The development of psychological contract breach and violation: A longitudinal study', *Journal of Organizational Behavior*, 21, 525-546.

Roehling, MR & Boswell, WR 2004, 'Good cause beliefs in an at-will world? A focused investigation of psychological versus legal contracts', *Employee Responsibilities and Rights Journal*, 16, 211-231.

Rousseau, DM 1989, 'The "problem" of the psychological contract considered', *Journal of Organizational Behavior*, 19, 665-671.

Rousseau, DM 1990, 'New hire perceptions of their won and their employer's obligations: A study of psychological contracts', *Journal of Organizational Behavior*, 11, 389-400.

Rousseau, DM 1995, *Psychological contracts in organizations: Understanding written and unwritten agreements*, Sage, Thousand Oaks.

Rousseau, DM 2004, 'Psychological contracts in the workplace: Understanding the ties that motivate', *Academy of Management Executive*, 18, 120-127.

Rousseau, DM & Aquino, K 1993, 'Fairness and implied contract obligations in job terminations: The role of remedies, social accounts and procedural justice', *Human Performance,* 6, 135-149.

Rousseau, DM & Greller, MM 1994, 'Human resource practices: Administrative contract makers', *Human Resource Management*, 33, 385-401.

Rousseau, DM & Tijoriwala, S 1996, 'It Takes a Good Reason to Change a Psychological Contract', Presented at the *Society of Industrial Organizational Psychology*, April, San Deigo.

Shore, LM & Tetrick, LE 1994, 'The psychological contract as an explanatory framework in the employment relationship' in CL Cooper & DM Rousseau (eds), *Trends in Organizational Behavior*, 1, John Wiley & Sons, Somerset, NJ.

Sims, R 1994, 'Human resource management's role in clarifying the new psychological contract', *Human Resource Management*, 33, 373-382.

Tekleab, A, Takeuchi, R & Taylor, MS 2005, 'Extending the chain of relationships among organizational justice, social exchange, and employee reactions: the role of contract violations', *Academy of Management Journal*, 48, 146-157.

Thomas, HDC & Anderson, N 1998, 'Changes in newcomers' psychological contracts during organizational socialization: A study of recruits entering the British army', *Journal of Organizational Behavior*, 19, 745-767.

Tversky, A & Kahneman, D 1991, 'Loss Aversion in Riskless Choice: A Reference Dependent Model', *Quarterly Journal of Economics*, 106, 1039-1061.

Vandenberg, R J & Scarpello, C 1990, 'The matching model: An examination of the processes underlying realistic job previews', *Journal of Applied Psychology*, 75, 60-67.

Van Dyne, L & Ang, S 1998, 'Organizational citizenship behavior of contingent workers in Singapore', *Academy of Management Journal*, 41, 692–703.

Winter, R & Jackson, B 2006, 'State of the psychological contract: Manager and employee perspectives within an Australian credit union', *Employee Relations*, 28, 421-34.

Zhao, H, Wayne, SJ, Glibkowski, BC & Bravo, J 2007, 'The impact of psychological contract breach on work related outcomes: A meta-analysis' *Personnel Psychology,* 60, 647-680.

Case study: Should I stay or should I go?

Jim Woods was a senior IT analyst for a leading national food company. Jim had been with the company for 25 years beginning work at the company initially as a summer casual whilst completing his university degree. On completion of his biology degree he took up a full-time position with the organisation's head office in Essendon Victoria, working initially in the food hygiene section. However, over the years Jim undertook a variety of positions as he moved up through the organisation. With little experience in the area, Jim joined the IT section as it expanded and rose to the position of senior analyst quickly. As a result of his skills and knowledge of the company's new IT system, and his communication skills, he was approached by senior management to help set up the system in other states where they were still working on manual arrangements that relied on the tacit knowledge of the senior logistics people. Whilst this tended to work at a local level, the increasing need to manage the systems and logistics nationally meant that these local systems had to be integrated into the new system.

An initial discussion with the consultants who helped design and install the current system indicated that they would charge over $250,000 to train and develop the staff in the other states. The company balked at the cost and in a meeting of senior management it was suggested that Jim fly over to Perth and Adelaide to spend a week in each plant helping train the logistics and IT staff in the new system. The senior logistics manager called Jim to his office to ask him to undertake the role, pointing out that it would provide an opportunity to broaden his skill base and would reflect well in his next performance appraisal. In addition, the senior logistics manager indicated that Jim's work would be rewarded in his end of year bonus – 10 per cent of the saving the company could make that year with the successful implementation of the system (estimated at $150,000).

Jim readily took the opportunity and in the two weeks successfully implemented the system despite the initial hostility at the two sites. His success was attributed to his effective communication skills and sound knowledge of the system from an operator's perspective. These attributes gave Jim strong credibility with the IT people that he wasn't just another consultant pushing another company's product. Jim also worked 13-hour days to ensure he covered both shifts at the plants. On his return to head office his manager said little, but pointed to the backlog of work that had accrued whilst he was away. However, he knew with the new systems in place that the backlog and integration problems would be quickly eliminated, and after all he had his bonus to look forward to.

At the end of the year Jim sat down with his manager to undertake his performance appraisal. As the meeting progressed to its conclusion, Jim was increasingly concerned that the issue of his interstate work was not raised and when he raised it his manager said that the work he did was not his concern. When Jim asked about the cost saving and his bonus, his manager said that his agreeing to go interstate and help had in fact caused major problems and backlogs in the Victorian plants at Carrum Downs and Essendon and he should be happy he was getting the same bonus as everyone else, considering the problems he had caused.

Jim left the meeting stunned as he had expected to be commended for his work and get some indication of his bonus. Jim went back to his office and thought about the situation. That night he updated his CV and the next day sent it to three recruitment agencies specialising in IT work. As he waited for the recruitment companies to respond to him he worked his required hours, rather than the hours of unpaid overtime he used to undertake and spent that time networking for a new position.

Written by: Peter Holland.

Case study questions

1. What type of psychological contract did Jim have with his organisation prior to the performance management? Explain.

2. What type of psychological contract did Jim have with his organisation after the performance management? Explain.

3. How would you describe what has occurred to change Jim's attitude to his workplace?

4. What lessons can be learned from this experience?

Discussion questions

1. Define the psychological contract.
2. Compare and contrast the traditional (relational) with the new (transactional) psychological contract.
3. What is the difference between psychological contract violation and psychological contract breach?
4. What are the effects of change in work status on psychological contracts and how do the psychological contracts of temporary/contingent employees differ from the psychological contracts of permanent employees?
5. How do human resource policies and practices influence the psychological contract?

Chapter 6

CAREER MANAGEMENT IN THE 21ST CENTURY

INTRODUCTION

The way in which many individuals construct their careers has been transformed in recent years due to a number of significant environmental and attitudinal changes. Traditional career theories have generally been unable to explain or interpret these novel and burgeoning career paths, and therefore new approaches – such as the protean and boundaryless perspectives of career – have emerged. This chapter describes the changes that have impacted on careers, and explain the protean and boundaryless perspectives of career development. Recently, some commentators (e.g. Baruch 2003) have suggested that there has been inordinate emphasis in the careers literature on individual initiatives for managing non-traditional careers without sufficient consideration of organisational practices. To redress this oversight, this chapter examines the human resource management functions that can positively influence career management in the 21st century.

Traditional perspectives of career development

Established conceptions of career development – for example, Holland's (1973) theory of congruence and Super's (1953) life-span, life-space theory – tend to view career choice as a decision undertaken in early adulthood, and invariably careers are conceived as unfolding in a lockstep, stable-state, predictable and linear fashion. Thus, according to traditional perspectives the young adult, following some early exploration of potential career options, settles on an occupation and proceeds to advance in his or her career. These traditional theories of career were largely developed between the 1950s and 1970s, and they certainly reflected the career experiences of employees in industrialised societies up until that time. For most of the previous millennium, individuals were typically employed by the same organisation throughout the course of their careers. Workers who changed career were regarded as poor decision-makers, and those who had experienced multiple career transitions were considered unstable.

Most organisations were quite paternalistic and assumed much of the responsibility for managing the careers of their employees. Consequently, workers were largely dependent on opportunities provided by their organisation and had to trust that their employer would evaluate their career interests when making decisions. The training offered to employees was often quite focused on developing firm-specific skills that were not readily transferable. The traditional career was based on the relational psychological contract between the employee and the employer (see *Chapter 5: Psychological Contracts*) where loyalty and continued organisational membership were offered in exchange for job security. Organisations were typically bureaucratic, and employees could expect to advance up the promotional hierarchy. Thus, career success was measured according to position within the hierarchy as well as the attendant benefits of higher salary, greater status and increased responsibility (Sullivan 1999).

Environmental and individual changes

A number of major changes in recent years have significantly influenced the world of work and the construction of careers. Many organisations have downsized by cutting large numbers of staff, and have restructured by removing multiple levels from their promotional hierarchies. This is evident in research which indicates that 62 per cent of Australian organisations downsized some aspect of their operations between 1997 and 1998. During that same period 35 per cent of Australian organisations reduced their employee numbers by between one and ten per cent (Jensen & Littler 2000), and it has been reported that 3.3 million fulltime workers were retrenched in Australia between 1986 and 1997 (Cleary 1997). According to recent data, 454,100 Australian employees (4.2 per cent of the total workforce) were retrenched or lost their jobs due to their employer going out of business in the 12-month period leading up to February 2010 (*Australian Bureau of Statistics* 2010). While Australia has not experienced the same level of impact from the 2008 global financial crisis (GFC) as many North American, European and Asian countries (e.g. Australia avoided going into technical economic recession), the GFC appears to have had some effect. For example, a recent longitudinal study tracking labour force experiences from 2006 to 2009 (van Wanrooy, Wright, Buchanan, Balwin & Wilson 2009) found that job insecurity among Australian workers rose from seven per cent in 2008 to 12 per cent in 2009. It should be noted, however, that this level of job insecurity is still considered very low when compared with levels in other developed countries in the wake of the GFC.

Over the preceding 25 years there has also been a marked increase in the participation by women in the workforce. In 1986 women represented 48.3 per cent of the Australian workforce, however this figure rose to 53.8 per cent in 1996 and increased to 59.2 per cent in 2011 (*Australian Bureau of Statistics*

2011). Greater participation by women in the workforce has also engendered an increase in the number of dual income families.

Another major change in recent years is that organisations are increasingly outsourcing their human resource management – including recruitment, training, and payroll – as well as finance, accounting, information technology and procurement functions in order to focus on their core business. A recent study conducted by the business analysis company IDC Asia Pacific (2009) valued the Australian outsourcing market at A$6.4 billion in 2008, and they estimated a compound annual growth rate of four per cent. This suggests that the Australian outsourcing market will reach nearly A$8 billion by 2013. Beaumont and Costa (2003) found that the three most important factors driving outsourcing in Australia were: access to skills; improved service quality; and increasing managers' ability to focus on core business activities.

Additionally, in order to achieve greater flexibility and to improve responsiveness to changing market conditions, organisations are making much greater use of part-time and casual labour. Indeed, between 1985 and 2011, the proportion of part-time employees in Australia increased from 18 per cent to 30 per cent (*Australian Bureau of Statistics* 2011). Similarly, the number of Australians employed in casual jobs rose from 1.4 million in 1994 to over 2.1 million in 2009 (*Australian Bureau of Statistics* 2009) and accounted for approximately 21 per cent of the Australian workforce. Recently there has also been a global increase in the number of temporary agency workers (TAWs). TAWs are workers who are employed by an agency, though placed on assignment with a client organisation (Burgess, Connell & Rasmussen 2005). According to the International Confederation of Private Employment Agencies (CIETT), the number of TAWs increased globally from 700,000 in 1996 to 1.2 million in 2008 (CIETT 2010), and the agency work industry is one of the largest private employer groups in Europe (CIETT 2007).

There has also been an increase in recent years in the number of workers experiencing both job and career change. According to data published by the Australian Bureau of Statistics, nine per cent of the 10.9 million Australians working in February 2010 had changed employer or business in their main job in the previous 12 months, and 22 per cent of those individuals had also changed their occupation (*Australian Bureau of Statistics* 2010). Recent data (van Wanrooy *et al.* 2009) also indicate that the average job tenure of Australian employees is seven years, which is shorter than that experienced by workers in the majority of countries in the European Union.

The expectations, goals and values of many individuals have also shifted during this period. Some employees have grown weary of the stress and demands associated with climbing organisational ladders, and instead have declined promotions in order to focus on personal development (Ibarra 2003). Others have abandoned organisational careers and have attempted to gain greater work-life balance by establishing their own businesses that allow greater alignment of work and non-work activities (Moore 2002). It would also appear that some employees have felt constrained by the rigidity of their roles and have switched to jobs that offer greater flexibility or part-time work hours (Higgins, Duxbury & Johnson 2000). Dispositional factors may also influence the decision to switch organisations or change career. For example, Vinson, Connelly and Ones (2007) found that individuals who were higher on extraversion, openness to experience and conscientiousness – three of the dimensions in Costa and McRae's (1992) five factor theory of personality – were more likely to change employer than those who were lower on these constructs.

Contemporary career perspectives

In the context of the significant changes that have occurred, traditional theories of career appear anachronistic due to their inability to adequately represent contemporary career paths. Consequently, nascent perspectives such as boundaryless careers (Arthur & Rousseau 1996) and protean careers (Hall & Mirvis 1996) have emerged to interpret the changing nature of careers.

Boundaryless career perspective

Arthur and Rousseau (1996) applied the term *boundaryless* to describe their theory in order to underscore the notion that workers no longer consider themselves bound to a single organisation. According to this theory, boundaryless workers operate as free agents moving easily between organisations and careers. Thus the boundaryless career does not describe a specific career form but rather represents a range of career manifestations that confound traditional career expectations and assumptions. In contrast to traditional perspectives, the boundaryless approach does not presume that an individual's career will consist of predictable and invariant advancement within a single organisation. Rather, according to Arthur and Rousseau, it is more likely that an individual's career will be comprised of lateral moves, occasional career plateauing and stagnation, periods outside of the labour market for familial reasons or to acquire human capital (i.e. education), and radical career change (Marler, Barringer & Milkovich 2002). Individuals following boundaryless career paths will need to apply a much broader set of criteria for gauging their career success by focusing on outcomes such as meaningful work, skill utilisation, work-life balance and fulfilling relationships (Hind 2005).

In order to successfully navigate these unwieldy career paths, boundaryless workers will need to demonstrate agency, have strong internal and external marketability, be motivated by skill development rather than formal organisational rewards such as promotion or tenure, and be willing to take risks to capitalise on emergent career opportunities – all the while remaining confident in their 'saleability' in the labour market. A consistent theme in the literature regarding boundaryless careers is that they are liberating, as workers have greater autonomy, more flexibility to combine work and non-work activities, and expanded career options.

Protean career perspective

The protean career approach has many characteristics in common with the boundaryless career perspective. The term *protean* is derived from the Greek god Proteus, who could transform himself into any form at will (Hall 1996; Hall & Mirvis 1996). This metaphor is used to evoke the image of an adaptable, flexible and independent worker, capable of reinvention in order to redirect and manage his or her career. Thus, protean careers are influenced more by the individual than the organisation, and they may be refocused periodically to accommodate individual needs and circumstances. According to Hall (1996), protean workers are motivated by psychological success, continuous self-directed learning, autonomy, flexibility and self-fulfilment. Recent research conducted in Australia indicated that the two most important personal values of individuals with a protean career orientation were making a contribution to society and maintaining work-life balance (Sargent & Domberger 2007).

The protean career perspective also holds that careers should not be thought of as being nested in any one organisation or occupational field. Rather, this approach advocates a radical redefinition of the relationship between employee and employer where concepts such as job security, trust in the relational contract and loyalty are seen as irrelevant residuals from a bygone era (Hall 1996).

Traditional perspectives have invariably coupled career with paid employment and work that is performed within the formal organisation, with little emphasis placed on non-work influences. However, Hall and Mirvis (1996) have argued that this is too circumscribed in a protean career context and instead have advocated the enlargement of career space. This involves the recognition that the demarcation between domains such as work and family are becoming diffuse and that work and non-work activities intersect and interact in a dynamic fashion to mutually shape the protean worker's career (Sullivan 1999).

Traditional career theories typically view the organisation's needs as the primary consideration in career development decisions and view the employee's needs as secondary. From the protean perspective, however, the individual is seen as 'the figure' and the organisation is conceived as 'the ground' or context in which the protean worker can realise his or her aspirations. In this new relationship, the burden of responsibility for career development is shifted from the organisation to the individual and thus requires that protean workers self-manage their careers. Consequently, those individuals who are following the protean career path need to be flexible, self-directed, able to take risks in uncertain environments and focused on acquiring and developing their human capital.

Cautionary issues

Some researchers have raised concerns about the impact of increased job mobility on organisational commitment, particularly given the well-established relationships between this construct and important variables such as turnover (Allen & Meyer 1996), absenteeism (Hackett, Bycio & Hausdorf 1994), job performance (Meyer, Stanley, Herscovitch & Topolnysky 2002), and organisational citizenship behaviour (Meyer *et al.*). Kondratuk, Hausdorf, Korabik and Rosin (2004) found that external career mobility (i.e. the number of external job moves throughout a career) was negatively related to normative commitment (i.e. commitment to an organisation based on loyalty). This study also indicated that affective commitment (i.e. commitment to the organisation based on emotional attachment) and continuance commitment (i.e. commitment to the organisation based on a perceived lack of alternatives and investments that would be lost by leaving) were both significantly lower for external movers prior to exiting their organisation when compared with non-movers. However, it should be noted that some studies have not provided support for the notion that workers with a protean career orientation are less committed to their organisation. For example, Briscoe and Finkelstein (2009) found that self-directed career management and values-driven attitudes (characteristics of protean careerists) were not related to affective, continuance or normative commitment.

While the number of workers following protean career paths is certainly increasing, it is important to note that the traditional career has not vanished from the organisational landscape. Reitman and Schneer (2003) longitudinally tracked a sample of MBA alumni over 13 years and found that 38 per cent were pursuing a protean career; however, a not insubstantial 34 per cent were following a traditional career path. (The residual 28 per cent of the sample was excluded from analysis due to classification difficulties.) As Baruch (2006) has suggested, the descriptions in the literature of traditional and protean careers are best thought of as archetypical anchors at the extremes of the same continuum, with all careers falling somewhere along the continuum and most clustering towards the middle. Rodrigues and Guest (2010) have also questioned the inordinate emphasis that the boundaryless career perspective places on the individual as the primary agent for career management. These authors argued that this notion is implied rather than substantiated, and that the empirical research indicates that individuals are less agentic in managing their careers than espoused by the boundaryless career perspective. It is also important to bear in mind that protean career paths are uneven in their distribution of risks and opportunities; for well-educated and high-skilled workers these careers can provide challenges and avenues for self-development, however for poorly educated and low-skilled workers such careers can provide precarious and discontinuous employment and may well engender stress and uncertainty.

Human resource management and career management

While the boundaryless and protean conceptions of career development place considerable emphasis on individual employees taking much of the responsibility for managing their career, there are a number of human resource management practices that can assist career development in the 21st century. Indeed, research indicates that human resource practices have a significant influence on the career management of employees (Portwood & Granrose 1986), and satisfaction with organisational career management practices has been found to be negatively related to turnover intention (Herriot, Gibbons, Pemberton & Jackson 1994). Moreover, effectively managing the career development of employees can make a significant contribution to the organisation attaining a competitive advantage from within (Garavan & Coolahan 1996). Thus the goal of human resource management practices that focus on career development is the alignment and mutual satisfaction of employee and organisational needs (Herriot & Pemberton 1996).

Succession planning

In light of the fact that organisational commitment and loyalty continue to decline and employees are frequently changing employers, succession planning – i.e. evaluating the promotion potential of each manager and deciding on a replacement for every management position – is a critical human resource management practice. However, there is evidence to suggest that many organisations are not placing sufficient emphasis on succession planning. For example, a recent study conducted in the United States found that 45 per cent of leading corporations have no succession plan in place, and 50 per cent rated their organisation as less than effective in terms of CEO succession (National Association of Corporate Directors 2006). Similarly, a survey conducted by the global consultancy firm Development Dimensions International found that 91 per cent of Australian organisations experienced difficulty finding talent at all levels, however this problem was particularly acute at the more senior echelons (O'Hagan 2002). Hirsh (1990) examined succession planning undertaken by organisations and identified four distinct approaches: *as and when* – where a position is filled when it becomes vacant and there is no forward planning; *one step* – where successors are identified from the level below; *planned development* – where successors are identified from the level below but there is also fast tracking for high potential employees; and *developing potential* – where the employee rather than the position is the focus of the strategy, and consequently vacant positions are posted openly and there is a strong emphasis on training and development.

Paradoxically, the very factors cited above – i.e. declining loyalty and commitment, and increasing turnover – as rationales for the importance of succession planning also limit its predictive ability (Baruch 2004). As a consequence, succession planning needs to be flexible and broad in scope in order to adapt to the vagaries of the current context. Indeed, Leibman, Bruer and Maki (1996) have developed a dynamic approach that they refer to as succession management. With succession management: leadership templates rather than position descriptions are used as assessment criteria; replacement strategies are based on having cadres or pools of talent rather than on slating an individual to a specific position; and the assessment criteria are based on competence and networks rather than on skills and experience. While succession management typically involves senior managers and line mangers, human resource managers also play a vital role. Specifically, human resource managers can contribute by developing and facilitating the process, managing important cross-boundary job transitions, ensuring that minority groups are not disadvantaged, and providing counselling and informational support to employees (Hirsh 2000). Human resource managers also need to have extensive networks *within* the organisation in order to sense potential departures, but they also need excellent networks in the *external* labour market in order to identify potential replacements (Baruch 2004).

Lateral moves and secondments

Lateral moves and secondments provide employees with cross-functional experience in order to improve their skill development and extend their networks. Recent research (Hall, Gardner & Baugh 2008) indicates that employees are opting for lateral, or even downward, job shifts in order to realise their personal needs. The extent to which lateral moves and secondments can occur in organisations may be limited by prescriptive policies and procedures (Garavan & Coolahan 1996). Consequently, human resource managers should attempt to 'free up' rigid and restrictive practices when developing their organisation's approach to lateral moves and secondments. There is clear evidence to indicate that cross-functional assignments have a positive influence on career development. For example, Malamed (1996) found that the number of intra-organisational position changes was positively associated with managerial level and, similarly, Rosenbaum (1989) found that the amount of time individuals spent in their first job in an organisation was negatively related to the level of advancement they finally achieved. While lateral moves may be beneficial in terms of advancement in the longer term, employees may interpret these transitions pejoratively. Thus, human resource managers are advised to explain to employees that advancement does not require vertical progression and that these horizontal shifts should be interpreted as successes rather than failures as they will improve their internal as well as their external marketability (Baruch 2004).

Outplacement

In light of the significant job losses resulting from downsizing, human resource managers should consider offering outplacement services. Outplacement involves the organisation providing specialised career counselling to employees who have been terminated in order to assist them in finding employment elsewhere. The purpose of outplacement is to reduce disruptions for both the organisation and the individual by providing a smooth transition process. Outplacement also minimises the potential for litigation and grievance proceedings, improves the morale of remaining employees, and protects the public image of the organisation. Traditionally, outplacement services have focused on activities such as resume writing, interest assessment, and interview training; however, in the context of boundaryless and protean careers they should also emphasise values exploration, the identification of transferable skills, developing and capitalising on networks, and improving career resilience (Butterfield & Borgen 2005).

Executive coaching

It has been estimated that approximately 50 per cent of individuals in managerial and executive positions are not performing to expectations, and as a consequence their career progression is limited (Burke & Cooper 2006). Recently, executive coaching – which is a one-on-one relationship between a manager and an external coach in order to further the manager's professional development – has become a popular career management practice (McCauley & Hezlett 2001). In the UK, 95 per cent of managers reported in a survey that the extent of coaching had increased in their organisation in the preceding year (Pemberton 2006), and in 2003 there were 10,000 professional coaches in the US (Ferguson & Whitman 2003). The outcomes of executive coaching will benefit those following boundaryless or protean careers as they are focused on enhancing skill development, modifying interaction styles, improving performance, building career resilience, increasing adaptability to change, attaining work-life balance, and facilitating career advancement (Witherspoon & White 1996). As executive coaching is quite a nascent practice, there is little empirical evidence of its effectiveness; however, Smither *et al.* (2003) found that executives who worked with coaches – compared to those who did not – set more specific goals, were open in sharing their feedback, received action ideas from their supervisors, and improved their multi-source performance rating scores.

Dual ladders

As organisational hierarchies are increasingly being de-layered and as the number of highly-educated employees competing for fewer promotional opportunities expands, organisations are increasingly introducing dual promotional ladders. A dual ladder is a parallel promotional hierarchy that affords technical and professional employees advancement, remuneration and recognition without having to move to managerial positions. Moreover, it is often the case that very competent technical and professional staff do not necessarily make effective managers and perhaps have no aspiration to move into managerial roles. Thus, dual career ladders enable organisations to capitalise on the expertise of their technical and professional staff who are often in pivotal roles and whose knowledge is a source of competitive advantage. Many large organisations – particularly those in the health, education and science fields – utilise dual ladders. For example, Unilever recently introduced an alternative career pathway whereby highly-skilled scientists could progress to become the equivalent of senior managers.

Mentoring

As much greater responsibility is being placed on individuals to manage their career development, the importance of having an effective mentor is particularly acute. Mentoring occurs when a senior, more experienced employee (i.e. the mentor) provides career related (e.g. sponsorship and coaching) and psychosocial (e.g. friendship and counselling) support to a junior, less experienced employee (i.e. the protégé) (Eby, Lookwood & Butts 2006). Many mentoring relationships are informal and occur naturally and spontaneously as a result of unstructured social interactions, mutual identification and interpersonal comfort. However, it is increasingly more common that organisations are introducing formal programs where mentors are assigned or paired with protégés. Unlike informal mentoring relationships, their formal counterparts are structured by the organisation and often last for a predetermined duration.

In a meta-analytical review involving 14 studies, Underhill (2006) found that mentoring was associated with increased job satisfaction and with perceived promotion or career advancement opportunities. Additionally, Wanber, Kammeyer-Mueller and Marchese (2006) assessed formal mentoring relationships and found that the extent to which mentoring occurred was related to positive outcomes such as improved career clarity for both protégés and mentors. Additionally, this study indicated that mentor proactivity – i.e. taking responsibility for initiating meetings and maintaining contact – was positively related to both career mentoring and psychosocial mentoring. Research also indicates that organisational agents such as human resource managers play an important role in establishing, shaping and reinforcing the values that facilitate effective mentoring relationships. In organisations where mentoring is supported, senior employees are more likely to devote the time and energy required to establish relationships in order to develop junior employees. Allen, Poteet and Burroughs (1997) found that the most important factor for facilitating mentoring relationships was perceived support by the organisation for employee learning and development. Similarly, Eby *et al.* (2006) found that as perceived management support for mentoring increased, there was a concomitant increase in the extent to which career-related mentoring occurred.

Despite the clear benefits of mentoring, there is some evidence to suggest that this career management practice may be under-utilised. For example, McAlearney (2005) found that only one third of healthcare organisations in her sample had formal mentoring programs. Additionally, none of the executives and fewer than one quarter of chief executives who responded to the survey indicated that they had participated in formal mentoring programs as a protégé. The reluctance to participate in mentoring programs may be due to the difficulties that can potentially occur in these relationships. Eby and Lockwood (2004) examined the problems encountered in mentoring relationships and found that they related to factors such as mentor-protégé mismatches, problems with scheduling meetings, geographic distance, mentor neglect (by protégés), unmet expectations (by protégés), structural separation from mentors (by protégés), and perceptions of personal inadequacy (by mentors). Sullivan and Baruch (2009) argued that single mentoring relationships are no longer sufficient to satisfy the complex needs of protégés. They have recommended that employees establish multiple within-firm mentoring relationships (and in some cases external mentoring relationships) in order to cope with growing performance pressures and increased protégé career mobility.

Performance management and career management

A number of scholars (Baruch 2004; Boswell & Boudreau 1999; Hall, JL, Posner, BZ & Harder 1989; Soens & De Vos 2007) have highlighted the importance of establishing close links between the organisation's performance management system and career development. Additionally, Baruch (2004) has argued that as careers become more boundaryless or protean in nature, a robust performance management system is essential as it can identify employees who are eligible for promotion, those requiring skill development through training, and those who should be considered for redundancy during periods of downsizing. Moreover, the assessment should be oriented towards 'meta-criteria', such as the capacity to learn and adaptability in response to change as well as context performance (i.e. extra-role behaviours), the extent to which networks are maintained and extended, and the individual's contribution to team performance.

Facilitating career self-management

Career self-management – i.e., the extent to which an employee gathers information and plans for career decisions) – by definition is largely the responsibility of the employee, and indeed research conducted by Chiabura, Baker and Pitariu (2006) indicates that proactivity is positively related to career self-management. However, this study also found that the relationship is mediated by career resilience. Given the mediating role of this variable, human resource managers should consider introducing interventions to build career resilience, including: providing support for skill development, offering positive rewards for performance, using reinforcement contingencies, and providing opportunities for success. Organisations should also consider introducing explicit career self-management training programs where employees are encouraged to demonstrate agency in their own career building: by increasing their self-knowledge, through commitment to their career goals, and by the quality of their career plans. Indeed, Raabe, Frese and Beehr (2007), using a quasi-experimental design, found that these three variables were related to career self-management behaviours which in turn were related to career satisfaction.

Human resource development activities should also focus on helping employees develop *know-why*, *know-how*, and *know-whom* competencies in order to successfully manage boundaryless careers (DeFillippi & Arthur 1994). Know-why competencies require that employees acquire an understanding of their motivations, career goals and personal values. Know-why competencies also involve recognising the linkages between successive careers, thereby integrating these perhaps diverse work experiences into a coherent conception of one's career. Know-how competencies concern the extent to which employees are able to construct a portfolio of skills that are readily transferable between jobs and careers. Know-whom competencies relate to the establishment and maintenance of mentoring relationships, as well as networks that provide support, guidance, influence and tacit knowledge (i.e. knowledge that is not written down and only available from experienced individuals concerning issues such as what is rewarded by organisations, future directions, or shifts within industries, etc.). While empirical research examining the importance of these competencies in relation to boundaryless careers is scant, initial evidence has been generally supportive. For example, Colakoglu (2011) found that career boundarylessness was positively related to both know-why and know-how competencies, however it was unrelated to know-whom competencies. Additionally, this study found that all three competencies were positively related to career autonomy, which in turn was predictive of subjective career success.

Integration

In order to be effective, the human resource management practices discussed above should not be introduced in isolation. Rather, these practices should be combined to form an integrative career system. Of course the sophistication of an integrated career system will vary according to organisational size, with larger firms requiring more complex systems. Additionally, larger organisations with internal labour markets are more likely to focus on career development with explicit policies and to offer greater training opportunities (Herriot *et al.* 1994). Baruch (2003) has argued that an organisation's career system requires integration at both the internal and external levels. Internal integration requires coordination of the various human resource practices; for example, in order for executive coaching to yield maximum results it should be guided by performance management data and supported by an internal mentor (Wasylyshyn 2003). External integration, according to Baruch (2003), occurs when the career management system is aligned with both the organisational culture and strategy.

Conclusions

The traditional career theories – based on advancement, predictability, the relational psychological contract and organisational career management – have struggled to cope with the significant changes experienced by many individuals in the work environment. In response to these changes, new conceptions of career – i.e. boundaryless and protean career – have emerged which emphasise horizontal job moves, coping with uncertainty, transactional psychological contracts, networking and personal satisfaction. While career self-management is a hallmark of these new and increasingly-common career paths, human resource managers can assist employees in the development of protean and boundaryless careers through initiatives such as succession planning, lateral moves and secondments to increase cross-functional experience, outplacement, executive coaching, dual ladders, mentoring, performance management, and explicit training in career self-management. It is important to note, however, that these practices should not be introduced in isolation, but rather as an integrated career management system.

References

Allen, NJ & Meyer, JP 1996, 'Affective, continuance, and normative commitment to the organization: An examination of construct validity', *Journal of Vocational Behavior*, 49, 252-276.

Allen, TD, Poteet, M.L, & Burroughs SM 1997, 'The mentor's perspective: A qualitative inquiry and future research agenda, *Journal of Vocational Behavior*, 51, 70-89.

Arthur, MB, & Rousseau, DM 1996,' The boundaryless career as a new employment principle', in MB Arthur & DM Rousseau (eds.), *The Boundaryless Career,* Oxford University Press, New York, pp. 3-20.

Australian Bureau of Statistics 2009, *Australian Social Trends,* cat. no. 4102, Australian Government Printing Service, Canberra, ACT.

Australian Bureau of Statistics 2010, *Labour Mobility,* cat. no. 6209, Australian Government Printing Service, Canberra, ACT.

Australian Bureau of Statistics 2011, *Labour Force,* cat. no. 6202, Australian Government Printing Service, Canberra, ACT.

Baruch, Y 2003, 'Career systems in transition: A normative model for organizational career practices', *Personnel Review,* 32, 231-251.

Baruch, Y 2004, *Managing careers: Theory and practice,* Pearson Education, Harlow, England.

Baruch, Y 2006, 'Career development in organizations and beyond: Balancing traditional and contemporary viewpoints', *Human Resource Management Review,* 16, 125-138.

Beaumont, N & Costa, C 2003, 'Information technology outsourcing in Australia', in M Khosrow-Pour (ed.), *Advanced Topics in Information Resources Management,* IGI Publishing, Hershey, PA, USA

Boswell, WR & Boudreau, JW 1999, 'Separating the developmental and evaluative performance appraisal uses', Working Paper 99-09, Center for Advanced Human Resource Studies, Cornell University.

Briscoe, J & Finkelstein, LM 2009, 'The new career and organizational commitment: Do boundaryless and protean attitudes make a difference?' *Career Development International,* 14, 242-260.

Burgess, J, Connell, J, & Rasmussen, E 2005, 'Temporary agency work and precarious employment: A review of the current situation in Australia and New Zealand' *Management Review,* 16, 351-369.

Burke, RJ & Cooper, CL 2006, 'The new world of work and organizations: Implications for human resource management', *Human Resource Management Review,* 16, 83-85.

Butterfield, LD & Borgen, WA 2005, 'Outplacement counseling from the client's perspective', *Career Development Quarterly,* 53, 306-316.

Chiaburu, DS, Baker, VL, & Pitariu, AH 2006, 'Beyond being proactive: What (else) matters for career self-management behaviors?', *Career Development International,* 11, 619-632.

CIETT 2007, *More work opportunities for more people: Unlocking the private employment agency industry's contribution to a better functioning labour market.* Brussels, CIETT.

CIETT 2010, *The agency work industry around the world,* Brussels, CIETT.

Cleary, P 1997, 'A revolution in the nation's workplace', *Sydney Morning Herald,* 20 October, 1-7.

Colakoglu, SN 2011, 'The impact of career boundarylessness on subjective career success: The role of career competencies, career autonomy, and career insecurity', *Journal of Vocational Behavior,* doi:10.1016/ j.jvb.2010.09.011.

Costa, PT Jr. & McCrae, RR 1992, 'A five-factor theory of personality', in LA Pervin and OP John (eds.), *Handbook of Personality: Theory and Research*, The Gilford Press, New York, pp. 139-153.

Defilippi, RJ & Arthur, MB 1994, 'The boundaryless career: a competency-based perspective' *Journal of Organizational Behavior, 15,* 307-324.

Eby, LT & Lookwood, A 2004, 'Protégés' and mentors' reactions to participating in formal mentoring programs: A qualitative investigation', *Journal of Vocational Behavior*, 67, 441-458.

Eby, LT, Lookwood, AL, & Butts, M 2006, 'Perceived support for mentoring: A multiple perspectives approach', *Journal of Vocational Behavior*, 68, 267-291.

Ferguson, N, & Whitman, M 2003, 'Corporate therapy', *Economist*, 369 (8350), 61.

Garavan, TN & Coolahan, M 1996, 'Career mobility in organizations: Implications for career development – part 1', *Journal of European Industrial Training*, 20, 30-40.

Hackett, RD, Bycio, P, & Hausdorf, PA 1994, 'Further assessment of Mayer and Allen's (1991) three-component model of organizational commitment', *Journal of Applied Psychology*, 79, 15-23.

Hall, DT 1996, 'Protean careers of the 21st century', *Academy of Management Executive*, 10, 8-16.

Hall, DT, & Mirvis, PH 1996, 'The new protean career: Psychological success and the path with a heart', in DT Hall (ed.), *The Career is dead - long live the career*, Jossey Bass, San Francisco, CA, pp. 15-45.

Hall, DT, Gardner, W & Baugh, SG 2008. *'The questions we ask about authenticity and attainability: How do values and beliefs influence our career decisions?'* Careers division theme session panel discussion presented at the Academy of Management, Anaheim, CA.

Hall, JL, Posner, BZ & Harder, JW 1989, 'Performance appraisal systems', *Group and organizational studies*, 14, 51-59.

Herriot, P & Pemberton, C 1996, 'Contracting careers', *Human Relations*, 49, 757-790.

Herriot, P, Gibson, P, Pemberton, C, & Jackson, RJ 1994, 'An empirical model of managerial careers in organizations', *British Journal of Management*, 15, 113-131.

Higgins, C, Duxbury, L, & Johnson, KL 2000, 'Part-time work for women: Does it really help work and family?', *Human Resource Management*, 39, 17-32.

Hind, P 2005, 'Making room for career change', *Career Development International*, 10, 268-274.

Hirsh, W 1990, 'Succession planning: Current practices and future issues', *IMS Report 184*, Brighton.

Hirsh, W 2000, 'Succession planning demystified', *IMS Report 372*, Brighton.

Holland, JL 1973, *Making vocational choices: A theory of careers*, Prentice Hall, Englewood Cliffs, NJ.

Ibarra, H 2003, *Working Identity: Unconventional strategies for reinventing your career*, Harvard Business School Press, Boston, MA.

IDC Asia Pacific 2009, *Australia Outsourcing Services Market Forecast and Analysis 2009-2013*, IDC.

Jensen, B & Littler, CR 2000, 'Downsizing in Australia', *Australian Social Monitor*, 2, 134-138.

Kondratuk, TB, Hausdorf, PA, Korabik, K, & Rosin, HM 2004, 'Linking career mobility with corporate loyalty: How does job change relate to organizational commitment?, *Journal of Vocational Behavior*, 65, 332-349.

Marler, JH, Barringer, MW, & Milkovich, GT 2003, 'Boundaryless and traditional contingent employees: Worlds apar',. *Journal of Organizational Behavior*, 23, 425-453.

McAlearney, AS 2005, 'Exploring mentoring and leadership development in health care organizations', *Career Development International*, 10, 493-511.

McCauley, CD, & Hezlett, SA 2001, 'Individual development in the workplace', in N Anderson, D Ones, HK Sinangil, & C Viswesvaran (eds.), *Handbook of industrial, work, and organisational psychology*, 2, London, Sage, pp. 313-335.

Melamed, T 1996, 'Career success: An assessment of a gender-specific model', *Journal of Occupational and Organizational Psychology*, 69, 217-242.

Meyer, JP, Stanley, DJ, Herscovitch, L, & Topolnysky, L 2002, 'Affective, continuance, and normative commitment to the organization: A meta-analysis of antecedents, correlates, and consequences', *Journal of Vocational Behavior*, 61, 20-52.

Moore, DP 2002, *Careerpreneurs: Lessons from leading women entrepreneurs on building a career without boundaries*, Davies-Black Publishing, Palo Alto, CA.

National Association of Corporate Directors 2006, 'Corporate boards still challenged by CEO succession planning', Media release, Washington, DC: September 12, 2006.

O'Hagan, J 2002, 'My career: Our leadership crisis', *Sydney Morning Herald*, 15 June, 1-2.

Pemberton, C 2006, *Coaching to Solutions: A manager's toolkit for performance delivery*, Elsevier Ltd, Oxford.

Portwood, JD, & Granrose, CS 1986, 'Organizational career management programmes: What's available? What's effective?', *Human Resource Planning*, 19, 107-119.

Raabe, B, Frese, M, & Beehr, TA 2007, 'Action regulation theory and career self-management', *Journal of Vocational Behavior*, 70, 297-311.

Reitman, F & Schneer, JA 2003), 'The promised path: A longitudinal study of managerial careers', *Journal of Managerial Psychology*, 18, 60-75.

Rodrigues, RA & Guest, D 2010, 'Have careers become boundaryless?', *Human Relations*, 63, 1157-1175.

Rosenbaum, JE 1989, 'Organization career systems and employee misperceptions', in MB Arthur, DT Hall and BS Lawrence (eds), *Handbook of Career Theory*, Cambridge University Press, New York.

Sargent, LD & Domberger, SR 2007, 'Exploring the development of a protean career orientation: values and image violations', *Career Development International*, 12, 545-564.

Smither, JW, London, M, Flautt, R, Vargas, Y, & Kucine, I 2003, 'Can working with an executive coach improve multisource feedback ratings over time? A quasi-experimental field study', *Personnel Psychology*, 56(1), 23-44.

Soens, N & De Vos, A 2007, 'Career counseling within organizations: Isolation or integration?', Working Paper 6482/10, Vlerick Leuven Gent Management School, Belgium.

Sullivan, SE 1999, 'The changing nature of careers: A review and research agenda', *Journal of Management*, 25(3), 457-484.

Sullivan, SE & Baruch, Y 2009, 'Advances in career theory and research: A critical review and agenda for future exploration', *Journal of Management*, 35, 1542-1571.

Super, DE 1953, 'A theory of vocational development', *American Psychologist*, 8, 185-190.

Underhill, CM 2006, 'The effectiveness of mentoring programs in corporate settings: A meta-analytical review of the literature', *Journal of Vocational Behavior*, 68, 292-307.

Van Wanrooy, B, Wright, S, Buchanan, J, Balwin, S, & Wilson, S 2009, *Australia at Work: In a Changing World*, Report published by the Workplace Research Centre, University of Sydney, November 2009.

Vinson, G.A, Connelly, BS, & Ones DS 2007, 'Personality and organization switching: Implications for utility estimate',. *International Journal of Selection and Assessment*, 15, 118-133.

Wanberg, CR, Kammeyer-Mueller, J, & Marchese, M 2006, 'Mentor and protégé predictors and outcomes of mentoring in a formal mentoring program', *Journal of Vocational Behavior*, 69, 410-423.

Wasylyshyn, K M 2003, 'Executive coaching: An outcome study', *Consulting Psychology Journal: Practice & Research*, 55(2), 94-106.

Witherspoon, R, & White, R, P 1996, 'Executive coaching: A continuum of roles', *Consulting Psychology Journal: Practice & Research*, 48, 124-133.

Case study: Becoming protean

David had been working for ABC Bank for 20 years and had risen steadily through the ranks. He was initially employed in a general customer service role, but after demonstrating some flare had been promoted into the lending area. Over the years, David was promoted up through the ranks of personal and commercial lending and was now a senior lending manager. David had witnessed and been a part of many changes throughout his banking career, and had embraced and adjusted to these changes well. However, during a merger with XYZ Bank his work situation changed dramatically. David was now reporting to a new manager from XYZ Bank who was completely changing the way things worked. The new manager was extremely sales focused and set stringent targets for his lenders to meet. David had great difficulty adjusting to this new style and was concerned that his customer relationships were suffering due to the new aggressive sales approach. David was now also working long hours just to get everything done, and was not being remunerated or even recognised for the extra hours he was working. He also felt that he was constantly monitored as he was having to provide endless statistics on new leads and on the activity to generate them as well as having to report on sales results. David was indeed unhappy in this new work situation and his work began to suffer. What was once a rewarding and fulfilling position now became a chore, and David lost interest in his work. Eventually, as staff cuts were made to incorporate the new employees from XYZ Bank, David was made redundant and was referred to a recruitment agency for outplacement services.

Although David's career had plateaued somewhat, he was devastated that his career was over with XYZ Bank and was extremely concerned about his future employment options. He believed that, although he had developed sound skills in banking – particularly in lending – he would be very limited in new career opportunities outside of those areas. However, after several consulting sessions with the outplacement service, David realised that he had indeed developed many skills throughout his career that were transferable to other work contexts.

Similarly, during David's banking career he had established quite a network of contacts and it was through these contacts that David was soon offered a position as an insurance broker with DEF firm. DEF had an excellent reputation in the industry and placed strong emphasis on induction and training of new staff as well as on the professional development of existing staff. Having completed the induction programme, David embarked on his new career armed with his company car and new laptop. David enjoyed much success in his new role and was an instant hit with his new clients, as they were impressed with his knowledge and experience. DEF offered flexible work arrangements including variable work schedules to their employees to accommodate both their brokers' as well as their clients' needs. David enjoyed the option of working from home on certain days to avoid distractions, and was even able to structure his time so that he could collect his children from school each day. In addition, David found that he could manage his time more effectively by completing all of his processing work early in the morning, which was when he worked best. In terms of remuneration, David was now receiving a similar base salary to his previous role, however in his current role as an insurance broker he was also eligible for commissions on each sale that he made. This was a rewarding incentive to increase sales that he had not previously enjoyed. In his previous role David had avoided training and development programmes as he thought they were a bit of a waste of time. He thought he was too old to learn new skills, and he had already risen to a fairly senior level within the organisation and was comfortable at that level. David now regularly attends professional development programmes and industry conferences in his new role, as he sees them as valuable opportunities to further develop and refine his skills as well as a chance to establish important networking contacts.

After three fulfilling and successful years as an insurance broker, David became aware of a fantastic new opportunity for a sales training manager with a new company establishing a finance and insurance business. With such an excellent sales and customer service record, well-developed presentation skills and strong previous management experience, he succeeded in securing the role. David couldn't believe what a difference a change in career had made to his life and how much he now enjoyed his work. Having originally worked in an organisation that he thought he would be with for life that had a very rigid organisational structure and fairly traditional values, he was now in a position that he loved with flexible working arrangements in a progressive and dynamic industry.

Written by: Ross Donohue.

Case study questions

1. What aspects of David's experience suggest that he is following a protean or boundaryless career?

2. What human resource management initiatives could be introduced at the new finance and insurance company that David has joined to assist his career development?

Discussion questions

1. Discuss the environmental and attitudinal changes that have occurred in recent years which have given rise to protean and boundaryless careers.

2. Why have some researchers raised concerns about emerging perspectives of career such as the protean and boundaryless approaches?

3. How can lateral moves and secondments positively influence career management in the 21st century?

4. Explain why mentoring appears to be underutilised, despite its positive benefits in terms of career development.

5. Why is it important to adopt an integrative approach to human resource management practices focused on career development?

Chapter 7

HRM AND SERVICE WORK

INTRODUCTION

Within the resource-based view of the firm, there are three types of resources that act as sources of competitive advantage: physical capital, organisational capital and human capital (Barney & Wright 1998). Increasing levels of technological sophistication and the speedy transfer of this information has diminished the competitive advantage that was once available through the first two resource bases. Products are now more readily copied and processes replicated, and the result is that often the remaining sources of differentiation rest either with the people who generate new ideas or, alternatively, with those who deliver the product. There is increasing recognition, therefore, of the potential of the latter of these three resources, human capital, to make a substantial and lasting impact on sustainable competitive advantage (Barney & Wright 1998; Wright, McMahan & McWilliams 1994). The elevation of human assets as a possible source of competitive advantage has been further reinforced with the emerging dominance of service work where attention is focussed on the nature and quality of services provided to customers (Morris & Feldman 1996). This chapter considers the challenges and opportunities that service work presents for employees and employers, and discusses the contribution that the human resources (HR) function can make in the management of some of the related issues.

The rise of service work

During the late nineteenth century, the industrial revolution set the trend for a strong manufacturing base for employment in advanced market economies. During the twentieth century, however, automotive developments reduced the intense labour requirements that had previously been associated with manufacturing assembly processes. Declining employment in the sector continued to fall near the end of the century, with the trend to exporting manufacturing work to low-wage job markets overseas. As a result, the primary focus of employment in many developed countries has increasingly become service oriented. By the late 1980s, more than 60 per cent of employees in the OECD as a whole were working in the services sector (Blyton 1989). By the mid 1990s in the United States, for example, approximately 3 per cent of US jobs were in agriculture, and about 70 per cent of work had shifted to service employment (Macdonald & Sirianni 1996). In the UK in the years between 1971 and 2000, the number employed in manufacturing in Britain fell by almost 4 million – or almost 50 per cent. In the same period the number of employees in services rose by almost 7 million – or an increase of over 60 per cent. As a consequence, by 2000 more than four and half times as many people were employed in the service sector in Britain as in manufacturing (Noon & Blyton 2002).

In Australia the industry composition of labour has similarly changed considerably. Historically, the manufacturing industry has provided the largest source of work for Australian employees but its contribution to the number of employed people has been in decline. As recently as 1990-91, the manufacturing industry was the main source of employment, but in 2004-05 manufacturing was ranked third after retail trade and the property and business services industries. By 2007-08, the services-producing industries' overall contribution to the total production of goods and services in the Australian economy (gross domestic product) was 55% (*Australian Bureau of Statistics* 2010).

What is service work?

The United Nations has provided an overview of the types of work that might fall within the service work category. Work associated with the following industries has been identified: wholesale, retail, certain kinds of repair, hotel, catering, transport, postal, telecommunications, financial, insurance, real estate, property services, computer-related work, research, professional work, marketing and other business support work, government, education, health, social, sanitation, community, audiovisual, recreational, cultural, personal and domestic services (United Nations 2002:8). The breadth of these work categories raises the question of what it is about service work that gives it distinction.

Korcynski (2002) suggests that there are five traditional attributes of a service: intangibility, perishability, variability, simultaneous production and consumption, and inseparability. First, with respect to intangibility, a service is not presented in a form that can be touched. The manufacturing process usually results in a three dimensional product that has mass and weight and can be handled. A service, however, does not possess these physical dimensions and its quality assessment therefore becomes more difficult as it is measured through the recipient's perceptions. The second characteristic of a service is its perishability – or temporary nature. This means that the service cannot be produced or stored in advance and taken out when needed; it has to be produced at the time it is required. Third, a service is characterised by variability where the interaction between the provider and the customer contributes an added possible level of difference to each interaction. When a customer deals with a manufactured product, the product is usually relatively inert and predictable; with the creation of a service, however, the product relies on an interpersonal interaction and although the provider may be following a script and be trained to respond in a particular fashion, the interaction between each provider and customer has the potential to create quite a different outcome. Fourth, consistent with the perishability characteristic noted above, the service is produced and consumed simultaneously. Finally, inseparability refers to the active role that the customer takes in the service interaction, as often the service relies on the information interaction between the provider and the customer.

Having identified these characteristics that differentiate manufacturing work from service work, Korcynski (2002) has noted that types of service interactions vary considerably. Mills (1986) has argued that three basic types of service organisation can be identified. First is the 'maintenance-interactive service organisation' where the service provider effectively dispenses a product. Examples include sales assistant work, banking, and fast food service. Second is the 'task-interactive service organisation' where employees not only dispense the service but produce it as well – for example, working in made-to-order sandwich outlets or as a beauty therapist. Finally, Mills terms a service as a 'personal-interactive service organisation' where the service provided does not involve a *separate* product, but the service *is* the entire product, for example, psychological therapy, teaching or the assessment provided by a medical physician.

Macdonald and Sirianni (1996) highlight a further distinction between types of service work by distinguishing between white collar service providers and the 'emotional proletariat'. The emotional proletariat are generally front-line service workers and paraprofessionals, whereas white collar service providers generally reside in managerial and professional roles. This differentiation on the basis of professional status is often accompanied by different guidelines about how the service is to be provided. For members of management and professional groups, for example, guidelines for appropriate emotional labour approaches (see full discussion of emotional labour in *Chapter 8: Managing Emotional Labour in the Workplace*) will be generated collegially, and these individuals are to a great extent self-supervised. Front line service jobs, however, are more likely to be given very explicit instructions concerning what to say and how to act, e.g. call centres.

Having identified these broad characteristics the service work label covers quite a wide variety of interactions. Specifically, service work categories can be distinguished by the extent to which a separate product is associated with the service (Mills 1986), and also the level of professionalism of the service (Macdonald & Sirianni 1996). The following sections highlight particular HR challenges faced by service providers in a range of situations as well as possible approaches to dealing with these challenges.

HR challenges and opportunities in the services sector

A prominent feature of employment conditions in the service sector is flexibility in work arrangements (Smith 2005). Australian studies suggest evidence of the common pattern seen in other industrialised countries: employment is moving from the 'traditional' forms of full-time, permanent, work towards a wider variety of working arrangements including part-time work, temporary employment and contract employment (Kalleberg 2000; Van den Heuvel & Wooden 1997). In 2004-05, 71 per cent of employed people were working in full-time employment. Full-time workers are those who usually work 35 hours or more per week in all jobs. Part-time workers are those who usually work fewer than 35 hours a week, and this classification of worker now accounts for 28 per cent of all employed persons. With respect to gender mix, it is women who are most likely to work in part-time positions (*Australian Bureau of Statistics* 2010).

As well as the variation in working hours, another trend in Australia is the increasing number of workers now classified as 'casual'. In 2007, 25 per cent of employees were casual. These workers are defined as employees who are not entitled in their main job to paid annual leave and paid sick leave (*Australian Bureau of Statistics* 2009). Around two thirds of casual work is part-time, and the remaining third consists of full-time positions (Pocock, Buchanan & Campbell 2004). With respect to the current discussion, it is important to note that much of this casual work occurs within the services industry: over half of the employees in the accommodation, cafe and restaurant industry are casual (65 per cent), and 42 per cent of the workforce in the retail trade is registered as casual (*Australian Bureau of Statistics* 2009).

The increase in the number of casual workers is occurring for several reasons. A generalised erosion of the traditional employment contract, typically thought to be based on lifetime employment for dedicated service, is evident. Employers therefore no longer guarantee job security for their employees. As well as the impact of changing employment expectations there are considerable benefits to employers in adopting more flexible employment arrangements. Many companies have reduced the number of full-time employees in order to lower the associated labour costs and to give the organisation the flexibility to contract for skills when needed. Casual work can also be attractive from the worker's perspective as the work arrangements often allow employees to fit in child care responsibilities as well as other interests and employment opportunities (Burgess & Connell 2006).

Despite the benefits of flexibility offered by alternative forms of work in the services sector, the arrangements create numerous challenges both for employees and for organisations. For the employee, casual work is closely associated with poor work conditions including low hourly rates of pay, low and irregular earnings, reduced employment security, lack of access to notice and severance pay, reduced access to unfair dismissal rights, vulnerability to changes in schedules, loss of skill and age-related pay increments, and lack of representational rights (Pocock *et al.* 2004). In terms of work arrangements in 2007, casuals were less likely to have flexible working arrangements than employees with paid leave entitlements. However, the fact that many casuals work part-time may make some of these flexible working arrangements less important (*Australian Bureau of Statistics* 2009). The biggest difference between casual employees and other employees was in the ability to work extra hours to take time off. Just over half (52 per cent) of employees with paid leave entitlements could do this, compared with less than one-third (30 per cent) of casuals. Casuals were also less likely (77 per cent) than other employees (89 per cent) to be able to choose when to take their holiday leave (*Australian Bureau of Statistics* 2009).

For the employer, although there is the flexibility and often reduced costs associated with this category of worker, the arrangement does have potentially negative ramifications (Buultjens 2001). For example, casual workers, due to the transient nature of the terms of employment, are less likely to identify strongly with the organisation (Hall 2006) and as a result may not absorb and display appropriate organisational values and behaviours. And, they may also have high attrition rates.

The limited organisational investment in casuals also means that these employees may have less opportunity to develop necessary skills, and the contribution that they make may be limited to generic industry tasks rather than tasks that add real value as expected by some service providers. Lowry's (2001) investigation of the work arrangements for casual employees within the registered club industry in New South Wales indicated that casuals are employed on a primarily transactional basis, with an under-investment in employee development (Buultjens 2001; Lowry 2001). Over three quarters of Lowry's (2001) research sample reported that they had received some training, but the standard of the training was questionable and mainly consisted of *ad hoc* on-the-job training related to the immediate task. Furthermore, although over a half of the casual workers reported the availability of promotion opportunities, only a third of workers were progressing their careers. This is possibly because they were not willing to engage in or commit to the organisation. Respondents were also extremely critical of the lack of feedback and recognition for the work performed, and this had ramifications for the development of task skills and further detracted from the casual employees' willingness to commit to organisational needs.

The impact of an under-investment in HRM activities such as training and feedback has ramifications for the quality of the service delivery provided by casuals. Lowry's (2001) findings, for example, indicated that some employees were so dissatisfied with the lack of feedback and recognition that they made a conscious decision *not* to provide quality service. This finding is consistent with the previous research by Schneider, White and Paul (1998), who established a relationship between HRM practices, including training and supportive supervision, and the service climate.

The outcomes associated with a lack of organisational value alignment and the under-development of skills within the casual workforce is not only a problem in the hospitality industry but may affect other areas of service delivery as well. Using Mills's (1986) distinctions outlined above, when a service position involves dispensing a product (maintenance-interactive service organisation), problems can occur when the delivery of the product is accompanied by an inappropriate customer interaction style. An example of this would be in specialty retail stores that differentiate themselves on the basis of superior product knowledge and a required approach to customers. Alternatively, where the service is the entire product (personal-interactive service organisations) it becomes even more important that the employee has the appropriate skill base and that their behaviour aligns with the expectations of the organisation. In a university setting, for example, where casual staff are employed to take tutorials, problems can occur when these employees are not briefed appropriately on expected standards. With respect to HR's role in these circumstances, casual teaching staff may be asked to attend appropriate induction training programs and may also require close mentoring when first on the job. These systems have been activated in a number of leading universities in Australia where casual staff are required to attend training sessions before they are eligible to conduct tutorials. Casual teaching staff are usually also eligible to request student feedback through the formal central university teaching evaluation process. Performance feedback from other academics, however, is usually not formalised and relies on the willingness of other colleagues to provide appropriate mentoring.

Before leaving this discussion of the challenges associated with flexible work arrangements, it is important to consider the increasing presence of agency workers in service work. These workers are spread across a wide range of service industries – e.g. nurses, hospital support workers, teachers and sales assistants – and are defined as employees whose wages and labour costs are paid by an agency but who work for a host/client on a fixed-term basis (Hall 2006:159). Curtin (2004) points out that this class of worker is very prominent in Australia, ranked second in his sample of 17 OECD countries. The problem noted above of organisational value alignment within the casual workforce similarly exists with agency workers. This is especially the case with companies that require high involvement and high performance work practices. A hospital, for example, that differentiates itself in the market through particularly high levels of pastoral care for patients and achieves this through a high performance work culture would usually allow considerable employee autonomy and empowerment. The success of this approach, however, relies on the employee's alignment with, and understanding of, the organisation's culture. It may not be possible to achieve these goals when using a high number of agency workers.

This last example highlights the strategic HRM challenge for service industry companies that access these peripheral workers. In particular, strategic decisions have to be made about the nature of the tasks assigned to agency workers. Indeed, in Australia there is evidence that companies are using these workers to suit business needs. Hall (2006) has found that the workers are generally employed on a short-term basis, and they report that agency workers are less likely to be learning new skills and less likely to be doing work that is complex or difficult. The suggestion is, then, that companies that are using these workers are making the strategic decision to use them for less central tasks. Following on, Hall (2006) makes the point that the absence of intrinsically challenging work as a motivator for temporary agency workers requires that HR may have to apply higher levels of supervision, surveillance and direct authoritarian control than may be necessary for core, intrinsically motivated employees who are secure and committed.

In summary, the flexible work arrangements that characterise much of the service industry present challenges for employees and employers. When using casuals, HR can make a contribution by reviewing the level of training and mentoring provided to ensure that these workers are clear about what is expected of them in their interaction with customers. Socialisation programs and ongoing mentoring may help to diminish the fragmented approach to the work that can occur when an organisation draws from a large pool of casuals who work varied hours. When commitment to the organisation is a priority, the prospect of being able to transfer to permanent status or of gaining a promotion can also act as a motivator to casuals to align their behaviour with cultural expectations (Atkinson & Rick 1996). This is a process often employed in call centres when successful customer service operators are offered promotions to team leadership positions (Holman 2002). The problems of cultural fit and organisational commitment experienced with casual workers are similarly encountered with the use of agency workers (Geary 1992). Unlike casual workers however who may be employed on an ongoing basis with the company, agency workers are normally only employed for a limited term – and this presents even greater complexity for HR. In response, companies seem to be applying greater discretion about the type of tasks assigned and the autonomy given to these workers within their period of employment.

Managing the consequences of services sector work

Another major challenge experienced by those HR professionals involved in the service industry is managing the stress experienced by employees that is related to the nature of service work itself. A fundamental element of service work is the face-to-face or voice-to-voice interaction with customers (Macdonald & Sirianni 1996). As will be reviewed in *Chapter 8: Managing Emotional Labour in the Workplace*, these interactions involve high levels of emotional labour or 'the management of feeling to create a publicly observable facial and bodily display' (Hochschild 1983:7). In that chapter, the discussion reviews general issues associated with the management of differences between real and expected organisational displayed emotions and the role that HR can play in paying attention to clearly-stated organisational expectations and ensuring employee fit through careful recruitment, selection and training. The following discussion builds on that analysis to consider the role of HR in assisting employees in the management of emotionally-charged interactions with customers.

Undertakers, health professionals and counsellors take on their professions in the knowledge that they will often be dealing with people who are vulnerable and in distress. Accordingly, training and mentoring activities prepare these professionals for the emotional work that will be part of their job. Consideration may also often be given to a person's temperamental ability to deal with the intensity of the array of emotionally-charged situations that occur within the profession. It can be argued, however, that any service interaction has the potential to be characterised by high levels of emotional intensity that may be outside the expected scope of the position. This can often occur in the low paid front line 'emotional proletariat' work described by Macdonald and Sirianni (1996), who distinguish between these jobs and the services provided by white collar professionals.

The intensity of these potentially emotional encounters in front line work is highlighted in O'Donohue and Turnley's (2006) research that considered the compassion needed by newspaper employees who dealt with bereaved customers who contacted the newspaper to place *In Memoriam* notices on the anniversary of a close family member's death. The research reviews the sophisticated level of emotional interaction that can sometimes occur in seemingly mundane service exchanges in lower paid organisational positions. Newspaper employees could be consoling a distraught bereaved customer one moment and dealing with a routine classified advertisement in the next. Of particular interest in the research was the exploration of the factors that assisted these employees in coping with the emotional rollercoaster that their work involved. Using Korczyski's (2003) 'communities of coping' explanation, O'Donohue and Turnley (2006) note that the staff, who were mainly women, relied on each other to debrief about traumatic incidents or stories, and it was the collective support within the work environment that allowed the staff to cope with the potential distress of these situations.

Despite the emotional concentration of jobs where service workers are required to demonstrate care and compassion when dealing with customers, interactions with customers can also be an important source of pleasure and satisfaction. Workers who feel they are helping someone often find this interpersonal connection to be an intrinsically satisfying part of the job (Frenkel et al. 1999). Unfortunately, dealing with distressed customers does not always result in positive outcomes for customer service staff. An increasing amount of stress is generated in front line service roles by irate, and sometimes violent, customers. This interaction can be particularly distressing for service workers who start out with strong pro-customer attitudes. In these cases, the ongoing need to deal with difficult interactions may be a critical factor in 'burnout' of front-line workers (Korczynski 2002).

Specific examples of service industries that report increasing levels of violence include hospital staff, teachers, airline check-in employees, rail and bus service workers, and bank staff. A leading hospital in Melbourne, Australia, for example, reported an armed threat to nursing staff twice a week and an unarmed threat twenty times a week (Robinson 2004). Evidence has similarly emerged from the UK, with 40 per cent of nurses reporting abuse and threats from patients (Redford 2006). Teachers are also reporting increasing levels of violence and assault from parents and students as well as incursions onto campuses by angry and unstable people. The level of violence has now forced the Victorian Government in Australia to set up a committee that seeks to control inappropriate behaviour on school grounds. As a result, changes will be made to school offices to protect staff and teachers will be provided with specialised training that focuses on angry parents. Bad customer behaviour is also more common within the air travel business. The Australian Services Union has reported that rising violence against staff has resulted in Qantas recently testing 'duress buttons' at Melbourne airport check-in counters (Robinson 2004). These, and numerous other examples from employees working in rail and bus services as well as in the banking industry, highlight the stressful emotional interactions that can characterise service positions.

Another industry in which customer service operators can often face abusive clients is in call centres. There is actually more potential for abuse in these situations because of the removal of the face-to-face component of the service interaction. Telephone conversations create a social distance and the feeling that the customer service representative is a disembodied voice against which it is appropriate to vent one's rage (Korczynski 2002). The placement of some call centres offshore to countries such as India has exacerbated this level of abuse as customers incorporate racist abuse into existing complaints against the company (O'Malley 2006).

From these examples, it is apparent that most forms of service work can lead to emotionally intense interactions with customers that potentially place employees at risk. It becomes the responsibility of HR, therefore, to ensure that these interactions are minimised and that potential danger is averted. Occupational health and safety legislation in Australia ensures that organisations are legally responsible to provide a safe workplace and adopt a 'duty of care' with respect to both employees and customers. In practice this means that infrastructure changes need to be put in place that may include appropriate video surveillance of customer behaviour, access to employee assistance programs for employees to receive counselling, and closer communication with the security department to plan personal reaction strategies.

HR also has the responsibility for designing and communicating the organisation's policy on the prevention of occupational violence in the workplace. Effective policy development usually involves employees in the policy design process. The finalised policy clearly defines the range of violent interactions and the identification of risks, and reminds employees of common warning signs. An explanation is also provided of the employee's responsibilities for recognising signs and reporting them. Guidelines are usually provided about who to notify and what to do in various situations and training is set up on what policies and procedures actually involve. A confidential reporting system supports the effective operationalisation of the policy.

As well as these HRM policy initiatives, Korczynski (2003) emphasises the need to encourage and develop 'communities of coping', or the empathetic dynamic between colleagues that provides support in emotionally stressful service positions. This dynamic often arises informally and can be crucial to survival in the job. HR can assist in the creation of this coping mechanism by developing team structures that acknowledge the natural support mechanisms that often emerge among service workers. A necessary part of the success of these team structures is the design of HRM performance evaluation processes. Research has shown, for example, that performance-based pay in call centres works best when it is constructed on a team-basis rather than when it is developed as an individual reward (Fernie & Metcalf 1999; Korczynski 2002). Coupled with the importance of team dynamics, other research has reinforced the important role that the team leader has on employee well-being (Holman 2002; Rudewicz 2004). Care should be taken in the selection and training of team leaders to ensure that they are equipped to provide appropriate support. This can be especially important in call centres where customer service operators are often promoted to team leadership roles for their technical competency and may be relatively ill-equipped to cope with the emotional co-ordination of the team (Holman 2002).

Conclusions

Service work spans a wide range of possible interactions, but the essential component across all of these events is that the product is either partly or entirely associated with an interpersonal interaction between the provider and the customer. The management of employees, therefore, in the delivery of the organisation's business is critical. There are, however, a number of HR challenges that service work presents. With respect to HRM planning, the interaction cannot really occur unless the customer is present. Staff have to be available when the customer is there and are often redundant when the customer is absent, thus the employment of casual and agency staff becomes a necessity. The benefits of flexibility offered by this workforce are often outweighed by loyalty and skill deficiencies, and accordingly HR has to make strategic decisions about the types of tasks these employees are given and the return on investment in training and development initiatives. The personal nature of the 'product' can also present unexpected emotional intensity that HR has to manage for both the employee and the customer. Duty of care responsibilities, as well as the maximisation of company performance, may depend on how well HR attends to structural and policy design. At the broader level, the rise of the service sector has intensified the focus that is already being given to the impact human resources can make in organisations. The more that human capital emerges as a key resource base, the more important is the strategic impact that HR can make and this is highlighted in HR's role in dealing with challenges apparent in the service sector.

References

Appelbaum, E, Bailey, T & Berg, P 2000, *Manufacturing Advantage: Why High-Performance Systems Pay Off*, ILR Press, Ithaca.

Atkinson, J & Rick, J 1996, 'Temporary Work and the Labour Market', report 311, Institute of Employment Studies, UK.

Australian Bureau of Statistics 2006, *Yearbook Australia 2006*, cat. no. 1301.0, Australian Bureau of Statistics, Canberra.

Australian Bureau of Statistics 2010, *Yearbook Australia 2009-2010*, cat. no. 1301.0, Australian Bureau of Statistics, Canberra,
http://www.abs.gov.au/AUSSTATS/abs@.nsf/Lookup/1301.0Chapter22012009%E2%80%9310, accessed on Jan 12, 2011.

Australian Bureau of Statistics, Australian Social Trends, June 2009, cat. No. 4102.0
http://www.abs.gov.au/AUSSTATS/abs@.nsf/Lookup/4102.0Main+Features40June+2009 accessed on Jan 12, 2011.

Barney, J B & Wright, P M 1998, 'On becoming a strategic partner: the role of human resources in gaining competitive advantage', *Human Resource Management*, 37(1): 31- 46.

Batt, R 2000, 'Strategic segmentation in front-line services: matching customers, employees and human resource systems'. *International Journal of Human Resource Management*, 11 (3): 540-61.

Blyton, P 1989, 'Working population and employment', in R Bean (ed), *International Labour Statistics*, Routledge, London, pp. 18-51.

Bosch, G & Lehndorff, S 2005, *Working in the Service Sector: A tale from different worlds*, Routledge, Oxon.

Boxall, P 2003, 'HR strategy and competitive advantage in the service sector', *Human Resource Management Journal*, 13 (3): 5-20.

Buultjens, J 2001, 'Casual employment: A problematic strategy for the registered clubs sector in New South Wales', *The Journal of Industrial Relations*, 43(4): 470-477.

Burgess, J & Connell, J 2006, 'Temporary work and human resource management: Issues, challenges and responses', *Personnel Review*, 35(2): 125-40.

Curtin, R 2004, Affidavit of Dr Richard Curtin, no. IRC 4330 of 2003, Industrial Relations Commission of New South Wales, Sydney.

Fernie, S & Metcalf, D 1999, '(Not) hanging on the telephone: Payment systems in the new sweatshops', *Centre for Economic Performance Paper*, London School of Economics.

Frenkel, S, Korczynski, M, Shire, K & Tam, M 1999, *On the FrontLline: Work organization in the service economy*, ILR / Cornell University Press, Ithaca, NY.

Geary, J 1992, 'Employment Flexibility and Human Resource Management', *Work, Employment and Society*, 6(2): 251-270.

Hall, R 2006, 'Temporary agency work and HRM in Australia "Cooperation, specialization and satisfaction for the good of all"?, *Personnel Review*, 35(2): 158-174.

Hochschild, A R 1983, *The Managed Heart: Commercialization of Human Feeling*, University of California Press, Berkeley.

Holman, D, 2002, 'Employee wellbeing in call centres', *Human Resource Management Journal*, 12(4): 35-50.

Kalleberg, A 2000, 'Nonstandard employment relations: Part-time, temporary and contract work', *Annual Review of Sociology*, 26: 341-365.

Korczynski, M 2002, *Human Resource Management in Service Work*, Palgrave, Hampshire.

Korczynski, M 2003, 'Communities of coping: Collective emotional labour in service work', *Organization*, 10(1): 55-79.

Lowry, D 2001, 'The casual management of casual work: Casual workers' perceptions of HRM practices in the highly casualised firm', *Asia Pacific Journal of Human Resources*, 39(1): 42-62.

Macdonald, C & Sirianni, C 1996, 'The service society and the changing experience of work, in C Macdonald & C Sirianni, *Working in the Service Society*, The University Press, Philadelphia, pp. 1-26.

MacDuffie, JP 1995, 'Human resource bundles and manufacturing performance: organizational logic and flexible production systems in the world auto industry'. *Industrial and Labor Relations Review*, 48 (2): 197-221.

Mills, P 1986, *Managing Service Industries*, Ballinger, Cambridge, MA.

Morris, JA & Feldman, DC 1996, 'The dimensions, antecedents and consequences of emotional labour', *Academy of Management Review*, 21(4): 986-1010.

Noon, M & Blyton, P 2002, *The Realities of Work*, 2nd edn, Palgrave, Hampshire.

O'Donohue, S & Turnley, D 2006, 'Compassion at the counter: Service providers and bereave consumers', *Human Relations*, 59(10): 1429-1448.

O'Malley, N 2006, 'Indian call centre staff fed up with racist abuse', *The Age*, 20 March 2006, p. 5.

Pocock, B, Buchanan, J, & Campbell, I 2004, 'Meeting the challenge of casual work in Australia: Evidence, past treatment and future policy', *Australian Bulletin of Labour*, 30(1): 16–32.

Redford, K 2006,' Spotlight on violence in the workplace', *Personnel Today*, April 18, p. 35.

Robinson, P 2004, 'Violence at work all the rage', *The Age*, Insight, 29 May 2004, p. 4.

Rudewicz, F 2004, 'The road to rage', *Security Management,* February: 40-49.

Schneider, B, White, S & Paul, M 1998, 'Linking service climate and customer perceptions of service quality: Test of a causal model, *Journal of Applied Psychology*. 8 (2): 150-163.

Smith, M 2005, 'The incidence of new forms of employment in service activities', in C Macdonald & C Sirianni, *Working in the Service Society,* The University Press, Philadelphia, pp. 54-73.

United Nations 2002, Manual on Statistics of International Trade in Services, United Nations, Geneva,
http://www.oecd.org/dataoecd/32/45/2404428.pdf, accessed on Jan 12, 2011.

Wright, P, McMahan, G & McWilliams, A 1994,'Human resources as a source of sustained competitive advantage', *International Journal of Human Resource Management*, 5: 299-324.

Van den Heuvel, A, & Wooden, M 1997, 'Self-employed contractors and job satisfaction' *Journal of Small Business Management*, 35(3): 11-20.

Case study: Maintaining service quality in the wedding business

Escape Resorts International, founded in 1992, is headquartered in the UK. The organisation now has sites all over the world, including locations in Phuket in Thailand, Cairns in Australia, and a number of sites in The Bahamas, Jamaica, Antigua and Saint Lucia. The resorts operate primarily as 'couple only' retreats that cater to customers who are keen to enjoy romantic get-aways. The resorts offer amenities such as gourmet *à la carte* dining, entertainment and shows featuring well-known acts, and a range of outdoor activities including snorkelling, scuba diving and golf. In 2004, the company decided to offer a wedding and honeymoon package at the sites operating in The Bahamas, and trialled an offering that included a personal wedding consultant, a tropical wedding location, a celebrant, a wedding cake, a video and photograph package, a copy of the marriage licence, and arrangements that covered government and administration fees. Initially, the package generated a lot of bookings, including international interest from Europe as well as from North America. By 2009, however, demand had dropped dramatically and, although the wedding packages were not a core element of the experience offered by Escape Resorts, the downturn in sales attracted the attention of senior management in the UK. In response, a senior manager, Tom Height, was sent to the site to investigate the flow of the operation.

On arrival, Tom was greeted by the wedding co-ordinator, Rhea, who showed him into the area where all of the bookings and wedding arrangements were made with customers onsite. There were four couples waiting in the same room where an interview was currently underway. Tom asked why so many people were waiting at once, and Rhea explained that all the wedding arrangements took place on a Monday, and that the weddings then followed on the Tuesday. This arrangement freed staff to work in other areas of the resort for the remainder of the week. The next day, Tom was able to see the wedding program in progress, and was again surprised by the 'assembly line' approach to each wedding. He also had contact with the people who were working to provide videos and photos for the wedding parties, he noted that they were not engaged in the process and were keen to move people through quickly rather than to personalise each wedding. He was told that the wedding photographers did not actually work for the hotel but had been contracted to the resort to provide the service. The food that arrived after each wedding for a brief reception was also not co-ordinated properly in the kitchen, and often arrived late or in a poor condition.

> This was because the staff delivering the food were trying to fit their wedding reception food duties in between other duties associated with the main dining areas in the resort.
>
> Tom could see the frustration on the customers' faces, and overheard a number of guests comment that the service did not meet their expectations. One customer commented: 'We thought we were going to get a high quality experience, and instead we have been dealt with in a disorganised fashion by people who are not focussed on the job at hand.'
>
> Written by: Cathy Sheehan.

Case study questions

1. What are the key HR problems and issues associated with the running of the wedding business at Escape Resorts?

2. What changes could be made to HRM-related activities to improve the quality of the experience?

Discussion questions

1. Provide an in-depth definition of service work.

2. Identify possible reasons for the increasing dominance of the service sector.

3. What are the HR benefits and challenges associated with the flexible workforce that characterise much of the service sector, and how can HR deal with these issues?

4. What factors might determine HR's strategic decisions with respect to HR planning and the investment in employees within the service industry?

5. How can HR support employees who deal with emotionally-charged interactions with customers?

Chapter 8

MANAGING EMOTIONAL LABOUR IN THE WORKPLACE

INTRODUCTION

The examination of emotions in the workplace is emerging as a central area for research for those working in the broad field of management, and more specifically human resource management (HRM). The objective of this chapter is to review the challenges posed in organisations of increasing levels of emotional labour, with particular emphasis on the role that the human resources (HR) function can take in the management of these developments. This chapter is not designed, therefore, to provide a complete overview of the research related to emotions, but rather to consider some key emotional labour issues that are having a direct impact on the work of HR professionals.

Emotion and emotional labour

Hartel, Gough and Hartel (2008) acknowledge that despite the long history of investigation into the field of emotions the definition of the area has been characterised by disagreement and the definition has changed and evolved. Fineman (1993), in his book *Emotion in Organizations*, defined the area of inquiry into the nature of emotions to be focused on 'feelings'. Goleman (1996:289) extends this definition to incorporate physiological and behavioural aspects of emotions, and defines the phenomenon as 'a feeling and its distinctive thoughts, physiological and biological states and a range of propensities to act'. Mann (1999) concludes that emotions consist of a cognitive process, an experiential feeling, physiological change and a behavioural aspect.

Within the work environment, much of the discussion of feelings has focussed on the generation of these emotional states to fit in with job expectations. Hochschild (1983:7) developed the term 'emotional labour' to refer to 'the management of feeling to create a publicly observable facial and bodily display'. The term has been readily used in relation to work, as often the creation of a public face or bodily display is a central part of the delivery of the service or product. However, the delivery of a particular emotional interaction is not always easy to create, as often the expected emotion may be at odds with what an employee is actually experiencing. Using Weis and Cropanzano's (1996) classification of emotional experiences as depicted in Figure 8.1, an employee who is expected to generate cheerfulness or zest as part of the joy response in their job may struggle to do this when they are faced with a difficult customer whose behaviour elicits exasperation or irritation which is part of the anger reaction.

Figure 8.1 Classification of emotional experiences (Weis & Cropanzano 1996)

Anger	Fear	Joy	Love	Sadness	Surprise
Disgust	Alarm	Cheerfulness	Affection	Disappointment	(No sub-categories)
Envy	Anxiety	Contentment	Longing	Neglect	
Exasperation		Enthralment	Lust	Sadness	
Irritation		Optimism		Shame	
Rage		Pride		Suffering	
Torment		Relief		Sympathy	
		Zest			

Source: Adapted from Weiss, H M & Crapanzano, R 1996, Affective events theory: A theoretical discussion of the structure, causes and consequences of affective experiences at work, *Research in Organizational Behaviour*, 18: 1-74.

Emotional labour is heightened when the potential gap between real and displayed emotions widens; for example, when an employee is expected to display cheerfulness when they really want to express their irritation at the behaviour of a difficult customer or client. Morris and Feldman (1996) modelled the components of emotional labour to explain this concept in more detail. In line with the discussion above, their model included the impact of the psychological distress related to the internal conflict of displaying a certain emotion while actually feeling something quite different. The specific term used to describe this internal state is 'emotional dissonance'. These writers explain that the state of internal conflict is diminished when the required emotion is aligned with one's genuine emotional state. There should be little emotional labour required, for example, when selling a product that one genuinely believes in. Aligning one's emotional state with the behaviour of a difficult customer, however, is more difficult to achieve.

As well as reinforcing the impact of internal conflict on the level of required emotional labour, Morris and Feldman (1996) identified external conditions that intensify the need to exert emotional energy. The first of these external conditions may seem self evident, but it is still important to identify. It is related to the frequency of the required emotional display. An administration assistant working at a busy inquiries counter all day is more likely to be engaged in higher levels of emotional labour than someone who relieves that person at morning tea time because the incumbent will deal with a much higher number of variable interactions.

The second external condition that impacts on emotional labour is the requirement that people in the role attend to certain display rules – in other words, adhere to a particular protocol or script when dealing with customers. This factor consists of both the *duration* and the *intensity* of the emotional display. First, with respect to the *duration* of the emotional display, scripted interactions of a short duration may require minimal emotional labour output. For example, a customer service operator in a telephone directories call centre has an expected call turnaround of 18 seconds and is equipped with a set of regular prompts to help the caller refine their directory enquiry. Longer interactions with clients, however, can be associated with higher levels of emotional labour. The reasons for this are that it becomes more difficult to sustain the expected scripted approach as the interaction potentially creates a situation for which the employee has less information. It becomes more likely, then, that the employee may have to improvise, and it becomes harder for the employee to avoid showing their own personal feelings and only adhere to organisational expectations (Morris & Feldman 1996). Consider the situation of an airline attendant on a long haul flight. The attendant has a range of responses to the ongoing requests from passengers. As the flight progresses, however, everyone becomes more tired, and as the attendant gets to know more about particular passengers it becomes more difficult to maintain standard responses and the required smile. Therefore, due to the nature of these longer emotional displays, greater attention and emotional stamina are required.

The second aspect of required display rules, the expected *intensity* of the emotional display, is perhaps the most demanding of emotional display conditions. When employees are called upon to exhibit deep emotions that may be difficult to fake or to remain personally distant, the interaction can be draining for the employee (Morris & Feldman 1996). Neonatal intensive care nurses, for example, deal with babies and their parents who are going through some of life's most intense experiences. These nurses are expected to empathise and support parents, and yet remain professional and appropriate at all times. These expectations require sophisticated emotional management on the part of the nursing professional.

The final major dimension of emotional labour is the required variety involved in the work role. The expectation that the employee shifts from one emotion to another within a brief period of time requires the exertion of greater levels of psychological energy. A high school teacher on yard duty, for example, may have to react with enthusiasm to an eager grade seven student who is explaining that their debating team has just won the semi finals at the same time as restraining two grade nine students engaged in a fist fight.

Overall, these external components – the frequency of the emotional display, attentiveness to display rules and the variety of emotions expressed – along with the internal emotional dissonance often experienced by employees contribute to emotional labour requirements in any job. Mann (1999) explains that each of these dimensions on its own is enough to produce 'emotional labour', but the more dimensions that are experienced in any particular job the more emotional labour is being performed. Having explored the nature of the emotional labour challenge, the next section further investigates specific employee responses to the expectation that they display certain emotions.

Employee reactions

As mentioned earlier, portraying emotions that are not felt creates emotional dissonance, that is, a discrepancy between emotions felt and those expressed. The reaction of the employee to this state is similar to reactions to cognitive dissonance, which is the strain associated with inconsistencies between our beliefs, feelings and behaviour (Festinger 1957). Effectively, an individual cannot remain in this state of tension but seeks to reduce the stress by dealing with their internal state in a variety of ways. Mann (1999) identifies a number of strategies that the employee can use.

First, workers can try to change the expectations of the emotions that they are requested to feign. This results in an employee deciding to keep their internal emotional state intact and simply not align their responses with the required emotional display. The strategy may allow the employee to remain true to themselves and genuine in the interactions with the customer, but the choice of an alternative display may also result in behaviour that does not serve the organisation. An employee for a multinational fast-food chain, for example, who is expected to always be positive and enthusiastic about the quality of the product may decide to share cynical feelings about the organisation with a customer. This may reduce the employee's feelings of emotional dissonance, but ultimately the behaviour may lead to the employee being asked to exit the organisation as the refusal to adopt the display effectively implies a refusal to perform the required job.

A more probable employee reaction to dealing with emotional dissonance is to either fake what they feel or suppress what they feel. With both of these approaches, the employee makes some attempt to change their behaviour and emotional response to move in line with corporate expectations. The employee will therefore say the right lines and provide the necessary smile or empathetic reaction. There will be variation however in how aligned the employee can actually become in their acceptance of the required emotional state. As noted, some employees will fake the responses, produce the required phrases and protocols, but keep their own emotions separate and thereby remain internally emotionally intact. Effectively, these employees reduce the emotional dissonance by explaining to themselves that this is part of their job and that the emotional display is necessary because they need the work, or alternatively there are other aspects of the job that compensate for the task at hand. The self-explanation reduces the dissonance and helps the employee to keep their internal emotional balance.

Other workers may move more in line with the emotions expected by the organisation, and this may mean that these workers actually suppress their own emotions. At the extreme, these workers deny their own emotions and as a result can acquire both psychological and physical problems. There has been a long tradition of research that has identified the negative consequences of 'bottling up emotions'. Suppression of emotions has been shown to lead to conditions such as hypertension and coronary heart disease (Friedman & Booth-Kewley 1987; Gentry 1985; Goldstein, Edelberg, Meier & Davis 1988).

Whether the employee fakes what they feel and provides a very superficial show of the required emotion or makes a more substantial attempt to carry out the organisation's emotional requirements by suppressing their own emotion, the pressure to express emotions that are genuinely not felt may cause the individual to feel false, cynical and alienated from their work (Ashforth & Humphrey 1993). As well as the personal cost associated with these emotions, there are implications for the organisation as well as for employees who seek out emotional labour coping strategies.

A simple coping mechanism is for employees to retire to 'staff only' areas where they can let off steam and retreat from customer demands (Martin, Knopoff & Beckman 1998). An associated outcome of this strategy is that employees get to share their experiences with other co-workers, and this solidarity helps them cope with the work demands (Karabanow 1999). Other coping strategies impact more directly on the customer interaction, and these include behaviours where the employee avoids eye contact with the customer or says the right things but does not try to really engage with the customer. Taylor and Bain (1999:113) provide the following example of resistance from an operator in a telecommunications centre:

> *Some customers are just a pain…But I've worked out a way of saying things that put them in their place. If you choose your words carefully, there's no way they can pull you in and dig you up for what you've said.*

Workers in this situation are engaging in deviant behaviour. Consistent with the dyadic nature of the service encounter, Browning (2008) has shown that such deviant behaviour is more likely when the attitude and behaviour of the customer becomes difficult to manage. Ultimately, in these situations where employees engage in coping behaviours that do not serve organisational goals, at a minimum the customer interaction loses spontaneity and authenticity and at the extreme customers feel that they have been dealt with in a condescending and disrespectful manner. The question emerges, therefore, of what HR can do to assist in the management of these interactions.

What can HR do to manage emotional labour requirements?

To return to Morris and Feldman's description of the dimension of emotional labour, there are two main factors that intensify the need to exert emotional energy: 1) internal emotional dissonance, and 2) external conditions that include the frequency of the emotional display, attentiveness to display rules (including duration and intensity of emotional display), and the variety of emotions expressed. HR's management of the stress associated with excessive emotional labour should therefore consider each of these sources of emotional stress.

Dealing with internal emotional dissonance

First, with respect to internal emotional dissonance, an individual will experience the strongest dissonance when their own emotions are not aligned with expected display emotions. A number of factors may determine the alignment or fit between the emotions experienced by an employee and those espoused by the organisation. One potential determinant of internal harmony is that of value alignment. Pruzan (2001) has argued that employees seek out work not just for traditional benefits such as wages and opportunities for advancement, but employees also look for work that is meaningful and aligned with their personal values.

Theoretically, values have been subdivided into instrumental and terminal values (Rokeach 1973). Terminal values are self-sufficient end-states of existence that a person strives to achieve (e.g. a comfortable life, wisdom) whereas instrumental values are modes of behaviour (e.g. honesty, helpfulness) rather than states of existence. The relationship between instrumental and terminal values is such that instrumental values describe behaviours that facilitate the attainment of terminal values (Rokeach 1973). Put more simply, Meglino and Ravlin (1998) suggest that values are a person's internalised belief about how he or she should or ought to behave. With respect to work values, they suggest that we add the qualifier 'at work'.

For the purposes of the current discussion about emotional alignment, values are believed to have a substantial influence on the affective and behavioural responses of individuals (Rokeach 1973). Values provide a personal standard of conduct, and as a consequence any actions that are inconsistent with these values will result in feelings of guilt, shame or self-depreciation (Kluckhohn 1951). Emotional labour requirements therefore that highlight a gap between an employee's personal values and the organisation's enacted values (i.e. values-in-use) may result in emotional dissonance that is very uncomfortable for the employee.

The question then arises as to how HR can deal with this source of emotional dissonance. One way in which inconsistencies in values may be minimised is to ensure that organisational values are explicit and clearly articulated. Many organisations spend considerable time and money in the development of espoused values, or values to which members of the organisation wish to aspire. These value and mission statements may be developed, however, to create a positive public image rather than reflecting the enacted values or the values that are actually in use in the organisation. The HR department can take an active role in ensuring that espoused values are actually put into operation. Making sure that declared organisational values are based in reality is, however, a demanding role for HR professionals. Nevertheless, writers such as Wright and Snell (2005), Meisenger (2005) and Elliot (2004) argue that a key HR leadership role is to challenge, mentor and support the organisation's top-level leadership team in value commitment. When key business decisions potentially conflict with organisational values, HR has to act as the organisation's conscience. Drawing from the example of Delta Air Lines, where HR became complicit in a cost reduction emphasis, Wright and Snell (2005) highlight the challenge for HR professionals to maintain a focus on core values rather than being caught up in short term solutions such as agreeing to the development of a 'commodity' workforce rather than a 'capability' workforce.

One of the clear benefits of a comprehensive enactment of values in an organisation is that prospective employees, at the point of recruitment and selection, can access accurate information about what is expected from them as employees (see also *Chapter 2: Managing the War for Talent*). Following on, if the tasks involve a particular emotional display, potential recruits can then make informed decisions about their personal level of comfort with organisational expectations. Behaviours and expected emotional displays at Virgin Blue, for example, are clearly articulated on the Virgin website[9]. The following comments from the website makes it clear what will be expected from someone who wishes to become a Virgin employee:

> *Virgin people are easy to spot. They act in unusual ways as it's the only way they know how. But it's not forced – it's natural. They are honest, cheeky, questioning, amusing, disruptive, intelligent and restless… Virgin people are smart.*
>
> *I joined Virgin because I wanted rock 'n' roll. I wanted the big challenge, the big job, the big car, but I wanted rock 'n' roll as well, and that comes from a stuffy old Finance Director!*

---

[9] <http://www.virgin.com/aboutvirgin/howitallworks/whatwearelike/default.asp>. Accessed 5th December 2006.

A Virgin person would typically:

- have a passion for new ideas;
- think 'differently';
- have signs of creativity;
- be able to smell new business opportunities; and
- always listen to customers.

In interactions with customers, a Virgin Blue booking agent or flight attendant would be expected to be fun, warm, innovative and a bit cheeky. If someone were uncomfortable with the expected level of gregarious behaviour, they could make the decision to look for a position at another airline that does not expect employees to be as expressive.

In Australia, Qantas is the major competitor to Virgin Blue. A search of the Qantas website[10] reveals that, although there are similarities in expectations about customer service, the emotional disposition expected of airline attendants seems to be more sedate and considered. In a description of what they look for in a flight attendant, the following guidelines are provided:

- An understanding of the needs and comfort of our customers who travel with us – whether they are regular flyers or customers who have never flown before.
- An ability to build rapport and trust in a team to positively contribute to the team's performance.
- An ability to adapt to any situation that may present itself in a sensible, warm and safe way.
- An appreciation of cultural diversity and sensitivity towards customers who may need extra help, such as unaccompanied minors, those who are nervous about flying or people who may not have English as their first language.
- A caring approach when offering our customers food, beverages and any other assistance they may need on board.

Further on, in the description of what is important at Qantas, the following is included:

> *Our Flight Attendants have a significant opportunity to influence our customers' perception of our airline through their ability to provide high standards of service in a sensitive and empathetic manner.*

---

[10] <http://www.qantas.com.au/info/about/employment/flightAttendants#jump0>. Accessed 5th December 2006.

> *We expect our Flight Attendants to be of the highest calibre with superior communication and service skills and an ability to care for our customers in all circumstances. They are selected for their empathy, cultural sensitivity and respect for their colleagues.*

The emotional expectation at Qantas is that employees focus more on empathy and sensitivity. Again, for prospective employees this is useful information that can help them form a decision about personal levels of comfort with these emotions. HR has an active role to play in helping to distinguish these expectations at the recruitment entry point and to ensure that potential employees are clear about the emotional displays that will be expected from them on the job.

As well as providing clear signals about organisational values at the recruitment level, HR may further enhance the possibility of achieving employee emotional fit at the point of employee selection. Thompson, Warhurst and Callaghan (2001) review a number of case studies where social and emotional skills were more important to the work than technical skills. At one call centre, Telebank, where the work was routine, standardised and simple, the company used sophisticated recruitment and selection processes in order to achieve the required social and emotional fit with the call centre's objectives to have a workforce that communicated with energy and enthusiasm. To achieve that end, the company used a number of interactive selection techniques including telephone interviews and role plays with a range of possible customer profiles.

As well as interactive selection that includes group interviews, role plays and structured interviews built around scenarios, many companies are incorporating emotional fit inventories into selection processes. One such approach is the measurement of emotional ability or emotional intelligence (EQ). John Mayer with his colleague Peter Salovey provided the first formulation of this concept that was later popularised by Daniel Goleman. Goleman (2005) explains that emotional intelligence is made up of the following five dimensions:

1. Self awareness – or knowing one's emotions – is the first dimension, and it is considered to be a fundamental requirement in developing overall effective emotional intelligence. The ability to monitor one's own feelings from moment to moment is crucial to self understanding.

2. Managing emotions – or self regulation – builds on the ability to read one's own emotions. Employees who have a high capacity to self regulate their emotions are less likely to react negatively to customers who are irritating and difficult, and more likely to think through the consequences of making flippant or inappropriate remarks.

3. Motivating oneself involves directing emotions towards a specific goal, stifling impulsiveness and delaying gratification. The ability to stay focused on the task at hand allows the individual to maintain expected standards, and to be optimistic even when they do not achieve their goals.

4. Recognising emotions in others – or empathy – is another fundamental people skill. This ability allows people to understand and be sensitive to the feelings, thoughts and situations of others. Employees who are empathetic will be more attuned to the subtle social signals that other people display.

5. Handling relationships – or social skills – builds on the ability to read the emotions of other people. Effectively, this dimension refers to the art of relationship building and allows people to guide the way that other people act. These abilities underlie popularity, leadership and interpersonal effectiveness.

Goleman (2005) points out that it is possible to be well developed on some of these dimensions but less developed in others. Some people may be adept at handling their own emotions, for example, but find difficulty in managing the emotions of others. When looking at positions that draw on the emotional resources of an employee, the more an employee understands their own emotions and is capable of motivating themselves to stay focused on the goal, the more likely it is that the employee will remain optimistic when matching real and required display emotions.

A very good example of the importance of the ability to manage one's own emotions is found in the position of sporting referees. The Australian National Rugby League in recruitment and selection processes, for example, has made a conscious attempt to incorporate a measure of prospective referees' emotional management ability. Steve Brown, who sits on the Australian rugby league's board of directors, explains 'It's a very high pressure job to be in charge of 26 players on a football field and deal with a crowd as well' (*Human Resources* 2002:23). In order to find a right fit, the League, working with an EQ vendor, put together a specification that could be filled out by candidates online. Each candidate was then provided with feedback about their suitability and the likelihood that they would be considered for the position (*Human Resources* 2002).

As with most measurement instruments, there is some debate about appropriate approaches to the assessment of EQ. The Emotional Quotient Inventory is very popular, self-reported and easy to conduct. The measure does attract criticism, however as reviewers suggest that it relies too heavily on personality attributes and measures of self esteem rather than on emotional intelligence as defined by Goleman. Another tool, the Emotional Competency Inventory, is a multi-rater measurement approach which provides 360 feedback. Its strength lies in its ability to measure how *others* perceive the candidate's emotional intelligence. A further measure is the Mayer-Salovey-Caruso Emotional Intelligence Test (MSCEIT). This is an ability-based model that measures potential emotional intelligence using pictures and scenarios to see how candidates respond. The criticism of this measure is that it only measures a person's potential to respond appropriately and not whether a person is motivated enough to put the skill into use (Hoffman 2006).

Despite the controversy surrounding the measurement of the dimension, the important issue for HR is the recognition that EQ is becoming an increasingly important selection tool that may actually supersede IQ – especially in situations where employees are required to manage their own emotions and the emotions of others. Once staff have been selected, on-going training programs are being used as a way of reinforcing organisational expectations and refining employee emotional management skills. Australian organisations as disparate as the New South Wales training academy for prison officers[11] and the accounting firm Bellmores (*Human Resources* 2002) are using emotional management approaches to assist staff in dealing with emotional pressures.

Dealing with external sources of emotional stress

The second set of factors that intensify the need to exert emotional energy or labour, as identified by Morris and Feldman (1996), come from pressures within the external environment. Specifically, emotional energy is heightened when the employee is required to display the behaviour often, when the display is required over a long period of time and with intensity, and when the required emotion display is characterised by variety. It follows, then, that the more an organisation expects in terms of these emotional labour requirements the more likely it is that employees struggle to maintain standards and forget or neglect to adhere strictly to company requirements. Employers, and HR by default, have to develop mechanisms to monitor and control the behaviour of employees to ensure that the correct emotional response is being delivered. Covert monitoring can involve the use of 'mystery shoppers' who are hired by the company and disguised as customers to gauge the performance of company representatives. Fast food outlets, for example, often use this technique to ensure that appropriate standards of customer interaction are being met. Van Maanen and Kunda (1989) reported that at Disneyland supervisors actually hid in areas of the park in order to watch the interactions between 'guests' and employees. Unfortunately, controls that are too tightly specified or too intrusive in making sure that employees provide an appropriate interaction may actually run the risk of having the opposite effect, as employees devote their cognitive

---

[11] http://www.abc.net.au/catalyst/stories/s581804.htm, accessed 1st June, 2011.

resources to dealing with anxiety rather than focussing on a quality customer experience (Holman 2002).

Intrusive forms of monitoring have also been shown to have negative outcomes on employee well-being. In a survey of customer service representatives working in call centres, Holman (2002) identified that the factors most highly associated with employee well-being were high control over work methods and procedures, a low level of monitoring, and having a supportive team leader. Deery and Kinnie (2002) suggest that, as well as often resulting in stressful outcomes for employees, there are other limitations to the rigid and prolonged adherence to standard work procedures. Where the personal interaction between an employee and the customer requires subjective interpretation and personal judgement on the part of the employee, for example, standardised control of employee behaviour is inappropriate. Customers may present unusual requests and behaviours, and employees who are trained to work within tightly prescribed behavioural responses may not be able to respond appropriately to unusual requests. Finally, customers are also very sensitive to the authenticity displayed by the employee, and tightly scripted and routinised responses can interfere with the warmth of the exchange. In response, organisations are recognising the value of normative control or self initiated adherence to organisational goals. In such situations companies concentrate on developing an awareness within employees of what is important and allowing employees to respond as required. To return to the Telebank example, Thompson *et al.* (2002) explain that, in the call centre, trainees are encouraged to make the necessary changes to 'their state of mind' in order to generate rapport and improve sincerity. One outcome of this approach is that the organisations will adopt what Macdonald and Sirianni (1996:7) refer to as an 'empowerment approach' where through careful training employers '...create the kinds of people who would make decisions that management would approve'.

Conclusions

A great deal of the literature related to the management of emotions in the workplace has focussed on emotional labour, or the production of emotional displays that fit with the job requirements. This chapter has considered conditions under which emotional labour is heightened, such as internal conflict when displaying required emotions and external conditions that exacerbate emotional labour requirements. The HR function can assist in the management of these internal and external sources of emotional stress in a number of ways. First, HR can take a more proactive role in refining, communicating and framing espoused organisational values as well as reinforcing enacted values. Greater clarity around what these values involve provides an important source of recruitment information. Prospective employees are able to more accurately decide whether they are comfortable with possible emotional displays that may be associated with the defined organisational value set. Second, the use of emotional intelligence measures in selection – and later as part of on-going training – further assist in achieving appropriate employee fit with the organisation's expectations. Finally, in dealing with external sources of emotional stress, HR can review the conditions under which employees are expected to cope with expected display rules. Rigid adherence to certain display rules over long periods of time, or emotional displays that involve high levels of intensity and variety, create situations of potentially high levels of emotional stress on employees. Heavy monitoring of employees that is focussed on controlling employee reactions in these situations rather than assisting in the development of these employees is potentially destructive with respect to both the employee's well-being and the authenticity of the interaction with the customer. HR can assist in promoting normative control rather than overt monitoring as a way of empowering workers and returning control to them in order to allow them to cope with any stress presented in the situation.

References

Ashforth, BE & Humphrey R 1993, 'Emotional labour in service roles: The influence of identity', *Academy of Management Review*, 18(1): 88-115.

Browning, V 2008, 'An exploratory study into deviant behaviour in the service encounter: How and why front-line employees engage in deviant behaviour', *Journal of Management and Organization*, 14, 4, 451 – 473.

Deery, S & Kinnie, N 2002, 'Call centres and beyond: a thematic evaluation', *Human Resources Management Journal*, 12(4): 3–13.

Elliot, G 2004, 'HR's role in instilling core values', *Employment Relations Today*, Summer, pp. 25-32.

Festinger, L 1957, *A Theory of Cognitive Dissonance*, Row Peterson, Evanston, IL.

Fineman, S 1993, 'Organizations as emotional arenas', in S Fineman (ed), *Emotions in Organizations*, Sage Publications, London, pp. 9-35.

Friedman, HS & Booth-Kewley, S 1987, 'Personality, type A behaviour and coronary heart disease: The role of emotional expression', *Journal of Personality and Social Psychology*, 53: 783-792.

Gentry, WD 1985, 'Relationship of anger-coping styles and blood pressure among Black Americans', in M A Chesney & R H Rosenman (eds), *Anger and Hostility in Cardiovascular and Behavioural Disorders*, Hemisphere Publishing Corporation, New York, pp. 139-148

Gioldstein, HS, Edelberg, R, Meier, CE & Davis, L 1988, 'Relationship of resting blood pressure and heart rate to expressed anger', *Psychomatic Medicine*, 50: 321-329.

Goleman, D 1996, *Emotional Intelligence: Why it can matter more than IQ*, Bloomsbury, London.

Goleman, D 2005, *Emotional Intelligence: Why it can matter more than IQ*, 2nd edn, Bantam Dell, New York.

Hartel, C, Gough, H & Hartel, G 2008, 'Work group emotional climate, emotion management skills and service attitudes and performance', *Asia Pacific Journal of Human Resources*, 46, 1, 21-37.

Hochschild, AR 1983, *The Managed Heart: Commercialization of Human Feeling*, University of California Press, Berkeley.

Hoffman, L 2006, 'Something more than feelings', *Human Resources*, 4 April, pp. 16-17.

Holman, D 2002, 'Employee well-being in call centres', *Human Resource Management Journal*, 12(4): 35–50.

Human Resources 2002, 'EQ Testing: Passing fad or functional tool?', November: 22-23.

Karabanow, J 1999, 'When caring is not enough: Emotional labor and youth shelter workers', *Social Service Review*, 73(3): 340-357.

Kluckhohn, C 1951, Values and value-orientations in the theory of action, in T Parsons & E Shils (eds), *Toward a general theory of action*, Harvard University Press, Cambridge, pp. 388-433.

Korczynski, M 2002, *Human Resource Management in Service Work*, Palgrave, Hampshire.

Lee, RT & Ashforth, BE 1996, 'A meta-examination of the correlates of the three dimension of job burnout', *Journal of Applied Psychology*, 81, 2 123-133.

Macdonald, CL & Sirianni, C (eds) 1996, *Working in the Service Society*, Temple University Press, Philadelphia.

Mann, S 1999, 'Emotion at Work: To what extent are we expressing, suppressing or faking it?', *European Journal of Work and Organizational Psychology*, 8(3): 347-369.

Martin, J, Knopoff, K & Beckman, C 1998, 'An alternative to bureaucratic impersonality: Bounded emotionality at The Body Shop', *Administrative Science Quarterly*, 43: 429-469.

Meglino, BM & Ravlin, EC 1998, 'Individual values in organizations: concepts, controversies, and research', Journal of Management, 24(3): 351-390.

Meisinger, SR 2005, 'The four Cs of the HR profession: Being competent, curious, courageous and caring about people', *Human Resource Management*, 44: 189-194.

Mitchell, R & O'Neal, M 1994, 'Managing by values: Is Levi Strauss' approach visionary - or flaky?', *Business Week*, August 1: 46-52.

Morris, JA & Feldman, DC 1996, 'The dimensions, antecedents and consequences of emotional labour', *Academy of Management Review*, 21(4): 986-1010.

Nord, WR, Brief, AP, Atieh, JM, & Doherty, EM 1988, 'Work values and the conduct of organizational behavior', in LL Cummings & BM Staw (eds), *Research in Organizational Behavior*, CT: JAI Press, Greenwich, vol. 9, pp. 1-42.

Pruzan, P 2001,' The question of Orgnizational Consciousness: can Organizations have values, virtues and visions?, *Journal of Business Ethics*, 29(3): 271-284.

Rokeach, M 1973, *The nature of human values*, Free Press, New York.

Saxton, MJ, Phillips JS, & Blakeney, RN 1991, 'Antecedents and consequences of emotional exhaustion in the airline reservations service sector', *Human Relations*, 44, 583-602.

Schein, EH 1985, *Organizational culture and leadership*, Jossey-Bass, San Francisco.

Taylor, P & Bain, P 1999, 'An assembly line in the head: Work and employee relations in a call centre', *Industrial Relations Journal*, 30(2): 101-117.

Taylor, S & Tyler M 2000, 'Emotional labour and sexual difference in the airline industry', *Work Employment and Society*, 14(1): 77-95.

Thompson, P Warhurst, C, & Callaghan, G 2001, 'Ignorant theory and knowledgeable workers: Interrogating the connections between knowledge, skills and services', *Journal of Management Studies*, 38(7): 923-942.

Van Maanen, J & Kunda, G 1989, 'Real feelings: Emotional expression and organizational culture', in LL Cummings & BM Staw (eds), *Research in Organizational Behaviour*, CT: JAI Press, Greenwich, pp. 43-103.

Weiss, HM & Crapanzano, R 1996, 'Affective events theory: A theoretical discussion of the structure, causes and consequences of affective experiences at work', *Research in Organizational Behaviour*, 18: 1-74.

Wright, PM & Snell, SA 2005, 'Partner or guardian? HR's challenge in balancing value and values', *Human Resource Management Review*, 44: 177-182.

Case study: Emotional stress in call centres

TelBus is an American telecommunications company that provides voice, video, data, internet telecommunications and professional services to businesses, consumers and government agencies. During its long history, TelBus set up operations in international locations in Europe, Asia and Australia. Central Call centre operations for the Australian division were located in Melbourne. The call centre was devoted to in-bound calls, which meant that customers could ring in and make bill or service-related enquiries. Although call centre staff were required to keep call times within an acceptable range, their primary role was to make sure that customers had their questions answered and to create a sense that customers had been listened to respectfully. TelBus also ran a number of out-bound 'cold call' campaigns where the purpose was to ring existing customers, or potential new clients, and provide information about new products and services with a view to increasing sales and market share. These calls were outsourced to another call centre in Sydney that specialised in sales and the arrangement worked quite well.

During routine call monitoring at the Melbourne in-bound call centre, it was noted that there were quite a number of opportunities for the call centre operators to sell new products to customers. Despite call centre operator efforts to provide some information about upgrades and new products, it became clear to senior management that call centre operators did not push through and close the sale. In response, senior management re-thought the divide between in-bound and out-bound calls and decided to place a greater emphasis on selling as part of the normal in-bound calls taken by the Melbourne call centre operators. Effectively, this meant that each in-bound call became a potential sale. Even though customers did not ring up to enquire about new products, it became part of the operators' responsibility to finish the call with information about the latest telecommunication offering and to make suggestions to customers that could result in a sale.

In response to the change in operator responsibilities, new performance criteria were designed and put in place. Previously operators had been required to keep calls within a ten minute window, but the changed expectations led to much tighter controls on time as well as on sales target quotas. The new criteria included sales targets, dollars logged per hour, average talk time, wrap time per call, adherence to scheduled breaks, and sales call quality. The reaction among the call centre staff was one of dissatisfaction. A number of staff left, and management observed that their exit was probably in everyone's best interest. Senior management did recognise the morale problem, however, and decided to invest more heavily in the training of the team leaders. The call centre had always been organised into groups and the team leaders had held a central role in maintaining staff morale and in providing development and training for new members. The training for the team leaders focused on team morale management, but a key objective was also to assist team leaders in getting more out of the team so that sales targets could be met.

A number of team leaders began to question the intention of the training, and pointed out that morale was already low and that call centre operators did not need further pressure from the team leader. Eventually, stories of worker stress and two cases of severe bullying were leaked to the media. The union became active in representing the case and senior management were asked to account for the negative outcomes at the call centre.

Written by: Cathy Sheehan.

Case study questions

1. What are the key HR problems and issues associated with the running of the TelBus Melbourne call centre?

2. What changes could be made to HRM-related activities?

Discussion questions

1. How can emotions be defined and what are some of the basic categories of emotions?

2. Explain the term 'emotional labour' and the internal and external conditions which may impact on the level of required emotional labour.

3. What are some of the strategies that HR can apply to enhance the management of emotional labour requirements in the workplace?

4. Answer the following:
   - Identify the different types of emotional labour that might be expected from a funeral director; an airline attendant; a tour guide. Specify what you think HR might be able to do when recruiting, selecting, training and monitoring employees in these jobs.
   - Provide three examples of jobs that you think require a different type of emotional labour. Again specify what you think HR might be able to do when recruiting, selecting, training and monitoring employees in these jobs.

Chapter 9

EMPLOYEE HEALTH AND WELL-BEING IN THE WORKPLACE

INTRODUCTION

Decades of research has demonstrated that the structure and fabric of the organisation, and how it functions, can have a wide-ranging impact on the health and well-being of employees, and ultimately on the effectiveness of the organisation itself. According to the UK Labour Force Survey (2007) in 2005/2006, an estimated 2 million people suffered from ill-health which they thought was work related. Evidence from Europe, North America and Australia also confirms that the high and rising costs of workplace absenteeism due to work-related ill-health, particularly workplace stress, are a significant problem (Houtman & Jettinghoff 2007).

However, health and well-being are often seen as something separate from the daily running of the organisation – something that is 'nice to have' rather than integral to the effectiveness of the organisation. The fact that the financial burden directly and indirectly attributable to work-related ill-health is said to run into billions provides a powerful argument for organisations to pay special attention to the health and well-being of their employees (Bejean & Sultan-Taieb 2005; Nielsen, Randall, Holten & Gonzalez 2010). The growth of occupational health and safety legislation across industrialised countries also means that increasingly organisations also have a broad duty of care to ensure that employees are not at risk of injury or made ill by their work.

This chapter looks at what is meant by employee health and well-being in an organisational context, the key causes or predictors – both individual and organisational – of poor employee health and well-being, the consequences for both individuals and organisations of poor employee health and well-being, and how organisations can intervene to improve the health and well-being of their employees.

Health and well-being

Definitions

Traditionally, the definition of employee health has been negatively conceptualised as the absence of disease, illness and sickness. Recently, however, a broader and more positive conceptualisation has been adopted that goes beyond a disease-based definition. Under this broader definition, employee health is said to not only be characterised by an absence of disease, but also by a sense of purpose, by positive self-regard, and by quality relationships with others (Quick, Macik-Frey & Cooper 2007).

Similarly well-being – which at times in the literature is also referred to as psychological well-being – is also generally conceptualised as a multifaceted construct characterised by both the presence of positive emotions and attitudes, and the absence of unpleasant emotions (Diener, Suh, Lucas & Smith 1999). Poor work-related employee well-being is therefore said to be characterised by: a) emotional discomfort or a tense state of emotional and mental exhaustion; b) bodily uneasiness characterised by fatigue and body tiredness; c) task impairment or a reduction in employee task quality and quantity; d) employee organisational distance or detachment/isolation from co-workers; and e) a dragging workday with the employee perceiving the workday to be very long or excessively slow (Martin 2010). Importantly, employee well-being is said to be subjective in nature. That is, employees are high in well-being to the extent that they believe themselves to be.

Both employee health and employee well-being have been found to be caused or predicted by similar factors, with evidence suggesting that both individual factors and organisational factors play a role in the extent to which an employee is healthy and has a positive sense of well-being. The key individual and organisational predictors of employee health and well-being are discussed in detail next.

Individual predictors of employee health and well-being

Age

Job-related well-being is lowest between the ages of 30 and 40, with higher levels around 60 and under 25 (Clark, Oswald & Warr 1996; Johnson 2009). The lower level of well-being, when individuals are in their 30s and 40s, coincides with a time when financial and family demands are generally highest. The greater job-related well-being of older workers relative to those around 30 is also thought to be partly due to the more attractive job features, such as greater income and opportunity for personal control, that these workers have compared to younger workers.

Gender

Research indicates that female managers score higher on negative stress-related health outcomes compared to their male counterparts (Burke &

Richardson 2009; Davidson & Cooper 1992). Studies have also revealed that managerial women experience unique sources of stress related to their minority status and gender, which negatively affect their well-being (Fielden & Davidson 2001). For example, research has found female managers report more emotional stress than men related to relationships and perceived responsibilities for caretaking both at work and at home, and more stress related to the challenge of balancing home and work aspects; whereas men report more physical health problems and stress related to technology (Iwasaki, MackKay & Ristock 2004). Women also report more stress because of lack of communication, lack of support from superiors, and having to perform better than men to have the same chance of promotion (Lundberg & Frankenhaeuser 1999). Men and women also differ in terms of the job features they regard as important in terms of their well-being, with women placing greater emphasis on mutually-supportive relations with colleagues and convenient work schedules, and men tending to see autonomy, skill use, income and job security as more important (Warr 2008).

Personality

Three key personality characteristics have been recognised as being associated with employee health and well-being. The first is a type A behaviour pattern which is characterised by a sense of time urgency or impatience, by competitiveness, and by a strong need for achievement (Burke & Fiksenbaum 2009). People exhibiting type A behaviour have been shown to have higher levels of stress, psychological distress and coronary heart disease than individuals who do not exhibit this behaviour pattern (Burke & Fiksenbaum 2009).

The second key personality characteristic is workaholism, which is said to be when an individual has an excessive involvement in work and feels compelled or driven to work because of inner pressures (Burke & Fiksenbaum 2009). Individuals who exhibit type A behaviour are also more likely to exhibit workaholic tendencies (Burke & Fiksenbaum 2009). Not surprisingly then, workaholism has also been shown to be associated with poorer psychological and physical well-being (Burke 1999).

Locus of control is the third important personality characteristic. This is an individual's belief regarding the extent to which they feel outcomes at work are determined by themselves (internal locus of control) or by external forces (e.g. luck, chance, fate) (Spector 1999). Individuals with an external locus of control – because of their belief that outcomes are externally determined and not influenced by them – tend not to be proactive in dealing with problematic work situations and therefore tend to cope less effectively with stress. Consequently, individuals with an external locus of control, as compared to individuals with an internal locus of control, tend to experience poorer health and well-being.

Self-efficacy

Self-efficacy refers to an individual's beliefs about their ability to perform the behaviours necessary to achieve work-related goals or, more generally, to perform the tasks required to succeed in their job (Spector 2009). Those with stronger self-efficacy beliefs are likely to hold more optimistic expectations about their ability to succeed in their job and to obtain the work-related outcomes they value, and this in turn has been found to translate positively into good health and well-being (Spector 2009).

Organisational predictors of employee health and well-being

Work hours and schedules

There is compelling evidence that the more hours an individual works the more negative health symptoms they are likely to experience, with individuals who work more than forty-eight hours a week being particularly susceptible to psychological and physical health problems (Cartwright 2000; Sparks, Cooper, Fried & Shirom 1997). Overall, research has shown working long hours negatively affects the cardiovascular system through chronic exposure to increases in blood pressure and heart rate, placing individuals at a significant increased risk of heart disease (Burke & Fiksenbaum 2009). Working long hours has also been shown to produce sleep deprivation, with the lack of recovery time between work leading to chronic fatigue and poor health-related behaviours such as excessive alcohol consumption (Benson, 2005; Liu & Tanaka 2002; Meijman & Mulder 1998). The total number of hours worked can also impinge upon an individual's family commitments and life off the job, and can contribute to reduced levels of work-life balance (Kirkcaldy, Levine & Shephard 2000).

In addition to work hours, work schedules and – in particular – shift work have also been found to negatively impact the health and well-being of employees (Folkard 1996). This negative effect is thought to result mainly from the way in which working shifts interrupts the body's normal circadian rhythm. Shift work can also make social relationships outside of work problematic, and issues of work-life balance are often exacerbated as a result of the individual's non-typical work schedule.

Workplace relationships and leadership

The quality of relationships that an individual has with his or her peers and supervisor has been shown to play an important role in their health and well-being (Leung & Lee 2006; Rousseau *et al.* 2008; Settoon & Mossholder 2002). For example, autocratic and authoritarian leadership styles have generally been observed to induce strain among employees (Seltzer & Numerof 1988), whereas more participative and democratic leadership has typically been found to enhance employee well-being (Marklund, Bolin & von Essen 2008; Martin *et al.* 2005; O'Driscoll & Beehr 1994). Interestingly, though, research indicates that it is the relationship an individual has with their peers, as compared to their relationship with their immediate supervisor, which has the stronger effect on well-being (Rousseau *et al.* 2008). It has been argued that this is probably because individuals frequently spend more time with their peers than with their supervisor. Not surprisingly, the importance of peer relationships also seems to increase when the level of teamwork and collaboration required is higher. Importantly, though, the *combined* effect of good supervisor relationships and good peer relationships is stronger than either element in isolation (Rousseau *et al.* 2008). This implies that neither good peer relationships nor good supervisory relationships alone are sufficient to optimise employee well-being.

Work demands and level of control

The demand-control model was first introduced by Robert Karasek (1979) and has proved popular in research investigating organisational predictors of employee health and well-being. The demand-control model proposes that stress and ill-health at work results from a distinct job task profile defined by two dimensions: the demands put on the employee, and the degree of control available to the employee. A low level of control can manifest itself in two ways: first, as a lack of decision authority over one's tasks; and, second, as a low level skill utilisation in the case of monotonous and repetitive work. Jobs where individuals have high demands and low control have been found to be related to an elevated risk for employees of absence due to sickness and depression (Marmot, Siegrist & Theorell 2006; Spector 2009). These types of jobs are classified as 'high strain jobs'. Conversely, situations where individuals have high demands but also have high control are less stressful. These jobs are classified as 'active jobs', are health protective, and may even be health promoting in some cases (Ganster, Fox & Dwyer 2001).

Role demands

Three major role demands – role conflict, role overload and role ambiguity – have been identified as contributing to employee stress and poor well-being. Role conflict is when there is a lack of compatibility between different expectations arising from a job role or position. Role overload refers to a situation where an employee's role places excessive demands on their time and energy, which makes them feel uncertain about their ability to perform their job adequately. Finally, role ambiguity refers to a situation where the employee lacks clarity in relation to key aspects of their role. In excess, each of these three role demands has consistently been found to contribute to lower levels of employee well-being and health (Bakker, Demerouti & Euwema 2005; Jex & Elacqua 1999).

Levels of effort versus levels of reward

Another popular model used by researchers to understand the organisational predictors of employee health and well-being is the effort-reward imbalance model. This model builds on the notion of social reciprocity, or the extent to which the employee feels that their effort in relation to their job tasks and obligations are adequately rewarded (Siegrist 1996). Rewards can include: income, esteem, and career opportunities including job security. Research has demonstrated that a lack of reciprocity – or where employees feel they are exerting high levels of effort but only receiving low levels of rewards – has been found to elicit strong negative emotions in individuals with reciprocal negative long-term effects for health (Hasselhorn, Tackenberg & Peter 2004).

Technology

Most jobs these days invariably involve the use of some form of technology, often in the form of computers, mobile phones and/or smart phones (e.g. iphones, blackberries). While potentially useful from a productivity perspective, these devices can cause several different types of strain which can be detrimental to an employee's health. These strains can take the form of physical problems (e.g. musculoskeletal disorders) and/or mental pressures (e.g. stress from new technology). Modern technology, because of its ability to facilitate 24/7 communication, also has the potential to exacerbate other stressors like role overload and to hamper an individual's ability to achieve work-life balance.

Job insecurity

Job insecurity can be in the form of insecurity by an individual about holding onto their job, or in the form of a lack of opportunity to advance their career. These issues are usually particularly salient during mergers between companies, downsizings in industries, or efforts to reduce management layers in organisations. There is substantial evidence that both insecurity about holding onto their job (Kinnunen *et al.* 2000) and a lack of career development opportunities (Sullivan 1999) can induce severe strain in employees and undermine their well-being. Indeed, the fear of job loss has been identified as one of the more important sources of employee stress (O'Driscoll & Cooper 1996). Research has also found that those employees with job insecurity report a greater incidence of physical health conditions and higher levels of anxiety and depression (Probst 2003).

Individual employee health and well-being consequences

People with higher levels of well-being are healthier (mentally and physically), have happier lives and live longer (Cartwright & Cooper 2008) but importantly, research also shows that they are also likely to take a more positive approach to their work and their relationships with colleagues.

People with higher levels of well-being learn and problem-solve more effectively, and are more enthusiastic about and accepting of change (Cartwright & Cooper 2008). Additionally, individuals experiencing low levels of well-being as a result of their work will often use potentially harmful coping mechanisms that can further contribute to health problems, such as excessive alcohol or caffeine intake, and over- or under-eating.

A key individual employee consequence of poor health and well-being is 'burnout'. Burnout is a response to chronic interpersonal stressors on the job. Broadly, burnout refers to a condition where an individual feels overextended and depleted of their emotional and physical resources as a result of the work that they do. It is a condition that is characterised by three key symptoms: emotional exhaustion, depersonalisation, and reduced personal accomplishment. Of the three symptoms, emotional exhaustion is recognised as being the most central and is characterised by: a wearing out, loss of energy, depletion, debilitation, and fatigue (Maslach, Leiter & Schaufeli 2009). Depersonalisation refers to a negative shift in feelings towards others and is often characterised by an inappropriate callous attitude towards clients/customers, irritability, loss of idealism, cynicism, and withdrawal or detachment from the job (Maslach, Leiter & Schaufeli 2009). The third and final symptom, reduced personal accomplishment, is characterised by low self-esteem, low morale, reduced productivity, and an inability to cope (Maslach, Leiter & Schaufeli 2009). Research has demonstrated that the second two symptoms result from the individual first experiencing a sense of emotional exhaustion (Maslach, Leiter & Schaufeli 2009). As a result of the high level of interaction with others and the emotionally taxing nature of their work, some of the key occupations affected by burnout are teachers, call centre workers and healthcare workers including nurses, social workers and ambulance officers (Shaufeli, Leiter & Maslach 2009). However, anyone in a job which requires emotional work or labour can be affected (see chapters 7 and 8).

Organisational health and well-being consequences

Employee well-being has been shown to be related to a number of different indicators of organisational effectiveness, such as absenteeism, work accidents and productivity (Danna & Griffin 1999; Hardy, Woods & Wall 2003; Van Dierendonck, Haynes, Borrill & Stride 2004). For example, in relation to productivity, employee well-being has been shown to be related to job performance, with as much as 25 per cent of the variance in job performance being found to be associated with differences in well-being (Donald et al. 2005; Wright 2010). Indeed, well-being has been shown to be a predictor of job performance even after including demographic variables such as employee age, gender, tenure with the organisation, and education level (Wright 2010).

Interestingly, research has also shown that, even for the most satisfied employees, if they are also low on well-being, then their high job satisfaction is less likely to be reflected in increased job performance (Wright, Cropanzano & Bonett 2007). Evidence indicates that there is a stronger relationship between job satisfaction and performance when well-being is high, and a weaker relationship to performance when well-being is low (Wright *et al.* 2007). Not surprisingly, research also indicates that individuals with low levels of well-being are six times more likely to have any lost days of work than individuals with high levels of work-related well-being (Keyes & Grzywacz 2005). Strong relationships have also been found between employee well-being and turnover (Page & Vella-Brodrick 2009).

Employee health and well-being interventions

Cooper and Cartwright (1997) summarise three levels of interventions that organisations can take to prevent poor levels of employee health and well-being: primary, secondary and tertiary.

Primary intervention approaches attempt to eliminate the source of poor employee health and well-being in the work environment. Due to their focus on changing the work environment, these interventions take place at the organisational rather than at the individual level. Primary intervention strategies that have been shown to be effective include: job redesign, the establishment of flexible work arrangements, the implementation of participative decision-making, the provision of social support and feedback, the development of cohesive work teams, the reduction of ambiguity in relation to employees' future job prospects or their likely future opportunities for career development, and the enhancement of organisational communication (Probst 2009). Obviously, the suitability of any of these interventions will depend on first having a clear understanding of the primary causes of poor employee health and well-being in the organisation.

Secondary interventions are focused on assisting employees to manage and cope with the work environment and their job more effectively, rather than eliminating the source of the health and well-being problems. These interventions typically focus on assisting employees to re-evaluate how they perceive stressors, and on helping them to become more resilient to stress.

Finally, tertiary intervention strategies are focused on treating and compensating employees who are already experiencing symptoms associated with poor health and well-being. Tertiary interventions can include such things as counselling, and workers' compensation and injury management programs.

Unfortunately, when thinking about health and well-being interventions, organisations often adopt a compliance mindset which normally results in a defensive approach to employee health and well-being and an emphasis on secondary and tertiary interventions. This can be counterproductive because it means that the underlying causes of the employees' health and well-being issues are not being addressed and the effectiveness of these interventions is therefore only likely to be short lived (Guthrie, Ciccarelli & Babic 2010). To be effective, interventions need to be mutually reinforcing and to contain both individual-focused (secondary and tertiary) interventions and organisational-focused (primary) interventions (LaMontagne & Shaw 2004).

The intervention process

Interventions, no matter what type they are, have the best chance of having a significant impact if they follow a structured, systematic and participatory intervention process (Nielsen, Randall, Holten & Gonzalez 2010). With this in mind, there are a number of key steps that should be taken in designing and implementing all employee health and well-being initiatives. First, the findings of many research studies emphasise the importance of establishing a steering group to serve as a guiding coalition for the intervention (Nielsen *et al.* 2010). It is important that this group contains employee representatives, with research indicating that interventions are significantly more likely to be successful if there has been employee participation in the intervention design and implementation process (Hatinen, Kinnunen, Pekkonen and Kalimo 2007).

The second step in the intervention process is to ensure that there is a detailed understanding of the current levels of health and well-being in the organisation, and what specific issues might be negatively affecting employees' health and well-being. Commonly, data is collected from employees in relation to: demands (e.g. workload, work environment), control (i.e. how much say an employee has in how they do their work), support (i.e. the encouragement and resources provided by the organisation/line manager), relationships (e.g. extent to which positive working relationships versus conflict is present), and role clarity or sense of purpose. It can also be useful to measure health outcomes and self-reported productivity to get a sense of the extent to which the specific issues are linked with reported physical and psychological outcomes. It may also be useful to measure more positive work-related attitudes such as organisational commitment and motivation in order to also gauge how these attitudes are being affected. Gathering this data will help to ensure that any health and well-being intervention that is planned is treating the underlying causes and not just the symptoms.

As part of the audit of employee health and well-being, an assessment also needs to be made in relation to the numbers of employees suffering from lower levels of health and well-being (i.e. is it everyone in the organisation or only people in certain roles?) and to the severity of effects (e.g. how many unplanned employee absences on average is it causing?). This data will then help prioritise issues (i.e. for which issue are the severity of the effects greatest and most broadly distributed amongst employees?) and also help reveal which specific employees should be targeted by the intervention. Companywide surveys, human resource records (e.g. absenteeism, voluntary turnover rates), focus groups and discussions with key stakeholders can all be used to gather this data.

The previous step will generally result in a number of different areas that are negatively impacting employee well-being and around which interventions could be developed being identified. However, the impact – and therefore the importance of these issues – is likely to vary considerably. The health and well-being issues should therefore be prioritised to identify those issues that need immediate attention. Once priorities have been identified, a business case for the employee health and well-being intervention needs to be constructed. Overall, the business case should provide a clear picture of what is trying to be achieved, and should highlight how improving the health and well-being of the employees will assist in enhancing business-level outcomes. These outcomes can include sickness-absence rates, turnover and productivity. Highlighting the organisational benefits of the employee health and well-being, intervention will also assist in securing the support of senior management. This is crucial because employees are unlikely to embrace initiatives if they feel that they are not genuinely supported by senior management, or that these initiatives are only a superficial attempt to address health and well-being issues within the organisation.

In relation to each of the selected business-level outcomes, improvement goals also need to be established. These goals need to be based upon an understanding of what is realistic and achievable. These goals should clearly specify: the target for the intervention (e.g. all workers on shift A), the specific level of amount of improvement that the initiative is expected to achieve (e.g. a 7 per cent decrease in unplanned absences by employees), and the timeframe in which the change should occur (e.g. the decrease will be achieved within the next 12 months). Establishing goals in this way can assist with the evaluation process once the intervention is complete and serve as benchmarks against which the success of the intervention can be measured.

Next, an implementation action plan for the intervention needs to be developed which specifies who will be responsible for overseeing the intervention, the financial and other resources that have been allocated to the intervention, and when and how the intervention will be undertaken. Then, periodically during the implementation phase, checks should be carried out to ensure that the intervention is being implemented in accordance with the action plan, that implementation tasks are being completed to a high standard, and that any barriers to effective implementation are being identified and addressed. It is important that the degree to which the intervention is being well received by the employees it is targeting is also assessed. It is also crucial during the implementation phase not to underestimate the importance of communicating the ongoing progress of the implementation of the health and well-being initiatives. If employees are given little information about the progress of initiatives, they are likely to believe that the intervention has either only been slightly effective or not been effective at all.

Finally, once the implementation phase has concluded and the health and well-being program or intervention has been operating for some time, information needs to be collected to assess the extent to which the goals of the intervention have been met and to determine whether the implementation methods were appropriate. This information can then be used to make adjustments to the existing health and well-being intervention, and also to improve the design and implementation of future health and well-being interventions and programs.

Conclusion

The health and well-being of employees is not just represented by an absence of physical or psychological illness, but rather is more broadly conceptualised to include an employee's sense of purpose at work, the degree to which they experience positive work relationships, and the presence more generally of positive work-related attitudes and emotions. Given work constitutes a huge part of most people's lives, it is a major determining factor in individuals' health and well-being. Employee well-being has also been shown to be a key factor in determining an organisation's long-term profitability, with many studies showing a direct link between productivity levels and the general health and well-being of the workforce. For these reasons the importance placed on employee health and well-being by organisations is increasing.

Employee health and well-being is influenced by both individual and organisational factors, with the degree to which employees have control or influence over the work they do and the adequacy of rewards being two of the main contributing factors. Organisations wishing to improve the health and well-being of their employees should ensure interventions are multi-layered (individual and organisational focused), integrated, and targeted at specific areas. Employees should be involved in the intervention design process, with employee participation being shown to be important in determining the success of health and well-being programs. Finally, it is important to ensure clear metrics are in place through which the success of health and well-being initiatives can be evaluated.

Case study: MV Health

MV Health is an integrated health care organisation that owns and operates a large number of nursing homes in Victoria, Australia. MV Health was formed through the merger of two smaller companies. MV also acquired some nursing homes that had previously been operated by the Government. The goal of the merger and restructure was to create a more coordinated and integrated system of care, maximising profit through improvements in the efficiency with which care for the elderly was provided.

Before the merger and restructure, individual nursing homes were given almost complete autonomy to manage their operations without interference from senior management. When the merger and restructuring took place, however, the management of all of the homes was brought together under one senior management team. This senior management team was given a mandate to operate the nursing homes as one unified group, with a heavy emphasis placed on increasing the profitability of the group. The following section describes some of the changes that were implemented and the perceptions of one senior nurse regarding the impact of the changes.

Sarah is a nursing supervisor at the Balwyn Nursing Home, and has held the position for the past seven years. Sarah studied part time and completed her postgraduate geriatric nursing studies three years ago.

She says that since the merger she has had a lot more paperwork to complete. She finds this paperwork extremely complicated and dislikes doing it. She feels it takes her away from what she was trained to do – what she likes most about her job – spending time providing 'hands on' care to the elderly residents. The paperwork takes up so much of her time that she feels like she rarely has time anymore to just sit and talk to a resident, spend time brushing a resident's hair, or read a book to them. Not having time to do this anymore really upsets Sarah, as it was one of the aspects of her job that she enjoyed the most. She also feels doing things like this is a really important component of providing high quality care for residents.

Senior management at MV have also cut all registered nurses' working hours, in accordance with changes in government legislation. The changes mean that operators no longer require one registered nurse to be on duty for every eight high-care residents. Rather, this change has meant that only one registered nurse is now required to care for 15 high-care residents (who are in two different wards on different floors of the nursing home). These changes have also meant that MV is increasingly hiring employees on a casual rather than permanent basis.

Today Sarah is sitting in the staff room eating her lunch alone: because of changes to the rosters no one has breaks at the same time any more. In fact, as she takes a bite of her apple, she tries to remember the last time she saw Diane, one of the other more senior nurses. Just as she is packing up her leftovers from lunch, Diane walks into the tearoom and says, 'I've been looking for you. Did you know that we are out of bandages and that they're now letting people who aren't qualified give out medications to residents?' (Diane is referring to the change in policy that allowed care assistants to dispense medication.) 'It's like all our experience and training counts for nothing. We are put on the same level as someone who comes in off the street with no experience.' Diane collapses into one of the chairs and says, 'What's happened to resident care? That's what we're here for. I just think everything is wrong – there's just too much emphasis placed on the almighty dollar. I just don't think I can take it much longer, I've lost all heart. When did they think it was a good idea to add cleaning the floors to our list of duties?' Sarah sympathises with Diane and says, 'I know we have to do more and more with less and less. I've had so many fights with management that I think I'm just hitting my head against a brick wall.'

As Sarah walked back to her office from the staff room, she thought about how her job had changed over the past year or so. They had run out of bandages again because these days every little purchase had to be approved by senior management in head office, and this always seemed to take forever. Fellow nurses seemed to frequently be in her office complaining about the changes and telling her how unhappy they were. Morale was certainly very low, and the rostering changes and increased workloads meant that Sarah found it almost impossible to foster the old team atmosphere. Sarah thought that senior management were out of touch with the realities of what the work was actually like. They didn't seem to understand that caring for the elderly was a difficult and extremely demanding job.

As she reached her office and remembered the huge pile of paperwork she had to try to get through before her shift ended later that afternoon, Sarah felt a wave of exhaustion come over her. She wasn't sure how she'd find the energy to last the rest of her shift – much less till she had two days off in five days' time. Sarah just didn't feel like she could cope much longer with all the stress and pressure. Maybe, she thought, it was time she started looking for another job.

Written by: Belinda Allen.

Case study questions

1. What do you think are the likely levels of health and well-being amongst the employees and MV? What health and well-being symptoms are the employees at MV demonstrating?

2. Identify the key causes of the levels (be they high or low) of employee health and well-being at MV.

3. What initiatives could be introduced by management to improve the health and well-being of employees working in the nursing homes?

Discussion questions

1. From a job design perspective, what are some of the key causes of poor health and well-being amongst employees?

2. Summarise the demand-control model and explain how it can be used to understand employee health and well-being.

3. Explain why it is beneficial for organisations to promote the health and well-being of their employees.

4. What are some of the interventions that organisations can introduce to improve the health and well-being of their employees?

Contemporary Issues and Challenges in HRM

Overview case:
Understanding the work environment

Of all the jobs that require the use of emotional labour, a high degree of service and supportive health and well-being strategies, the nursing profession is amongst the most demanding and high profile. This is no more demonstrated than in the role of critical care nurses in intensive care units. The following case illustrates the demanding nature of the job and the associated management issues of continual skills shortages and turnover. This is an ongoing issue in Australian hospitals and, with an ageing population, it is only likely to get worse if current strategies are maintained. The following case illustrates the holistic and integrated nature of the issues discussed in the last three chapters.

Case study: Just managing

Critical care in intensive care units

Background

HospitalCo intensive care unit (ICU) is a 20-bed level 3 unit (which is the highest and most complex with the sickest patients) with a 90 per cent bed occupancy rate. Because of a nursing shortage, on most days the rostered number of nurses on a shift is insufficient for the 18 or 19 patients, and continually puts pressure on staff. The nurse-to-patient ratio for mechanically ventilated patients is one-to-one, plus a shift coordinator and an admissions/resource nurse. So, for each shift, four or five extra nurses are needed.

Casual pool or agency nurses are employed on a shift-by-shift basis. These nurses choose this lifestyle for flexibility, and to suit their family, childcare, travel or study needs. Some nurses are regular extras to the HospitalCo unit; some are unknown to the regular staff, and can be unfamiliar with the environment. These staff are usually allocated less complex patients, and so take a lighter patient load than the regular experienced staff. They often also need supervision and support to safely care for their allocated patients, thus putting more strain on the workload of core staff.

Last year, a 12-hour shift roster pattern was introduced to the HospitalCo ICU. Advantages to 12-hour shifts are that nurses work fewer shifts per roster, which can be desirable for some. More than 50 per cent of nurses chose this option, with the remainder preferring to work the traditional 8, 8, 10 hour shift pattern. Disadvantages of the 12-hour shift pattern include: nurses working 50 per cent of their shifts on nights, long and tiring shifts, and longer recovery time. In addition, there is less opportunity for professional development and unit communication. And, managing the two roster patterns to ensure that there is always a nurse to care for each patient is complex.

The national recommended standard for the number of critical care (CC) qualified nurses is a minimum of 50 per cent. In the HospitalCo unit, 40 per cent of the nurses also hold a recognised qualification. Some casual pool and agency nurses hold a CC qualification, but this varies on a shift-by-shift basis. The past few years' annual turnover of staff in the ICU has been 20 per cent, reflecting the national average for critical care nursing. This has also impacted upon the roster profile, as there are usually five or six graduate nurses and nurses new to the intensive care environment on any given shift – all requiring supervision and support.

Case profile

Jo is a clinical nurse in the ICU. She has worked there for seven years, and has held the position for the past four years. Jo completed a postgraduate certificate in intensive care nursing five years ago. On most shifts, Jo is the coordinator or admission nurse, and these roles are the most senior on the shift – and both can be stressful. One evening, Jo arrived on night duty at 2100 to find that there were only 14 rostered nurses – including three new graduate nurses and two nurses on orientation – to care for the 19 patients in the ICU. This wasn't an unusual situation, and the hospital manager was still ringing the nursing agency trying to find more staff to cover the shift. Two of the regular staff on days off had agreed to work an extra shift, and two nurses from the evening shift had agreed to work double shifts. While this would be great for that shift, it would mean that they wouldn't be working the next day and so the morning shift would be short. This was an on-going problem, and a further potential source of tension between shift managers. The medical consultant on duty had agreed that the one patient who was not mechanically ventilated could be transferred out to a ward. This would help relieve the ICU staffing problem, but Jo was well aware that transfers out of ICU out-of-hours are associated with high risk, and that this was less than ideal.

Finally, it looked as if there were going to be enough staff for the patients for the night. Now Jo had to work out how to safely allocate nurses to the patients, factoring in the skill mix (that is, the capacity of nurses to care for the complexity of the patients) and the supervision and support required by the inexperienced nurses. As usual, the pressure was on the experienced ICU staff to take on their own complex patients as well as the extra load of supervising the inexperienced staff. In addition, Jo needed to have a plan to staff for an unexpected admission during the night. She also needed to be able to attend a MET or code call anywhere in the hospital, as the ICU shift coordinator was a member of the resuscitation team.

Jo had allocated one of the graduate nurses, Pam, to a young male patient, Ash, who was physiologically stable. He was recovering from chest trauma, had a tracheostomy, and was on a ventilation weaning regime. That would be simple enough on its own, but it appeared that Ash was becoming agitated. Pam had no experience in dealing with this type of patient, and her support person was busy with her own unstable patient. The support staff member was well-known in the unit for not being friendly to junior staff. Once she had reviewed the sickest patients on the shift with the night registrar, Jo had planned to spend some time with Pam to discuss how to assess and manage Ash's agitation. Before she got to Pam and her patient, however, Jo heard the emergency alarm ringing in that direction and so hurried over. Ash had pulled out his tracheostomy tube and tried to get out of bed, and Pam had tried to restrain him – with both of them falling to the floor. Jo called for help and calmly managed the event, Jo's attention then turned to Pam, who had hurt her back and was distressed.

'What a terrible start to a career in ICU', Jo thought, and felt guilty that she had not been able to provide more support to Pam. Jo had many pressures at the beginning of that shift, she had felt unsupported herself, and now she felt that she had let down Pam. She wouldn't be surprised if Pam didn't want to continue working in the ICU anymore, and wondered if she really needed all this stress herself.

Written by: Fenella Gill, Curtin University.

Discussion questions

1. From an organisational perspective, there are seven predictors of employee health. Identify how these factors impact upon the work of critical care nurses in HospitalCo.

2. What key burnout factors do you see in this case study?

3. What intervention strategies would you recommend in the short term?

4. What intervention strategies would you recommend in the long term to reduce the turnover rate of 20 per cent?

References

Bakker AB, Demerouti E & Euwema MC 2005, 'Job resources buffer the impact of job demands on burnout', *Journal of Occupational Health Psychology*, 10, 170-180.

Bejean S, & Sultan-Taieb H 2005, 'Modelling the economic burden of diseases imputable to stress at work', *European Journal of Health Economics*, 50, 16–23.

Benson H 2005, 'Are you working too hard?', Harvard Business Review, Nov, 53-58.

Burke RJ 1999, 'Workaholism in organisations: Psychological and physical well-being consequences', *Stress Medicine*, 16, 11-16.

Burke RJ & Fiksenbaum L 2009, 'Work hours, work intensity, and work addiction: Risks and rewards', in CL Cooper & S Cartwright (eds) *The oxford handbook of organisational well-being* (267-299), Oxford UK, Oxford University Press.

Burke RJ & Richardson AM 2009, 'Work experiences, stress and health among managerial women: Research and practice', in CL Cooper, JC Quick, MJ Schabracq (eds) *International Handbook of Work and Health Psychology* (3rd edn), West Sussex, Wiley-Blackwell.

Cartwright S 2000, 'Taking the pulse of executive health in the UK', *Academy of Management Executive*, 14, 16-23.

Cartwright S & Cooper, CL 2008, *The Oxford handbook of Personnel Psychology*, Oxford, Oxford University Press.

Clark AE, Oswald AJ & Warr, P 1996, 'Is job satisfaction U-shaped in age?' *Journal of Occupational Psychology*, 69, 57-81.

Cooper CL & Cartwright S 1997, 'An Intervention Strategy for Workplace Stress', *Journal of Psychosomatic Research*, 43, 7-16.

Danna K & Griffin RW 1999, 'Health and well-being in the workplace: A review and synthesis of the literature', *Journal of Management*, 25, 357-384.

Davidson MJ & Cooper CL 1992, *Shattering the glass ceiling: The woman manager*, London, Paul Chapman Publishing.

Diener E, Suh M, Lucas E & Smith H 1999, 'Subjective well-being: Three decades of progress', *Psychological Bulletin*, 125, 276-302.

Donald I, Taylor P, Johnson S, Cooper C, Cartwright S, & Robertson S 2005, 'Work environments, stress and productivity: An examination using ASSET', *International Journal of Stress Management*, 12, 409-423.

Fielden SL & Davidson MJ 2001, 'Stress and the woman manager', in J Dunham (ed), *Stress in the workplace: Past, present and future* (109-129), London, England, Whurr Publishers Ltd.

Folkard S 1996, 'Biological disruption in shiftworkers', in WP Colquhoun, G Costa, S Folkard & P Knauth (eds), *Shiftwork: Problems and Solutions* (29-61), Frankfurt, Peter Lang.

Ganster DC, Fox ML & Dwyer DJ 2001, 'Explaining employees' health care costs: a prospective examination of stressful job demands, personal control, and physiological reactivity', *Journal of Applied Psychology*, 86, 954-964.

Guthrie R, Ciccarelli M, & Babic A 2010, 'Work-related stress in Australia: The effects of legislative interventions and the cost of treatment', *International Journal of Law and Psychiatry*, 33, 101-115.

Hardy GE, Woods D, & Wall TD 2003, 'The impact of psychological distress on absence from work', *Journal of Applied Psychology*, 88, 306-314.

Hasselhorn HM, Tackenberg P, & Peter R, 2004, 'Effort-reward imbalance among nurses in stable countries and in countries in transition', *International Journal of Occupational and Environmental Health*, 10, 401-8.

Hatinen M, Kinnunen U, Pekkonen M, & Kalimo, R 2007, 'Comparing two burnout interventions: Perceived job control mediates decreases in burnout', *International Journal of Stress Management*, 14, 227-248.

Houtman I & Jettinghoff K 2007, *Raising awareness of stress in developing countries*, Geneva, World Health Organisation.

Iwasaki Y, MacKay K, & Ristock J 2004, 'Gender-based analyses of stress among professional managers: An exploratory qualitative study', *International Journal of Stress Management*, 11, 56-79.

Jex SM & Elacqua, TC 1999, 'Time management as a moderator of relations between stressors and employee strain', *Work & Stress*, 13, 182-191.

Karasek RA 1979, 'Job demands, job decision latitude, and mental strain: Implications for job redesign', *Administrative Science Quarterly*, 24, 285–308.

Keyes CLM & Grzywacz JG 2005, 'Health as a complete state: The added value in work performance and healthcare costs', *Journal of Occupational and Environmental Medicine*, 47, 523–532.

Kinnunen U, Maumo S, Naetti J, Happonen M, 2000, 'Organisational antecedents and outcomes of job insecurity: A longitudinal study in three organisations in Finland', *Journal of Organisational Behaviour*, 21, 443-460.

Kirkcaldy BD, Levine R, & Shephard RJ 2000, 'The impact of working hours on physical and psychological health of German managers', *European Review of Applied Psychology*, 50, 443-449.

Labour Force Survey 2007, Available at http://statistics.gov.uk.

LaMontagne A & Shaw A 2004, *Evaluating OHS Interventions: A Worksafe Victoria Intervention Evaluation Framework.*, Melbourne: University of Melbourne and Worksafe Victoria.

Leung DYP & Lee WWS 2006, 'Predicting intention to quit among Chinese teachers: differential predictability of the components of burnout', *Anxiety, Stress & Coping. An International Journal*, 19, 129-141.

Liu Y & Tanaka H 2002, 'Overtime, work, insufficient sleep, and risk of non-fatal acute myocardial infarction in Japanese men', *Occupational Environmental Medicine*, 59, 447-451.

Ulf L & Frankenhaeuser M 1999, 'Stress and workload of men and women in high ranking positions', *Journal of Occupational Health Psychology*, 4,142-151.

Marklund S, Bolin M, & von Essen J 2008, 'Can individual health differences be explained by workplace characteristics?—a multilevel analysis', *Social Science Medicine*, 66, 650–662.

Marmot M, Siegrist J, Theorell T 2006, 'Health and the psychosocial environment at work', in M Marmot M & RG Willdnson (eds), *Social Determinants of Health* (97-130), Oxford, Oxford University Press.

Martin AD 2010, 'Work-related negative experience: A unification model of poor employee well-being and work-related mental ill-health and substance consumption', *European Psychologist*, 15, 109-120.

Martin R, Thomas G, Charles K, Epitropaki O, & McNamara R 2005, 'The role of leader-member exchanges in mediating the relationship between locus of control and work reactions', *Journal of Occupational and Organisational Psychology*, 78, 141-147.

Maslach C, Leiter MP, & Schaufeli, WB 2009, 'Measuring burnout', in CL Cooper & S Cartwright (eds) *The Oxford Handbook of Organisational Well-Being* (86-108), Oxford UK: Oxford University Press.

Meijman TF & Mulder G 1998, 'Psychological aspects of workload', in P Drenth, H Thierry & C DeWolff (eds), *Handbook of Work and Organisational Psychology* (5-33), Hove, Psychology Press.

Nielsen K, Randall R, Holten AL & González ER 2010, 'Conducting organisational-level occupational health interventions: What works?', *Work & Stress*, 24, 234 – 259.

O'Driscoll M.P. & Beehr TA 1994, 'Supervisor behaviours, role stressors and uncertainty as predictors of personal outcomes for subordinates', *Journal of Organisational Behaviour*, 15, 141-155.

O'Driscoll, MP & Cooper, CL 1996, 'Sources and management of excessive job stress and burnout', in PB Warr (ed) *Psychology at Work* (188-223), Hammondsworth, England: Penguin.

Page KM & Vella-Brodrick DA 2009, 'The 'what', 'why' and 'how' of employee well-being: A new model', *Social Indicators Research*, 90, 441-458.

Probst, TM 2003, 'Exploring employee outcomes of organisational restructuring: A Solomon four group study', *Group and Organisation Management*, 28, 416-439.

Probst, TM 2009, 'Job insecurity, unemployment, and organisational well-being: Oxymoron or possibility?', in CL Cooper & S Cartwright (eds), *The Oxford Handbook of Organisational Well-Being* (387-410), Oxford UK: Oxford University Press.

Quick JC, Macik-Frey M, & Cooper CL 2007, 'Managerial dimensions of organisational health: The healthy leader at work', *Journal of Management Studies*, 44, 206-221.

Rousseau V, Aubé C, Chiocchio F, Boudrias JS, & Morin E 2008, 'Social interactions at work and psychological health: the role of leader-member exchange and work group integration', *Journal of Applied Social Psychology*, 38, 1755-1777.

Seltzer J & Numerof RE 1988, 'Supervisory Leadership and Subordinate Burnout', *Academy of Management Journal*, 31, 439-446.

Shaufeli WB, Leiter MP, & Maslach C 2009, 'Burnout: Thirty-five years of research and practice', *Career Development International*, 14, 204-220

Siegrist J 1996, 'Adverse health effects of high effort-low reward conditions at work', *Journal of Occupational Health Psychology*, 1, 27-43.

Sparks K, Cooper C, Fried Y, & Shirom A 1997, 'The effects of work hours on health: A meta-analytic review', *Journal of Occupational and Organisational Psychology*, 70, 391-408.

Spector PE 1999, 'Objective versus subjective approaches in the study of job stress', *Journal of Organisational Behavior*, 20, 737.

Spector PE 2009, 'The role of job control in employee health and well-being', in CL Cooper, JC Quick, MJ Schabracq (eds) *International Handbook of Work and Health Psychology* (3rd edn), West Sussex, Wiley-Blackwell.

Sullivan S 1999, 'The changing nature of careers: A review and research agenda', *Journal of Management*, 45, 457-484.

Settoon RP, Mossholder KW 2002, 'Relationship quality and relationship context as antecedents of person- and task-focused interpersonal citizenship behaviour', *Journal of Applied Psychology*, 87, 255-267.

van Dierendonck D, Haynes C, Borrill C & Stride C 2004, 'Leadership behaviour and subordinate wellbeing', *Journal of Occupational Health Psychology*, 9, 165-175.

Warr PB 2008, 'Work values: Some demographic and cultural correlates', *Journal of Occupational and Organisational Psychology*, 81, 751-775.

Wright TA 2010, 'The role of psychological well-being in job performance, employee retention and cardiovascular health', *Organisational Dynamics*, 39, 13-23.

Wright TA, Cropanzano R., & Bonett DG 2007, 'The Moderating Role of Employee Positive Well-Being on the Relation between Job Satisfaction and Job Performance', *Journal of Occupational Health Psychology*, 12, 93-104.

Chapter 10

TRADE UNIONS AND THE NEW WORKPLACE

INTRODUCTION

Australian trade unions have witnessed a marked erosion in their power base in workplaces, industry and society over the course of the 20th century, and particularly over the past two decades. In the 21st century, union density – that is, the proportion of the workforce who are unionised – currently stands at less than 20% (see section on Australian union decline on page 196). Declining union density has paralleled important social, economic and political changes in Australia, leading to new preferences on the part of employees and employers in the employment relationship. These external changes have led to a fundamental reshaping of Australian workplaces, forcing unions to adopt new strategies and techniques for the recruitment and organisation of members in order to survive. Revitalisation, regeneration or renewal – as it has been variously labelled – has become an urgent task for Australian unions who now must redefine their operation, success and ongoing effectiveness in workplaces (Cooper, Westcott & Lansbury 2003).

This chapter explores union decline in Australia alongside important social, economic and political changes that have fundamentally reshaped workplaces, and the strategies and approaches of trade unions over the past two decades. It begins by reviewing the explanations for the decline in union density and by considering other external changes that have contributed to the changing nature of Australian workplaces to establish a need and urgency for union renewal. This discussion is then followed by a consideration of the strategic responses of Australian trade unions to the threats and challenges they face. Australian unions' strategies in the new workplace are evaluated with reference to their relative success, before a review of union innovation under a hostile legislative environment is undertaken. It is without doubt that Australian unions are at a critical juncture. Understanding the ways in which unions have responded to external change is paramount in order to analyse the strategies and

Australian unions in decline

As can be seen from Table 10.1, Australian unions enjoyed relatively high levels of membership and density until the late 1980s. Since 1998, patterns of trade union membership and density in Australia indicate a significant decline (in terms of density, approximately 1% per annum). Whilst the decline has been less marked in recent years, trade unions now represent less than 20 per cent of the Australian workforce. In the private sector where the majority of employment is located, union density is less than 15 per cent (*Australian Bureau of Statistics* 2010). Union penetration remains at low levels in industries including agriculture, forestry and fishing, wholesale trade, accommodation and food services, professional, scientific and technical services and administrative and support services (*Australian Bureau of Statistics* 2010). Nevertheless, the positive story for unions in 2009, amongst a significant economic downturn in most advanced market economies (AMEs), was the increase in membership (both at aggregate level and as a proportion of the workforce who are unionised). Unions in a number of sectors also cited significant increases in membership (Hannan 2009; Brigden 2010), and Brigden (2010) suggests that the increase in union membership was largely among women, with the gender union gap closing to just 0.2 percentage points.

Table 10.1 Patterns of Australian union membership & density: 1988-2009

Year	Aggregate union membership ('000)	Union density %
1988	2.535.9	42.0
1990	2,659.6	40.5
1992	2,508.8	39.6
1993	2,376.9	37.6
1994	2,283.4	35.0
1995	2,251.8	32.7
1996	2,194.3	31.1
1997	2,110.3	30.3
1998	2,037.5	28.1
1999	1,878.2	25.7
2000	1901.8	24.7
2001	1,902.7	24.5
2002	1,833.7	23.1

Year	Aggregate union membership ('000)	Union density %
2003	1,866.7	23.0
2004	1,842.1	22.7
2005	1,911.9	22.4
2006	1,786.0	20.3
2007	1,696.4	18.9
2008	1,752.9	18.9
2009	1,835.1	19.7

Source: Compiled from the Australian Bureau of Statistics 1988-2010; Cooper *et al.* 2003.

Research examining the causes of declining union membership and density in Australia and other AMEs is extensive. In Australia, the causes of decline have been categorised into four areas: structural shifts in the economy; macroeconomic variables; institutional and organisational factors; and individual decision factors. A summary of these categories and relevant research that both supports and challenges these causes is provided in Table 10.2.

Table 10.2 The causes of union decline in Australia: A summary

Cause	Examples	Relevant research: national & international
Structural factors	Inter-sectoral industry changes (e.g. growth of female participation in the labour market, growth of service sector), changes in occupation and firm size, public and private sector employment changes.	Drago & Wooden (1998) Peetz (1998) Turnbull (1996)
Macroeconomic factors	Unemployment, wage levels and price levels.	Bain & Elsheikh (1976) Kelly (1990) Visser (1990)
Institutional and organisational factors	The roles and strategies of governments (particularly legislation, changes to bargaining structures), the roles and strategies of employers (e.g. changed attitudes and style), and the roles and strategies of unions (e.g. amalgamations and the Accord – see page 217).	Dabscheck (1995) Fairbrother, Svensen & Teicher (1997) Freeman & Pelletier (1990) Kenyon & Lewis (1992, 1996) Western (1997)

Cause	Examples	Relevant research: national & international
		Baird (2002)
		Cooper, Ellem, Briggs & Van den Broek (2009)
		Holland, Pyman, Cooper & Teicher (2009)
Individual factors	Individual decision factors such as attitudes, job and personal characteristics (e.g. employee qualifications, labour mobility), public attitudes towards unions, and societal values (e.g. individualism).	Bearfield (2003) Peetz (1998) Savery & Soutar (1996)

Source: Compiled from Griffin 2006; Griffin & Svensen 1996.

While the causes of union decline are well established in the literature, the proportion of the decline attributable to these factors over different time periods remains the subject of much debate (Pocock 1998). For example, while the structural explanation for union decline is compelling at face value – and Peetz (1998) has shown that structural change was the dominant factor explaining union decline in Australia in the 1980s – the reduction of compulsory unionism through changes in the law has been identified as the critical factor in the 1990s (Griffin 2006). Turnbull (1996) has also questioned structural factors as a robust explanation of decline on the basis that evidence in most advanced western market economies shows density has declined across all industries and sectors, rather than just being an idiosyncratic feature of particular sectors. The Australian data confirms this (Griffin 2006).

The effects of governments and legislation on declining union density have also been keenly contested, primarily due to the limits of causality. In the Australian case, the limitations of institutional arguments are illustrated by the fact that the rate of union density decline was comparable under the national Labor government during the 1990s to that experienced under the Liberal-National government from 1996-2007 (Griffin 2006). In summary, while there are criticisms of, and unconvincing empirical evidence related to, each of the major causes of union decline, it is important to view the decline as a by-product of all four factors. No one single factor can explain the decline, although some causes may be more or less important in explaining a proportion of the decline in different time periods.

In order to understand and analyse contemporary union decline in greater depth, and the erosion of Australian unions' power more generally, it is also critical to examine and analyse key external changes that have reshaped the industrial relations system and the climate of employment relations in Australia since the 1980s. As Griffin (2006) points out, during the 1980s the dismantling of tariff protection (particularly in manufacturing), the development of new forms of work organisation, changes in the composition of the workforce and the ending of a fixed currency exchange rate were major drivers of change in Australian labour markets and increasingly challenged the role of trade unions. Proactive changes in the management of the employment relationship on behalf of employers – including the adoption of individually-driven direct management styles embedded in individual employment contracts with greater pay flexibility – also had an impact on unions during the 1980s (Griffin 2006). Mining companies Rio Tinto and BHP are often cited as instigators of the shift toward a more antagonistic management style as a result of their high profile attempts to marginalise both collective bargaining rights and the role of unions in general, through the introduction of individual employment contracts (Bachelard 2001; Robinson 2001). Attempts to introduce individual employment contracts in the traditional heartlands of union membership have since followed in other companies, including: Telstra; the major banks, e.g. the Commonwealth Bank; and the public sector, e.g. government agencies and authorities (Cooper *et al.* 2003; Robinson 2001).

Changes in employer behaviour were, and continue to be, intimately linked both to increasing competitive pressures in a globalised economy and to the competitive forces upon managers at workplace level to enhance flexibility and productivity (e.g. Cooper *et al.* 2003; Teicher & Bryan 2006). However, the change in employer behaviour also encapsulates an ideological dimension. Australian employers in the 1980s were increasingly influenced by 'new right' economic philosophies that were promoted and encouraged by leading employer associations including the Business Council of Australia (BCA) and the HR Nicholls Society (Griffin 2006; Isaac 2005). These new-right philosophies were built around the notion of direct individualised employment relationships and a free market approach, thus promoting the exclusion of trade unionism through decentralised determination of wages and conditions, the use of individual employment contracts, and state intervention as a last resort (Griffin 2006; Isaac 2005). The focus on the individual and unitarist assumptions of shared goals and common objectives between employers and employees is also linked to the emergence of new HRM approaches which strongly advocate individualised employer-employee relations over and above employer-union relations.

Post 1990, several factors can be identified as important in challenging Australian unions' power and influence, and exacerbating the decline in membership and density. One of the most significant changes that defined the 1990s was the introduction of legislation at the federal level by the Keating Labor government in the form of the *Industrial Relations Reform Act*

1993 (Cth). This legislation constituted a radical revision of the long established arbitral system (McCallum 1994). In particular, the Act enshrined enterprise bargaining as the primary form of wage determination, in addition to introducing non-union enterprise agreements (known as Enterprise Flexibility Agreements - EFAs), a right to strike, and good faith bargaining provisions (e.g. Naughton 1994).

The Howard Liberal-National government's enactment of the *Workplace Relations and Other Legislation Amendment Act* 1996 (Cth) (WRA) at the federal level represented a watershed in Australian industrial relations, challenging trade unions in a myriad of forms (e.g. Cooper *et al.* 2003; Quinlan 1998). Not only were the roles and influence of the Australian Industrial Relations Commission (AIRC) and trade unions circumscribed based on the assumption that the role and influence of 'third parties' should be minimised, two further radical changes were also introduced. For the first time in the history of Australian industrial relations, the WRA introduced both, freedom of association provisions giving employees the right to join or not join a trade union, and, provisions for individual employment contracts – known as Australian Workplace Agreements (AWAs). Whilst there was significant debate as to whether the WRA represented continuity and/or change with respect to the earlier legislative amendments introduced by Keating's Labor government in 1993, it is clear that the WRA amounted to radical changes in relation to the marginalisation of union and third party intervention in wage determination and the employment relationship.

The highly controversial *Workplace Relations Amendment (Work Choices) Act* 2005 (Cth) introduced by the Howard Liberal-National government (1996-2007) represented one of the most significant changes to Australian industrial relations in the past century. As Teicher, Lambert and O'Rourke (2006) outline, some of the most contentious changes resulting from *Work Choices* included: the creation of a national workplace relations system; changes to the setting of minimum wages; the curtailment of minimum conditions, the role of the AIRC and trade unions; the streamlining of agreement making; the narrowing of unfair dismissal laws; and further restrictions on the right of employees to take lawful industrial action. This legislation, in conjunction with the ongoing decline in union density, raised important questions regarding the effectiveness of trade unions, their legitimacy as a representative voice for workers, and changes and patterns in employee voice more generally.

It is important to acknowledge, however, that the significance of the industrial relations changes introduced by the Howard Liberal-National government extended beyond legislative innovation. The Howard government intensified the neo-liberal agenda of political and economic reform, vigorously pursuing, for example, privatisation of publicly-owned companies, corporatisation, contracting out and the deregulation of labour, product and financial markets (e.g. Cockfield & Lazaris 2007; Cooper *et al.* 2003; Teicher & Bryan 2006). However, Australia is no exception in this regard. Much of the globalisation debate and economic and industrial reforms in the US and UK, for example, have been underpinned by neo-liberal ideology and practice, and the associated drive for increased labour market flexibility, productivity and global competitiveness (Williams & Adam-Smith 2006). As Teicher *et al.* (2006) argue, the ideology of neoliberalism – which is in competition with social democracy and derives from the free market model of global competition – is central to any effort to understand the legislative interventions introduced by the Howard Liberal-National government and their consequences over the period 1996-2007.

The external changes discussed above have served not only to radically reduce the power and influence of trade unions, but also to completely reshape the nature of Australian workplaces. The reshaping of the Australian labour market – including a decline in manufacturing employment, an increase in service sector employment, a decline in full-time male employment and a growth in atypical employment, e.g. part-time, casual and sub-contracting – have also served to undermine and challenge unions (Pocock 1998). Collectively these changes mean that unions no longer play a central role in the Australian workplace, although in some highly-organised industries unions do retain the balance of power. Under a hostile legislative environment during the Howard Liberal-National government's reign, and in light of the increasing 'juridification'[12] of industrial relations, employers were more willing to challenge and resist trade unions (e.g. Carter & Cooper 2002; Cooper 2005; Peetz 2002), leaving unions little scope to extend their power and influence. On the other hand, the challenges and threats to trade unions in Australia also spurred a debate about the prospects for union renewal, that is, the ability and opportunity for unions to exercise strategic choices as a means of improving membership growth and rebuilding power and influence in the workplace and society (e.g. Cooper 2005; Cooper *et al.* 2003; Pocock 1998).

The notion of union renewal focuses on organisational and institutional changes implemented by unions that seek to facilitate the development of new strategies designed to rebuild and redefine the role of the union, of officials and of the rank-and-file members (Cooper *et al.* 2003). Much of the literature on union renewal has focused on the use of innovative organising strategies in the workplace (e.g. Bronfenbrenner 1997; Bronfenbrenner, Friedman, Hurd, Oswald & Seeber 1998; Grablesky & Hurd 1994). However, one of the core assumptions that underpins the union renewal literature is the notion of agency, that is, that unions can and do have the capacity to determine their own fate. Whilst some exogenous factors in the

---

[12] 'Juridification' is a term used to describe the increased legalism and complexity of the industrial relations system (Creighton & Stewart 2000).

external environment are beyond their control, they also 'own' endogenous strategic choices that can be implemented to respond to, and to mitigate, external changes and circumstances (e.g. Carter & Cooper 2002; Cooper et al. 2003; Griffin 2006; Pocock 1998). As Pocock (1998) notes, successful organising transformations have occurred historically – usually in response to crises – and a responsive capacity and a unifying leadership have proved critical to success.

The concept of union renewal in Australia has been further heightened under changed industrial relations and legislative conditions since 2007. The Howard-Liberal National Coalition government lost the election in November 2007, with the Australian Labor Party coming to power under the leadership of Kevin Rudd.[13] The policy document 'Forward with Fairness' (Rudd & Gillard 2007) that Labor took to the federal election in 2007 made a commitment to replace *Work Choices* with laws for 'Fair Work'. Labor's policy document represented an effort to quell public concerns about the erosion of employment conditions under the Howard-Liberal National Coalition government's *Work Choices Act* (Sutherland & Riley 2010).

The *Fair Work Act 2009* (Cth.) received royal assent on 7th April 2009 and promised to bring greater stability and simplicity to Australia's workplace relations system (Sutherland & Riley 2010). Significant sections of the *Fair Work Act 2009*, and notably the new collective bargaining framework, came into operation on 1st July 2009, with the remainder of the Act taking effect from 1st January 2010 (Cooper 2010). One of the marked changes that resulted from the enactment of the *Fair Work Act 2009* is the movement of Australia's industrial relations laws to a national system. In 2009, all states, with the exception of Western Australia, referred their powers over industrial relations matters to the Commonwealth, meaning that the majority of Australian private sector employees are now covered by the national Fair Work system (Cooper 2010; Sutherland & Riley 2010).

As Cooper (2010) and Brigden (2010) note, the provisions of the *Fair Work Act 2009* came into effect in a turbulent economic context, as a result of the global financial crisis, and therefore at a time when many unions were immersed in negotiations to mitigate the worst effects of the downturn on their members. At the same time, unions had been heavily engaged in the award modernisation process[14] which began under the auspices of the AIRC in March 2008, following the Labor government's election, as a means

---

[13] The Rudd Labor government was elected in 2007. Julia Gillard replaced Kevin Rudd as the leader of the Labor party and Australian Prime Minister in June 2010. The Gillard Labor government was re-elected for a second term in November 2010.

[14] The award modernisation process resulted in the ceasing of over 1,500 awards and associated instruments, as a result of the review by the AIRC. At the end of the process, s 122 modern awards based on industry or occupation had been created (Gillard 2009b).

to simplify and streamline industrial relations processes, to reduce business costs and to promote productive, flexible workplaces (Gillard 2009a). Changes to awards were not without controversy among Australian unions, and involved considerable time and resource commitments throughout the process (Cooper 2010).

For unions, some of the key changes enacted by the *Fair Work Act 2009* are: the creation of a new governing institutional body Fair Work Australia[15]; legislated national employment standards (NES); and, changes to collective bargaining (See Cooper 2010 for additional details). The national minimum employment standards, together with awards, are designed to guarantee a fair and simple minimum safety net for Australian employees (Gillard 2009b). The list of ten NES are provided in Table 10.3.

Table 10.3 The National Employment Standards (NES): *Fair Work Act 2009* (Cth)

NES	Legislated minimum
Maximum weekly hours of work	38 hours
Request for flexible working arrangements	For parents of under school age children, and children with a disability
Parental leave and related entitlements	12 months unpaid and a right to request a further 12 months (unpaid)
Annual leave	4 weeks per year with an extra week for some shift workers
Personal/carer's leave and compassionate leave	10 days personal/carer's leave; 2 days compassionate leave
Community service leave	For emergency services and jury duty
Long service leave	National long service leave standard in development
Public holidays	A paid day off on a public holiday, except when reasonably requested to work that day
Notice of termination and redundancy pay	Up to 5 weeks' notice and up to 16 weeks redundancy pay (depending on length of service)
Fair work information statement	To be provided to all new employees by their employer outlining rights and responsibilities

Source: Adapted from Cooper 2010.

---

[15] Fair Work Australia replaces the AIRC and other previous tribunals and agencies.

One of the key questions for unions, and particularly in the context of renewal, is the extent to which the new legislation embodies collectivist principles (Cooper 2010). Given that the promotion of collective bargaining was a cornerstone of the 'Forward with Fairness' policy document (Rudd & Gillard 2007), what will the new legislation mean for management-union relations and the realities of work in Australian workplaces? In terms of collectivism and bargaining, the *Fair Work Act 2009* provides for union involvement in enterprise bargaining in many ways. The laws require, for example, employers to provide a notice period to employees about their right to representation in the bargaining process, with the union as the default representative for union members (Sutherland & Riley 2010). There are also new good faith bargaining rules which subsequently require employers to recognise employees' representatives (Sutherland & Riley 2010). The Act also introduces a low-paid bargaining stream which offers a new form of multi-employer bargaining. Bargaining is supervised by the new institutional regulator, Fair Work Australia, with some capacity to intervene and make orders during the bargaining process (Cooper 2010). One of the notable developments under the new collective bargaining laws in the *Fair Work Act 2009* has been the significant progress made in major, ongoing, long-running disputes that began under *Work Choices*, with employers being brought back to the table to negotiate with unions (Brigden 2010).

Given the 'recency' of the *Fair Work Act 2009*, it is too early to assess its impact on unions, management-union relations, employees and workplaces. Such analyses will be a key task for industrial relations academics and practitioners over the next three years (Cooper 2010). Whilst many trade union leaders have been, in the main, supportive and positive about the Fair Work system (particularly in relation to its predecessor *Work Choices*), there is evidence of optimism and pessimism among academics in relation to the role of unions and collectivism under the Act (Cooper 2010:268). Forsyth (2009), for example, has suggested that 'union rights' are not provided for in the *Fair Work Act 2009*, and Hardy and Howe (2009:322) have suggested that the new legislation means that unions are just one of a number of possible bargaining agents at the enterprise level, rather than the central regulatory actors in the system. Some academics have further argued that the new system has much in common with *Work Choices* with respect to the regulation of collective action, particularly industrial action and pattern bargaining (McCrystal 2009, 2009-2010). Whatever the future impact of the new legislation on unions is, one positive story to emerge in 2009 was the increase in union membership, both in aggregate and as a proportion of the workforce unionised (see Table 10.1).

Australian union strategies in the new workplace

A variety of strategic responses have been adopted by Australian trade unions to redress and counteract the decline in union membership and density since the 1980s. There are three identifiable responses: restructuring via mergers and amalgamations; the establishment of organising works; and a conscious shift to the organising model of unionism. Each of these strategies is briefly reviewed and evaluated below.

Award restructuring: mergers and amalgamations

The first formal endorsement of union mergers occurred in 1987 at the Australian Council of Trade Unions (ACTU) biennial conference. Influenced by the Federal Prices and Incomes Accord (see page 217) and the Scandinavian model of industrial relations, the 'Future Strategies for the Trade Union Movement' policy was formally adopted (Griffin 2006). A key plank of this policy was the recommendation of union mergers. Unsurprisingly, many unions were resistant to change and there was little formal take-up of mergers in the early period (Griffin 2006).

The ACTU Congress in 1989 provided the impetus for a restructuring of the Australian union movement, by which time mergers and amalgamations were strongly supported by unions (Griffin 2006; Hose & Rimmer 2002). Legislative change also facilitated the process, with the federal Labor government implementing several amendments to the *Industrial Relations Act* 1988 (Cth) in 1990 including the removal of requirements that amalgamations could not take place without 25 per cent of membership approval (Griffin 2006). One of the most significant restructuring initiatives supported by the ACTU and the federal government at the time was a move to 20 industry-based 'super unions' (Carter & Cooper 2002). The rationale for these 'super unions' was that they would create economies of scale for the provision of union services, thus freeing up resources for the building of membership (Cooper *et al.* 2003). Restructuring was a successful strategy in a short period of time in terms of a reduction in the aggregate number of Australian unions. From 1990 to 1994, 132 mergers occurred, and the total number of unions decreased from 295 to 157 (Griffin 2006). The number of federally-registered unions also dropped from 134 to 52, with these 52 unions accounting for more than 85 per cent of total union membership in 1994 (Griffin 2006).

The overarching success of the restructuring of the Australian union movement has been widely questioned (Costa & Duffy 1991; Pocock 1998). If measured on the criterion of union membership, it was largely unsuccessful (e.g. Carter & Cooper 2002; Cooper *et al.* 2003) as between 1990-1996 union density fell by almost 10 per cent. Organisational restructuring initiatives also had an adverse effect on workplace organisation and activity as a result of greater centralisation of decision-making structures (Carter & Cooper 2002; Cooper *et al.* 2003). Similarly, Pocock (1998) argues that amalgamations failed to generate positive outcomes for union democracy in terms of improvements to union services, improved contact with union officials, increased commitment among members or the union's ability to deal with workplace issues. However, using an alternative criterion of success, there are very few examples of unions withdrawing from prior amalgamations, despite the fact that provision was made for disamalgamation in the WRA (Ellem 2001).

Organising works

From the 1990s onwards, the primacy of enterprise bargaining for wage determination led many union leaders to rethink the role and importance of union structures at the local workplace. A key turning point in the Australian union movement's strategy came in 1993 following an ACTU-led delegation of union officials to North America in search of innovative ideas for the building of membership – primarily through organising and recruitment. The US and Canada were seen as an appropriate comparators based on the notion that these unions were also operating in hostile political and legal environments (Holland 1999; Carter & Cooper 2002; Cooper *et al.* 2003; Griffin 2006; Pocock & Wishart 1999). One of the major outcomes of the delegation's report was a recommendation to introduce an organising centre, modelled on the American Federation of Labor and the Congress of Industrial Organisation's (AFL-CIO) organising institute. The AFL-CIO Institute was designed to recruit, train and place field organisers as a means of increasing the quantity and quality of union organisers (Griffin 2006).

In August 1993, the recommendations of the ACTU delegation and its executive were given formal effect, with the executive agreeing on a program:

- to select and train young persons for recruitment and organising;
- to devote more resources to recruitment and organising activities; and
- to ensure that organising reflected a diverse background of union membership and potential membership, particularly with regard to gender, age and ethnicity.

Source: Griffin 2006:128.

The philosophy underpinning the organising centre became known as the organising model (discussed in the next section). Under the banner of organising unionism, the ACTU established 'Organising Works' in March 1994. In alignment with its American counterpart, Organising Works was developed as a means for recruiting, training and supporting new union organisers, particularly young people, women, and those from non-English speaking backgrounds (Pocock 1998). Under this program, training was primarily embedded in the participating federal union, with the organisers spending four days on average in the employing union and one day in training (Griffin & Moors 2004). Over the past decade (1994-2004), approximately 450 graduates have successfully completed the program, with approximately 50 per cent of these graduates being female and under 30 years of age (Griffin 2006).

As Holland (1999) suggests, if one takes absolute membership figures and union density as barometers of strategic success, the Organising Works program has – just like amalgamations – failed to halt the decline. However, as Griffin (2006) rightfully points out, tangible gains at the micro level can be identified, particularly in relation to the development of a new cadre of trained activists committed to the principles of the organising model. Carter and Cooper (2002) also suggest that the success of a number of high-profile organising campaigns in retail and hospitality are testament to the effectiveness of Organising Works[16]. Pocock (1998) extends these arguments, suggesting that Organising Works has been an inspiring initiative in two ways. First, it has resulted in recruitment and organisation in traditionally difficult, yet growing areas of employment such as call centres, casinos and hospitality. Second, it has provided the union movement with an influx of relatively young organisers willing to critique Australian unionism's traditional habits of servicing. New organising tactics have developed as a result, including organisation outside the workplace, one-to-one organising, and activist development (Cooper *et al.* 2003).

Despite the success of the Organising Works program across a range of criteria, important questions and doubts have been raised in relation to whether the program and its graduates have successfully impacted on the entrenched cultures and models of unionism in Australia (e.g. Griffin & Moors 2004; Pocock 1998). The 'iron-cage' nature of union culture, working methods and structures has also been recognised elsewhere in the Australian literature, with Pocock (1998) labelling such barriers to union transformation as a case of 'institutional sclerosis'. In terms of the Organising Works program, experiences of culture shock have been common, whereby new trainee organisers have met with entrenched opposition from long serving full-time officials – whether due to their tertiary education, sex, age or experience (Cooper *et al.* 2003; Pocock 1998).

---

[16] Cooper *et al.* (2003: 195-198) advance a similar argument and discuss two case studies of unions' organising experiences in Australia. One case focuses on the Liquor, Hospitality and Miscellaneous Workers' Union's attempts to organise hotel workers, and the other on the experiences of the Community and Public Sector Union in organising call centre workers.

The organising model

The organising model is typically contrasted with the servicing model of unionism. The former is characterised as an inclusive, empowerment-based approach, where the members at the workplace level – or what is termed the 'grass roots' level – constitute 'the union' and are active in the establishment of an agenda (Cooper 2005; Griffin 2006; Holland 1999; Tarrant 2001). Indeed, the focus is on organisers providing assistance to self-reliant rank-and-file members where members are active participants rather than passive consumers (Carter & Cooper 2002). The key then is the localised organisation of the members through their own initiative, activism and leadership to establish a culture of unionisation in the workplace (Carter & Cooper 2002; Grabelsky & Hurd 1994; Heery, Simms, Simpson, Delbridge & Salmon 2000; Robinson 2001). The aim of the organising model is to increase internal democracy, build alliances with the community and develop capacities for strategic campaigning (Cooper *et al.* 2003). In contrast, the servicing model views the union as a form of insurance – a third party which attempts to solve problems for members if and when necessary (Griffin 2006; Holland 1999). Whilst the two models are often portrayed as polar opposites in the literature, the reality is that unions will need to pursue both organising and servicing in order to enable recruitment and retention of members (Boxall & Haynes 1997; Pocock & Wishart 1999).

As noted above, the organising model came to underpin the Organising Works program as a result of the influences of the US experience – namely the commitment of a new breed of leaders at the AFL-CIO to organising, strategic planning and a vision of inclusive unionism (Carter & Cooper 2002; Pocock 1998). However, in more recent times the ACTU and federally-registered unions have demonstrated a conscious strategic shift towards a more deeply embedded organising approach. This is exemplified by the two most recent ACTU manifestos: Unions@Work (1999) and Future Strategies (2003).

Not dissimilar to Organising Works, Unions@Work (1999) is a policy document that emanated from an overseas ACTU delegation, this time to Britain, Ireland, Belgium, Canada and the US. The policy is underpinned by the organising approach, emphasising workplace activity and the devotion of union resources to recruitment (Griffin 2006). Four key building blocks were promoted by Unions@Work (1999) as being necessary foundations for strong and effective unionism, and in turn, a just and fair Australian society. Each of these four major building blocks was linked to a series of pre-requisite actions. The major building blocks of Unions@Work (1999) are summarised in Box 10.1.

Box 10.1: The building blocks of Unions@Work

1) Strength in the workplace

- Establishing and strengthening delegate, activist and collective structures in the workplace;
- Educating and activating delegates to recruit, bargain and handle grievances;
- Creating industrial and organising rights for delegates and activists; and,
- Enhancing the role of union organisers in developing delegates.

2) Growth in new areas

- Recruiting and organising new members in growing industries;
- Developing an organising function within unions with a coordinator and specialist organising teams;
- Developing new organising and campaign methods;
- Educating and involving delegates and activists in campaigns outside the workplace; and,
- Sending staff to gain organising experience in unions overseas.

3) Technology for the times

- Ensuring all delegates and activists are online;
- Using the internet and email to provide information and services;
- Modernising and simplifying the delivery of union services through call centres;
- Enhancing democracy and efficiency through modern management and structures; and,
- Creating national and international networks and developing campaign capacity.

4) A strong union voice

- Developing modern, comprehensive campaign and pressure tactics;
- Building a union media capacity to market messages;
- Involving and recruiting new members around contemporary issues;
- Fighting for decent wages, a decent wage system, safety and job security; and,
- Forming strong alliances with other groups in the community.

Source: Adapted from ACTU (1999:2).

Future Strategies (2003) built upon the 1999 Unions@Work policy to offer a broader vision of the Australian union movement (Griffin 2006). Three themes were central to the 2003 policy: unions and the wider society; unions and the workplace; and unions reaching out to new members. Each of these three themes was related to underpinning strategies. These themes are summarised in Box 10.2.

> **Box 10.2: Future strategies**
>
> **1) Unions and the wider society**
> - Building and promoting union values;
> - Political activity;
> - Building a cooperative industrial relations culture;
> - Improving access to unions;
> - Quality and value-for-money union services; and,
> - Developing an ACTU call centre hotline.
>
> **2) Unions and the workplace**
> - Building union delegate numbers and networks;
> - Building representative decision-making processes in unions;
> - Building communication and campaigning capacity; and,
> - Commitment, structures and resources for union growth.
>
> **3) Reaching out to new members**
> - Resources, research and planning for growth;
> - Innovative organising tactics and union organisation;
> - Commitment to existing areas of organisation and coverage; and,
> - The responsibility to organise.

Source: Adapted from ACTU (2003).

Two of the core underpinnings of the organising model and the recent policy approaches of the ACTU are: activism and the development of union structures, and representation at the workplace. The two are interdependent. It could be argued that potential barriers to the diffusion of an organising model of unionism in Australia are the historically underdeveloped nature of workplace union structures and the uneven presence of union delegates at the workplace level (Carter & Cooper 2002; Pocock 1998). Indeed, the importance of union structures and local delegates are reinforced by Peetz's (1997) analyses which showed that workplaces with active union delegates and active union-management relations experienced, on average, lower levels of declining density. These findings support the notion that a focus on activism and the development of localised workplace structures are central priorities for Australian unions in the future.

It is also important to note that the 1999 and 2003 policy documents developed by the ACTU were a by-product of a sea-change in styles and leadership at the national peak body as part of a process of modernisation and a return to traditional grass roots organising values (Carter & Cooper 2002; Cooper *et al.* 2003; Robinson 2001). Greg Combet, the former Secretary of the ACTU, was at the vanguard of organising unionism and the redefinition and re-emergence of organised labour, continuously reinforcing and acknowledging the need for unions to innovate in the face of difficult challenges – particularly in response to political and legislative hostility (Griffin 2006; Robinson 2001). The publication of the 1999 and 2003 policy documents signalled a deeper practical and political commitment to organising unionism on the part of the leadership of the union movement (Carter & Cooper 2002). However, the effectiveness of the strategic responses adopted by Australian unions can still be questioned on the basis of membership growth because the fact remains that there has not been a turnaround in the long-term rate of union density decline.

It is also important to note that organising unionism goes to the very heart of union strategy, ideology, democracy and activism, and it is a commitment to change at the level of the individual union that is critical, rather than at the level of the peak council (Carter & Cooper 2002; Cooper *et al.* 2003). Not dissimilar to the Organising Works experience, there is some evidence of fear and resistance to change among unions, thus stifling the move toward organising unionism and proactive changes in strategic direction (e.g. Carter & Cooper 2002; Burchielli & Bartram 2009). Organising unionism does however also have significant implications at lower levels in the hierarchy, particularly in relation to the role of organisers and the union's approach to building workplace membership (Cooper *et al.* 2003; Burchielli & Bartram 2009).

In 2009, the ACTU Congress launched 'Australian Unions – Working for a Better Life', which endorses a new union agenda for job security, workers' rights and a better Australia (ACTU Congress 2009). The agenda builds on existing policies and priorities set by the ACTU executive, including: a voice for working Australians; improving wages and working; creating a fairer Australia; growing union membership; organising workplaces, industries and sectors; and, connecting with communities (ACTU Congress 2009). The three priority areas addressing the future of work, organising and a fair society are summarised in Box 10.3.

Box 10.3: Future strategies: Australian unions – Working for a better life

1) A plan for the future of work that gives workers:

- safe, secure and rewarding jobs in sustainable industries;
- the right to bargain and organise collectively;
- fair wages, pay equity for women, and family-friendly working conditions;
- access to training, skill development and support throughout their careers;
- a rich and rewarding life outside work, including in retirement; and,
- jobs that provide greater security for individuals and for the planet.

2) An organising and growth strategy that:

- safeguards and extends the same rights for all workers;
- builds strong, democratic and growing unions which are effective in representing their members;
- closely involves the wider community and other organisations on shared issues of concern; and,
- is able to influence and achieve lasting political and social change.

3) A vision for a fairer society where:

- everyone has access to good healthcare, appropriate housing, quality education and other essential community services;
- the lives of working people are made easier and our communities are strengthened through access to transport, communications and public services;
- the most vulnerable members of the community are supported to enable their participation in economic and social life;
- laws are applied equally to all citizens;
- government plays a positive role in stabilising the business cycle to secure jobs and living standards;
- the economy provides benefits to the whole community;
- Australia participates in international arenas to promote peace,

> security, human rights, labour standards and prosperity through fair trade arrangements; and,
>
> - there is strong and urgent action to tackle climate change

Source: ACTU Congress (2009).

Union innovation under a hostile legislative environment: 1997-2006

Australian trade unions pursued and implemented a range of novel strategies during the reign of the Howard Liberal-National Coalition government from 1996-2007, in an attempt to respond to and counteract political and legislative hostility at the federal level. The Howard government reforms were labelled as anti-union (e.g. Carter & Cooper 2002; Cooper *et al.* 2003; Robinson 2001), forcing Australian unions to re-engage with members and strategy on a different level. As Cooper *et al.* (2003:185) noted, fundamental to the new strategies adopted by unions was a re-definition of their relationship with the state to ensure more autonomy[17]. Through re-building unionism at a grass roots level using an organising approach, unions sought to minimise their susceptibility to changes in industrial legislation (Cooper *et al.* 2003). In addition to the responses discussed above, a canvassing of research on union innovation reveals three distinct strategies: corporate campaigning, creative compliance and community unionism. These strategies are discussed below.

Corporate campaigning

Corporate campaigning has its origins in the social activism campaigns in the US in the 1960s and the writings of social campaigner Saul Alinsky (Klein 2000; Manheim 2001). The fundamental theme underpinning social activism and trade union corporate campaigning is the recognition of the corporation as a social institution, integrated within society through its diverse and multiple stakeholders (Freeman 1984; Thompson, Wartick & Smith 1991). It is the ability of unions therefore, to mobilise these interests against the corporation that provides the power base for effective campaigning. Using Alinsky's metaphor of 'political jujitsu', Klein (2000) emphasises the dynamic nature of corporate campaigning in using one part of the organisation's power structure (stakeholders) against another (management) to provide a power base to effect organisational change. However, as Greven and Russo (2003) point out, when the concept first

---

[17] It is argued that Australian unions have traditionally been seen as dependent on the State. This is known as the 'dependency thesis'. Developed by Howard (1977), he argued that Australian unions were dependent on the state, as a product of the compulsory arbitration system. See also Griffin and Scarcebrook (1990).

emerged in the US it was not popular with conservative union leaders who emphasised a cooperative employment relationship and focused on servicing the membership.

The catalyst for union adoption of social activism strategies in the US since the 1970s has been the increasingly adversarial legal and political environment; a declining union base; and, the global mobility of capital (Brown & Chang 2004; Craypo 1997; Greven & Russo 2003). The refocusing of labour relations issues from a broader perspective of corporate and industrial citizenship (e.g. McCallum 2005) has also provided a new strategic approach for union-based campaigns against organisations. In a global context, corporate campaigning can be seen as a way of negating the increasing power imbalance between labour and multinational corporations.

Despite the discrete objectives of corporate campaigning, defining the concept remains difficult, primarily due to the different perspectives that it can be analysed from. These include financial, economic and public relations perspectives. Definition is also difficult due to the diverse nature and focus of such campaigns. For example, do they complement or substitute for strike action and organising activities (Jarley & Maranto 1990; Kochan, Katz & McKersie 1986; Perry 1996)? Despite these difficulties, Manheim (2001:xiii) developed a comprehensive definition which reflects the broad nature of the concept:

> *'Corporate campaign' is a term of art referring to a coordinated, often long-term, and wide ranging program of economic, political, legal, and psychological warfare; usually, but not exclusively, initiated by a union or by organised labour in general. It is directed against a corporation that has opposed unionisation, declined to accept contract terms a union deems critical, or in some other way refused to yield on some issue of great importance to the organisation launching the campaign. It is warfare waged in such disparate venues as Wall Street, Capitol Hill, the regulatory agencies, the courts, and the market place. Most of all, it is warfare waged in the media, where the unions or other groups seek to redefine the image and undermine the reputation of the targeted company through systematic and unrelenting pressure ... to cause so much pain and disruption that management is forced to yield to their will.*

Whilst the context and focus of corporate campaigns will be wide and varied, Greven and Russo (2003) identify three defining elements: strategic research and planning; an effective media strategy; and escalation. Research indicates that media strategies are often framed as metaphors or symbols designed to effect corporate decision making: for instance, 'David versus Goliath'; 'Social Justice'; 'For the Common Good'; or 'Betrayal' (Greven & Russo 2003; Keiser 1993; Perry 1987). In effect, unions attempt to seize the moral high ground (Brown & Chang 2004). From this vantage point, the campaign develops both vertical and horizontal strategies (Perry 1987). Vertical strategies include focusing on stakeholders, such as shareholders, customers and corporate alliances, and attacking the organisation's public image and any particular weakness in the organisational power structure (for example, government contracts or alliances). Horizontal strategies include coalition building with international unions or local community groups such as churches and political parties.

Corporate campaigning has been criticised by some as representing a sign of union weakness, in the sense of constituting a search for alternate strategies that seek to protect the union's position and its members from hostile regulatory systems, managerial resistance and the global power of corporations (e.g. Greven & Russo 2003; Perry 1996). Despite these criticisms, corporate campaigning remains an effective union strategy, particularly when coordinated across international boundaries. As Burgmann (2003:169) has noted, in a modern society, workers' movements – in order to play a meaningful role – must engage all industrial, political, social and moral struggles affecting working people as a whole, or, as Perry (1987) argues, utilise a 'cafeteria of confrontational tactics'.

The value of corporate campaigns is often in their clandestine operation, meaning that management cannot know what to expect or what affect a corporate campaign will have. Indeed, the knowledge that a union is planning a corporate campaign as opposed to strike action may be significant enough to induce management to negotiate. In addition, the outcomes of corporate campaigning can be far more effective and less costly than strike action because it does not necessarily require a loss of wages and may not involve legal costs (Greven & Russo 2003; Perry 1987). Evidence from the US also indicates that unions adopting corporate campaigning strategies are more successful in recruiting new members than those who do not (Bronfenbrenner & Juravich 1998; Fiorito, Jarley & Delaney 1995; Voss & Sherman 2000).

Several key features of effective corporate campaigns have also been identified in the literature. These features include: in-depth research of the corporation's power structures and relationships; the timing of the campaign; national union involvement; mobilisation of the rank-and-file; targeting an identifiable, company-specific product or service; and the building of alliances and networks of power (e.g. Brown & Chang 2004; Greven & Russo 2003; Juravich & Bronfenbrenner 1999; Perry 1987, 1996). Gangemi and Torres (1996) also note that the coordination and concentration of activities are seminal features of a corporate campaign as a means of inflicting economic damage, operational disruption, management disorganisation, loss of customer confidence, community support, employee loyalty and ultimately the destruction of business and jobs.

The ability to use 'multiple scales simultaneously', that is, to be able to escalate the conflict on all fronts (Herrod 2001), is also critical since it is never clear from one case to the next which tactic will prove the most effective (Voss & Sherman 2000). Similarly, Greven and Russo (2003) argue that a dynamic approach and the continuous refinement of strategies will avoid what they describe as 'pattern targeting' in which employers and corporations develop successful counter measures based on patterns and past experiences.

Corporate campaigning in Australia

In Australia, the concept of corporate campaigning has developed in parallel with the US model, despite Australian unions traditionally having far more power and density than their US counterparts. The Australian union movement has a long history of involvement in social issues dating back to the first decade of Federation, and the fight for a minimum 'living wage' (widely known as the Harvester Judgement 1907). However, corporate campaigning has its origins in what became known as the 'green bans' of the early 1970s. In response to often speculative commercial developments in the central business district of Sydney, the development of housing and the protection of culturally and architecturally significant buildings were largely over-ridden. In response, the New South Wales Builders' Labourers Federation (NSW BLF) initiated and led a campaign to stop further speculation on significant sites (Burgmann & Burgmann 1998).

The BLF claimed the right to intervene in the decision-making process to insist that all work performed should be socially useful and of an ecologically benign nature (Munday 1988 cited in Burgmann 2003). This altruism was despite the fact that the BLFs stance could potentially have had an adverse affect on BLF members' employment. The first ban was on the last open bushland within Sydney. With no support from the local state representatives or the Premier of NSW, the BLF – in coalition with local residents – proceeded to black ban the site and picket work. The builders, AV Jennings, initially attempted to continue with non-union labour. However, as Burgmann (2003:170) notes:

> ...building workers on a Jennings office project in North Sydney sent a message to the company which said "If you attempt to build on Kelly's Bush, even if there is the loss of one tree, this half completed building will remain so forever, as a monument to Kelly's Bush." This had a sobering influence on Jennings, and alarmed property developers more generally.

By 1974, 42 green bans had been initiated. However, with the political downfall of the NSW BLF leadership that year, the green bans collapsed. The campaign is credited however with saving over 100 buildings considered worthy of preservation by the national trust, and as being the catalyst for more stringent state and federal laws on protecting sites of special value (Burgmann 2003). The 'green' political agenda around the world has its origins in this campaign (Allaby 1983; Burgmann 2003).

Corporate campaigning as a strategy lay dormant in Australia over the next 20 years as the Labor party gained power federally and forged a close alliance with the unions through the Prices and Incomes Accord. The 'Accord', as it became known, was a mechanism to increase the role of the ACTU in the negotiation of wages, economic and social policies in return for the tempering of wage claims (Cooper *et al.* 2003; Isaac 2005). During this period, union density declined by approximately 1 per cent per annum, from 50 per cent in 1976 to 35 per cent in 1994. In 1996, the conservative Howard coalition government was elected with a more hostile agenda towards unions (see previous discussion of legislation). During this period, unions rediscovered the corporate campaign and have used this strategy across a variety of sectors to address a broad spectrum of issues. One of the main issues to attract the focus of unions has been the liability of organisations in relation to occupational health and safety as seen in the James Hardie case study on page 232.

Creative compliance

The practice of creative compliance has been studied primarily in accounting, and more specifically in terms of financial reporting and taxation. The essence of creative compliance is evasion of the intended impact of a law. Pyman (2005) found evidence of opportunistic and proactive approaches being utilised by federally-registered unions as a means of counteracting the WRA at the national level. Examples included creative attempts by unions to evade the intended impact and spirit of the law whilst simultaneously maintaining compliance with the letter of the law. Similar strategies have been identified in the US literature in relation to corporate campaigning, for example, and the manipulation of government agencies to achieve ends other than those intended by the law (e.g. McGuiness 1996). Literature in the US has also identified incidences of employer-initiated creative compliance in relation to the manipulation of, and opposition to, union organising campaigns (e.g. Voss & Fantasia 2004).

Pyman (2005) revealed two particular types of creative compliance tactics being used: work-to-rule and the exploitation of loopholes. Work-to-rule involved the adaptation and reshaping of legal rules. Examples of this tactic included the exploitation of award provisions as a means of maintaining and preserving award content in the face of the legal rationalisation of awards through a process known as award simplification[18].

---

[18] One of the key reforms introduced by the WRA was award simplification. This process involved the rationalisation of federal awards. Awards were only permitted to cover the 20 allowable matters listed in the statute.

The exploitation of loopholes tactic represented a more deliberate technique involving the manipulation of the content of the law – that is, the actual wording of the statute – to secure favourable outcomes and thwart the spirit of the legislation (Pyman 2005:86). A primary example of this tactic was identified in relation to union rights of entry to the workplace. The legislation required unions to provide 24 hours notice of their intention to enter an employer's premises. As a means of retaining spontaneity in access to workplaces, the unions' would notify an employer of their intention to enter over an extended period of time, such as a week or a fortnight, and often across multiple workplaces or a larger geographical area. This tactic therefore enabled the unions to retain spontaneity and an element of surprise in their visits to workplaces as a means of minimising employer preparation for union visits.

Pyman (2005) concluded that the use of creative compliance tactics by the unions studied facilitated positive industrial outcomes, particularly in relation to the reduction of managerial prerogative and in engendering behavioural and strategic change in their methods and processes of operation. These research findings substantiate the earlier discussion of union renewal and strategic choice, reinforcing the notion that unions are not captives of their external environment. Instead, they have a zone of strategic choice and they can use this proactively to their advantage to implement strategic and behavioural change, or to build and extend organisational competencies and influence at the workplace.

Community unionism

Increased interest in union renewal and innovative organising strategies has spurred a parallel interest in union-community relationships, particularly in the form of networks, coalitions and alliances (Tattersall 2004, 2005, 2006, 2007). Various different types of union-community relationships have been identified in practice, ranging from simple instrumental relationships, to union-community coalitions, to community unionism (Tattersall 2005). Community unionism is a strategy and practice that has the potential to increase unions' capacities, power and effectiveness. Engagement with community organisations can enhance union power by broadening their bargaining and campaigning agendas to wider social issues and using social pressure from mobilised communities as a novel tactic (Tattersall 2006, 2007). It has been argued that, in addition to neo-liberal economic reform, increased diversity in rank-and-file membership in terms of gender and ethnicity, for example, have driven a shift toward community unionism strategies (Tattersall 2004).

Community unionism is a broad encompassing term that has been used to describe a range of activities. A lack of theoretical development has generated ambiguity and complexity in the terminology used to describe union behaviour of this kind (e.g. Cockfield & Lazaris 2007; Tattersall 2004).

Tattersall (2004:6) defines the term community unionism broadly to entail the practice and process of unions focusing their activity on social and community concerns. Tattersall (2005) distinguishes community unionism from other types of union-community relationships by identifying the existence of union participation as central. Thus, community unionism depicts a high level of integration and reciprocity between the participating union and the campaign of a coalition, and is focused on mutual interests (Tattersall 2005). At the core of a community unionism strategy is a multi-pronged community agenda that complements traditional campaigning methods (Cockfield & Lazaris 2007; Tattersall 2004). High profile campaigns in the US and the UK, including the Justice for Janitors[19] and Living Wage[20] campaigns have popularised union-community relationships (Tattersall 2006). However, much of the literature in the US has been criticised for focusing on labour-community coalitions rather than community unionism itself (Ellem 2003).

Community unionism has obvious overlaps with the organising model in terms of the latter's objectives of increased membership participation and activism through the use of local or regional organising initiatives and as a strategy for proactive organisational change (Tattersall 2004). Community unionism also resonates with corporate campaigning and social movement theory in terms of unions using their relationships with community organisations to operate as agents of social change and to exercise not only workplace power, but also social, economic and political power (Cockfield & Lazaris 2007; Tattersall 2004). For example, rather than just actively representing their members on traditional or sectional workplace issues, unions need to pursue a broader social vision and demonstrate activism on issues such as education, health, infrastructure and trade and globalisation, e.g. wage equality and the distribution of wealth (Cockfield & Lazaris 2007; Tattersall 2004, 2007). The range of community organisations that unions can align their activities with include, but are not limited to: political organisations, non-governmental organisations (NGOs), faith/religious organisations, environmental groups, ethnic groups, youth groups, student groups, sporting clubs and of course the public at large (Tattersall 2004).

In Australia, community unionism is an underdeveloped yet growing area of research, and there is increasing evidence of union engagement with community organisations in practice (Tattersall 2007). The most recent and commonly-heralded incidence of community unionism was the ACTU-led campaign against the Howard government's *Work Choices Act* – the 'Your Rights at Work' campaign (ACTU 2005c). Ellem (2003), however, in a significant contribution to the research literature identified the importance

---

[19] See Erickson, Fisk, Milkman, Mitchell and Wong (2002) for an overview of the Justice for Janitors campaign.
[20] See Wills (2004) for a discussion of the Living Wage campaign in East London.

of the intersection of work and community in Australia's Pilbara mining towns. The 1998 waterfront dispute was also notable for the establishment of community pickets (e.g. Trinca & Davies 2000). In fact, union engagement with the community has been explicitly adopted and encouraged by the ACTU since 2001. The ACTU has mounted various campaigns to build a positive social profile and to pursue equity and fairness in the community (Cooper *et al.* 2003). Notable examples of these campaigns include a claim to the AIRC to extend parental leave arrangements and a claim to the AIRC for reasonable hours and submissions to National Wage Case hearings on behalf of the union movement. Many of these campaigns were stimulated by the 2001 'Our Future at Work' discussion document released by the ACTU which identified work-life balance, casualisation, inequality of wealth, and job security as issues of paramount concern to workers (Cooper *et al.* 2003). There is also evidence to suggest that state peak councils have attempted to pursue campaigns that move beyond a narrow, traditional focus on wages and conditions to encompass the broader community (Cooper *et al.* 2003). Other community unionism initiatives that have been recognised in the literature include the Labor for Refugees campaign and the Walk against the War campaign coordinated by Unions NSW (Tattersall 2007).

Bramble (2005) conducted an in-depth analysis of the ACTU resistance strategy against *Work Choices*. *Inter alia*, Bramble (2005) identified the building of support in the wider community as a notable initiative in the campaign. The building of community support was achieved through a series of highly-effective television advertisements designed to raise community awareness of the threats posed by *Work Choices*. Other key tactics used by the ACTU included leafleting local community events such as football matches in parks and public spaces, the display of banners on prominent buildings in the central business district of Melbourne, media events, and mass community mobilisation in the form of a national week of action in June-July 2006, followed by a national day of action four months later (Bramble 2005).

The relative success of the community unionism campaign against *Work Choices* has been noted in several forms. First, opinion polls post implementation of the Act suggested a changing tide of public opinion, with a majority opposed to the new legislation and reports of greater sympathy for trade unions (Bramble 2005). Second, the Howard government reacted defensively to the campaign, using their own television advertisements for example to quell community concerns, suggesting that the ACTU-led action and increased community awareness struck a chord with the government (Bramble 2005). Third, the mass community mobilisations witnessed in response to the legislation were the largest recorded in Australian history, reaffirming mass sentiment among the community to mobilise (Bramble 2005). Ultimately, the ACTU campaign resulted in a resounding success from an electoral viewpoint, with the election of a Federal Labor government in 2007.

Despite the tangible benefits to be gained from community unionism, there are several implications for unions. The effective practice of community unionism, much like organising unionism, requires significant changes to the operation and structure of unions (Tattersall 2004). First, engagement with community organisations requires unions to decentralise decision making and power and control (Tattersall 2004). Second, community unionism must be underpinned by common interests in order to be effective (Tattersall 2007). Third, there must be genuine commitment or 'buy in' from the trade union to a strategy of community unionism, including support from leadership and membership ranks (Tattersall 2007). Union members play a key role in eliciting the support of the community (Cockfield & Lazaris 2007). Fourth, community union strategies must be used alongside traditional campaigning tactics: they do not act as a replacement for such methods (Cockfield & Lazaris 2007). Fifth, Cockfield and Lazaris (2007) argue that a clear and coherent communication strategy is vital to community unionism campaigns in shaping and gaining wider support. In light of these implications, community unionism, just like the other two innovative strategies discussed above, does not represent a universal panacea for union decline or union renewal.

Outsourcing trade union membership recruitment

An emerging union strategy, and a contentious issue in the recruitment of members is the adoption of the business tactic of outsourcing; ironically, a process through which many unions have lost members. One argument underpinning this approach to union membership recruitment is the notion that trade unions are not equipped with the skills or resources to undertake effective recruitment campaigns at the grass-roots level. Leading unions utilising such a recruitment strategy are the Australian Education Union (AEU) and the Communications, Electrical and Plumbing Union (CEPU). The organisation they have engaged to help recruit new members is Work Partners. The founder of Work Partners, Stuart McGill, describes the organisation (employing 90 staff) as a professional service and marketing provider (Hannan 2010).

The focus of Work Partners is to sell the benefits of trade union membership to potential members. For the AEU, they have focused on a general approach to recruitment. Under the schools recruitment scheme, school principals are approached to provide permission for Work Partners recruiters to speak one-on-one with non-unionists. The CEPU, however, have asked Work Partners to focus recruitment on specific organisations: Telstra and Australia Post (Hannan 2010). The Victorian secretary of the AEU – Brian Henderson – acknowledges that the fee paid to Work Partners is $500, which roughly equates to one year's union subscription.

Criticism of the strategy has come from both inside and outside the union movement. Paul Howes, the national secretary of the Australian Workers Union (AWU), argues that the strategy constitutes outsourcing of a core activity of the union movement (Hannan 2010). However, Ed Husic, National President of the CEPU, argues that this model complements day-to-day union activities in the workplace, freeing up the time of union officials (Hannan, 2010). Karen Batt, Victorian Secretary of the Community and Public Sector Union (CPSU), suggested that the use of Work Partners was part of a wider strategy to membership recruitment. She also pointed out that, like any organisation, trade unions use a variety of external professional services such as legal and communications organisations (Hannan 2010). External criticism of the strategy has come from industrial relations consultants, like Grace Collier, who argues that these high pressure sales strategies intimidate workers into joining the union (Palmer 2010). This approach is linked to the concept of 'chugging', or charity mugging, which has been successful for the charity sector where groups of charity workers aggressively target people at train stations and in other high density locations. McGill, however, argues that the results his organisation is obtaining are more to do with the representation gap than high pressure sales strategies (Palmer 2010). Evidence of the success of the model will take time to analyse, but initial figures from the AEU show an increase in membership of 20 per cent, to 35,000 members since the introduction of an outsourcing strategy (Hannan 2010), which equates to 250 new members per week (Palmer 2010).

Future issues

The future of Australian unions is uncertain yet interesting. Whatever the future holds for Australian unions, they will continue to face challenges and threats – both external to the workplace and internally. In this light, one thing remains certain: Australian unions, as they have continually demonstrated over time, will continue to represent a proportion of the Australian workforce through adaptation to change and the exercise of strategic choices. The innovative strategies being pursued by some Australian unions will continue to evolve and develop, alongside the broad organising and fair working principles encouraged and promoted by the ACTU. Diffusion of innovative strategies among a larger group of federally-registered unions will also shape future success. Whether Australian unions will be able to rebuild their power and influence in the workplace – and in society more generally – remains to be seen. Their efforts and successes will continue to be influenced by organisational and workforce restructuring, global competition and the increasing deregulation of labour markets in pursuit of improved business productivity and flexibility. Union strategies in the new workplace will also be shaped by future government strategies and the way in which the industrial relations system – particularly the legal environment – continues to evolve and develop.

Conclusions

The power and influence of trade unions in Australia declined dramatically during the 20th century. This decline has continued into the 21st century, with trade unions currently representing less than 20% of the Australian workforce. Alongside the decline in union membership and density, fundamental economic, social and political changes have occurred, reshaping the nature of Australian workplaces. Internal and external changes have prompted a rethinking of union strategy, leading to the adoption of new techniques in the management of the employment relationship and the representation of members. Union revitalisation or renewal, as it has been termed, has become a central objective of the Australian union movement, particularly under conditions of political and legislative hostility.

This chapter has outlined important internal and external changes that have contributed to the decline in trade unionism in Australia, and has considered the ways in which unions have responded over the past two decades. It has also considered examples of contemporary strategic responses among Australian unions. Four strategies are notable: the development of corporate campaigning, creative compliance strategies, community unionism and the outsourcing of union recruitment. Whilst Australian trade unions appear to be at a critical juncture, research evidence suggests that they have shown an ability to adapt to internal and external change, and in this respect will continue to play a role in representing the interests of employees. Whether unions will reclaim the historic levels of power and influence that they once enjoyed in Australia remains to be seen, but will be shaped by, on the one hand, an increasingly globalised marketplace driven by short termism and shareholder needs, and, on the other hand, a more favourable legislative environment. It is without doubt, however, that the ability of unions to renew themselves internally in the workplace – and in society – will be critical determinants of their success in addressing ongoing challenges in the 21st century and in attracting workers who have historically not joined unions. As Pocock (1998) cautioned, the capacity of unions to engage in self-transformation is an essential yet far from sufficient condition for regeneration.

References

Allaby, M 1983, *Macmillan Dictionary of the Environment*, 2nd edn, Macmillan, London.

ALP 2005, *Labor Welcomes ACTU Agreement With James Hardie*, viewed 1 June 2005, <http://www.alp.org.au/media/1204/mscgr210.php>.

Australian Bureau of Statistics 2010, *Employee Earnings, Benefits & Trade Union Membership Australia*, cat. no. 6310.0, Australian Government Publishing Service, Canberra.

Australian Bureau of Statistics 2005, *Employee Earnings, Benefits & Trade Union Membership Australia*, cat. no. 6310.0, Australian Government Publishing Service, Canberra.

Australian Bureau of Statistics 2004, *Employee Earnings, Benefits & Trade Union Membership Australia*, cat. no. 6310.0, Australian Government Publishing Service, Canberra.

Australian Bureau of Statistics 2003, *Employee Earnings, Benefits & Trade Union Membership Australia*, cat. no. 6310.0, Australian Government Publishing Service, Canberra.

Australian Bureau of Statistics 2002, *Employee Earnings, Benefits & Trade Union Membership Australia*, cat. no. 6310.0, Australian Government Publishing Service, Canberra.

Australian Bureau of Statistics 2001, *Employee Earnings, Benefits & Trade Union Membership Australia*, cat. no. 6310.0, Australian Government Publishing Service, Canberra.

Australian Bureau of Statistics 2000, *Employee Earnings, Benefits & Trade Union Membership Australia*, cat. no. 6310.0, Australian Government Publishing Service, Canberra.

Australian Bureau of Statistics 1999, *Employee Earnings, Benefits & Trade Union Membership Australia*, cat. no. 6310.0, Australian Government Publishing Service, Canberra.

Australian Bureau of Statistics 1998, *Weekly Earnings of Employees (Distribution) Australia*, cat. no. 6310.0, Australian Government Publishing Service, Canberra.

Australian Bureau of Statistics 1997, *Weekly Earnings of Employees (Distribution) Australia*, cat. no. 6310.0, Australian Government Publishing Service, Canberra.

Australian Bureau of Statistics 1993, *Weekly Earnings of Employees (Distribution) Australia*, cat. no. 6310.0, Australian Government Publishing Service, Canberra.

Australian Council of Trade Unions (ACTU) 2009, 'ACTU Congress 2009 Resolution: Australian Unions – Working for a Better Life',
<http://www.actu.org.au/Images/Dynamic/attachments/6577/d12b_2009_mr_ACTU%20Congress%202009%20-%20final%20policies%20+%20resolutions%20-%20REVISED%2025%20Nov%202009%20Executive%20_retirement%20policy%20clause%2013_.pdf >.

Australian Council of Trade Unions (ACTU) 1999, 'Unions@Work: The Challenge for Unions in Creating a Just and Fair Society', report of the ACTU overseas delegation, August, ACTU, Melbourne.
<http://www.actu.asn.au/Archive/Papers/unionswork.aspx>.

Australian Council of Trade Unions (ACTU) 2003, 'Future Strategies', ACTU Triennial Conference, August, ACTU, Melbourne.
<http://www.actu.asn.au/Archive/Congress2003/FinalPolicies/FinalCongressPolicies.aspx>.

Australian Council of Trade Unions (ACTU) 2005a, *James Hardie a Lemon in Orange County*, viewed 22 November 2005, <http://www.actu.asn.au/cgi-bin/printpage/printpage.pl>.

Australian Council of Trade Unions (ACTU) 2005b, *Unions & Asbestos Groups Secure James Hardie Compo Agreement*, viewed 22 November 2005, <http://www.actu.asn.au/cgi-bin/printpage/printpage.pl>.

Australian Council of Trade Unions (ACTU) 2005c, *Your Rights at Work*, <http://www.rightsatwork.com.au/>.

Bachelard, M 2001, 'Steel Fist, Velvet Glove', *The Weekend Australian*, Inquirer, 19-20 May, p. 23.

Baden, S 2005, 'Long-awaited Hardies deal signed, but victory rests on tax', *The Epoch Times*, viewed 1 December 2005, <http://en.epochtimes.com/news/5-12-1/35227.html>.

Bain, G & Elsheikh, F 1976, *Union Growth and the Business Cycle: An Econometric Analysis*, Basil Blackwell, Oxford.

Baird, M 2002, 'Changes, Dangers, Choice and Voice: Understanding What High Commitment Management Means for Employees and Unions', *Journal of Industrial Relations*, 44(3): 359-375.

Bearfield, S 2003, 'Australian Employees' Attitudes to Unions', Working Paper no. 82, ACIRRT, University of Sydney.

Boxall, P & Haynes, P 1997, 'Strategy and Trade Union Effectiveness in a Neo-Liberal Environment', *British Journal of Industrial Relations* 35(4), December: 567-591.

Bramble, T 2005, 'Resisting Howard's Industrial Relations 'Reforms': An Assessment of ACTU Strategy', *Journal of Australian Political Economy*, 56, December, 254-267.

Brigden, C 2010 'Unions and Collective Bargaining in 2009', *Journal of Industrial Relations*, 52(3): 321-334.

Bronfenbrenner, K 1997, 'The Role of Union Strategies in NLRB Certification Elections', *Industrial and Labor Relations Review* 50(2): 195-212.

Bronfenbrenner, K, Friedman, S, Hurd, RW, Oswald, RA & Seeber, RL 1998 (eds.), *Organising to Win: New Research on Union Strategies*, ILR Press, Ithaca, New York.

Bronfenbrenner, K & Juravich, T 1998, *It takes more than a house call: Organising in the Public Sector: An Analysis of State Elections*, ILR Press, Ithaca, New York.

Brown, EL & Chang, T 2004, 'PACE International Union vs Imerys Gruope: An Organizing Campaign Case Study', *Labor Studies Journal*, 29(1): 21-41.

Burchielli, R. & Bartram, T 2009 'What Helps Organizing Work? The Indicators and Facilitators of Organizing', *Journal of Industrial Relations*, 51(5): 687-707.

Burgmann, V 2003, *Power, Profits and Protest: Australian Social movements and Globalisation*, Allen & Unwin, Crows Nest, NSW.

Burgmann, M & Burgmann, V 1998, *Green Bans, Red Union. Environmental activism and the New South Wales Builders Labourers' Federation*, UNSW Press, NSW.

Carr, B, Combet, G & Banton, B 2004, *Jackson report on James Hardie asbestos*, press conference, 21 September, Premier Bob Carr and representatives on release of Jackson report – James Hardie.doc.

Carter, B, & Cooper, R 2002, 'The Organizing Model and the Management of Change: A Comparative Study of Unions in Australia and Britain', *Relations Industrielles*, 57(4), Fall: 712-743.

CFMEU 2004b, *Thousands protest outside James Hardie meeting*, viewed 1 June 2005, <http://www.cfmeu.asn.au/construction/press/nsw/20040915_hardies2.html>.

Cockfield, S & Lazaris, M 2007, 'Building Community Support for Union Campaigns', in D Buttigieg, S Cockfield, R Cooney, M Jerrard & A Rainnie (eds.) *Trade Unions in the Community: Values, Shared Interests and Alliances*, Heidelberg Press, Melbourne, 201-214.

Cooper, R 2010, "The 'New' Industrial Relations and International Economic Crisis: Australia in 2009", *Journal of Industrial Relations*, 52(3): 261-274.

Cooper, R 2005, 'Life in the Old Dog Yet? 'Deregulation' and Trade Unionism in Australia', in J Isaac & R Lansbury (eds.) Labour Market Deregulation: Rewriting the Rules, The Federation Press, Sydney, 93-106.

Cooper, R, Ellem, B, Briggs, C & Van den Broek, D 2009, 'Anti-unionism, Employer Strategy and the Australian State 1996-2005', *Labor Studies Journal*, 34(3): 339-362.

Cooper, R, Westcott, M & Lansbury, R 2003, 'Labor Revitalization? The Case of Australia', *Labor Revitalization: Global Perspectives and New Initiatives*, 11: 183-205.

Costa, M & Duffy, M 1991, *Labour Prosperity in the Nineties: Beyond the Bonsai Economy*, Federation Press, Leichhardt, NSW.

Crapo, C 1997, 'The Impact of Changing Corporate Strategies on Communities, Unions, and Workers in the United States of America', *Journal of Law & Society*, 24(1): 10-25.

Creighton, W B & Stewart, A 2000, *Labour Law: An Introduction*, The Federation Press, Sydney.

Dabscheck, B 1995, *The Struggle for Australian Industrial Relations*, Oxford University Press, Melbourne.

Drago, R & Wooden, M 1998, *The Changing Role of Trade Unions in Australian Workplace Industrial Relations*, Australian IR Discussion Paper Series no. 3, National Institute for Labour Studies, Flinders University, Adelaide.

Ellem, B 2001, 'Trade Unionism in 2000', *The Journal of Industrial Relations*, 43(2): 196-218.

Ellem, B 2003, 'New Unionism in the Old Economy: Community and Collectivism in the Pilbara's Mining Towns', *The Journal of Industrial Relations*, 45(4): 423-441.

Erickson, CL, Fisk, CL, Milkman, R, Mitchell, DJB & Wong, K 2002, 'Justice for Janitors in Los Angeles: Lessons from Three Rounds of Negotiations', *British Journal of Industrial Relations*, 40(3), September, 543-567.

Fairbrother, S, Svensen, S & Teicher, J 1997, 'The Ascendancy of Neo-Liberalism in Australia', *Capital & Class*, 63: 1-12.

Fiorito, J, Jarley, P & Delaney, J 1995, 'National Union Effectiveness in Organizing: Measurements and Influences', *Industrial Relations Review*, 48:613-635.

Forsyth, A 2009, '"Exit Stage Left", now "Centre Stage": Collective Bargaining Under Work Choices and Fair Work', in A. Forsyth and A. Stewart (eds.) *Fair Work: The New Workplace Laws and the Work Choices Legacy*, Federation Press, Sydney: pp. 120-140.

Forsyth, A & Sutherland, C 2006 "From 'Uncharted Seas' to the 'Stormy Waters': How Will Trade Unions Fare under the Work Choices Legislation?", *The Economic and Labour Relations Review*, 16(2): 215-236.

Freeman, RE 1984, *Strategic Management: A Stakeholder Approach*, Pitman, Boston, MA.

Freeman, R & Pelletier, J 1990, 'The Impact of Industrial Relations Legislation on British Union Density', *British Journal of Industrial Relations*, 28(2): 141-164.

Gangemi, CR & Torres, JJ 1996, 'The Corporate Campaign at Caterpillar', *Journal of Labor Research*, XVII(3), Summer: 377-394.

Gillard, J 2009a *Request Under Section 576C(1), Award Modernisation, Original Request*, AIRC, Original Request, AIRC Melbourne, 2 April.
<http://www.airc.gov.au/awardmod.request.httm>

Gillard, J 2009b *Modern Awards Delivered*, Minister for Education, Minister for Employment and Workplace Relations, Minister for Social Inclusion, Deputy Prime Minister, Minister's Media Centre, Media Release, 4 December
<http://www.deewr.gov.au/ministers/gillard/media/releases/pages/article_091204_170009.aspx>

Gillard, J 2009c Address to ACTU Congress, Minister for Education, Minister for Employment and Workplace Relations, Minister for Social Inclusion, Deputy Prime Minister, Minister's Media Centre, 3 June
<http://www.deewr.gov.au/Ministers/Gillard/Media/Speeches/Pages/Article_090603_131653.aspx>

Grabelsky, J & Hurd, R 1994, 'Reinventing an Organizing Union: Strategies for Change', *Proceedings of the 46th Annual Meeting of the Industrial Relations Research Association*, Boston.

Greven, T & Russo, J 2003, 'Transnational Corporate Campaigns: A Tool for Labour Unions in the Global Economy?', *13th International Industrial Relations Association (IIRA) World Congress*, Berlin, September 8-12.

Griffin, G & Scarcebrook, V 1990, 'The Dependency Theory of Trade Unionism and the Tole of the Industrial Registrar', *Australian Bulletin of Labour*, 16(1): 21-31.

Griffin, G & Svensen, S 1996, 'The Decline of Australian Union Density – A Survey of the Literature', *Journal of Industrial Relations*, 38(4), December: 505-547.

Griffin, G & Moors, R 2004, 'The Fall and Rise of Organising in a Blue-Collar Union', *Journal of Industrial Relations*, 28(2): 141-164.

Griffin, G 2006, 'Employees and Unions', in J Teicher, P Holland & R Gough (eds.), *Employee Relations Management: Australia in a Global Context*, Pearson Education, Australia, pp. 117-137.

Hannan, E 2009 'Union Membership Boost under Kevin Rudd', The Australian (September 14).

Hannan, E 2010 'Unions Employ Ultimate in Outsourcing'. The Australian (March 10).

Hardy, T & Howe, J 2000 'Partners in Enforcement?: The New Balance Between Government and Trade Union Enforcement of Employment Standards in Australia', *Australian Journal of Labour Law*, 22(3): 306-336.

Heery, E, Simms, M, Simpson, D, Delbridge, R & Salmon, J 2000, 'Organizing Unionism comes to the UK', *Employee Relations*, 22(1): 38-57.

Herrod, A 2001, 'Labor internationalism and the Contradiction of Globalisation', *Antipode*, 33(3): 407-426.

Holland, P 1999, 'Organising Works: Meeting the Challenge of Declining Trade Union Membership', *International Employment Relations Review*, 5(1): 63-74.

Holland, P & Pyman, A 2006, 'The Role and Influence of Corporate Campaigning in Australia: The Case of James Hardie', paper presented at The Organizing Society – The 22nd EGOS Colloquium 2006, Bergen, Norway 2006, July 6-8.

Holland, P, Pyman, A, Cooper, B & Teicher, J 2009, 'The Development of Alternative Voice Mechanisms in Australia: The Case of Joint Consultation', *Economic and Industrial Democracy*, 30(1): 67-92.

Hose, K. & Rimmer, M 2002, 'The Australian Union Merger Wave Revisited', *Journal of Industrial Relations*, 44(4): 525-544.

Howard, W A 1977 'Australian Trade Unions in the Context of Union Theory', *The Journal of Industrial Relations*, 19(3): 255-273.

Isaac, J 2005, 'The Deregulation of the Australian Labour Market', in J Isaac & R Lansbury (eds.), *Labour Market Deregulation: Rewriting the Rules*, The Federation Press, Sydney, 1-14.

Jarley, P & Maranto, CL 1990, 'Union Corporate Campaigns: An Assessment', *Industrial and Labor Relations Review*, 43(5): 505-524.

Juravich, T & Bronfenbrenner, K 1999, *Ravenswood: The Steelworks Victory and the Revival of American Labor,* ILR Press, Ithaca, New York.

Keiser, K 1993, 'Framing the Fight. Media Savvy Bolsters Corporate Campaigning', *Labor Research Review*, 12(2): 71-79.

Kelly, J 1990 'British Trade Unionism 1979-89: Change, Continuity and Contradictions', *Work Employment and Society*, Special Issue, May, 29-65.

Kenyon, P & Lewis, P 1992, 'Trade Union Membership and the Accord', *Australian Economic Papers*, 31: 325-345.

Kenyon, P & Lewis, P 1996, 'The Decline in Trade Union Membership: What Role Did the Accord Play?', Discussion Paper 96/8, Centre for Labour Market Research, Murdoch University, Perth.

Klein, N 2000, *No Logo*, London, Flamingo.

Kochan, T, Katz, H & McKersie, R 1986, *The Transformation of American Industrial Relations*, Basic, New York.

Manheim, J 2001, *The Death of a Thousand Cuts: Corporate Campaigns and the attack on the corporation*, LEA, New Jersey.

McCallum, R 1994, 'Voluntary Trade Unionism in New South Wales: Timely Innovation or Backward Step?', *Australian Journal of Labour Law*, 7: 1-32.

McCallum, R 2005, 'Industrial Citizenship', in J Isaac & R Lansbury (eds.), *Labour Market Deregulation: Rewriting the Rules*, The Federation Press, Sydney, 15-36.

McCrystal, S 2009 'The New Consensus: The Coalition, the ALP and the Regulation of Industrial Action', in A. Forsyth and A. Stewart (eds.) *Fair Work: The New Workplace Laws and the Work Choices Legacy*, Sydney, Federation Press: pp. 141-163.

McCrystal, S 2009-2010 'The Fair Work Act 2009 (Cth) and the Right to Strike', *Australian Journal of Labour Law*, 23: 3-38.

McGuiness, JC 1996, 'Legal and Regulatory Responses to Corporate Campaigns', *Journal of Labor Research*, 17(3): 417-424.

National Nine News 2004, *Thousands rally against James Hardie*, 15 September, viewed 1 June 2005, <http://news.ninemsn.com.au/article.aspx?id=18384>.

Naughton, R 1994, 'The New Bargaining Regime Under the Industrial Relations Reform Act', *Australian Journal of Labour Law*, 7: 147-169.

Palmer, T 2010, 'Outsourcing Union Membership'. ABC TV: 7:30 Report (March 11).

Peetz, D 1997, 'The Shrinking foothold: Changes in union membership within the Australian workplace', paper for the Third International Conference on Emerging Union Structures, Australian National University, Canberra, Australia, 2 December 1997.

Peetz, D 1998, *Unions in a Contrary World: The Future of the Australian Union Movement*, Cambridge University Press, Melbourne, Australia.

Peetz, D 2002, 'Decollectivist Strategies in Oceania', *Relations Industrielles*, 57(2): 252-281.

Perry, CR 1987, *Union Corporate Campaigns*, Industrial Relations Research Unit, The Wharton School, University of Pennsylvania, Philadelphia, Pennsylvania.

Perry, CR 1996, 'Corporate Campaigns in Context', *Journal of Labor Relations*, 27(3): 329-343.

Pocock, B 1998, 'Institutional Sclerosis: Prospects for Trade Union Transformation', *Labour & Industry*, 9(1), August, pp. 17-37.

Pocock, B & Wishart, J 1999, 'Organising Our Future', *Centre for Labour Research*, Adelaide, pp. 1-46.

Prince, P, Davidson, J & Dudley, S 2004, 'In the Shadow of the Corporate Veil: James Hardie and Asbestos Compensation', Parliamentary Library Research note no. 12, Parliamentary Library, Department of Parliamentary Services, Canberra, August 2004.

Pyman, A 2005, 'Creative Compliance in Labour Relations: Turning the Law on its Head', in D Lewin & B Kaufman (eds.), *Advances in Industrial and Labor Relations*, 14: 67-100.

Quinlan, M 1998, 'Industrial Relations Policy Developments 1977-1988: A Critical Review', *Journal of Australian Political Economy*, 42: 75-105.

Savery, L & Soutar, G 1996, 'Community Attitudes to Industrial Relations Issues in Perth, 1974-1993', *International Journal of Employment Studies*, 4: 23-25.

SBS News 2004, *James Hardie signs $4B compo deal*, 22 December, viewed 1 June 2005, <http://www9.sbs.com.au/theworldnews/region.php?id=101644&region=7>.

Sutherland, C & Riley, J 2010, 'Industrial Legislation in 2009', *Journal of Industrial Relations*, 52(3): 275-287.

Robinson, P 2001, 'Fighting Back!', *The Age*, Features, (February 16): p. 13.

Rudd, K & Gillard, J 2007 *Forward with Fairness: Labor's Plan for Fairer and More Productive Australian Workplaces*, April. Canberra: Australian Labor Party.

Tarrant, L 2001, *Organising Unionism - Back to Our Roots*, Australasian Organising Conference, ACTU, Sydney.

Tattersall, A 2004, 'Community Unionism: A Strategy for Union Power Under Neoliberalism', paper presented at the 18th AIRAANZ Conference: 'New Economies: New Industrial Relations', Griffith University, Noosa, QLD, 3-6 February.

Tattersall, A 2005, 'Understanding what makes union-community coalitions effective: A framework for analysing union-community relationships', paper presented at the 19th AIRAANZ Conference: 'Reworking Work', University of Sydney, 9-11 February, 227-234.

Tattersall, A 2006, 'Labor's place in coalition: How and when unions build powerful labor-community coalitions', UALE Conference, Research Paper, Cornell University, US, 1-17.

Tattersall, A 2007, (forthcoming), 'Variations in union-community coalitions: A look at union engagement in NSW', in D Buttigieg, S Cockfield, R Cooney, M Jerrard & A Rainnie (eds.), *Trade Unions in the Community: Values, Shared Interests and Alliances*, Heidelberg Press, Melbourne: 113-126.

Teicher, J & Bryan, R 2006, 'The Australian State and The Global Economy', in J Teicher, P Holland & R Gough (eds.), *Employee Relations Management: Australia In A Global Context*, 2nd edn, Pearson Education Australia, Frenchs Forest.

Teicher, J, Lambert, R & O'Rourke, A 2006, *WorkChoices: The New Industrial Relations Agenda*, Pearson Education, Australia.

Thompson, J K, Wartick, S L & Smith, H L 1991, 'Toward a substantive definition of the corporate issue construct: A review and synthesis of the literature', *Business & Society*, 33: 293-311.

Trinca, H & Davies, A 2000, *Waterfront: The Battle that Changed Australia*, Doubleday, Milsons Point.

Turnbull, P 1996, 'Organising Works in Australia: Can It Work in Britain?', Working Paper no. 97, Department of Management and Industrial Relations, University of Melbourne.

Visser, J 1990, 'In Search of Inclusive Unionism', *Bulletin of Comparative Labour Relations*, 18.

Voss, K & Fantasia, R, 2004, 'The Future of American Labor: Reinventing Unions', *Contexts*, 3(2): 35-41.

Voss, K & Sherman, R 2000, 'Breaking the Iron Law of Oligarchy: Union Revitalization in the American Labor Movement', *The American Journal of Sociology*, 106(2): 303-349.

Western, B 1997, *Between Class and Market: Postwar Unionization in the Capitalist Democracies*, Princeton University Press, Princeton, NJ.

Williams, S & Adam-Smith, D 2006, *Contemporary Employment Relations: A Critical Introduction*, Oxford University Press, Oxford.

Wills, J 2004, 'Organising the Low Paid: East London's Living Wage Campaign as a Vehicle for Change', in G Healy, E Heery, P Taylor & W Brown (eds.), *The Future of Worker Representation*, Palgrave Macmillan, Basingstoke, 264-282.

Case study: James Hardie

The ACTU led a national corporate campaign against James Hardie (JH) in relation to compensation owed to asbestos victims and their families. The campaign was prompted by a corporate restructure by JH which resulted in the transfer of the company headquarters – along with assets worth almost two billion dollars – from Australia to the Netherlands in October 2001. It is important to note that the Netherlands is a country that Australia does not have a legal treaty with. This meant that the victims were unable to pursue or enforce compensation claims in a Netherlands court.

The corporate campaign led by the ACTU centred on ensuring that the actions of JH were unsuccessful and that Australian victims could successfully prosecute claims against the assets of the company responsible for their illness. Greg Combet, the then Secretary of the ACTU, was the lead negotiator representing unions. Asbestos interest groups and the NSW government were also involved in the campaign to ensure JH provided funding for its compensation liabilities to current and future victims. Two other key individuals prominent in the corporate campaign were the then NSW Premier Bob Carr, and the Acting President of the Asbestos Diseases Foundation of Australia, the late Bernie Banton – himself a victim of asbestos-related lung cancer.

Key elements of the campaign

The key elements of the ACTU campaign included: a public boycott of JH products; the building of alliances and support networks with other unions, both nationally and internationally; mobilisation of community and interest group support; shareholder pressure; a targeted media campaign; and, government pressure. Each aspect of the campaign is discussed below.

Public boycott

A public boycott on JH products by Australian building workers, municipal councils, consumers and state governments was a central tactic in the campaign. The commitment of the NSW government to the boycott, particularly as the biggest state government in Australia and a purchaser of approximately 8% of JH products, served as a strong pressure point on the company (Carr, Combet & Banton 2004). The NSW state government also extended the ban to state government contracts when it instructed Multiplex to ban JH products from the refurbishment of the NSW Trades Hall Council. This ban was taken up by the NSW Labor Council in addition to receiving endorsement from 20 local government authorities. The federal Labor opposition (at the time) also supported the boycott and pledged public commitment for a further boycott of JH products in all commonwealth construction and public works, if elected, in the event that JH continued to refuse to negotiate and pay victims due compensation. Construction unions in Victoria also supported the ban on JH materials (Prince, Davidson & Dudley 2004).

Building alliances & support networks

The ACTU built support for the campaign with other unions, the NSW Labor Council and the Victorian Trades Hall Council (VTHC). Government support for the ACTU campaign was critical – both from state and territory governments and from other state premiers. Alliances were also built with unions in the 'trades' industry. International support from unions in the US – particularly the International Metalworkers Federation (IMF) – was also a defining feature of the campaign and critical to its success, given that more than 80% of JH's earnings are derived from the sale of building products to the US market. US unions and community groups held a protest rally in September 2004 in support of Australian asbestos victims outside JH's Californian headquarters.

Mobilisation of community support & pressure: public rallies

A hallmark of the campaign against JH was a national day of action by Australian unions and asbestos groups on 15 September 2004, designed to coincide with the JH shareholders information meeting in Sydney. Approximately 5,000 people – including victims and their families – attended a rally in Sydney, while as many as 20,000 workers rallied across the country in Brisbane, Melbourne, Adelaide and Hobart in support of sufferers, calling on JH to meet all future compensation claims (National Nine News 2004). In solidarity, all building sites across the central business district in Sydney were closed down, with Construction Forestry Mining and Energy Union (CFMEU) members joining the rally to demand fair compensation for victims. Mobilisation of community support for the campaign was sustained with more traditional campaign tactics including the production and distribution of campaign stickers, leaflets and posters.

Shareholder pressure

As part of the national day of action, the ACTU led attendance at the JH Australian Shareholders Information Meeting at Sydney's Darling Harbour Convention Centre on 15 September 2004, calling on the Board of Directors to meet all compensation payouts to victims. The then Secretary of the ACTU, Greg Combet, plus CFMEU National Assistant Secretary Lindsay Fraser, the then CFMEU NSW Secretary

Andrew Ferguson and the then Australian Manufacturing Workers Union (AMWU) NSW Secretary Paul Bastion, attended the shareholders meeting with asbestos victims and their supporters (ACTU 2005a, CFMEU 2004).

Australian unionists and asbestos groups also attended the Annual General Meeting in the Netherlands on 17 September 2004 (ACTU 2005a). At this meeting, JH declined to present its annual accounts. This decision followed a campaign by unions and asbestos groups who wrote to fund managers and shareholders asking them to vote against the adoption of the accounts because they made no provision for future asbestos liabilities (ACTU 2005a).

A targeted media campaign

The targeted media campaign led by the ACTU, asbestos groups and the NSW government was multidimensional but had a central objective: to attack the reputation of JH to cause utmost disruption and damage. One of the most visible aspects of the media campaign was a public commitment by the ACTU on behalf of all the parties concerned to pursue JH and the moral rights of victims at all costs. That is, to ensure that JH unconditionally committed to compensating all the victims of JH's asbestos products (Carr *et al.* 2004).

Using the campaign as a platform for health and safety awareness and, in particular, developing national public awareness of the dangers of asbestos was a second visible element of the media strategy. The success of the ACTU on this dimension can be seen in entries in individual web logs (blogs) at the time of the campaign calling for community mobilisation and action to support victims' legal rights to compensation payouts. The use of public pressure to attack JH's image and to question their morality and ethics was also a defining feature of the media campaign. Greg Combet continually made public comments throughout the campaign using emotive language to attack JH's morality and ethics. The reputations of the CEO and Chief Financial Officer were also attacked publicly as they were seen as bearing principal responsibility for JH's actions. To reinforce these actions, the ACTU publicly refused to negotiate with these two individuals.

Government pressure

Government and political pressure was maintained throughout the duration of the campaign, and was also critical to its success. Several aspects of government pressure can be illustrated. First, the ACTU repeatedly called on the federal government to formalise a treaty between Australia and the Netherlands – and between Australia and the USA – to permit recovery of all assets from JH. These calls were supported by state governments and the federal labor opposition at the time. Second, political pressure on JH was particularly strong from the NSW state Labor government. The steadfast position of this government that JH had to negotiate with the ACTU and receive their approval, the approval of the Labor Council and the approval of victims added to the political pressure on JH.

The federal Labor opposition also exerted political pressure. The JH case featured as a key issue in the federal election campaign of 2004, with the opposition pledging public support for victims, asbestos groups and the ACTU. The then leader of the federal Labor opposition, Mark Latham, placed additional pressure on JH by supporting the public boycott of JH products and returning all political donations received from JH to asbestos victims (ALP 2005). This latter tactic reinforced the opposition's public stance on the campaign.

Toward a resolution

In September 2004, JH made a public commitment to negotiate with the ACTU regarding their moral obligation to provide ongoing financial compensation to asbestos victims and their families. On 21 December 2004, a landmark $1.5 million dollar Heads of Agreement was concluded between the ACTU, Unions NSW, asbestos groups and JH identifying how the compensation arrangements would operate (ACTU 2005b). This agreement was believed to be the largest personal injury settlement in Australian history, worth over $4 billion dollars over a 40 year period (Baden 2005, SBS 2004).

The Heads of Agreement was designed to provide the basis for a legally-binding 'Principal Agreement' which was to be concluded by June 2005, yet would have to be voted on and accepted by JH shareholders. Upon the deal being made public, JH's share price increased and the announcement was welcomed by unions and the then federal opposition.

Despite the conclusion of the Heads of Agreement in December 2004 and a commitment to finalise the legally binding arrangements by June 2005, negotiations took a further 12 months to complete, prompting threats of a second campaign. Combet threatened renewed union, community and government action, making a public commitment to urge the NSW government to introduce legislation compelling JH to pay should the company not finalise the deal. A resolution came shortly afterwards with JH agreeing to fund all compensation payouts for victims both now and in the future.

Written by: Holland & Pyman.

Case study questions

1. Why did the ACTU pursue a corporate campaign against James Hardie?
2. Analyse the key characteristics of the campaign. Do you believe the campaign was a success? Justify your answer with reference to theory.

Discussion questions

1. What are the four major causes of union decline identified in the literature?
2. What other external changes in Australia need to be considered alongside declining union density? Include a brief discussion of these factors in your answer.
3. What have been the primary strategic responses of Australian unions to the decline in union density since the 1980s?
4. How effective has the take-up of the organising model been by Australian unions? Justify your answer.
5. Define corporate campaigning. Why have unions adopted this strategy in Australia?

Chapter 11

THE CONTESTED TERRAIN OF MONITORING AND SURVEILLANCE IN THE WORKPLACE

INTRODUCTION

Whilst the concept of monitoring and surveillance has been part of the workplace for centuries, the advancements in information technology – combined with diminished costs – have created a significant shift in the type, availability and intensity of monitoring and surveillance at the start of the 21st century. Issues such as drug testing, for example, were once seen as applicable for critical incident professions (such as pilots) and were associated with large organisations that had the resources to undertake such operations. However, drug-testing is now within the realms of most organisations. In addition, the movement of work into cyber-space has created a further dimension in monitoring employees' time usage and website visits. Even issue such as genetic testing of employees and tagging through radio frequency identity devices (RFID) and global positioning systems or GPS are now within the reach of most organisations. The nature of the issues and debates traverse a range of theoretical perspectives including human resource management, employee relations, labour process theory and ethics, and provide new challenges to the employment relationship. As a result, organisations need to make decisions on the extent of monitoring and surveillance and on the cost-benefits – both tangible and intangible. This chapter explores two major areas of debate within monitoring and surveillance – drug testing and electronic or ecommunication (email and internet usage). The chapter also identifies some of the emerging aspects and trends in workplace monitoring and surveillance including genetic testing and tagging. As these issues permeate the workplace, there are increasing challenges to privacy and trust – the bedrock of good human resource management (HRM) and employment relations. The issues and the debates that surround the implementation of these processes, therefore, need to be more fully understood.

Drug-testing in the workplace

Alcohol and illicit substance abuse in the workplace are increasingly becoming a major human resource and employee relations issue. Whilst more sophisticated measures have been developed to test and monitor drug use in the workplace, and despite tacit trade union support on the grounds of occupational health and safety (OH&S), the implementation of drug testing procedures remains a contentious issue. This section examines the arguments for and against drug testing in the workplace.

The issue of substance abuse at work

Substance abuse and the potential dangers it poses in the workplace are well documented. For example, Wall (1992) identifies that both illicit substance abuse and 'recreational' substance use, (alcohol), impact negatively upon almost all industries in Australia causing substantial costs in both human and economic terms. Whilst acknowledging the lack of accurate data concerning drug use in the workplace, the National Health and Medical Research Council (NH&MRC) (1997) found that 22 per cent of the working population drank alcohol at harmful levels and that up to 27 per cent of the working population experienced alcohol-related problems annually (Allsop, Phillips & Calogero 2001; Allsop & Pidd 2001). Wilke (1998) estimated that substance abuse in Australia accounts for 10 per cent of work-place deaths and 25 per cent of workplace accidents.

From an alternative viewpoint of human costs, Richmond, Heather, Holt and Hu (1992) argue that illicit drug use is responsible for harm because it stems from negligence in the workplace. This is an important issue because OH&S legislation in each Australian state ensures there is an obligation upon employers to provide a safe workplace for all employees and visitors to their sites. Employers are subject to strict liability under this law and face significant fines if found to be in breach. Employer liability extends to their employees' actions and/or omissions regardless of their state of mind, highlighting a need for drug testing in the workplace.

Drug testing is commonplace in the US. Research indicates that the use of drug testing programs in both employment and pre-employment testing has been a major factor in the reduction of absenteeism and accidents, and is the most popular method of removing the issue of substance abuse in the workplace (Flynn 1999; Hartwell, Steele, French & Rodman 1996). These points provide a compelling case for drug testing in the workplace, first, to ensure that the employee is meeting his/her contractual obligations to a satisfactory standard and, second, to meet the employer's requirements of duty of care under OH&S legislation (DesJardine & McCall 1990). Implicit in these points is the potential that employers who do not have drug testing policies and programs are maintaining an unsafe workplace (Redeker &

Segal 1989). However, the cost-effectiveness and overall value of drug testing is questionable (Gip 1999:16):

> *The American Civil Liberties Union cites analysis by a committee of the National Academy of Sciences (NAS) which found that most workers who use illicit drugs never use them at work, and when they use drugs on their own time, they do so in a way that does not affect work performance.*

Moving away from the issues of human and economic costs, within the scope of a contract of employment, performance is an important and related consideration in the drug testing debate. As DesJardine and McCall (1990:203) point out: To what level of performance are employers entitled? If an employee's productivity is satisfactory and he/she is meeting contractual obligations, the knowledge of drug use on grounds of productivity is not pertinent. Secondly, whilst the issue of duty of care is important, not every job has the potential to do harm. DesJardine and McCall (1990:204) argue that by saying employers can use drug testing to prevent harm is not to say that every employer has the right to know about the drug use of every employee. In this context therefore, less intrusive testing alternatives such as impairment testing to determine fitness for work are likely to be more effective and are less likely to raise privacy and fairness concerns. These are important considerations for employees and their unions when drug testing is implemented in the workplace.

From an employee perspective, the principal consideration is the right to privacy. Using Mills' principle of liberty, Bowie and Duska (1990:89) argue that employees have the right to do whatever they wish as long as it does not harm the employer. In this context, if a person chooses to partake of illicit drugs outside of their work commitments, it is of no concern to the employer so long as it does not impinge on work performance (Bowie & Duska 1990). In addition, drug testing can suffer from accuracy problems. Typically, drug tests cannot determine whether the effects of illicit drugs, which may remain in the system for days and even weeks, will substantially impair or affect performance. Webb and Festa (1994) also note that the link between drug usage and on-the-job injuries is tenuous at best. Drug testing may also uncover other medical conditions or the use of over-the-counter or prescribed drugs by employees (such as Viagra or metabolites of morphine), which have the potential to affect the employment status of workers. As Wasserstrom (1978) argues, employees have a right to 'informational privacy'. This is supported by DesJardine and McCall (1990:202) who state:

> *...an employee's right to privacy is violated whenever personal information is requested, collected or used by an employer in a way or for a purpose that is irrelevant to or in violation of the contractual relationship that exists between employees and employers.*

Thus, the argument that the innocent have nothing to fear from drug testing is erroneous, because it may violate employee rights – particularly if testing has the potential to provide the employer with generic medical information which is not relevant to the contractual relationship (Cranford 2001). In addition, mandatory testing may be open to improper or malicious use of procedures to intimidate or target employees who undertake activities that may be unpopular with management such as union activism (Webb & Fester 1994). Therefore, the use of drug testing within the workplace may create an atmosphere of insecurity, oppression and anxiety in employees, and may actually result in lower performance and higher turnover (Redeker & Segal 1989). Indeed, Bohle and Quinlan (2000) have noted that this has been an important consideration for Australian managers of US-based organisations that have pursed the introduction of drug testing procedures. Zwerling, Ryan and Oraw (1990:2643) argue that, due to methodological problems, many assertions justifying pre-employment drug screening have been exaggerated. In addition, Bahls (1998:82) notes that the internet is filled with tips on how illicit drug users can evade drug tests and detection.

Within the larger context of the employment relationship, work culture and the social environment have also been identified as critical and complex factors in the drug testing debate. For example, a culture of drug use – both legal and illicit drugs – in geographically isolated locations has been linked to the notions of culture and environment and the physical location of work. As Allsop and Pidd (2001:5) note:

> *In a variety of cultures, formal and informal pressures still encourage weekly after-work team building and relaxation based on alcohol consumption. Sanctioned drugs such as caffeine and tobacco have been embraced in ritualised breaks in worktime.*

Indeed, a study of alcohol consumption in the Pilbara mining region of Western Australia (WA) found that consumption of alcohol was 64 per cent above the state level (Daly & Philp 1995). A subsequent study by Midford, Marsden, Phillips and Lake (1997) of workforce alcohol consumption in mining related worksites found that alcohol consumption was greater than the national average. Drinking in the top risk category was on a par with the national average, and binge drinking was more prevalent and was related to shift work and isolation from family.

Aside from the explicit focus on the mining industry, a burgeoning body of research has focused upon the link between the nature of work in general and associated drug use. Issues of control, alienation and stress – linked with individuals' perceptions of their powerlessness – have been identified as factors related to drug use in the workplace (Ames & Grube 1999; Greenburg & Greenburg 1995; Seeman & Seeman 1992; Tices & Sonnenstuhl 1990). As Midford (2001:46) argues:

Chapter 11 – The Contested Terrain of Monitoring and Surveillance in the Workplace

In the workplace, holding the view that drug use is a problem for the individual worker is functional from the point of view of the employers, because it avoids any exploration of how the workplace may contribute to the problem. However, to gain an understanding of workplace drug problems, one must look at a full range of factors that influence patterns of drug use.

The union view

The Australian Council of Trade Unions (ACTU) does not support the introduction of any form of biological testing of workers for alcohol or other drugs in the workplace, except in very limited circumstances and subject to joint union and employer agreement (Mansfield 2001). They argue that the introduction of testing cannot be seen as a quick fix solution and is unacceptable and inappropriate in most circumstances. The ACTU does not consider that the introduction of a testing program is an effective strategy for the workplace. Testing for alcohol and other drugs is usually an inappropriate feature of any prevention program for a number of reasons, including: the inaccuracy of test results, both positive and negative; the fact that drug testing measures exposure not impairment, particularly in the case of illicit drugs; the problems and errors with interpretation of test results; the impact of prescribed medication and over-the-counter drugs on tests; the focus on the individual; the infringement of individual rights; the problems associated with the right to privacy; and the disruption to industrial relations (Mansfield 2001). The ACTU position is that there must be joint development of any drug testing policy by unions and employers, particularly where the misuse of alcohol or illicit drugs are identified as workplace issues. Indeed, any policies dealing with workplace hazards and OH&S should be jointly developed and implemented. The ACTU policy framework on the subject focuses on: safety at work; full participation and joint control by workers and their representatives; applicability to both workers and management; addressing the causes of alcohol or illicit drug misuse in the workplace; a consultative, educative and rehabilitative approach rather than a punitive approach; and the maintenance of confidentiality at all levels (Mansfield 2001).

This pluralist stance adopted by the ACTU is based upon the argument that it is only when drugs and alcohol are misused to the extent that the user cannot properly and safely carry out regular duties that a need for control and prevention measures arise. In any consideration of an appropriate response in particular workplaces, there must first be involvement of union representatives as well as second an examination of the broad environmental factors pertaining to the individual workplace or industry. The ACTU also argues that rehabilitation action should be undertaken during working hours or through schemes that include paid leave. A key issue the ACTU promotes is that the misuse of alcohol and other drugs may be symptomatic of other problems which are in the control of the employer.

For example, the ACTU list the following as key issues in the use and misuse of alcohol and other drugs:

- shift work;
- long hours of work;
- hazardous work;
- boring, monotonous and repetitive work;
- poor work environment;
- unrealistic deadlines;
- job insecurity;
- lack of participation and/or control;
- inadequate training and/or supervision; and
- stress.

Source ACTU 2006.

This perspective is supported by the work of Hagen, Egan and Eltringham (1992) who found a link between higher alcohol consumption and work pressure, stress, lack of control and over-work. Philips (2001:39), in summarising the work of Roman, Johnson and Blum (2000) on the relationship between stress at work and increased alcohol consumption, states:

> *Much of this increase [in stress] has been stimulated by changes in work organisation that have occurred in the second half of the twentieth century. Among the changes: jobs have become more complex; responsibility has been devolved to less senior personnel; employer organisations have become larger and more global; manual labour has been mechanised; machines have become more 'intelligent'; and continuous production schedules have disrupted daily life patterns and resulted in more people working for extended periods.*

Indeed, the fatigue generated by these factors combined with increased deregulation of the labour market in Australia raises major issues regarding OH&S in the workplace (ACIRRT 1999). As Nolan (2000:2) points out:

> *Employees and unions have questioned why random drug testing has assumed such priority in an industrial climate where increasing demands have been placed upon workers to work twelve-hour shifts. Evidence suggests that it is fatigue and not impairment through drugs and alcohol abuse that leads to the majority of accidents.*

If management is truly interested in these issues, the ACTU argues that a more holistic approach should be adopted, for example, to include fatigue monitoring and management systems (Mansfield 2001). This broadens the drug testing debate and raises the critical issue of fitness for duty.

Holistic approaches and fitness for duty

The issue of fitness for duty often raises a more subtle and complex issue – control in the workplace. Unions often see the introduction of measures such as drug testing as management exercising increased control under the guise of 'managerial prerogative', and as a strategy to marginalise the countervailing power of unions, particularly where there is no consultation on the subject. As Webb and Festa (1994:101) note:

> *On a broader scale, the notion of testing programs, especially if introduced unilaterally and without reference to or consultation with employees and their representative bodies, is philosophically at variance with labour relations in Australia.*

However, this perspective has come increasingly under review with the emergence of human resource management, underpinned by a unitarist philosophy. This can potentially see testing becoming a major issue of conflict between management, employees and their unions. The need to strike a balance between the employer's legal obligations and employees' rights is a complex and sensitive issue in the development of drug policies. Similarly, Nolan (2000:63) points out those legal obligations that are too dogmatically defined can easily clash with industrial relations.

It is perhaps the impracticality of a dogmatic approach to drug testing that is leading to the development of a broader concept of fitness for duty. Although this concept is most prevalent in the mining industry where it is embodied in regulations made pursuant to OH&S legislation, it is also appearing in industries such as road and public transport. Traditionally, the concept of fitness for duty meant little more than pre-employment screening of employees to determine their capacity to meet the requirements of the job. More controversially, as explained above, fitness for duty is often manifest in testing regimes designed to detect impaired capacity to perform the duties of a position. Such approaches have often proved controversial due to the process by which regimes are implemented as well as deficiencies in the tests themselves.

The need for a more holistic and pragmatic approach has led to advocacy of a non-discriminatory testing regime for a wide range of physical and psychological factors which may impair performance (Nolan & Nomchong 2001). While the search for appropriate tests remains problematic, the philosophical underpinning of this approach is that the causes of impairment are not confined to circumstances within the employee's control and may be impacted by workplace conditions under the employer's control.

eCommunication in the workplace

In advanced market economies (AMEs), both email and the internet have become standard work tools. The ease of access and its potential use and misuse throws up major issues and challenges to be managed in the workplace. As Paterson (2002:1) notes in discussing workplace ecommunications:

> ..... when coupled with the legal dangers which they pose and the illusion of anonymity that such activities create, it gives rise to some very complex legal and policy issues. Employers face legal as well as financial imperatives to ensure that employees do not make inappropriate use of these facilities and are increasingly resorting to blanket or broad-brush electronic surveillance as a solution. Such an approach may not necessarily be the most effective and may expose them to a number of potential legal pitfalls.

Whist the implications of ecommunication are increasingly being understood by both employees and employers, there still remain both moral, legal and managerial issues that are yet to be fully tested. The following section explores these issues and includes suitable approaches employers can undertake to ensure appropriate use of technology.

The misconception of ecommunication

Many of the issues or problems associated with ecommunication in the workplace stem from misconceptions regarding its privacy and permanency. The first misconception is privacy of email. Because email is sent via the organisation's computer system, an electronic trace is created. This leads to the second misconception about lack of permanency. Whist the sender and receiver may both delete the email, the message can remain on both the sender's and receiver's hard drive and/or server. As Miller and Jentz (2002) note, it is increasingly common for email and other electronic communications to be requested for lawsuits. For this reason edocument retention policies and management are becoming increasingly important processes to develop in organisations. For employees unaware of this situation, these 'smoking guns' – as Miller and Jentz (2002) describe them – potentially can be more candid or defamatory than would be the case in other forms of communication. Several high profile cases have relied on email evidence, from the Monica Lewinsky-Bill Clinton relationship to the US Department of Justice case against Microsoft for uncompetitive behaviour.

Whilst the subject of informational privacy emerges as an issue here – and will be discussed in more detail later – as Nolan (2000) notes, in objective legal terms the computer system is regarded as a piece of office equipment and can therefore be potentially read by the system administrator and/or employer. At a more advanced level, organisations can use software to track and identify potentially problematic communication on the system.

Monitoring software

The use of filtering software to monitor ecommunication in an organisation is an obvious response by employers to protect themselves against potential problems. These software systems allow for a variety of monitoring and surveillance to take place. Examples include the tracking of employees' 'virtual' movements through websites and the time spent on these sites. More advanced software packages can even check email to identify information going out of the organisation. Such software can also target incoming email from 'head hunter' recruiters – which may be re-directed to the HR unit. More proactive software packages have a two-way purpose of both blocking incoming spam and viruses, and preventing or terminating connections to inappropriate websites which may range from pornography to recruitment websites. However, issues associated with security and its level need to be weighed against the ability of employees to do their jobs effectively. For example, whilst it might be appropriate to block access to sites using the word 'breast', would this be correct in the case of a doctor or student researching breast cancer? There is a need to strike a balance between the competing interests of employee's expectations to privacy and the requirements of their job, and the protection of employer's against liability or loss through time wasting or even espionage.

The issue of electronic surveillance at work

Advances in technology have allowed employers to monitor employees' virtual work time in both real time and through the ability to quickly and easily retrieve and archive employees' electronic work patterns (Miller & Weckert 2000; Townsend & Bennett 2003). This has led to increasing interest and debate around electronic surveillance. The first point is, what is the appropriate level of monitoring? Second, what is the suitable amount of personal or private usage – if any – an employee can undertake? Thirdly, to what extent does the employer have the right to encroach into this area? For example, should an employer have the right to read an employee's email, knowing, as Oliver (2002) points out, that this threatens employee privacy and is likely to result in the employer obtaining personal information about the employee, potentially breaching the element of trust in the employment relationship?

As noted, the misuse of electronic technology by employees can increase the risk of damage to an organisation's reputation as well as possible public embarrassment. As Turner (2003) found in an Australian study, almost half of internet use in the workplace is of a personal nature. The argument here is that inappropriate use of email and the internet can cause distraction. The potential for legal liability increases the more employees misuse the electronic equipment at their disposal (Henderson 2003). However, such facilities can also ensure that employees can deal with minor day-to-day issues such as banking online without having to physically leave work, go to the bank and queue (Stanton & Stam 2003). Allowing these types of activities can be seen to enhance productivity in the workplace. In addition, Oliver (2002) points out that preserving employees' autonomy can enhance productivity through ensuring independence of thought and creativity in the workplace. Studies by the International Labour Organisation (ILO) also indicate that monitoring and surveillance can have negative OH&S consequences as they have been linked to stress-related illnesses. However, the issue remains that the inappropriate use or misuse of electronic communication makes the organisation potentially liable. The decision of to what extent or how intrusive the monitoring and surveillance should be may therefore be determined by the underpinning HRM philosophy of the organisation in terms of the extent of trust and commitment that is to exist in the employment relationship.

These intangible issues can help provide a more balanced and considered long-term perspective when considered against the more tangible issue of potential loss of productivity and liability. This more holistic approach can negate potential problems associated with breaches of employees' rights to privacy and trust. The issue of trust in the employment relationship, therefore, needs to be considered as a pivotal factor in an employer justifying the implementation of electronic monitoring. Organisations who demonstrate a willingness to value trust can minimise the potential negative actions of their employees through education and a jointly developed policy approach (Colucci 2002; Cozzetto & Pedeliski 1997). To support this approach, Hartman and Bucci (1998) also argue that electronic surveillance concerns questions of ethical decision-making, arguing that the development of moral systems has not been able to keep pace with technological developments. In this context, an ethical approach to implementation decisions and/or the extent of electronic surveillance mechanisms can be a critical factor in maintaining trust, confidence and harmony in the workplace.

The issue of control

Whilst Mishra and Crampton (1998) note that electronic monitoring is a modern version of the supervision role of management, Sempill (2001) takes this a step further to argue that electronic monitoring can be used as a tool to reinforce employer power by promoting the enforcement of employee obedience. It is this imposition of technology by an employer which can be seen to contribute to the erosion of employees' rights and increased powerlessness in the employment relationship (Stanton & Stam 2003).

Whilst the extent and type of monitoring is not the focus of this chapter, several examples of the use of technology by management can easily be seen as ways of controlling employees and their activities. See Box 11.1 and Box 11.2.

Box 11.1: The Ansett case

The case of the *Australian Municipal, Administrative, Clerical and Services Union (ASU) v Ansett Airlines Ltd* (2000) FCA 441 illustrates the need for particular care where an employee is disciplined for activities associated with work – in this case, trade union activities. Justice Merkel found that the dismissal of the employee, Ms Gencarelli, breached the freedom of association provisions in the *Workplace Relations Act (WRA)* 1996 (Cth) because Ansett sacked Ms Gencarelli in her capacity as a union delegate for carrying out union activities.

In the course of enterprise bargaining negotiations, Ms Gencarelli distributed a union bulletin via email to union members advising of a meeting between the union and Ansett regarding the enterprise bargaining. Her employment was terminated on the grounds of misconduct. Ansett's policy regarding email stated that it must be 'for the purpose of performing authorised lawful business activities'. Justice Merkel stated that Ansett had entered into an agreement with the union to form a Joint Work Group to discuss employment issues, and that it was important to communicate the outcome of these meeting to employees. He took the view that Ms Gencarelli's use of the email system to distribute the information was implied within the policy as it was for authorised and lawful business purposes.

Justice Merkel emphasised the importance of procedural fairness. He found the employee who had dismissed Ms Gencarelli on behalf of Ansett had done so without adhering to its procedures regarding the investigation of misconduct in the workplace as he had not referred to the IT policy directly when conducting his investigation. Further, Justice Merkel found that the dismissal breached the 'freedom of association' provisions in the WRA, as Ms Gencarelli had been dismissed because of her position as a workplace delegate. As a result, Ansett was liable to a penalty.

Post script

Whilst the decision was hailed by unions and civil liberty groups as a landmark case, the Court emphasised that its decision did not mean that union delegates had a general authorisation to distribute union material via company email. Justice Merkel stated that the scope of an employee's use of company IT systems was situational dependent. According to the Court:

> *What is clear is the desirability of employees being made aware, in clear terms, of criteria establishing circumstances that constitute acceptable and unacceptable use of their employers' email and IT systems.*
>
> *Source*: Adapted from Australian Government Solicitor, Legal briefing no. 58, 27 February 2001, and *Australian Risk Management*, vol. 10, no. 4, 2001.

Monitoring and surveillance in the Australian workplace

With the variety and availability of monitoring and surveillance techniques – facilitated by advanced technology – increasingly being used in workplaces, it seems appropriate to review the nature and extent of monitoring and surveillance in the Australian workplace. In 2005, Sheehan, Holland and DeCieri undertook the Australian Human Resource Institute (AHRI) study on 'the state of play' of human resource management. This survey, undertaken every 10 years since the 1940s, provides a comprehensive view of the HR profession from its members. The online survey of AHRI members had a response of 1,372. For the first time in this study human resource managers were asked about monitoring and surveillance undertaken in their workplace.

The survey asked HR managers about the extent of monitoring and surveillance in their workplace, and whether there are explicit policies associated with the development of these processes involving employees or their representatives. The areas focused on included: drug testing, generic testing, video surveillance, GPS explicitly for employee surveillance, and key speed and time monitoring. The results showed that monitoring of key speed and time was the most widespread at 17 per cent, with 14.6 per cent of organisations having polices covering this issue. Whilst it is difficult to be clear about the actual nature of the jobs monitored, considering the amount of people undertaking keyboard work this could be considered to be both wide and varied.

The second most common area of surveillance was video monitoring at 15.5 per cent. This was closely followed by the contentious area of drug testing. 14.3 per cent of respondents stated that their organisation undertook drug testing, and 22.5 per cent said they had policies covering the undertaking of these tests in the workplace. However, what may be of concern – considering several high profile industrial disputes in Australia associated with the implementation of drug-testing in the workplace – was that only 11.3 per cent of workplaces involved the unions in the process. Research in this area indicates that a policy is likely to be more successful when the stakeholders are involved and are part of the solution.

The final areas explored in the snapshot of monitoring and surveillance in the workplace was GPS – specifically for employee surveillance – and genetic testing. Whilst GPS was used with only 1.7 per cent of the workforce – which may seem surprising considering the variety of systems available – this may be due to the fact that for most systems the priority is the tracking of *goods* rather than the movement of the people themselves undertaking the process. Finally, genetic testing was only evident in 0.7 per cent of workplaces examined. In all these cases, the concern associated with these more invasive systems was that fewer than half involved a union in the process.

While this is the first time these issues have been raised in Australia, a comparison with the US reveals that Australia's workforce is still relatively free of monitoring and surveillance. A survey of electronic monitoring and surveillance by the American Association of Management (2005) reveals 76 per cent monitor employee website connections, with 36 per cent tracking keystrokes. While only 7 per cent of US organisations used genetic testing and 8 per cent used GPS to monitor staff (significantly more than Australian workplaces), 53 per cent of companies employed smartcard technology to control access. In the area of video surveillance, 51 per cent undertook this process, of which 85 per cent also informed their staff.

Source: Sheehan, C, Holland, P & De Cieri, H 2005, 'Survey of the Australian Human Resources Institute Membership', *American Association of Management 2005 Electronic Monitoring & Surveillance Survey: Many Companies Monitoring, Recording, Videotaping – and Firing – Employees*, New York, May 18.

Policy development and monitoring and surveillance

It is clear that a formal, well-communicated company policy constructed in consultation with employees and/or their representatives can result in greater employee acceptance of the reasons why and the manner in which their electronic work will be monitored (Cappel 1995). These policies must also consider employee usage of IT outside the workplace and outside of normal working hours. As noted in the Ansett case, this is not always clearly defined or interpreted in the same way by all parties. In addition, the policy should identify what constitutes appropriate and inappropriate use. As Paterson (2002) notes, this also needs to be supported by ongoing education programs; simply relying on a set of statements is not enough. The alternative of indiscriminate surveillance is unlikely to eliminate the legal risks. Organisations therefore need to develop guidelines governing the use of IT and email by employees. One example is the guidelines encouraged by the Federal Privacy Commissioner which provide a framework upon which organisations can extend or adapt as they see fit. See Box 11.2.

> ### Box 11.2: Federal Privacy Commission guidelines on information technology and internet issues
>
> 1. **The policy should be promulgated to staff and management should ensure that it is known and understood by staff. Ideally the policy should be linked from a screen that the user sees when they log on to the network.**
>   - Consultation with staff may also be useful. A consultative process can engender an understanding by management of the sorts of legitimate activities staff are using email and web browsing for and increase the understanding by staff of the possible risk to the organisation associated with improper email and internet use.
>
> 2. **The policy should be explicit as to what activities are permitted and forbidden.**
>   - While it is for each organisation to determine what it considers to be appropriate usage of its system, to simply say that all activity must be 'work-related' may not be clear. There may be scope for guidelines outlining what personal use of email – both within the organisation and externally to other organisations – is appropriate. Other activities may be specifically prohibited, e.g. the use of email to harass, flame (to send abusive email) or defame or disclose information, or to transmit pornography.
>   - The issue of appropriate usage may be harder to define in respect to web browsing. It may not be possible to tell if a web page is relevant until it has been read. The operation of web search engines can result in surprising and irrelevant search results. Links on websites may also be misleading. Discussion with staff on the issue of work-related web use might help to clarify this issue. Where an organisation determines that usage is to be work-related only, it should clearly spell out what it considers to be work-related.
>   - The policy should refer to any relevant legislation. In the Commonwealth public sector this would include the Privacy Act, the Archives Act, the Freedom of Information Act, the Crimes Act, the Public Service Act, and the Australian Public Service (APS) Code of Conduct. APS regulations provide that employees must use Commonwealth resources in a proper manner and behave in a way that upholds the APS values and

the integrity and good reputation of the APS. For more information on the *Public Service Act* 1999, please visit the Public Service and Merit Protection Commission website at <www.apsc.gov.au>.

- The Sex, Race and Disability Discrimination Acts and workplace relations laws apply in both the public and private sectors. In particular, employers should be aware of their obligations under these Acts to protect their employees against sexual harassment, racial vilification and other forms of unlawful discrimination which could occur through email and internet use. The Corporations Law may also be relevant, as well as state and territory statutes.

- (Please refer to the Employers' Homepage on the Human Rights and Equal Opportunity Commission website at <www.hreoc.gov.au/info_for_employers/index.html>.)

3. **The policy should clearly set out what information is logged and who in the organisation has rights to access the logs and content of staff email and browsing activities.**

   - Staff email boxes will normally contain the emails they have sent and received. Back-ups and archives may also contain copies of emails that have been deleted by the user. As well as the actual content of messages, the date and time the message was transmitted, received and opened and the email addresses of the sender and recipients will normally be recorded.

   - With web browsing the URLs (uniform resource locaters or website addresses) of sites visited, the date and time they were visited and the duration of site visits may be logged. Normally, access rights to staff mail boxes and logs would be restricted to those with the responsibility for administering the system. Such access should be as limited as possible and who has access rights should be clearly set out in the policy. The policy should outline in what circumstances IT staff can legitimately access staff emails and browsing logs.

   - The policy should also indicate, in general terms, under what circumstances an organisation will disclose the contents of emails and logs. Many organisations will only do this on the production of a legal authority.

4. **The policy should refer to the organisation's computer security policy. Improper use of email may pose a threat to system security, the privacy of staff and others, and the legal liability of the organisation.**

> 5. The policy should outline, in plain English, how the organisation intends to monitor or audit staff compliance with its rules relating to acceptable usage of email and web browsing.
>
> 6. The policy should be reviewed on a regular basis in order to keep up with the accelerating development of the internet and information technology. The policy should be re-issued whenever significant change is made. This would help to reinforce the message to staff.
>
> *Source*: Federal Privacy Commission website <www.privacy.gov.au>, accessed 2 January 2007.

Emerging issues

RFID

IT technology continues to extend the boundaries of workplace issues and with it the implications of monitoring and surveillance within the employment relationship. Issues which are now starting to emerge may have seemed fanciful only a decade ago. For example, the use of RFID and GPS devices, which initially were seen as a way of tracking freight, can just as easily be used for the tracking of people – even through implants – as Box 11.3 illustrates.

> ### Box 11.3: RFID implant scheme
>
> A Cincinnati video surveillance company, CityWatcher.com, now requires employees to use Verichip human implantable chips.
>
> The news was reported by CASPIAN (Consumers Against Supermarket Privacy Invasion and Numbering), a US organisation that opposes the use of surveillance RFID cards.
>
> Although CityWatcher does not require its employees to take an implant to keep their jobs, they won't get in the data centre without it. CASPIAN's Katherine Albrecht says chipping sets an unsettling precedent. 'It's wrong to link a person's paycheck with getting an implant,' she says.
>
> CityWatcher argues that chipping employees is a move to increase the layer of security, as present systems can be compromised. However, CASPIAN warns that this can happen to implantable chips too. Security researcher Jonathan Westhues, the author of a chapter in a book entitled *Hacking the Prox Card*, recently demonstrated how the VeriChip can be skimmed and cloned by a hacker. A cloned chip theoretically could duplicate an individual's VeriChip implant to access a secure area.

Chapter 11 – The Contested Terrain of Monitoring and Surveillance in the Workplace

Source: Libbenga, J 2006, 'Video surveillance outfit chips workers', *The Register*, viewed 10 February 2006, <http://www.theregister.co.uk/2006/02/10/employees_chipped/>.

Genetic testing in the workplace

While there are not significant levels of genetic testing in Australia or the US at present, the implications on employment of such testing for genetic disorders and family history are considerable, and take monitoring and surveillance in the workplace to new level of intrusion and into the issue of informational privacy.

Genetic testing is the acquiring of information about an individual – either from them or from their family medical history. From a workplace perspective, the focus is on occupational health and safety related diseases, and can include:

- specific tests for employees at risk of a work-related disease;
- specific tests related to employee susceptibility to workplace chemicals;
- specific tests for people who have been exposed to harmful chemical; and
- specific tests for people who have been exposed to harmful radiation.

However, the concern remains about what the tests are actually testing. As research continues to indicate, genetic testing cannot clearly determine the susceptibility of an employee to these risks. It would also be expected that occupational health and safety legislation and the management of dangerous chemicals or radiation would prevent employees being exposed to such dangers.

Since the first edition of this book, the issue of generic testing has been increasingly prominent, as the case of NIB health insurance illustrates. Despite the claims that a test would not affect people's health cover, failure to disclose a genetic test for life insurance can make such a contract invalid. In addition, as Box 11.4 illustrates, DNA kits are now being sold in drug stores in the US. It could only be a matter of time before such tests are as common as drug and alcohol testing in the workplace.

Box 11.4: You bet your life: health insurer's cheap DNA test could prove costly

The insurer NIB has begun offering its customers cut-priced genetic tests, which could unwittingly expose them to higher premiums – or even leave them unable to get life insurance or insurance payouts.

But the company says that it has no ulterior motive and wants to help its members manage their health. In an Australian first, the company has sent a selected group of customers a letter inviting them to take a DNA test to assess their risk of getting preventable illnesses such as diabetes, heart attacks and some cancers.

However, experts warn that taking up the offer could lead to privacy and financial risks - which the company only admits to in fine print at the end of the letter. NIB has arranged a half-price deal with a US company, Navigenics, for a full genetic test that usually costs $1,000.

It is understood that a select group of 5,000 customers received the offer, but if it is successful it may be expanded. In the letter, the NIB Chief Executive, Mark Fitzgibbon, reveals he himself has had such a test himself. 'I found it to be an invaluable experience, and believe it could be something that you would be interested in, too.'

But a Sydney academic, Kristine Barlow-Stewart, a key government adviser on genetics technology, said that the move was concerning. 'It certainly raised red flags for me', she said.

> Once someone has taken a test, they can be forced to reveal the results to obtain life insurance, income protection, mortgage insurance, or even membership in some superannuation funds which include life insurance.

Insurers can then use the information to increase premiums. If a customer concealed the fact they'd had the test, the insurer could refuse to pay out the policy. Associate Professor Barlow-Stewart sits on the Federal Government's Human Genetics Advisory Committee. She has been researching cases of 'genetic discrimination', in which healthy people have been denied insurance cover due to the content of their DNA.

A spokesman for NIB said that the genetic test results would remain strictly confidential between Navigenics and the policy holder.

He said customers were warned of the implications in fine print on the letter, saying: 'you may be required to disclose genetic test results, including any underlying health risks and conditions which the tests reveal, to life insurance or superannuation providers.'

> The company also offered a counselling service for people who were worried or confused about the genetic test results.
>
> *Source*: Nick Miller - Sydney Morning Herald, 15 February, 2010.

Conclusions

This chapter illustrates the problems and complexity surrounding the development of monitoring and surveillance in the workplace. Appropriate levels of monitoring and surveillance are a vexed question. At what point does the prerogative of the employer's right to protect, manage and run their organisations conflict or infringe employees' right to privacy. It is clear from this overview that detailed assessments of both the tangible and intangible costs and benefits can be made in relation to monitoring and surveillance in the workplace. First, the issue of managerial prerogative versus employee privacy rights needs to be considered. Second, how monitoring and surveillance mechanisms are introduced and how and why the information is being used needs to be understood. Third, despite organisations having policies on drug and alcohol testing and email/internet usage, the issue of trust and commitment within the employment relationship cannot be underestimated – in other words, the fundamental question in this context is *why* organisations have decided to implement monitoring and surveillance programs? Without consideration of these issues, a breakdown of the employment relationship can occur. Understanding the views of all stakeholders is required to ensure all available options are considered, all available information is consulted, and the practicalities of monitoring and surveillance are fully understood.

References

ACIRRT 1999, *Australia at Work: Just Managing*, Prentice Hall, Sydney.

Allsop, S, Phillips, M & Calogero, C 2001, *Drug and Work: Responding to Alcohol and Other Drug Problems in Australian Workplaces* (eds), IP Communications, Melbourne.

Allsop, S & Pidd, K 2001, 'The Nature of Drug Related Harm in the Workplace', in S Allsop, M Phillips & C Calogero (2001) (eds), *Drug and Work: Responding to Alcohol and Other Drug Problems in Australian Workplaces*, IP Communications, Melbourne pp. 4-21.

Ames, G & Grube, JW 1999, 'Alcohol Availability and Workplace Drinking: Mixed Method Analysis', *Journal of Studies of Alcohol,* 60(3): 383-393.

ACTU 2006, Alcohol and Other Drugs in the Workplace Policy.

Bahls, JE 1998, 'Drugs in the Workplace', *HRMagazine*, February, pp. 81-87.

BHP Iron Ore Pty Ltd v. *Construction, Mining Energy Timberyards Sawmills and Woodworkers Union WA Branch*, WAIRC 130, 19 June 1998.

Bohle, P & Quinlan, M 2000, *Managing Health and Safety: A Multidisciplinary Approach*, 2nd edn, MacMillan, Melbourne.

Bowie, NE & Duska, RF 1990, *Business Ethics*, 2nd edn, Prentice Hall, New Jersey.

Cappel, J 1995, 'A Study of Individuals' Ethical Beliefs and Perceptions of Electronic Mail Privacy, *Journal of Business Ethics*, 14: 819-827.

Colucci, M 2002, *The Impact of the Internet and New Technologies on the Workplace: a Legal Analysis From a Comparative Point of View*, Kluwer Law International, The Hague.

Cozzetto, D & Pedeliski, T 1997, 'Privacy and the Workplace: Technology and Public Employment', *Public Personnel Management*, 26(4): 515-527.

Cranford, M 2001, 'Drug Testing and the Right to Privacy', *Journal of Business Ethics*, 17: 1805-1815.

DesJardine, JR & McCall, JJ 1990, *Contemporary Issues in Business Ethics*, 2nd edn, Wadsworth Publishing Company, California.

Flynn, G 1999, 'How to Prescribe Drug Testing', *Workforce*, 78(1): 107.

Gip, MA 1999, 'Drug Testing Assailed', *Security Management*, 43(12): 16.

Greenburg, E & Greenburg, S 1995, 'Work Alienation and Problem Alcohol Behavior', *Journal of Health and Social Behavior*, 36(1): 83-102.

Hartman, L & Bucci, G 1998, 'The Economic and Ethical Implications of New Technology on Privacy in the Workplace', *Business and Society Review*, 102/103: 1-24.

Hagen, R, Egan, D & Eltringham, A 1992, 'Work, Drugs and Alcohol', *Occupational Health and Safety Commission Inquiry into Alcohol, Drugs and the Workplace*, Victorian Occupational Health and Safety Commission, Melbourne.

Hartwell, TD, Steele, PD, French, MT & Rodman, NE 1996, 'Prevalence of drug testing in the workplace', *Monthly Labour Review*, 19(11): 35-42.

Holland, PJ, Pyman, A & Teicher, J 2005, 'Negotiating the Contested Terrain of Drug Testing in the Australian Workplace', *Journal of Industrial Relations*, 47(3): 326-338.

Kennedy v. *Cumnock No 1 Colliery Pty Ltd*, Print PR901496, March 2001.

Mansfield, B 2001, 'Impairment of Employees - The Union View', <http://www.actu.asn.au/public/news/1056670370_26248.html>.

Midford, R 2001, 'The Nature and Extent of Drug Related Harm in the Workplace', in S Allsop, M Phillips & C Calogero 2001 (eds), *Drug and Work: Responding to Alcohol and Other Drug Problems in Australian Workplaces*, IP Communications, Melbourne, pp. 42-56.

Midford, R, Marsden A, Phillips, M & Lake J 1997, 'Workforce Alcohol Consumption: Patterns at two Pilbara Mining Related Work Sites', *Journal of Occupational Health and Safety Australia and New Zealand*, 13: 267-274.

Miller, RL & Jentz, GA 2002, *Human Resources Management and E-Commerce*, Thomson Learning. United States.

Miller, S & Weckert, J 2000, 'Privacy, the Workplace and the Internet', *Journal of Business Ethics,* 28(3): 255-265.

Mishra, J & Crampton, S 1998), 'Employee Monitoring: Privacy in the Workplace?', *SAM Advanced Management Journal,* 63(3): 4-14

National Health and Medical Research Council 1997, 'Workplace Injury and Alcohol', A report prepared by a Working Party of the Health Advancement Standing Committee for the NHMRC, Department of Health and Family Services, AGPS, Canberra.

Nolan, J 2000, 'Unions Stuffed or Stoned', *Workers Online,* 71: 1-5, September.

Nolan, J & Nomchong, K 2000, 'Fitness for Duty – Recent Legal Developments', ACIRRRT Working Paper, no. 69.

Paterson, M 2002, 'Monitoring of Employee Emails and other Electronic Communications', *University of Tasmania Law Review,* 21(1): 1-19.

Richmond, R, Heather, N, Holt, P & Hu, W 1992, *Workplace policies and programs for tobacco, alcohol and other drugs in Australia*, AGPS, Canberra.

Redeker, J & Segal, J 1989, 'Profits Low? Your Employees May Be High!', *Personnel,* 66(6): 72-77, June.

Roman, RM, Johnson, JA & Blum, T 2000, 'The Workplace, Employer and Employee', in DB Cooper (ed.), Alcohol Use, *Radcliffe Medical Press Ltd, Abingdon, Oxen, pp. 121-133.*

Seeman, M & Seeman, AZ 1992, 'Life Strains, Alienation and Drinking Behaviour', *Alcoholism: Clinical and Experimental Research*, 16: 199-205.

Sempill, J 2001, 'Under the Lens: Electronic Workplace Surveillance', *Australian Journal of Labour Law,* 14: 111-144.

Stanton, JM, & Stam, KR 2003, 'Information Technology, Privacy and Power within Organizations: a View from Boundary Theory and Social Exchange Perspectives', *Surveillance & Society,* 1(2): 152-190.

Tices, HM & Sonnenstuhl, WJ 1990, 'On the Construction of Drinking Norms in Work Organisations', *Journal of Studies in Alcohol*, 51(3).

Townsend, A, & Bennett, J 2003, 'Privacy, Technology, and Conflict: Emerging Issues and Action in Workplace Privacy', *Journal of Labor Research,* 24(2): 195-205.

Turner, A 2003, 'Time Bandits', *The Age,* 26 August 2003, p. 5.

Wall, PS 1992, 'Drug Testing in the Workplace: An Update', *Journal of Applied Business Research,* 8(2): 127-132.

Wasserstrom, R 1978, *Today's Moral Problems*, 2nd edn, MacMillan, London.

Webb, G & Festa, J 1994, 'Alcohol and other drug problems in the workplace: Is drug testing the appropriate solution', *Journal of Occupational Health and Safety - Australia and New Zealand*, 10(2): 95-106.

Zwerling, C, Ryan, J & Orav, EJ 1990, 'The Efficacy of Pre-Employment Drug Screening for Marijuana and Cocaine in Predicting Employment Outcome', *Journal of the American Medical Association*, 264(20): 2630-2643.

Contemporary Issues and Challenges in HRM

Case study: BHP Pilbara mines

The Pilbara region in Western Australia (WA) is located 1,600 kilometres north of Perth. BHP produces approximately 65 million tonnes of iron ore per annum from its mines in the region. BHP Iron Ore has more than 1,563 employees and 1,300 contractors. The largest open cut mine is at Newman. This is linked to major ore processing, stockpiling and shipping facilities at Nelson Point and Finucane Island on opposite sides of the Port Headland harbour.

On the recommendations of the coroner following a fatal drug-related accident in 1994 and several other incidents, BHP sought to introduce drug and alcohol testing. Following the introduction of voluntary programs, BHP sought the implementation of a mandatory drug and alcohol testing program at each of its sites in the Pilbara. The introduction of a mandatory program stemmed from a philosophy that BHP had a responsibility to ensure the safety of all its employees. As Judith Thompson, Manager of Public Affairs for BHP Iron Ore in WA reiterated:

> *There's a duty of care that spreads among the workforce and from supervisory people to the workforce. Based on that duty of care, we have developed a policy in relation to drugs and alcohol on site, which is also consistent with WA mining legislation*[21] *(ABC Radio National 1996).*

The mandatory program proposed by BHP required that an employee, as a condition of employment, submit to random drug testing. If a test proved positive, on the first occasion the employee was liable to be sent home on paid special leave. On the second occasion and within a period of two years, the employee was liable to be sent home on unpaid special leave. On the third occasion within the same time period, the employee's continuing employment would be the subject of discussions with the company (*BHP Iron Ore Pty Ltd v. Construction, Mining Energy Timberyards, Sawmills and Woodworkers Union WA Branch, WAIRC 130, 19 June 1998*) [Hereafter *WAIRC 130, 19 June 1998*]. Education was a central part of the program, and there was also

---

[21] It is a requirement under the *Western Australian Mines Safety and Inspection Act* 1994, and associated regulations, that no drugs or alcohol are permitted on mine sites. Specifically, regulation 4.7 prohibits anyone from being in or on a mine while the person is affected by drugs or alcohol, and entitles the mine manager/supervisor to direct any employee reporting for duty – who in their opinion is adversely affected by alcohol or drugs – to leave the mine.

provision for assistance to those employees with a suspected alcohol or drug dependency. As Judith Thompson noted:

> *The policy includes education about the effects of drug and alcohol abuse and also offers counselling to people should they have trouble controlling their use of these substances (ABC Radio National 1996).*

Issues preceding the dispute

BHP held discussions with employees and the four unions in 1997 regarding the introduction and implementation of the program. The respective unions held separate meetings of members. A valid majority of employees approved the implementation of the program, with the exception of one union – the WA branch of the Construction Mining Timberyards Sawmills and Woodworkers Union. A majority of its members at the Newman and Finucane Island sites voted overwhelmingly to reject the program. Following lengthy negotiations with employees and the four unions, BHP did not implement the program. It was held to be impracticable if it did not apply to all employees. In addition, the three unions that supported the program did so on the proviso that it applied equally to all employees (WAIRC 130, 19 June 1998).

The main objection of the dissenting union was to drug testing. The union was initially opposed to both alcohol and drug testing, but by the time the case reached the WA Industrial Relations Commission (WAIRC), the union no longer objected to the alcohol testing. The union argued that drug testing constituted an unreasonable intrusion of an individual's privacy. The union also objected to the requirement that employees using prescribed or over-the-counter drugs that might impair them in their work, report this to the company, which would be required to maintain records of the employee's drug use for a minimum of two years (WAIRC 130, 19 June 1998).

Dispute over the introduction of drug and alcohol testing

The dispute over the introduction and implementation of drug testing at three BHP sites was referred to the WAIRC by BHP after two years of consultation with the workforce. The WAIRC was asked to consider the program as a whole, and specifically whether it was fair and reasonable.

Union position

The dissenting union put forward three key arguments in opposing the introduction of the program. Firstly, the union questioned the prevalence of drug use in the workplace and argued that there was no evidence to justify the introduction of such a program. For example, the union highlighted that while voluntary drug testing was in place at BHP sites during 1997-1998, there were no reported incidents. Secondly, the union questioned urine testing as a reliable indicator of impairment resulting from drug abuse. Thirdly, the union argued that BHP should not impose the program on its members simply because they had obtained the consent of the members of other unions (WAIRC 130, 19 June 1998).

Management position

BHP argued that the implementation of the program was necessary in order to enable the company to satisfy its common law duty to provide a safe workplace and in order to satisfy WA mining legislation. In response to the issue of privacy, BHP argued that the program protected the privacy of employees as far as possible by providing strict security measures. Such measures were designed to avoid publication of any test result and any other information given as part of the program. Responding to the union's second argument, BHP acknowledged the criticisms surrounding drug tests as an indicator of impairment. In fact, the company admitted that such tests were not a test of impairment. BHP maintained that the cut off levels of drugs allowed under the program before a positive result was returned were at such high levels that a positive result was a reliable indicator of safety issues. Finally, BHP argued that it should be free to implement the policy in accordance with the wishes of a significant majority of the workforce after having extensive consultation with the employees and unions regarding the implementation and implications of the program (WAIRC 130, 19 June 1998).

Both parties used expert witnesses to debate the extent to which drugs adversely affect safety in the workplace. This was a contentious and noteworthy issue throughout the dispute. The union argued that very little was known about the impact of drugs on workplace safety and that, in fact, some drugs could have positive effects. BHP, whilst accepting that little was known about the effect of drugs, argued that the effects of drugs on cognitive functions, psychomotor performance and other skilled tasks strongly predicted serious adverse effects on workplace safety (WAIRC 130, 19 June 1998).

Resolution of the dispute

On 19 June 1998, the WAIRC endorsed a requirement that BHP employees working on three sites – Newman, Finucane Island and Nelson Point – submit to random drug testing (Moodie 1998). On this basis, the WAIRC considered it reasonable for BHP to implement a scheme designed to detect, so far as possible, the level of consumption of drugs by employees and to implement procedures designed to deter the use of drugs in the workplace. The WAIRC decided the program was not unreasonable, harsh or unfair in BHP's attempt to satisfy its responsibility to provide a safe workplace for all employees (WAIRC 130, 19 June 1998).

Weighing up intrusion and privacy concerns against the legal obligation to provide a safe workplace, the WAIRC concluded that, whilst the program intruded on the privacy of individual employees, workplace health and safety requirements and community expectations were such that there would necessarily be some constraint on the civil liberties of employees. In addition, the program included elements that aimed to minimise intrusion of privacy. For example, urine samples were to be given in private and were not witnessed by the tester (WAIRC 130, 19 June 1998).

In reaching its decision, the WAIRC upheld several elements of the program as important, including the provision for formal education, counselling and rehabilitation. The fact that the penal elements of the program were subordinated to education and rehabilitation were also important in the WAIRC's assessment. For example, the program provided that, after the expiration of two years, any positive reading was expunged from an employee's record. Also important in the decision to endorse the program were the cut off levels set for a positive test. These cut off levels were determined to be relatively high and, unlike many other programs, they were significantly higher than the Australian standard. In a technical sense, the tests were regarded as rigorous, with experts identifying the probability for error in either test as less than 1% (WAIRC 130, 19 June 1998).

In summary, the WA IRC found insufficient merit for the union's objection to the program and endorsed BHP's extensive consultation with the workforce over the characteristics of the program. In endorsing the program, the WAIRC also noted the importance of a formal review mechanism as new, more efficient and effective drug and alcohol testing methods became available (WAIRC 13, 19 June 1998).

Written by: Holland, Pyman & Teicher.

Case study questions

1. With regards to the implementation of drug testing programs in Australia, identify the key features which make this case a benchmark for best practice.

Discussion questions

1. What are the major reasons for employers wanting to introduce monitoring and surveillance in the workplace?
2. What are the major concerns for employees regarding the introduction of monitoring and surveillance in the workplace?
3. 'With regard to drug-testing, the innocent have nothing to fear'. Is this correct? Why/why not?
4. What are some of the misconceptions employees have about electronic communication in the workplace?
5. What are the key principles for developing effective monitoring and surveillance policies and practices?

Chapter 12

RISK AND CRISIS MANAGEMENT

INTRODUCTION

The increasing interest in risk and crisis management has developed in response to a number of unexpected but devastating events that have presented serious threats to business continuity over the past 20 years. The widespread publicity of high profile failures in the late 1990s and early 2000s (e.g. WorldCom, Enron and HIH) has highlighted the possible impacts of poor financial risk management. Incidents, such as the September 11 terrorist attacks, hurricanes Rita and Katrina, the London bombings, the South Asia Boxing Day tsunami, the Queensland floods, the Christchurch earthquake in New Zealand, the nuclear disaster in Japan, and the BP oil spill in the Gulf of Mexico, have similarly contributed to increased public sensitivity to risk and the need for appropriate crisis responses. Customers have become more socially aware, and organisations have responded using a range of techniques – including the language of corporate social responsibility (CSR) to protect their businesses from the harmful ramifications of negative public perception. A core element in the prevention of these disasters has been the emergence of risk management. The Committee of Sponsoring Organizations of the Treadway Commission (COSO) defines enterprise risk management as a process: '… effected by an entity's board of directors, management and other personnel, applied in strategy setting and across the enterprise, designed to identify potential events that may affect the entity, and manage risk to be within its risk appetite, to provide reasonable assurance regarding the achievement of entity objectives' (2004:2).

This definition highlights that the process is designed to identify potential events that, if they occur, will affect the entity. At times, however, disasters come in unexpected forms as sudden, devastating events that pose serious threats to business continuity. These crisis events require a rapid response and force organisations to engage in crisis management. The following chapter reviews the steps taken within both risk and crisis management approaches, and the challenges and ramifications for human resource management (HRM). The chapter objectives are: to review the risk management process, to consider different approaches to understanding risk and the ramifications for HR, and to define crisis management and review the implications for HRM in response to some current crisis issues.

The process for managing risk

The international risk management standard, AS/NZS ISO 31000:2009, is based significantly on the 2004 edition of the *Australian/New Zealand Risk Management Standard*. It provides principles and guidelines for managing risk in a systematic and transparent manner across a range of contexts. Figure 12.1 depicts the proposed steps in the process. The first step is to define the internal and external parameters for the risk management policy. The next three steps are associated with the risk assessment: identifying the risk sources by finding, recognising and defining the risk, its causes and consequences; analysing the nature and level of the risk; and evaluating whether or not the risk is tolerable. The risk is then treated. The process also involves continuous monitoring, communication and consultation.

With respect to HRM, the risk management process, as specified by the standard, can be applied to a wide range of HRM decisions. The design of the HRM policy, procedures and practices for expatriate placement, for example, could be analysed using the process outlined in Figure 12.1. First, the parameters would include the strategic importance of target countries where the organisation seeks to conduct business, and the associated cultural, social and political conditions and relationships with key stakeholders in those countries. Next, the risk assessment would identify, analyse and evaluate the sources and consequences of potential risks. The risks of sending an Australian or American expatriate to New Zealand, for example, would be considerably different from sending someone to Columbia or the Philippines. An important source of expatriate risk in Columbia and the Philippines that is not present in New Zealand is kidnapping. Every year in Latin America some 15,000 people are kidnapped, with a significant number of these being foreigners on assignment (Briscoe & Schuler 2004). The Philippines, similarly, has a high rate of international kidnapping. The brutal kidnapping and murder of Coca Cola executive Betty Chua Sy prompted President Arroyo to vow to increase the focus on the prosecution of suspected kidnappers (Liou & Lin 2008). Other potential identifiable risks include access to health services in remote areas and consideration of location factors such as altitude on expatriates who suffer from asthma. More broadly, there is the substantial risk of sending expatriates who may not be sensitive to the language or cultural requirements of the host country (Mendenhall & Oddou 1985). A failure to ensure that expatriates are culturally sensitive when operating in the host country can lead to poor business relationships as well as to premature expatriate return (Dowling, Festing & Engle 2008).

Chapter 12 – Risk and Crisis Management

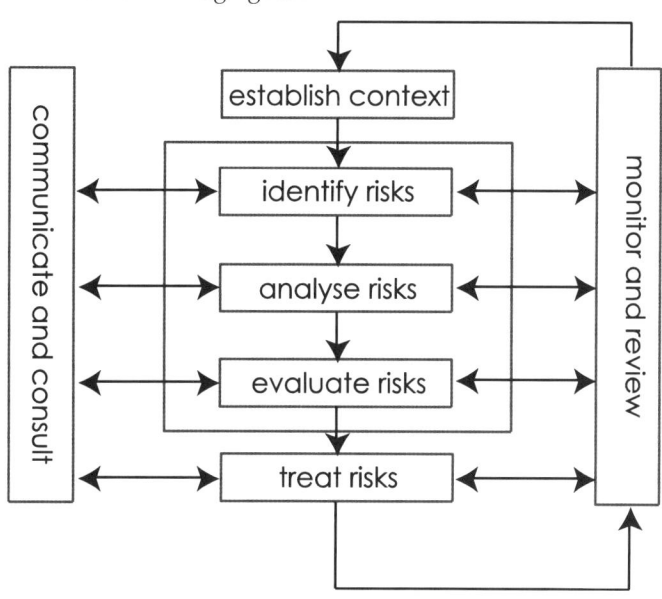

Figure 12.1 Process for managing risk

```
                    ┌─────────────────────┐
                    │  establish context  │
                    └─────────┬───────────┘
                              ↓
  ┌──────────┐      ┌─────────────────────┐      ┌──────────┐
  │          │ ←──→ │   identify risks    │ ←──→ │          │
  │ communi- │      └─────────┬───────────┘      │ monitor  │
  │ cate and │                ↓                   │   and    │
  │ consult  │ ←──→ │   analyse risks     │ ←──→ │  review  │
  │          │      └─────────┬───────────┘      │          │
  │          │                ↓                   │          │
  │          │ ←──→ │   evaluate risks    │ ←──→ │          │
  │          │      └─────────┬───────────┘      │          │
  │          │                ↓                   │          │
  │          │ ←──→ │    treat risks      │ ←──→ │          │
  └──────────┘      └─────────────────────┘      └──────────┘
```

Source: Adapted from Australian/ New Zealand Standard AS/NZS ISO 31000, 2009:vi.

As part of risk assessment, risk identification, therefore, for expatriate placement considers specific risks associated with that country. Risk analysis would then review criteria to determine who are most at risk in particular situations. For example, high profile executives are more likely to be at risk of kidnapping, while expatriates with pre-existing health conditions and who are travelling with a family are more likely to need health support. Expatriates who have had limited language training and cultural exposure represent higher risk than those who are appropriately trained and experienced. Risk evaluation, then, involves a judgement about the suitability and value of sending a particular expatriate, and includes a review of the extent of the danger, how likely the danger is, and who is exposed. A decision is then made about how to treat the situation. For example, in a situation where the range of available expatriates are not deemed appropriate, a treatment decision may be to train a host country national. Alternatively, to reduce the risks associated with unhappy trailing spouses, the company may adopt a flexpatriate approach. This is where companies opt for short-term, unaccompanied business travel assignments rather than long-term placements of expatriates accompanied by their families. These employees have a job in a home office and also carry a workload in other countries (Mayerhofer, Muller & Schmidt 2010). The benefits of 'flexpatriate' arrangements are that employees can be placed for shorter periods of time and the risks associated with family pressure can be minimised.

Within the risk management process described above, decision points assume a rational perspective. The following section reviews additional perspectives and the challenges in the risk management process.

Approaches to risk

All of us are exposed to risk every day; indeed, successful risk taking is a necessary component of personal and business growth. Horlick-Jones (2005) has commented on the increasing focus on risk in business and made the observation that, in the past decade and a half, many professionals have found their everyday work to be articulated in the language of risk to the point that '... it has assumed the status of an all-purpose language of administration" (p. 268). From an HRM perspective, risk management is closely tied to the area of occupational health and safety (OH&S), an area that focuses on the duty of care that an organisation has to the safety, health and welfare of employees. HRM is also concerned about the impact of risk management on employer branding: the organisation's reputation as an employer. The following section considers the approaches to risk, including the technical, economic, cultural and psychometric, and the contribution that these approaches make to the management of HRM safety and reputation concerns.

The technical approach to risk has its origins in engineering and the hard sciences, and adopts an objective assessment that helps to identify and eliminate hazards. An established and popular approach in the design of OH&S standards, this approach measures risk as **Risk = Probability x Magnitude**. Objective scientific sources of evidence are used to identify, estimate, analyse, evaluate and communicate risk issues associated with the likelihood and impact of any risk. For example, according to a Wall Street Journal, analysis of US Federal accident records in oil industry platforms that are 20 years old or more accounted for more than 60 per cent of fires and nearly 60 per cent of serious injuries aboard platforms in 2009. These platforms are subject to extreme ocean currents, corrosive salt water and frequent hurricanes, and age has become a determinant in platform safety. Such information suggests that there is an infrastructure issue confronting the industry that needs to be addressed (Casselman 2010). A primary focus in the approach, therefore, is to identify the relevant hazard, rank the risk according to consequences, assess the probably of the event, and then impose managerial control. The process ties in with regulatory frameworks including legislative and compliance requirements. Internal company mechanisms can also be used to reinforce company policy and ongoing measurement, and feedback can include inspection checklists, safety audits and risk assessments (Glendon, Clarke & McKenna 2006). Within the field of OH&S, much time is spent in the development of appropriate work safety standards, and there is a concentration on worker behaviour modification to follow patterns of behaviour in order to reduce accidents and increase productivity.

In contrast to the technical approach that is focused on the elimination of harm, the economic approach considers the benefits of risks, and uses mathematical and statistical techniques to view the elements of risk, bringing the future into the present and making it calculable (Rose 1999). Tools and techniques can include cost benefit analysis (CBA) and expressing benefits and 'disbenefits' as monetary values. This approach depends on all relevant consequences being valued and on determining process and probabilities objectively to estimate tolerable levels of risk (Glendon, Clarke & McKenna 2006).

Both the technical and economic approaches adopt a rational perspective and assume that people are risk averse and act to prevent harm. Herbert Simon has proposed, however, that people, rather than being perfectly rational, engage in satisficing behaviour (Simon 1963). Satisficing, or bounded rationality, involves looking for an outcome that is *good enough*, rather than the absolute best, and this makes sense in a world where information is costly, incomplete, and rapidly changing. For individuals working in complex organisations faced by competing demands and pressures to produce results quickly, even when clear guidelines for risk management may be thought through, other perspectives help to explain how reduced risk sensitivity may impact on rational decision-making. In healthcare, for example, medical staff are expected to follow strict guidelines to ensure the reduction of personal injury and the transfer of disease between patients. Yet in a report on nurse behaviour in South Africa, despite a range of policies aimed at reducing the risk of accidental HIV needlesticks or other exposures to blood, nurses reported a resistance to wearing gloves because they created a physical barrier between nurse and patient and an impression that patients were 'untouchable' (Zelnick & O'Donnell 2005). Risk management in these settings sometimes needs, therefore, to go beyond policy and rules to address cultural pressures. In response, a cultural theory approach recognises how groups in society interpret danger, and how emergent values and values impact on the interpretation of safety expectations.

The value of cultural theory is in understanding that key social groups' attitudes and values can translate into behaviours that impact on the established order. In a large organisation, uniform risk management standards may be challenged when applied not only across country borders but also across workplaces that have sub-cultures that have developed different perceptions of risk (Hallowell 2010). Sinclair (2010), in a review of safety culture in an Australian coal mining company, identified substantial and persistent differences across five mine sites in OH&S performance. Reasons given for the development of a site-led 'bottom up' safety culture as opposed to a management-led 'top down' safety culture include the geographical remoteness of the mine sites and the longevity and insularity of the workforce. Mine workers are physically remote from both corporate management and from localised mine site management. A lack of computer access at underground work sites also means that workers are, effectively, isolated from a key source of management communication. Another relevant feature in the development of a bottom up safety culture in a mine is the longevity and insularity of the workforce. The average age of workers is 50, and many of the workers have spent their entire working lives at a single mine, or at a very small number of mines. This means that many of these workers have worked side-by-side with a common set of colleagues, often in small team environments, in very confined spaces for the majority of their working lives. The shared experience in relatively remote locations has created an emergent set of expectations about of how things are to be done (Sinclair 2010).

The commercial shipping industry is similarly characterised by operational sites distanced from corporate offices where crews work in close proximity to one another for long periods. In response, the shipping industry has begun to recognise the importance of fostering a positive safety culture on individual ships rather than across the fleet as a whole (Wake, 2005). The development of site-specific responses to risk raises important HRM policy implications. It seems that corporate-driven policy and expectations are likely to be re-interpreted when individual sites are isolated or form close shared communal expectations. These findings present a strong case for focusing on a range of bottom-up, site-specific HRM risk management approaches that take into account historical and cultural factors rather than reliance on corporate-level risk management directives.

A final perspective on risk is the psychometric approach. This view of risk includes the impact of individual factors on risk perception as a subjective cognitive (within the head) phenomenon. Risk perceptions, among other factors, can be impacted by voluntariness, familiarity, novelty, degree of control, chronic-catastrophic potential, immediacy of effect, and the severity of the consequences (Glendon *et al.* 2006). The ramifications of this perspective require a shifting of perceptions of risk away from statistics and towards personalising the impact. An organisation may have very clear guidelines about appropriate management of hazardous waste, for example, but unless an individual has had some personal experience of the impact of the risk, the rules may be seen as burdensome controls that hinder getting the job done rather than as parameters that protect workers from danger.

Overall, the risk management process, as described above (ISO 31000), provides a useful overview for the management of approaches to risk control. The standard outlines a constant process of identifying, analysing and treating risks supported with ongoing monitoring and communication. An exploration of some of the perspectives on risk have shown, however, that the process is far from simple and, despite the development of clear company policy and guidelines, cultural and individual factors can impact on the implementation of risk directives. Glendon *et al.* (2006) advises that, from an HRM perspective, underlying priorities in the risk management process include an active and personal involvement from senior management on a routine basis, open communication links between workers and management, a stable workforce with good industrial relations procedures, workforce empowerment to take responsibility for safety, a strong emphasis on training, and the ongoing collection of safety data. These recommendations incorporate a top down approach (as suggested by the Australian Risk Roundtable 2008), but also reinforce the importance of bottom up involvement and an organisation-wide understanding of the priority given to any risk management initiative.

Crisis management

Liou and Lin (2008) characterise a crisis event as one that: possesses high ambiguity with unknown causes and effects, has a low probability of occurring, requires a rapid response, poses a serious threat to the survival of the organisation and its stakeholders, and presents a dilemma necessitating a decision that will result in positive or negative change. Examples of crises that impact on a business include major accidents and destructive natural events, health and environmental disasters, technological breakdown, economic and market failures, or the actions of rogue employees (*Harvard Business Essentials* 2004). Crisis management models generally include before, during, and after phases. Campbell's model, depicted in Figure 12.2 below, classifies the identification stage as one that occurs before the crisis occurs. Preparation, response and recovery occur during the crisis period, and then learning can be consolidated in the wake of the event (see Box 12.1). Heath's (1998) crisis management model similarly includes a before stage, and he refers to this as prevention.

Box 12.1: Valuable lessons in adversity

The Australian Red Cross was charged with a mammoth task during Queensland's ongoing flood and cyclone crisis: to establish, co-ordinate and run dozens of evacuation centres, which would accommodate thousands of evacuees from across the state.

Volunteers – the lifeblood of the Red Cross, the world's largest humanitarian organisation – were called at a moment's notice to help establish temporary shelters and provide 24-hour care – including food, first aid and support.

'The scale of the crisis is far greater than anything we have seen in my lifetime', Brisbane-based Australian Red Cross emergency services co-ordinator Tim McInerny says. '[The challenge has been] the number of evacuation centres that we have managed and the complexity of those centres.' We had only managed a handful over the past couple of years, just due to the nature of those [flooding] events in Queensland, but we have managed dozens of them in the space of four weeks. [It was obvious that the] community is stretched and our personnel are stretched. 'We have learned a big lesson about how to prepare people to step into that environment, and manage it in a safe, economical way that maintains human dignity.'

McInerny has played a central role in ensuring Australian Red Cross's workforce, which draws on 60,000 members and volunteers, is prepared for any emergency. He runs training programs for volunteers and the organisation's incident management team, and has undertaken courses at the Australian Emergency Management Institute, part of the Attorney-General's department in Canberra and established in 1956 (originally named the Civil Defence School). He's running an intensive one-day course for volunteers on the establishment and management of evacuation centres, and the needs of the people in them. During the next two months, McInerny will train hundreds of volunteers in Queensland to try to build the organisation's long-term capacity in the state and to improve its flood and cyclone response. 'It's about human capacity, having more trained people who can respond, and up-skilling people to take on leadership roles,' McInerny says. 'One of the big challenges for us is time. Usually the identification, recruitment, training and getting someone on the system takes weeks. Now what we are trying to do is condense that into a day. It's a matter of making sure those processes are streamlined, so we can bring people through and very quickly they can step into a uniform and be able to go out and add value rather than be a risk or create extra challenges for our leadership out there in the field.'

During training, volunteers are introduced to the principles and history of the Red Cross, the emergency services environment in which they're operating, the services it provides, and its relationship with the community. They learn about safety, potential hazards and the physical and mental requirements of working in an emergency environment. 'Fatigue is a big issue,' McInerny says. Mentoring is crucial. Volunteers are partnered with more experienced personnel in areas where they have skills. A volunteer who has worked in a warehouse, for instance, may be directed into logistics. Some undertake additional training at the Australian Emergency Management Institute, which offers vocational and professional development courses with the aim of building disaster resilience by ensuring there is consistency of practice between state and territory jurisdictions.

'Demand for the courses offered here has been consistently high over the years, and in the past couple of years volunteers and local government participants have featured in the nominations for the range of courses offered,' institute executive director Raelene Thompson says. 'The institute has recently conducted a training needs analysis in the emergency management sector, and is now engaged in a curriculum redevelopment phase to ensure our courses remain highly relevant and strategically targeted to ensure the sector is well-serviced by the education opportunities offered.' Participants at the institute include emergency management practitioners from all levels of government and emergency management organisations, such as fire, State Emergency Service and ambulance, as well as non-government organisations such as the Red Cross.

One of the most popular courses is manage recovery functions and services, which covers the competency required for financial assistance, personal support programs and health services. However, real-life experiences remain the most compelling, and it is the lessons learned during the Queensland floods that will help shape future training programs at Australian Red Cross. Already, McInerny is reshaping and updating the training program to make it more interactive. A videographer is recording interviews with personnel who had key roles in the flood emergency response to better prepare volunteers for field experiences. 'So, when new people come from interstate, or people are about to take on a new role, they can watch a 15-minute walk-through of the role to give them a solid understanding before they get a hand-over, mentor and then step into it,' McInerny says. 'It's about gaining the perspective of people who have been working in the field who are in our command centre now.'

Source: P McLeod, *The Weekend Australian Professional Section – Executive Training*, p. 4, 19-20 February 2011.

Figure 12.2 Crisis process continual improvement

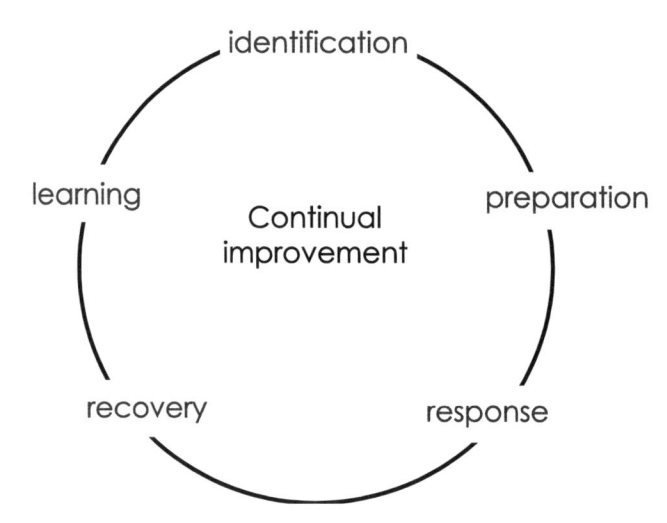

Circular diagram showing: identification → preparation → response → recovery → learning, around "Continual improvement"

Source: Campbell, R 1999, *Crisis Control: Preventing and Managing Corporate Crisis*, Prentice Hall, Wollongong.

Liou and Lin (2008) recognise the interactive nature of these models and the importance of the opportunity for learning. But, as they point out, September 11 showed that the crisis management process actually often begins with the response phase and, because by definition a crisis is an unexpected event, crisis managers must often solve complex events without the information they require. Nevertheless, Lockwood (2005) has argued that the devastating impact of the September 11 terrorist attacks warrants a generalised increase in disaster preparedness plans and has argued that the HRM function has a key strategic role to play in the management of crisis awareness. During such times, the HRM function has the opportunity to offer substantial leadership before during, and after the crisis. During a crisis there is a tendency to focus on systems, operations, infrastructure and public relations – with people last on the list. Consistent with the ongoing priority now being given to employees as a key source of competitive advantage (Wright, McMahan & McWilliams 1994), organisations should prioritise the management of their people's safety during a period of unexpected threat. To ensure that this is promoted, HR can make the business case for the link between a focus on people within the crisis management plan, and performance indicators and critical success factors that rely on personnel deliverables.

As well as emphasising the strategic imperative of a crisis management plan, HRM can be active in the development of leadership qualities through the senior workforce to ensure that they are capable of handling the communication and integrity issues necessary during a crisis. During a crisis event managers with crisis management and leadership talents are extremely valuable, as these people are used to operating in circumstances where there is little time to gather necessary information to make informed decisions (Sayegh, Anthony & Perrewe 2004). Lockwood (2005) has used the classic example of Johnson & Johnson's sound leadership in the handling of the Tylenol crisis. In October of 1982, Tylenol, the leading paracetamol pain-killer medicine in the US at the time, was taken off the shelves when an unknown suspect replaced Tylenol capsules with cyanide capsules, resulting in the deaths of seven people. In line with the company's strategic priority of protecting people first and property second, the leadership group of McNeil Consumer Products, a subsidiary of Johnson & Johnson, immediately released media information and recalled about 31 million bottles with an associated loss of more than $100 million dollars[22] In such situations, it is the CEO who communicates and represents the message of corporate involvement and honesty. When the CEO is less prepared to deal with such a crisis event, the result can be a loss of faith in the good intentions of the company. Tony Hayward, CEO of BP, for example, was thrust into a media spotlight following a rig explosion that killed 11 workers and caused the worst oil spill in US history. The BP CEO made a number of ill-considered remarks in the confusion that followed the event, including, 'I'd like my life back.' The public and media reaction to his comments was negative and, on 27 October 2010, BP announced that Robert Dudley would replace Haywood as CEO.[23]

In view of the pivotal role played by senior management in a crisis situation, Sayegh *et al.* (2004) propose that HRM managers should become more aware of the role that emotions play in rapid decision-making, and should provide awareness training for senior managers. For example, in a crisis event, how do managers react? Is the event perceived as a threat, a challenge or a loss? Managers can be trained to become aware of how such perception influence subsequent decisions and to become skilled in re-framing an event using more constructive interpretations.

Coupled with the strategic prioritisation of crisis management and the readiness of the leadership team to assume responsibility for its actions, Lockwood (2005) suggests the establishment of a crisis management team and the key positioning of the HR Director on that team. The HR role in the crisis management team is to provide support through important logistics and information, such as through access to personnel records, to assist information officers to reach affected individuals and their families, and to work to resolve all human issues created by the crisis. The HR role is also to ensure that required talent and succession planning is in place to enable the organisation to continue business.

---

[22] <http://iml.jou.ufl.edu/projects/Fall02/Susi/tylenol.htm>, accessed January, 7, 2011.
[23] <http://www.bp.com/genericarticle.do?categoryId=2012968&contentId=7063976, accessed January 7, 2011>.

Another issue that arises during a crisis situation is the influx of volunteer assistance. Rodsutti (2005), using the example of the tsunami experience in Thailand in December 2004, has explained that, in the aftermath of the tsunami, hundreds of volunteers, both from other parts of Thailand and from overseas, arrived to assist. Unfortunately, because of the lack of experience in the management of a volunteer workforce, many of the volunteers were not effectively deployed. HR in these situations can pre-empt such a void by planning based on the normal HR activities. For example, co-operation with the mass media can ensure effective and targeted recruitment of key professional groups. A well-designed application form can be an efficient selection tool and can also be used to determine job allocation. The form can be used, for example, to distinguish those people who had previous volunteer experience, those who may be useful in supervisory roles, and also the length of time that volunteers can be available. In terms of jobs to be performed, HR will also have a role in judging immediate and longer-term responsibilities, and can create project sign-up sheets that cover daily tasks as well as longer-term responsibilities. An orientation system also needs to be set up so that volunteers have appropriate expectations and preparation for the possible mental stress that the work might require, and also for the cross-cultural requirements of working with people who can be from quite different cultural backgrounds. If possible, a volunteer manual can assist in orienting staff, and attention can be given to basic accommodation and food in order to sustain current volunteers and attract new ones (Rodsutti 2005).

A key HR issue following a crisis is the loss of key talent and organisational knowledge due to low morale, fear, physical relocation and the death of co-workers. HR needs, therefore, to be involved in the crisis recovery plan, to ensure accessibility of the workplace and the organisation's resources and infrastructure, and to assist employees in regaining a sense of normalcy. HR can identify key personnel who are essential to the recovery effort, along with places to work and communication options. The following sections consider two crisis situations, the impact of terrorist-created events and the management of a pandemic. It also considers the specific roles that HR can take to assist in the crisis management process and in recovery.

Terrorism

Alexander, Valton and Wailkinson (1979: 4) have defined terrorism as 'the threat or actual use of force or violence to attain a political goal through fear, coercion or intimidation'. More recently Cinkota, Knight, Liesch and Steen (2010: 828) refined the definition to include broader objectives as follows: 'Terrorism is the premeditated, systematic threat or use of violence by sub-national groups to attain a political, religious or ideological objective through intimidation of a large audience'. Reasons given for the increase in terrorism since the 1980s include the globalisation of commerce, travel and information transfer. These developments have highlighted the difference between groups, and also provided collaborators with the capacity to communicate and move between nations more readily. There has also been an ascent in religious fundamentalism and its militant capacity (Crandell, Parnell & Spillan 2010). And finally, there has been an increase in the availability and capacity of weapons that can create deadly outcomes (Czinkota *et al.* 2010).

As well as the devastating personal loss that is part of terrorist action, such conflict has a substantial impact on business activity that has to be strategically managed (Henisz, Mansfield & Von Glinow 2010). In terms of which organisational functions should be involved Mankin and Perry, (2004) have observed that many areas consider the responsibility to be outside of their purview. In the government sector, for example, departments have considered that the relevant governmental emergency agency should assume responsibility. More broadly, the SHRM 2005 Disaster Survey Report indicated that, as a result of the September 11 terrorist attacks, 56 per cent of organisations created or revised their disaster preparedness plan, but special note was made that 45 per cent of organisations did not. Lockwood (2005) has raised concern about the lack of preparedness of these organisations, and has reinforced the important role that the HR department plays in the event of a disaster. Mankin and Perry (2004) similarly highlight that terrorist attacks in the past 30 years have been directed at government and business offices and, as a result, employees are at the forefront of the risk. A case is made above for the important role to be played by HR in strategic crisis management, but the function also has an important operational role during the event and in the post-event period.

Minimising injuries to staff and personnel relocation is a key HRM priority during a terrorist attack. During the attack on the World Trade Centre, Morgan Stanley was able to show the benefits of a plan for relocation that had been effectively communicated to staff prior to the event. Morgan Stanley was one of the organisations that had been affected by the previous 1993 bomb attack and had, in response, designed and practised floor-by-floor evacuations of staff. After the first plane crashed into the North Tower in 2001, Morgan Stanley staff quickly and efficiently evacuated their 22 floors (53rd to 74th) of the South Tower. By the time the second plane hit the South Tower, evacuation was under way (Liou & Lin 2008).

A further part of relocation is a plan to ensure business continuity. Terrorist attacks often result in building and structural damage that threaten both employees and business operations (Perry & Mankin 2005). Merrill Lynch was another organisation that were effective in the design and implementation of a previously thought through response to the 9/11 terrorist attack, and were able to re-locate business roles immediately. When the disaster occurred, the company activated its disaster recovery plan within minutes, and immediately began transferring business critical functions to its command centre in New Jersey. The New Jersey facility had been pre-designed as a corporate disaster response area, and all personnel had been previously briefed on how to enact the transfer of information (Stephens 2003). The reality of a terrorist attack is that there is the very real possibility of personnel shortage due to injury and loss. Transferring operations to another site, will assist with the coverage of employee loss at the affected site but the area that absorbs the increase in work then needs to be properly staffed to manage the increased load.

A further important aspect of employee welfare is communication with employees and their families, and Merrill Lynch had also devised a plan to use a telemarketing service along with the company's public internet site to communicate with displaced workers and their families (Stephens 2003). As part of the communication with staff, HR can be invaluable in providing accurate accounting of employee location to enable search and rescue activity and to keep families informed about employee welfare. In the time following the event, the HRM department must also co-ordinate the counselling of employees and their families, and may have established counsellor networks in place to assist with the recovery effort.

Overall, HRM can be active in advance terrorist scenario planning through the training and education of staff in emergency preparedness. As noted in the previous section on general crisis management, the HR function can also assist with the procurement and allocation of voluntary helpers who come to the affected area to assist in the recovery efforts. HRM can also be invaluable in a relocation plan for business continuity, including pre-designed role definition and plans for extended hours of operation and additional staff. In terms of assisting employees with managing the confusion of the event, HRM also has an important role in developing clear communication channels and providing up-to-date records of employee activity and location to assist emergency services and provide feedback to families about employee safety. Finally, HRM needs to provide and ensure appropriate psychological support for employees who are recovering from the disaster.

Pandemics

Pandemics are different from other threats and crises. Threats associated with bombs, or natural disasters such as fires, earthquakes and tsunamis, are over once the event has occurred. While the effects can be devastating and have long-term consequences, recovery can begin. A pandemic, on the other hand, is an unfolding global event that comes in waves that can sweep across the globe in a matter of weeks, and may take up to three months to manage (Staples 2006). Furthermore, the effects are mainly felt by people rather than by the infrastructure, and for that reason the potential inoperability of the workforce makes the disaster one in which HRM function will have to take a lead management role. Very high levels of absenteeism in the workforce could result from either the workers themselves becoming sick, or from indirect impacts such as the need to care for others or if a quarantine were to be enacted (Orsi & Santos 2010).

A pandemic is an infection that can spread globally and affect large populations (Orsi & Santos 2010). The World Health Organization (WHO) uses the following criteria to distinguish the severity of the rating of a pandemic: case fatality rate, severity of morbidity, unexpected nature of the mortality patterns, and unusual complications (WHO 2009). WHO distinguishes a number of phases for an influenza pandemic. Phases one to three refer to where the infection is mainly confined to animal infections with few human infections. Phase four indicates sustained human-to-human infection at the community level. Phases five and six indicate widespread human infection, and then post peak (possibility of recurrent events) and post pandemic (disease at seasonal levels) are reached (WHO 2009). There has been an increase in the rise of new infections, including the Sever Acute Respiratory Syndrome (SARS), avian flu (H5N1), and swine flu (H1N1), as well as the ongoing threat of bioterrorism. In response, experts believe that a pandemic is imminent and threatening. An influenza pandemic is particularly dangerous as it may mutate, overcome vaccines, or migrate rapidly (Orsi & Santas 2010). The following sections review previous influenza responses, along with a discussion of how HR can respond in such situations.

The SARS pandemic of 2003 demonstrated the economic ramifications of an influenza outbreak and the importance of ensuring the health and safety of workers. Economists have estimated $2 billion losses in tourism, retail sales and productivity, and $1 billion losses each in Japan, Hong Kong, Taiwan and Singapore. In Toronto, a major centre of the outbreak, the financial impact was estimated at $30 million a day at the height of the crisis. The workforce was significantly reduced because of illness and precautionary measures. Service areas such as tourism, transportation (airlines) and retailing were hard hit as the public went into 'demand shock' and simply stopped shopping and going out (Tan & Enderwick 2006). Twenty-five restaurants in HK, for example, were closed in the first two weeks of April, leading to the unemployment of 1600 restaurant staff (Lee & Warner 2005). The HR responses in the Hong Kong hotel industry were reasonably well handled, and mass layoffs and redundancies were avoided. Staff were requested to take accumulated leave or 'no pay' leave. Pregnant women in one hotel were given 'special leave' with full pay when their annual leave was cleared. In terms of preventative mechanisms, staff were requested to take their body temperature before going to work, and were required to wear masks. Public areas were constantly cleaned, and lift-buttons, for example, were treated every two hours with diluted bleach. With respect to communication, there were repeated emails reminding employees of the importance of rest, good personal hygiene and staying at home if unwell (Lee & Warner 2005).

WHO advises a number of preparedness and response recommendations: planning and co-ordination, situation monitoring and assessment, reducing the spread of the disease, continuity of health care provision, and communications. The HR function has an active role in all of these responsibilities. Specifically, the HR group is responsible for appropriate leadership selection and training to assist with the planning and co-ordination of a response. HR also plays a critical information role in registering absences and possible areas of infection spread. With respect to the reduction in the spread of the disease, HR will need to assist with measures that allow social distance between staff and also with customers. Advice on hygiene and decisions about reduced employee travel and who should be placed on leave and how leave arrangements can best be utilised will primarily fall within the ambit of the HR function. The management of the health of workers will also require thought to be given to whether the organisation will provide immunisation when available, and how that procedure will be co-ordinated. Finally, HR has a critical role in communicating with employees, with their families and also with the public about how they are managing disease spread and social distancing requirements. The WHO 2009 publication *Pandemic Influenza Preparedness and Response*[24] provides a useful guide to the steps that should be taken within each of the pandemic phases identified above. A further WHO publication, *Whole of Society Pandemic Readiness*, also provides a useful pandemic influenza business continuity and management checklist for businesses and government organisations.[25] See also the Pandemic Planning Checklist for businesses published in the Harvard Business Review (2006) that was adapted from one developed by the US Department of Health and Human Services and the Centres for Disease Control and Prevention (CDC).

Before leaving the discussion of the management of a pandemic special, recognition needs to be given to the care of 'first responder', that group of professionals who have initial contact with people affected by the disease. Sectors such as hospitals and ambulatory care services, for example, will likely play a large role in containing any disease outbreak, as well as minimising the number of infections and mortalities (Orsi & Santos 2010). Employers of workers in these sectors therefore need to be particularly mindful of the psychological and physical impact on their staff. There are psychosocial implications of perceived risk and consequences due to occupational exposure. Quarantine, personal infection and the risk of

---

[24] < http://www.who.int/csr/disease/influenza/pipguidance2009/en/index.html> accessed 12th January 2011.

[25] <http://www.un-ic.org/web/documents/english/WHO%20WOS%20Pandemic%20 Readiness%20 2009-05-05.pdf>, accessed 12th January 2011.

unknowingly transmitting infection to loved ones and colleagues represents a serious need to focus on the health and well-being of health care workers. In a Toronto hospital, for example, one diagnosis of SARS resulted in twenty four members of the unit team being put into quarantine. As well as their physical removal, these workers carried stigmatisation by the public and friends (CCH 2005). Training therefore has to prepare health care workers who, in disaster scenarios, are exposed to significant psychosocial stress as a result of their role in implementing triage procedures. Effectively they have to make decisions about the allocation of scarce resources for multiple patients and address other practical strategies involving vaccine programs which rely on stockpile supplies of vaccines and anti-virals (CCH 2005).

Conclusions

Unfortunate and largely unexpected events will occur in the life of any organisation. Globalisation, the associated increase in more complex communications and employee movement, along with changing social values have created a context for an increase in the likelihood of unforseen events. In response, risk and crisis management are becoming common elements of business strategy and implementation. As most risks and crises have the potential for major ramifications for employees, the HRM function has a key role to play in both the strategic design of relevant programs as well as in the delivery of immediate assistance during and following any event. Material in the chapter has included a number of resources that can be used in business to assist in the design of an appropriate risk and crisis management approach, as well as issues that need to be addressed by the HRM function. Along with involvement in strategic planning for an event, HRM can assist in the recruitment and selection of leaders who are capable and flexible during a crisis. The HRM role also extends to workforce disaster management training and expectations about possible changed roles during work flow disruptions including communication roles and responsibilities. The management and deployment of a volunteer workforce may also need to be given some pre-planning. During an event, the HRM function is invaluable in providing up-to-date information about the location of staff who may be missing and the duties gaps that need to be filled. Information also has to be disseminated to staff to inform them of unfolding company policy and advice about how to handle situations such as social distancing in the event of a pandemic. There are also relationships with other stakeholders such as employee families, the media and emergency services in which HRM will play a role. Following an event, there is the necessary re-allocation of tasks and assistance in getting staff back to health and assisting families with management of affected workers. All of these tasks fall within the HRM responsibilities of protecting the human resource within an organisation, providing a safe and healthy workplace for workers, and ensuring an ongoing positive view of the organisation as an employer of choice.

References

Alexander, Y, Carlton, D & Wilkinson, P 1979, *Terrorism: Theory and Practice*, Westview Press, Boulder, CA.

Australian/New Zealand Standard AS/NZS ISO 31000, 2009, Risk Management: Principles and guidelines, Sydney and Wellington: Standards Australia

Australian Risk Roundtable 2008, Risk Thinkers Pty Ltd, Melbourne.

Briscoe, D & Schuler, R 2004, *International Human Resource Management* 2e, Routledge, New York.

BP CEO Tony Haywood to step down and be replaced by Robert Dudley, http://www.bp.com/genericarticle.do?categoryId=2012968&contentId=7063976, accessed 7 January, 2011.

Campbell, R 1999, *Crisis Control: Preventing and Managing Corporate Crisis*, Prentice Hall, Wollongong.

Casselman, B 2010, 'Aging Oil Rigs, Pipelines Expose Gulf to Accidents', Wall Street Journal. (Eastern edition) Dec 15, 2010, 1.

CCH 2005 *Guide to Managing OHS risks in the Health Care Industry*. CCH Australia, Sydney.

Cinkota, M, Knight, G, Liesch, P & Steen, J 2010, Terrorism and international business: A research agenda, *Journal of International Business Studies*, 41: 826-843.

Committee of Sponsoring Organizations of the Treadway Commission (2004) Enterprise Risk Management: Integrated Framework,

<http://www.coso.org/Publications/ERM/COSO_ERM_ExecutiveSummary.pdf>. Accessed 28th November, 2010

Crandell, W, Parnell, JA & Spillan, JE 2010, Crisis Management in the New Strategy Landscape, Sage, Thousand Oakes, California.

Dowling, PJ, Festing, M & Engle, AD 2008, *International Human Resource Management* (5th edn). Thomson Learning, South Melbourne.

Effective Crisis Management, The Tylenol Scandal and Crisis management, 1982, http://iml.jou.ufl.edu/projects/Fall02/Susi/tylenol.htm, accessed 7 January, 2011)

Glendon, AI, Clarke, SG, & McKenna, E 2006, *Human Safety and Risk Management* (2nd Ed) Taylor Francis Group, Boca Ranton.

Hallowell, M 2010, 'Safety risk perception in construction companies in the Pacific Northwest of the USA', *Construction Management and Economics*, 28 (4): 403- 413.

Harvard Business Essentials, 2004, *Crisis Management: Master the Skills to Prevent Disasters*, Harvard Business School Press, Boston.

Harvard Business Review, 2006, *Preparedness: Pandemic Planning Checklist for Businesses*, May 25-26.

Harvey, M 1993, 'A Survey of Corporate Programs for Managing Terrorist Threats', *Journal of International Business Studies*, 24 (3): 465-478.

Heath, R 1998, 'Dealing with complete crisis – the crisis management shell structure', *Safety Science*, 30: 139-150.

Henisz, W., Mansfield, E., & Von Glinow, A 2010, Conflict, security and political risk: International business in challenging times, *Journal of International Business Studies*, 41: 759-764.

Horlick-Jones, T 2005, 'Informal logics of risk: Contingency and modes of practical reasoning', *Journal of Risk Research*, 8(3): 253-272.

Lee, G. O. M., & Warner, M 2005, 'Epidemics, labour markets and unemployment: the impact of SARS on human resource management in the Hong Kong service sector', *International Journal of Human Resource Management,* 16 (5): 752-771.

Liou, D. & Lin, C 2008, 'HRP on Terrorism and crises in the Asia Pacific Region: cross-national challenge, reconsideration and proposition from western experiences', *Human Resource Management,* 47 (1): 49-72.

Lockwood, N 2005 *Crisis management in today's business environment: HR's strategic role,* SHRM Research Quarterly, 4, Society for HRM

Mankin, L., & Perry, R. W. 2004, Commentary: Terrorism challenges for human resource management, *Review of Public Personnel Administration*, 24, 1, 3-17.

Mayerhofer, H., Muller, B., Schmidt, A 2010,' Implications of flexpatriates' lifestyles on HRM', *Management Revue*, 21(2): 155-173.

Mendenhall, M, & Oddou, G 1985, 'The Dimensions of Expatriate Acculturation: A Review', *Academy of Management Review*, 10: 39-47.

Orsi, M., & Santos, J 2010, 'Probabilistic modelling of work-based disruptions and input-output analysis of independent ripple effects', Economic Systems Research, 22(1): 3 - 18

Perry, RW & Mankin, LD 2005, Preparing for the unthinkable: Managers, terrorism and the HRM function, *Public Personnel Management*, 34(2): 175 – 193.

Rodsutti, M 2005, How HR can help in the aftermath of disaster, *Human Resource Management International Digest*, 13 (5): 18-20.

Rose, N 1999, *Powers of Freedom: Reframing Political Thought*, University Press, Cambridge, Cambridge.

Sayegh, L, Anthony, WP, & Perrewe, PL 2004, 'Managerial decision-making under crisis: The role of emotion in an intuitive decision process', *Human Resource Management Review,* 14: 179-199.

Simon, H 1963, 'Economics and psychology' in S. Koch (Ed.), *Psychology: A study of a science* (Vol. 6), pp. 685-723, McGraw-Hill, New York, NY.

Sinclair, D, 2010, 'The origins of safety culture in coalmining: 'top-down' versus 'bottom-up'', *Journal of Health, Safety and Environment*, 26 (3): 249 -259.

Staples, J 2006, A new type of threat, *Harvard Business Review*, May, 20- 22.

Stephens, DO 2003, Protecting records, *Information Management Journal*, 37 (1): 33-40.

Tan, W & Enderwick, P 2006, Managing threats in the global era: The impact and response to SARS, *Thunderbird International Business Review*, 48 (4): 515-536.

Wake, P 2005, 'Leadership: a training need.' *The International Maritime Human Element Bulletin*, 6.

World Health Organization 2009, *Pandemic Influenza Preparedness and Response*, WHO, Geneva, http://www.who.int/csr/disease/influenza/pipguidance 2009 en index.html, accessed 12 Jan, 2011.

World Health Organization 2009, Whole of Society Pandemic Readiness, WHO, Geneva, http://www.un-pic.org/web/documents/english/WHO%20 WOS%20Pandemic %20Readiness%202009-05-05.pdf, accessed 12 Jan, 2011.

Wright, P, McMahan, G & McWilliams, A 1994, 'Human resources and sustained competitive advantage: a resource-based perspective', *International Journal of Human Resource Management*, 5 (2): 301-326.

Zelnick, J, O'Donnell, M 2005, 'The Impact of the HIV/AIDS Epidemic on Hospital Nurses in KwaZulu Natal, South Africa: Nurses' Perspectives and Implications for Health Policy', Journal of Public Health Policy. 26 (2): 163 – 187.

Case study: The Beaconsfield Mine disaster

Beaconsfield is a small mining town situated in the northeast of Tasmania. In 1869, limestone mining in the area led to the discovery of gold, and since that time the mine has operated intermittently. In the mid 1990s gold mining was resumed and, on 25 April 2006, a small earthquake triggered an underground rock fall and information released to the media reported that three of the miners working underground were trapped. The rock falls were sparked by seismic events that geophysicists suspect were caused by the mine operation itself. All three miners had been working on an eleganter machine at the time of the incident, placing wire mesh designed to prevent rock falls in the tunnel. Rescue work managed to uncovered the rear of the machine that the miners had been working on, but tonnes of fallen rocks forced rescue crews to dig a new tunnel around the blocked area.

The mine collapse quickly attracted global attention and raised speculation about the possibility of whether the miners would survive. Trapped one kilometre underground, the miners were identified as a Beaconsfield man Todd Russell, a footballer and father of three in his 30s, Brant Webb, 37, from nearby Beauty Point, and Larry Knight, in his 30s, from Youngstown in Launceston. Early the following morning, rescue teams located a dead miner after the operator of a remote controlled camera-equipped earth-moving machine unknowingly transferred his body to a rock stockpile.

As more information became available, it became apparent that Larry Knight had been killed in the initial rockfall, but that Brant Webb and Todd Russell were still alive. These two miners were trapped in part of the vehicle in which they had been working at the time of the collapse, confined within a basket that was part of the equipment that they were working in. The cage was partially filled with rock, and the men were buried under some rubble.

After 14 nights, at 4:27 am, rescuers finally reached the men, one of them yelling 'I can see your light' when he broke through the ground which was separating him from the miners, to which the miners replied 'I can see your light too'. At 5:58 am, both men walked out of the lift cage unaided, punching their fists in the air to the cheers of the Beaconsfield crowds who had gathered outside the mine gate. Wearing their fluoro jackets and lit miner's helmets, the men switched their safety tags to 'safe' on the mine out board before embracing family members.

In the period following the rescue, media attention and the Australian Workers Union (AWU) review opened fire on the Beaconsfield mine, detailing for the first time a succession of safety failures before the rock fall that killed one miner and trapped Webb and Russell for 14 days.

After meeting miners, the AWU revealed:

- It could not identify one underground miner who had received OH&S training at the site.
- Miners had complained of a reduction in the amount of cement used to harden concrete that they used to backfilled exploited areas of the mine.
- Key 'crown' pillars meant to provide support had been removed from deep workings.
- Steel safety mesh bolted to the walls of the mine - used to stabilise the workings - had failed to contain rocks. The rocks were active and were 'blowing out' - that is, blowing the safety protection off the walls.

Tasmania's premier at the time met the then AWU's federal secretary, Bill Shorten, after the union meeting at Beaconsfield. Mr Shorten raised pressure for an independent inquiry, but he held open the possibility that miners could return to parts of the mine declared safe. However, he warned: 'If the current mining methods are sought to be pursued, most of them won't go back down'.

Sources:

New bid to reach missing miners, *Sydney Morning Herald*, 27 April, 2006, http://www.smh.com.au/articles/2006/04/27/1145861446863.html, accessed 12 Jan, 2011.

A Disaster waiting to happen, *Sydney Morning Herald*, Andrew Darby 16 May, 2006, http://www.smh.com.au/news/national/a-disaster-waiting-to-happen/2006/05/15/1147545265579.html, accessed 12 Jan, 2011.

Beers, tears and cheers at Beaconsfield, *NineMSM*, Emma Chamberlain, 9 May, 2006, http://news.ninemsn.com.au/article.aspx?id=99319, accessed 12 Jan, 2011.

Case study questions

1. Using ideas from the chapter, identify the responsibilities that would have been taken on by the HRM function during the mine collapse and the wait for the release of the miners.

2. What plans could an HRM function put into place following such a disaster?

Discussion questions

1. Apply the proposed management of risk process as set out by The international Risk Management Standard, AS/NZS ISO 31000:2009 to risk of sending an Australian expatriate to Indonesia.

2. What contributions are made by the technical, economic, cultural and psychometric interpretations of risk to the management of HRM safety and reputation concerns?

3. Why have risk and crisis management become more prominent business concerns in the past 20 years?

4. Specify key HRM responsibilities before, during and after a crisis.

Chapter 13

THE GREENING OF SKILLS IN THE 21ST CENTURY

INTRODUCTION

From public discussions to major reports commissioned by the Australian federal government (see the Garnaut reports 2008a; 2008b), it is clear that the development of a progressively more sustainable economy is growing. The foundations of this will be the development of 'green-collar' jobs underpinned by 'green-collar' skills. The tightrope that needs to be managed in this context is the relationship between economic growth and environmental considerations. This is where research by Hatfield-Dodds, Turner, Schandi and Doss (hereafter the CSIRO Report) (2008:1) has argued that well-designed policies in this area can substantially decouple economic growth from environmental pressures, and have limited impact on national employment. This is because the CSIRO report notes the high potential for employment across a variety of sectors in this respect. However the CSIRO caveat on this projection is 'a massive mobilisation of skills and training'. This CSRIO report argues that there needs to be a two-pronged focus: firstly, in equipping new workers with the appropriate skills; and secondly, enabling appropriate changes in practices by workers already working in key sectors where change opportunities have been identified. This chapter explores the emerging issues in the developing field of a growing 'green-collar' economy from an employment perspective, and looks at the issues HR professionals will have to consider – particularly in a training and development context.

Defining green skills

The concept of 'green-collar' jobs as the vanguard for a 'green-collar' economy has a simple yet appealing resonance with the challenges increasingly being faced in developing a progressively more sustainable economy. However, when it comes to defining 'green-collar' jobs, the definition becomes difficult to clearly articulate. This is because, at one level, the varying interpretations of sustainability, environmentalism, occupation and industry make it difficult to clearly define the sector (IEANZ 2009). And, at a second level, there is an assumption that green-collar jobs are linked with 'clean and green' forms of energy efficiency and sustainability, when the reality is that much of the innovation needs to come from traditional sectors such as heavy industry (Bill, Mitchell & Weller 2008; Pearce & Stillwell 2009). As such, the definition by Armadale, Morrison-Sanders and Duxbury (2004) provides a broader spectrum, focusing on innovative practices to reduce the negative impact on the environment of 'dirty industries', while also focusing on jobs that are designed specifically for sustainability. The key element to this definition is that there are *two* areas for developing new jobs and skills, since it is additionally looking at transitioning traditional sectors to a more sustainable focus.

Developing green skills – a theoretical perspective

As advanced market economies (AMEs) move increasingly from a manufacturing to a knowledge base, the development of employees' knowledge, skills and abilities (KSAs) has become an increasingly significant aspect of contemporary HRM. Indeed, as Hadfield-Dodds *et al.* (2008) point out:

> *Human capital is the most valuable component of the economic wealth of nations, accounting for more than 75% of the total asset base of high income nations, and 40-60% in developing nations (see Hamilton 2006).*

The key literature providing a theoretical perspective to understand the strategic approach linked to the long-term development of the organisation's human resources is human capital theory. Human capital theory links investment in the organisation's key asset, employees, to increased productivity and sustained competitive advantage (Schultz 1959; Becker 1964; Smith 1998). The strategic aspect is the long-term enhancement of the firm's resource base by linking employee skill development with retention through training, development and career management (Garavan *et al.* 2001). As new markets emerge – e.g. the green economy – the focus is on an organisation developing their human resources through investments in human resource development (HRD) strategies to take advantage of the emerging sectors and economies. (Barney 1991; Walton 1999; Garavan *et al.* 2001), thus providing the essential elements for building sustained organisational competitive advantage (Boxall and Steenveld 1999; Delery and Shaw 2001; Wright, Dunford and Snell 2001; Garavan *et al.* 2001; and Boxall and Purcell 2003).

This strategic focus on the management and development of human resources can be linked to the deliberate promotion of human resource management and development strategies as a catalyst for the development of key human resources. This has led to an increased focus on HRD as a platform for building a competitive advantage. A critical element is the implementation of diverse strategies for staff enhancement and development as an important attraction and retention tool, creating a competitive advantage. Organisations taking this strategic course will seek a long-term and diverse approach to managing and investing in their human resources, and will ensure that appropriate training and development is available to all 'core' employees.

The management of learning and knowledge within organisations in more complex and competitive environments reflects a significant strategic role for HRD in the creation of competitive advantage – a theme which is increasingly reflected in the literature (Walton 1999; Garavan *et al.* 2001; Holland & De Cieri 2006). As such, the field of human resource development has been identified as an increasingly critical aspect of strategic HRM (Stewart and McGoldrich 1996; Prince and Stewart 2002; Homan and Macpherson 2005), and nowhere more is this important than in the development of 'green skill'. In a dynamic environment, this means that the organisations must commit resources to strategically develop a diverse and adaptive approach to ensure that each area within the organisation has access to appropriate levels of training and development to meet diverse organisational objectives.

Developing green skills – a historical perspective

> *The structural changes that will emerge in a low-emissions, growing economy will change requirements for human capital. In Australia, a history of skill development has been inherent in a globally successful resource sector. Australia should be structurally well placed to apply such skills to new activities (Garnaut 2008a).*

In the context of this new economic environment, organisations will need to adapt to this new paradigm in a variety of ways. The 'new' skills required will need to be defined and redefined as the skills requirements emerge and develop. In addition, 'traditional' employment skills will need to be realigned with the demands of the emerging 'green' economy. Management must, therefore, develop both structural and cultural conditions, including more diverse and proactive strategies around training and development as key aspects of sustained competitive advantage. What will be needed is a proactive approach to the management of human resources and, more particularly, to human resource development strategies linked to employee development and employability.

However, this shift needs to be seen in the context of the traditional Australian approach to training and development over the past century. The foundation of Australia, underpinned by protectionist industry policies reinforced highly rigid and hierarchical work patterns supported by strong trade unions, resulted in training and development in Australia remaining largely fragmented and narrowly focused around occupational skills and managerial control (McKeown and Teicher 2006:26). Supporting this approach was the reliance on waves of migration to alleviate the cycles of skill shortages and inter-firm mobility (poaching), which reinforced the insular, complacent and inwardly-focused approach of both industry and successive federal governments in the development of the Australian workforce (Ford 1990; Lansbury & McDonald 1999). Training and development in Australia therefore has a tradition of being *ad hoc* and crisis driven (McKeown & Teicher 2006), or what might be described as 'the Australian hegemony' (Holland, Sheehan & DeCieri 2007). Even with the dismantling of the trade and protection barriers from the 1970s and labour market deregulation issues associated with human resource development as a source of competitive advantage for industry and governments has waxed and waned. Federal government initiatives through the late 1980s and early 1990s, such as award restructuring where skill and remuneration were linked, only provided limited success and major programs such as the Training Guarantee Act (TGA) which developed as a catalyst for cultural change[26] (Smith & Freeland 2002), was seen more as a tax than a training incentive and the program was suspended in 1994 and abolished in 1996.

In regard to the Howard government period (1996-2007), it has been argued that the increased pace of deregulation resulted in limited progress on a human resource development agenda (McKeown & Teicher 2006), and that this has continued to make investment policies in training and development increasingly discretionary. These institutional attitudes are also appearing in research on the development of green skills. Research by CSIRO (2008) indicates that the knowledge of green skills and workforce capabilities is very poor, with no systematic gathering of information or data in these areas. From a long-term perspective, the CSIRO report also notes that there is no systematic collection of curricula that support the development of green skills training and development. CSIRO notes, therefore, in this situation that, due to this lack of data, employment growth is likely to be haphazard, and that skill shortages are likely to affect the ability of consumers to move to more energy efficient alternatives. The report also notes that the lack of adequately skilled workforce is affecting the take-up of solar energy use (NREL 2006:61).

---

[26] The TGA required organisation with payrolls in excess of A$200,000 to direct up to 1.5 per cent of payroll to training or be levied an equivalent amount (Smith & Freeland 2002).

Developing green skills – a policy perspective

The green skills agreement

In 2009, the Rudd federal Labor government proposed a national green skills agenda, in which green skills audits would be undertaken and in which all apprenticeship and vocational education and training (VET) would include green skills development. The agreement, developed between the Federal government and the states and territories, acknowledged the development of new skills and the application of existing skills to new work practices. The focus on the VET sector reflect the fact that over 1.7 million Australians participate in VET annually through 4,000 registered training providers (NCVER 2008). VET is therefore the critical platform upon which new and transition training can be provided to facilitate the change and development of skill policies and practices.

The principles of the agreement

The principles of the green skills agreement were to:

- deliver a nationally consistent and coordinated approach, while recognising the need for flexible and innovative approaches across jurisdictions, industries and workplaces;
- collaborate with employer and employee representatives, the VET sector and community organisations;
- complement and leverage existing national agreements, policies. programs and initiatives at jurisdictional levels;
- utilise the best available evidence to inform implementation;
- demonstrate transparency and accountability;
- align with the Australian Quality Training Framework (AQTF); and
- seek to achieve international best practice.

Source: Green Skills Agreement 2009:2.

However, in reflecting on these development, Tom Karmel, the Managing Director of the National Centre for Vocational Education Research (NCVER), has cautioned that, whilst acknowledging the push towards a green economy and a green skills base by policy makers, several cost-benefit issues need to be addressed. These concerns include the over-emphasis on green-specific skills, and developing an agenda before the skill requirements are clearly delineated. This, he notes, is because skill requirements develop relatively slowly in the labour market and are subject to changes in demand, to technological developments and to costs. As Karmel explains:

> *Plumbers may need to be able to install grey water systems, but they are still plumbers. The techniques they use will be driven by the way the technology is changing, and this is occurring independently of an sustainability issue (2009:8).*

Continuing the plumbing theme, Karmel notes, for example, that the cost issue driving change was the catalyst for the change in copper to plastic piping. Finally, at a macro or strategic level, Karmel argues that much of the policy development is predicated on current thinking about the issues of green economy and green skills. As we come to embrace these changes, new issue, and opportunities will develop, and conventional thinking and attitudes to cost and skill development will change. Karmel argues, therefore, for an incremental approach to education and training in the green skills area, so as not to create a false dawn of opportunities and potentially damage the development of this sector.

Box 13.1: Setting price will create '34,000 jobs'

Adam Morton, 28 February, 2011.

A carbon price aimed at cutting greenhouse gas emissions by 25 per cent by 2020 could help create 34,000 jobs in regional Australia, research says. To be launched today by independent MP Tony Windsor, the report by the Climate Institute predicts that a substantial carbon price, backed by renewable energy policies, would trigger tens of billions of dollars of investment in geothermal, large-scale solar, bio-energy, hydro, wind and gas.

In Victoria, the number of people employed in the electricity industry was projected to increase over the next two decades despite some job losses as coal-fired power plants closed. The new jobs would be concentrated in the state's Western District, central highlands and the Mallee. Climate Institute chief executive John Connor said the report, based on work conducted by consultants SKM-MMA and Ernst & Young, showed that clean-energy projects could provide an economic foundation to support strong regional populations.

It challenged claims that tackling climate change would cost jobs and hurt the economy. "It is important we have a discussion about the costs and how to manage them, but it is also important to look at the benefits and how you achieve those," Mr Connor said. Mr Windsor said the report showed regional Australia could be a big winner as renewable energy projects were developed. It is estimated nearly 6900 new electricity industry jobs could be created in Victoria by 2030.

Nearly 4600 would be in power plant construction and about 1200 in manufacturing. More than 1000 would be permanent roles running

> new plants. The total number of jobs in the industry would rise over the next five years as wind and gas plants were built, dip in the second half of the decade, but then grow dramatically after 2020 as more clean-energy technologies became commercially viable.
>
> The report suggests about 40 per cent of Victoria's electricity could come from clean sources by 2030, up from 5 per cent today. Gas-fired power, with about a third the emissions of brown coal, would also expand dramatically to provide about a third of the state's electricity. Specific projections for Victoria include:
>
> - More than 1500 jobs created in wind and geothermal energy in the south-west around Warrnambool, Portland and Hamilton.
> - Nearly 1200 new jobs relating to building and running large-scale solar plants in the Mallee.
> - About 600 new jobs in wind in the central highlands around Ballarat and Bendigo.
> - In the Latrobe Valley, the loss of about 500 permanent jobs in coal power, but the creation of 720 construction jobs building new gas and renewable plants.
>
> The modelling does not consider the impact of the possible implementation of carbon capture and storage technology. The jobs figures are based on a carbon price starting at $47 in 2012, the national 20 per cent renewable energy target, and policies to encourage clean technologies, including loan guarantees and tax credits. The research won the support of the ACTU and several energy companies.
>
> Tony Maher, the president of the mining and energy union, applauded the Climate Institute for focusing on jobs, skills and training as the key to Australia cutting emissions.
>
> *Source*: http://www.climateinstitute.org.au.

Developing green skills – an industry perspective

In attempting to bridge skills gaps, the ACTU, in conjunction with the Australian Conservation Foundation, commissioned a study into green skilling on the basis of an analysis of 30 green industries globally. To determine the keys to developing green skills and sustained completive advantage, the study used the following criteria:

- a strong projected domestic and global demand;
- an existing Australian industry and R&D base that is energetic, ambitious, leading the way on technological development, and

possessing the capacity to respond well to domestic policy levers; and

- the existence of policy options that can stimulate demand while increasing environmental protection and /or improving resource efficiency (2008:10).

Based upon these criteria, six key sectors where identified where the potential for growth: was high and, consequently, so was the opportunity for green skills and employment:

- *Renewable energy.* The focus here is on developing energy from renewable sources such as wind, sea and solar.

- *Energy efficiency.* This approach concentrates on reducing energy use in buildings and production systems.

- *Sustainable water systems.* Here the focus is on improving the efficiency of current technologies and on developing alternate technologies.

- *Biomaterials.* Derived from renewable resources such as sugar and vegetable oil biomaterials, biomaterials potentially use fewer resources such as water.

- *Green buildings.* This is a high potential area when retro fitting is taken into consideration. The prospect for high level energy and resources savings in construction and retro-fitting in a booming economy is likely to be significant.

- *Waste and recycling.* The most traditional of the green area – waste management and recycling domestically and internationally – will continue to grow.

Source: ACTU/ACF 2008.

Developing green skills – a practical perspective

From a human resource management and development perspective, the report estimates that the creation of a strong domestic market supported by government policies could create 500,000-plus jobs by 2030 (ACTU/ACF 2008). Significantly, however, the report highlights a major issue, that is, the failure to address skills and training bottlenecks which would see business and skills move overseas (ACTU/ACF 2008). A key recommendation of the report, therefore, is the fostering and development of green skills in the workforce by identifying key needs, industry skills, training bodies and stakeholder (ACTU/ACF 2008:4). This is also supported by the Cutler Review (2008), which recommended:

- investing in high quality human capital, which is critical to innovation; equipping people with the skills to innovate, which is essential for the generation and application of new knowledge; and using and adapting knowledge produced elsewhere.

- building high quality human capital by investing at all levels of education – from early childhood education and schooling, through vocational education and training and higher education, and on into the workplace – since public education spending has been waning both as a share of our own economy and relative to other countries (2008:1).

This final point is critical, as the historical development of skills in Australia has been deeply entrenched in the buy-in/poach model of human capital acquisition over a developmental approach. This was highlighted in research by Holland *et al.* (2007), which analysed the intent of human resource management in an Australia-wide survey. This research illustrates that, while there is a tacit understanding of the need to adopt new strategies in human capital development, active policies in the area of retention and development do not reflect this. The research found that, behind the rhetoric of an increasing focus on human resources as a source of sustained competitive advantage, Australian organisations are still coming to terms with the importance of human resource development as a source of competitive advantage. It appears that the Australian habit of relying on immigration and poaching remains deeply ingrained. And, this also needs to be seen in the context of a strong economy where high employment levels place a premium on currently scarce skill availability (CSIRO 2008).

> ### Box 13.2: Growth spurt for green jobs
>
> As an increasing number of organisations take action to implement sustainability strategies in the wake of debate on a carbon tax, many Australians are seeking pathways to green careers. Donald Munro, who has a Master of Arts in Economic Science and has worked in insurance for 15 years, turned his career around in just two years after being driven by a desire to do something about climate change. 'Who wants to be dealing with the exponentially increasing volumes of insurance claims in a climate change-ravaged world?' Munro asks.
>
> After completing a postgraduate certificate in sustainability at Melbourne's Swinburne University of Technology and a carbon accounting course, Munro landed a part-time role as sustainability manager at the Salvos Stores in Melbourne. He also lectures in carbon accounting at Swinburne's National Centre for Sustainability. Moving to a green career has not been without its challenges, and Munro says it is crucial to network and volunteer. While studying part time, he did volunteer work with the Environmental Jobs Network, an online resource for people wanting to move into the environmental sector.

Soon after, he was offered a part-time job as the EJN manager.

Towards the end of his course, he did a voluntary project for the Salvos Stores. When he presented the board with a 50-page report, he jokingly said: 'If you are serious about this and want to do this for real, you need to give me a job.' He was called back three months later and offered the position. Munro advises people who are considering a green career to try matching it with their existing skills. 'My background, in addition to working in insurance, is managerial, and includes business acumen and people skills,' he says. 'I'm doing that again, although I now have a green title. I have one eye to sustainability and am thinking: Can we do this in a better way?'

Lisa Tarry, Managing Director of Turning Green Recruitment, says sustainability is no longer treated within companies as a specialist subject, but as an integrated core business concern. 'Sustainability is now an economic imperative for many organisations, tracked through economic, environmental and social metrics over the business planning cycle,' Tarry says. 'One misconception of green jobs is that they operate in a rigid framework or industry that involves getting dirt under your nails and a degree in science or horticulture, when in actual fact they exist across every industry.'

KPMG's preview of its 2011 Global Corporate Sustainability report shows sustainability has moved up the corporate agenda in the past three years. Sixty-two per cent of companies surveyed have a strategy for corporate sustainability, up from just over half in February 2008. Turning Green has seen an increase in roles across all industries, and these roles also involve overall leadership and management of the organisations. There also has been an increase in executive leadership roles for key industry associations and non-profit organisations that advance the green agenda.

So, what are the opportunities for people who want to move into green jobs? Australia has no agreed definition for green occupations, which Tarry says makes it difficult to estimate what new and emerging occupations exist or are likely to be created. On a cautionary note, Tarry says that, even if you are lucky enough to secure your dream sustainability role, it doesn't mean that you won't encounter barriers such as a lack of broader organisational commitment and buy-in, or difficulties integrating your work with organisational values. She adds: 'Believe it or not, you could still find yourself struggling to engage employees, boards and management.' Making a green career change is not without risk. 'Unfortunately, gaining a Masters in Environmental Management or the like, with no previous experience, does not guarantee you a job,' Tarry says. 'It's really about demonstrating entrepreneurship, being an entrepreneur within your organisation, enterprise or venture and greening your established job.' Tarry says that business leaders and managers are being challenged by rising expectations of stockholders and stakeholders over corporate performance in areas of environmental, social and governance issues. She believes that Australia needs to put a price on carbon to help drive the transition to a low-carbon economy.

Jason Downes, Managing Director of Eco Recruitment, says that the global financial crisis had a serious effect on the recruitment industry, but that there have been marked improvements since the upswing. Eco Recruitment is a niche agency focused on sourcing candidates for the water, environmental and sustainability industries. Downes says that the data points to the environmental industry '...sitting on the cusp of a massive jobs explosion. Jobs are being created every week that really didn't exist three or four years ago. This is as a result of tighter legislation around environmental compliance, a community that is demanding great corporate social responsibility, and a technical workforce that wants to be involved in solving environment-related problems. The Australian industry lacks the skilled people necessary to fill the jobs being created. And, as a result, we are regularly asked to identify suitable individuals who may be located offshore.' Downes also says that Australia needs to invest in more education and training to ensure a continuing pipeline of qualified people with the required level of technical understanding.

Source: *The Weekend Australian*: *Professional Section*, J Stirling, p. 1.

Developing a framework for green skills

Acknowledging the critical skill shortage for green skill development, the ACTU/ACF (2008) report identified the need for a skills audit, as only through such a process would skill shortages, bottlenecks and deficiencies be identified. This is supported by the CSIRO (2008) report, which has proposed a national agenda and an education and skills development framework linked to workplace requirements. It also recommends:

- that accredited courses formally recognising green 'practitioners' should be further created and disseminated across vocations and professions;
- that a significant proportion of slots in the Commonwealth Productivity Places Program should be allocated to green skills development; and
- that national skill training bodies and stakeholders, including Skills Australia, should identify and promote the development of

the skills that will be required to create a low-carbon, sustainable future with a focus on current high-impact industries.

Source: CSIRO 2008:18.

Such a coordinated approach would help facilitate and develop training needs, training paths and accreditation to ensure that investments are clearly directed to critical areas of need.

Developing green skills – a case study perspective

Zoos Victoria

In 2009, as part of its new strategic 20-year plan to become an international leader in zoo-based conservation, Zoos Victoria undertook to develop the 'green skills' of its workforce. The 'Skill-Up Green' project, which in its first phase carries out a training-needs-analysis (audit) of the workforce, provides the opportunity to target skill-specific requirements and to develop appropriate programs to facilitate workforce development of green skills linked to conservation strategies. The catalyst for the program was the Federal Government's VET initiatives – 'skills for sustainability' – which provide the technical expertise for this new area of skill development.

Source: Zoos Victoria 2009.

Green electricians

The demand for environmentally efficient and sustainable buildings, both commercial and domestic (including retro-fitting), is providing the building industry with new challenges as well as new opportunities and skill sets. One of these initiatives is the Global Green Electricians accredited training program. The Global Green Electricians accredited course provides electrical workers with the knowledge and skills to develop this sector. The course, which is an initiative of the Electrical Trades Union (ETU) and of Electrical and Electronic Industry Training Ltd (EEIT), provides energy expertise and skills on energy efficiency, on the renewable aspects of building development, and on retro-fitting. In conjunction with partners Holmesglen TAFE and RMIT University, the five-day course skills electricians in reducing greenhouse emissions, in calculating and auditing energy uses, in providing options on reducing energy use, as well as in understanding the rebate and certification processes and the regulatory framework.

Source: ETU Victoria 2010.

Toyota Australia

The development and commercialising of energy efficient technologies in traditional heavy manufacturing has the potential to put Australia at the vanguard of these developments. An example of this is the development and market growth in fuel-efficient cars. Toyota has committed to the development of the hybrid Toyota Camry at the Altona plant in Victoria. With support for the Federal Government's Green Car Innovation Fund, it is estimated that the hybrid Camry will contribute $150 million to the Australian economy. Toyota is Australia's largest vehicle exporter.

Source: Invest Victoria 2008 and Allen Consulting Group 2009.

University challenge

The serious industry skill gaps in sustainability and green skills training in industry has seen several levels of education attempt to bridge this gap. Swinburne University, which incorporates both tertiary and vocational education sectors, has developed the National Centre for Sustainability (NCS) . The centre focuses on integrating sustainability into a wide range of national training packages. The Graduate Certificate program 'up-skills' trainers and shows how sustainability can be embedded throughout a curriculum instead of simply being an add-on. This qualification is being complimented at Swinburne by a professional development program for over 450 trainers from registered training organisations around Australia. The impetus for these programs comes from the demand for industry capability and skills, and from a shortage of experiences in green skills and qualified trainers equipped to contextualise training to the concepts of sustainability.'

Source: Building Skills: a Sustainable Workforce, Skills Victoria 2009.

References

ACTU/ACF Report (2008) Green Gold Rush: How Ambitious Environmental Policy can make Australia a Leader in the Global Race for Green Jobs. Melbourne.

Allen Consulting Group (2009) Victoria's Greenhouse Opportunity Set. Melbourne.

Armadale, D, Morrison-Saunders & Duxbury, L 2004, 'Regional Sustainability Initiative: The Growth of Green Jobs in Australia. *Local Environment*. 9(11): 81-87.

Barney, J 1991, 'Firm resources and sustained competitive advantage', *Journal of Management,* 17: 99-120.

Becker, GS 1964, *Human Capital: A Theoretical Analysis with Special Reference to Education*, New York: Colombia University Press.

Bill, A., Mitchell, W & Weller, R 2008, *A Just Transition to Renewable Energy. Economy In the Hunter Region*, Australia. GoFFE, Newcastle.

Boxall, P & Steenveld, M 1999, 'Human Resource Strategy and Competitive Advantage: A Longitudinal Study of Engineering Consultancies', *Journal of Management Studies*, 36(4): 443-463

Boxall, P & Purcell, J 2008, *Strategy and Human Resource Management*, 2nd edn, Basingstoke: Palgrave Macmillan.

Cutler, T 2008, Venturous Australia – Building Strength in Innovation. Report of the Cutler Review of the National Innovation System to the Department of Innovation. Sept.

Delery, J & Shaw, J 2001, 'The Strategic Management of People in Work Organizations: Review, Synthesis and Extension', *Research in Personnel and Human Resource Management*, 20:165-197.

De Cieri, H & Holland, P 2006, 'The strategic role of human resource development', in P Holland & H De Cieri (ed.) *Contemporary Issue in Human Resource Development*, Sydney: Pearson Education Australia, pp. 3-24.

Electrical Trades Union (ETU) Victoria 2010, Accredited Training for Electricians in: Renewable and Energy Efficiency. Melbourne.

Environmental Institute of Australia and New Zealand (EIANZ) 2009, What are the Green Collar Workers? Defining and Identifying Workers in Sustainability and the Environment. Connection Research/DECC NSW. Australia.

Ford. GW 1990, Rethinking skilling for a restructured workplace, 10th Occasional Paper, Commission for the Future, Canberra, ACT. Australian Government Publishing Service:

Garnaut Climate Change Review 2008a, Interim Report to the Commonwealth, State and Territory Governments of Australia. Melbourne.

Garnaut Climate Change Review 2008b, Final Report to the Commonwealth, State and Territory Governments of Australia. Melbourne.

Garavan, T Moreley, M, Gunnigle, P & Collins, E 2001, 'Human Capital Accumulation: The Role of Human Resource Development', *Journal of European Industrial Training*, 25: 48-68.

Green Skills Agreement 2009, Council of Australian Government.

Hamilton, K 2006, Where is the Wealth of Nations? Measuring Capital for the 21st Century. World Bank, Washington DC.

Hatfield-Dodds, S, Turner, G, Schandi, H, & Doss, T 2008, Growing the Green Collar Economy: Skills and Labour Challenges in Reducing our Greenhouse Emissions and National Environmental Footprint. CSIRO Report to the Dusseldorp Skills Forum. Canberra.

Holland, P & De Cieri, H 2006, *Human Resource Development: A Contemporary Perspective* (eds). Pearson Education. Australia. 1-26.

Holland, PJ Sheehan, C & DeCieri, H 2007, 'Attracting and Retaining Talent : Exploring Human Resource Development Trends in Australia Human Resources'. *Development International* 10(3): 247-261.

Homan, G & Macpherson, A 2005, 'E-Learning in the Corporate University', *Journal of European Industrial Training*, 30(1): 75-90.

Invest Victoria 2008, Victoria Chosen for Toyota Camry Hybrid manufacture. June 10.

Karmel, T 2009, Skilling and Re-skilling for our (Greener) future. Paper presented at the 2009 Economic and Social Outlook Conference. Melbourne.

Lansbury, R & McDonald, D 1999, 'Employment relations and the managerial revolution in the public sector', in R Morris, D Mortimer & P Leece (ed.), *Workplace reform and enterprise bargaining issues*. Harcourt Brace: Marrickville, NSW.

McKeown, T & Teicher, J 2006, 'Human Resource Management in a Deregulated Environment', in P Holland & H De Cieri (ed.) *Contemporary Issue in Human Resource Development*, Sydney: Pearson Education Australia, pp. 25-54.

National Renewable Energy Laboratory (NREL) 2006, Non-Technical Barriers to Solar Energy Use: Review of Recent Literature. Colorado. USA.

Pearce, A & Stillwell, F 2009, 'Green Collar Jobs: Employment Impacts of Climate Change Policies'. *Journal of Australian Political Economy*. 62:1-20. (March)

Prince, C & Stewart, J 2002, 'Corporate universities – an analytical framework', *Journal of Management Development*, 21(10): 794-811.

Schultz, T 1959, 'Investment in Man: An Economist's View'. *The Social Service Review*, 33(2):109-117.

Skills Victoria 2009, *Building Skills- A Sustainable Workforce*. Melbourne.

Smith, A 1998, *Training and Development in Australia*, 2nd edn, Sydney: Butterworth.

Smith, A 2003, 'Recent trends in Australian training and development', *Asia Pacific Journal of Human Resources*, 41(2):231-244.

Smith A & Freeland, B 2002, Industry training - Causes and Consequences. Leabrook, SA. National Centre for Vocational Research.

Stewart, J & McGoldrich, J 1996, *Human Resource Development: Perspectives, Strategies and Practice*, London: Financial Times Pitman Publishing.

Thomas, DC, Au, K & Ravlin, EC 2003, 'Cultural Variation and Psychological Contract', *Journal of Organizational Behaviour*, 24(4):451-471.

Walton, J 1999, *Strategic Human Resource Development*, London: Pearson Education Limited.

Wright, P, Dunford, B & Snell, S 2001, 'Human resources and the resource based view of the firm', *Journal of Management*, 27: 701-721.

Zoos Victoria 2009, Skill Up Green.

Chapter 14

JUSTICE AT WORK

INTRODUCTION

As the proceeding chapters have illustrated, the workplace is becoming an ever more dynamic, complex and pressured environment as new technology and globalisation challenges the way we think and work. From a human resource management perspective, it is an increasingly important responsibility to manage these key highly-skilled resources, which are increasingly mobile, in a way that will enable the organisation to retain them and become considered an 'employer of choice' for these employees to then recommend and return to in the future. Underpinning this is the notion that, in the midst of all this change, complexity and dynamism, the organisation's decision-making processes are underpinned by a sense of organisational justice. Indeed, this goes to the heart of contemporary human resource management, with its emphasis on building relationships between employee and management based upon mutual trust and respect (Lawler 2003).

As Burke (2008) notes, 'treating people right' is very difficult. As the chapters of this book illustrate, the nature of the issues faced by human resource managers are complex and require an in-depth understanding of the issues. For example, the psychological contract chapter illustrated that issues of breach and violation of contract are viewed by different people in different ways, based upon individual perceptions and perceived relationships with the organisation. The issues explored with regard to monitoring and surveillance illustrate how these policies can impinge on employee privacy and create an oppressive environment.

Whilst the complex and dynamic nature of the workplace can potentially be seen to overwhelm the ability of management to 'treat people right', Burke (2008) argues that, by placing strong emphasis on and resources into developing fair and equitable systems to manage these issues, organisations can attract and retain high skilled employees whilst motivating them to perform at higher levels. As Cropanzano and Randall (1993) note, whilst the research on justice largely emerged out of the field of social psychology, these concepts have increasingly been applied to human resource management issues and, from an applied perspective, offer new insights into the effective management of human resources. The consequences of not taking this approach manifest themselves in problems associated with a poor workplace climate, including health and well-being, morale, turnover, commitment and satisfaction. Indeed, Schabracq and Cooper (2000; 2003) argue that the way organisations approach these issues will become critical factors in competitiveness. So, what type of framework can an organisation develop to sustain itself as an organisation that is perceived to be 'treating people right'? This chapter explores issues associated with organisational justice as an issue in itself, and also in the context of the topics discussed in this book as a reflection of the workplace that people want to work in.

Justice at work – A theoretical perspective

A key aspect of employees' attraction, retention, development and general well-being is how the employee views and evaluates organisational decisions in terms of their perceived fairness, equity outcomes and treatment – or what has become increasingly understood as organisational justice (Boxall and Purcell 2008). As Gibson and Campbell-Quick (2008) note, the concepts of organisational justice – defined as the degree of equity and fairness employees are shown by the organisation – influence employee attitudes, emotions, trust, their sense of what is morally right and wrong, and increasingly whether this is an organisation that they want to work for or be associated with. Putting this in a human resource management context, the concept of organisational justice needs to be built upon trust, which is critical to developing employee commitment to organisations goals that are designed to increase organisational performance (Nicholls, Danford & Tasiran 2009). Because of the dynamic nature of the employment relationship, this reciprocity has both a positive and negative side. As such, the action of management towards employees is being continually evaluated and assessed by both employees and their representative. As Lewis and Welgert (1985) note, the actions by others imply reciprocal trust, and those actions that violate trust create an atmosphere of distrust and employees are thus less disposed to developing a committed relationship with management. Trust, therefore, becomes a key moderator in the relationship between HR practices and employee attitudes to management. As Sheahan (2005) in *Chapter 2: Managing the War for Talent* points out, organisations that have a serious negative image regarding their work practices will not attract in-demand talented people. So, if justice in the workplace is an increasingly critical issue, what is it and how can we manage it?

The concept of organisational justice

As a concept, the idea of justice can be taken back to Plato and Aristotle and, as noted, is bound with the concepts of fairness and equity. These ideas have been subsequently develop by Locke and Rousseau through to contemporary research by Rawls and Nozick (see Shaw & Barry 2004). With the increasing changes that have taken place in the workplace in terms of relationships (types of employment contracts) and the way we work (increasingly in cyberspace), the notion of justice has become an important area of research that focuses on better understanding and dealing with issues in the workplace that have never been conceived preciously, e.g. genetic testing, electronic offshoring, and social networking, which are discussed in this book. In this context, research indicates that the notion of justice has been developed to the extent that it is now seen to be made up of several components which need to be managed both separately and in unison in order for a robust framework to develop within an organisation. Organisational justice focuses on the perception of employees of the fairness and equity of the organisation's policies, processes and practices related to decision-making and the communication of information, the allocated resources, and the treatment of individual employees and other stakeholders in the organisation (Lewis, Thornhill & Sanders 2003). Within this context, organisational justice can be viewed from four inter-related perspectives: distributive justice, procedural justice, interactional justice, and informational justice. These perspectives are developed below.

Distributive justice

Distributive justice focuses on the fairness of the outcomes of a process or decision. One of the most important theories underpinning distributive justice is Adams' 'equity theory' (1965). Equity theory focuses the individual on social comparisons with similar employees. The individual assesses their effort and outcomes based upon their efforts or inputs (fairness) against other individual. Where there is a perceived disparity (either lower or higher), the employee will have a feeling of inequity (O'Donnell & Shields 2006). It is argued that the greater the perceived inequity, the greater the perceived discontent, and the greater is the motivation to achieve equity (Pratt & Bennett 1985). Thus, it is the perceived comparative reward rather than the absolute reward that determines satisfaction or dissatisfaction (Cropanzano & Randall 1993). The consequences of perceived inequity are reduced effort and commitment, and increased absenteeism and turnover.

Generally, Adams' equity theory is seen as a reasonable account of employees' responses to equity and inequity, with studies showing employees adjusting their behaviour and effort where the reward is perceived to be inequitable. For example, studies show that perceived status increase and decrease correlates with performance (Watson 1986; Greenberg

1988; Greenberg & Ornstein 1983). However, research on employees who are over-rewarded indicates that whilst improved performance can occur in response to the over-reward, employees are just as likely to rationalise this over-reward by inflating the perception of their performance through a 'self serving bias' and not increase their performance overall (Boxall & Purcell 2008; Kruger 1999). This appears, therefore, to support equity theory (Greenberg 1990). This is important, as distributive justice is very much focused on perceived fairness of outcomes, and potentially has major implications in an organisational context (Cohen-Charash & Spector 2001).

Interpersonal justice

Interpersonal justice refers to the social aspects of distributive justice and focuses on the consequences of the decision making (Crapanzano & Randall 1993). In practice, interpersonal justice reflects the way employees feel they have been treated in terms of respect and sensitivity to the issue or issues facing them, e.g. monitoring and surveillance. This is often seen as a reflection of the value an organisation puts on the individual (Greenberg & Baron 2006). This is also known as the group value explanation of organisational justice, where value and perceived importance to the organisation is interpreted from the effort made by the organisation to communicate decisions to the employees (Greenberg & Baron 2006).

Procedural justice

A key aspect of justice in organisations is the underlying system for determining decisions and outcomes, how they are made, whether they are fair and equitable, and if they are consistently enforced without prejudice or personal bias (Gilliland 1993). This is known as procedural justice. Procedural justice can mediate perceptions of distributive justice if the process has been seen to be fair and equitable (Cox 2000). This is particularly important where employees receive unfavourable decisions (Colquitt & Greenberg 2003). Increasingly in an era of declining trade union density and unitarist-based human resource management systems, the extent to which there is genuine employee voice is also an important factor is procedural justice as it ensures that employees have an opportunity to participate in and influence the decision-making process (Holland *et al.* 2011; Pyman *et al.* 2010; Boxall & Purcell 2008; Gilliland 1993). As Pearce, Bigley and Branyiczki (1998) note, studies focusing on the effects of voice in the workplace where it is perceived to be valued are positive in terms of fairness and equity. Importantly also in a period of increasing war for talent, procedural justice can be a way an employee evaluates the (on-going) relationship with management and with the organisation (Fischer & Smith 2004; Tyler & Lind 1992). Leventhal (1980) argues there are six rules which determine whether procedural justice has been followed. These are:

1. The consistency rule: Procedures should be consistent across all employees over time.

2. The bias-suppression rule: Self interest should be prevented from operating in decision-making processes.

3. The accuracy rule: The best quality information should always be used in decision-making.

4. The correctable rule: The system allows for the remedy of unfair decisions.

5. The representative rule: All stakeholders affected by a decision are represented.

6. The ethicality rule: Allocation of resources is undertaken in an ethical and moral way.

Interactional justice

To this point the concept of procedural justice has focused on the structural aspects of fairness. A further dimension to procedural justice is the social dimension. As Bies and Moag (1986) identified, individuals assess justice in organisations based on the quality of treatment and communication they receive throughout the process. This enacted characteristic of procedural justice has been termed 'interactional justice' (Crapanzano & Randall 1993). Specifically, interactional justice involves communicating information in a socially appropriate and respectful way (Tomlinson & Greenberg 2005; Colquitt 2001). Significant research into this aspect of justice across a range of organisational issues has identified several perspectives to interactional justice. These are truthfulness, respect, propriety and justification, and processes where an injustice may be rectified by an adequate justification (Crapanzano & Randall 1993). Research (Shapiro 1993; Bies 1987) indicates that an effective way of achieving this is by communicating to employees an account of the process and procedures undertaken in making a decision. This is what Cohen-Charash and Spector (2001) describe as the human side of organisational practices. Thus, a negative response to perceived interactional justice is more likely to focus on the individual supervisor rather than the organisation as would be the case with procedural justice (Crapanzano & Prehar 1999).

Contextual factors

Whilst the above framework clearly identifies the *content* of organisational justice, of equal important are the *contextual* elements, which include culture and organisational structures and how organisations manage status and power. As James (1993) notes, these issues have a very important and wide-ranging effect on justice behaviour and perceived injustice. Lewis, Thornhill and Sanders (2003) have noted the implications for justice on many aspects of human resources management. As noted, with the increasing complexity and speed of change in the workplace, it is important for organisations to have a solid foundation upon which policies, practices and processes are developed and reviewed in order to ensure that organisational justice is perceived by all stakeholders. Where decisions are made that will be unfavourable to stakeholders – i.e. employees – research indicates that where there is a sense of perceived fairness in the decision-making process, employees, whilst not necessarily agreeing with the outcomes, will more readily accept the decisions that are made. The alternative is a workforce that feels betrayal, and the repercussions that come from this including lower moral and commitment, and higher turnover, absenteeism and theft. As Cropanzano and Randall (1993) point out, from this applied perspective research in this area provides new approaches and recommendations for more effective human resource management.

Research on the issues of organisational justice has also identified the effects on the related aspect of employee voice (Folger 1977). Organisational justice and voice are linked by the scope of the subjects negotiated, the organisational decision-making approach to participation, and the perceived influence employee or their representatives have at arriving at a decision. Understanding this framework of justice can guide human resource managers in dealing with human resource issues as they develop in a way that, whilst possibly not perfect, will allow a sense that they are attempting to deal with the issues in a fair and equitable way with all stakeholder. It is clear that a culture of strong organisational justice can be critical to developing a workplace that is perceived by all stakeholders as a place where decision-making is undertaken in consideration of all and on a fair and equitable basis.

References

Adams, J 1965, 'Inequities in Social Exchange'. In L Berkowitz (eds) *Advances in Experimental Social Psychology.* 2. New York: Academic Press. pp. 267-299.

Bies, R 1987, "The Predicament of Injustice'. In L Cummings & B Shaw (eds). *Research in Organizational Behaviour.* Greenwich, CT: JAI Press. pp. 289-319.

Bies, R & Moag, J 1986, 'Interactional Justice: Communication Criteria of Fairness'. In R Lewecki, B Sheppard & M Bazerman (eds). *Research on Negotiation in Organizations.* 1. Greenwich, CT: JAI Press. pp. 43-55.

Boxall, P & Purcell, J 2008, *Strategy and Human Resource Management*, 2nd edn., Basingstoke. Palgrave Macmillan.

Burke, RJ 2008, 'Building More Effective Organisation's. In RJ Burke & CL Cooper eds, *Building More effective organisations.* Cambridge: Cambridge University Press.

Cohen-Charash, Y & Spector, P 2001, 'The Role of Justice in Organizations: A Meta-Analysis'. *Organisational Behaviour and Human Decision Process* 86(2): 278-321.

Colquitt, J 2001, 'On the Dimensionality of Organisational Justice: A Construct Validation Method'. *Journal of Applied Psychology.* 86: 386-400.

Colquitt, J & Greenberg, J 2003, 'Organisational Justice: A fair assessment of the state of the literature'. In J. Greenberg (eds) *Organizational Behaviour: The State of the Science.* 2nd edn, Mahwah: Erlbaum Associates.

Cox, A 2000, 'The Importance of Employee Participation in Determining Pay System Effectiveness'. *International Journal of Manpower Review.* 2(4): 357-375.

Cropanzano, R & Randall M 1993, 'Injustice and Work Behaviour'. In R Cropanzano, *Justice in the Workplace: Approaching a fairness in human resource management.* New Jersey: Lawrence Erlbaum Associates. pp. 3-20.

Cropanzano, R & Prehar C 1999, *Using Social Exchange Theory to Distinguish Procedural from Interactional Justice.* Paper Presented to the Annual Meeting of the Society for Industrial and Organizational Psychology. Atlanta.GA.

Fischer, R & Smith, P 2004, 'Values and Organizational Justice: Performance and Seniority-based allocation criteria in UK and Germany'. *Journal of Cross-Cultural Psychology.* 6: 669-688.

Folger, R 1977, 'Distributive and Procedural Justice: Combined Impact of Voice and Improvement on Experienced Inequity'. *Journal of Personality and Social Psychology.* 35: 108-119.

Gibson, A & Campbell-Quick, J 2008, 'Best Practice for Work Stress and Well-Being: Solutions for Human Dilemmas in Organisations'. In R. Burke & C. Cooper (eds) *Building More Effective Organizations.* Cambridge: Cambridge University Press. pp. 84-109.

Gilliland, S 1993, 'The Perceived Fairness of Selection Systems: An Organisational Justice Perspective'. *Academy of Management Review.* 18:" 694-734.

Greenberg, J & Omstein, S 1983, 'High Status Job Titles as Compensation for Underpayment. A Test of Equity Theory'. *Journal of Applied Psychology.* 68: 285-296.

Greenberg, J 1988, 'Equity and Workplace Status: A field experiment'. *Journal of Applied Psychology.* 73: pp .606-613.

Greenberg, J 1990, 'Organizational Justice'. *Journal of Management.* 16: 399-432.

Greenberg, J & Baron, S 2006, *Behavior in Organizations,* 9th edn, London: Prentice Hall.

Holland, P, Pyman, A, Teicher, J, & Cooper, B 2011, 'Industrial Relations Climate, Employee Voice and Managerial Attitudes to Unions. An Australian Study', *Human Resource Management.*

James, K 1993, 'The Social Context of Organizational Justice'. In R. Cropanzano *Justice in the Workplace: Approaching a fairness in human resource management.* New Jersey: Lawrence. pp. 21-50.

Kruger, J 1999, 'Lake Wobegon Be Gone! The 'Below Average Effect' and the Geocentric Effect of Comparative Ability Judgement'. *Journal of Personality and Social Psychology.* 27(2): 221-232.

Lawler, EE 2003, *Treating People Right,* San Francisco: Jossey –Bass.

Leventhal, G 1980, 'What Should be Done with Equity Theory?', In K Geergen, M Greenber. & R Willis (eds) *Social Exchange: Advances in Theory and Research*. New York: Plenum Press. pp. 27-55.

Lewis, J & Welgert, A 1985, *Trust as a Social Reality*. Social Forces, 63(4): 967-985.

Lewis, P, Thornhill, A & Sanders, M 2003, *Employee Relations: Understanding the Employment Relationship*. London: Prentice Hall.

Nicholls, T, Danford, A, Tasiran, A 2009, ,Trust, Employer Exposure and the Employment Relation'. *Economic and Industrial Democracy*. 30(2):241-265.

O'Donnell, M & Shields, J 2006, 'The New Pay: Performance Related Pay in Australia'. In J Teicher., P Holland & R Gough 2006, *Employment Relations in Australia*, 2nd edn, Pearson Education. Australia.

Pearce, J Bigley, G & Branyiczki, I 1998, 'Procedural Justice as Modernism: Placing Industrial and Organizational Psychology in Context'. *Applied Psychology*. 47: 371-396.

Pratt, K & Bennett, S 1985, *Elements of Personnel Management*. London:Von Nostrand `Reinhold.

Pyman, A, Holland, P, Teicher, J & Cooper, B 2010, 'Industrial Relations Climate, Employee Voice and Managerial Attitudes to Unions. An Australian Study', *British Journal of Industrial Relations*.

Shapiro, D 1993, 'Reconciling Theoretical Differences Among Procedural Justice Researchers'. In R Cropanzano, *Justice in the Workplace: Approaching a fairness in human resource management*. New Jersey: Lawrence Erlbaum Associates. pp. 50-78.

Schabracq, M & Cooper, C 2000, 'The Changing Nature of Work and Stress'. *Journal of Management Psychology*. 15: 227-241.

Schabracq, M & Cooper, C 2003, 'To be me or Not to be me: About Alienation'. *Journal of Counselling Psychology*. 16: 53-79.

Shaw WH & Barry, V 2004, *Moral Issues in Business*. Belmont CA: Thompson.

Sheahan, P 2005, *Generation Y: Thriving and Surviving with Generation Y at Work*. Melbourne: Hardie Grant Books.

Tomlinson, R & Greenberg, J 2005, 'Discouraging Theft by Managing Social Norms and Prioritizing Organizational Justice'. In R Kidwell & C Martin (eds) *Managing Organizational Deviance*. London: Sage Publications. pp. 200-221.

Tyler, T & Lind, E 1992, 'A Relational Model of Authority in Groups'. In M Zama (eds), *Advances in Experimental Social Psychology*. San Diego: Academic Process. pp. 101-120.

Watson, TJ 1986, *Management, Organisation and Employment Strategy: New Directions in Theory and Practice*. London: Routledge.

INDEX

A
AFL-CIO Institute, 206
attraction and retention, 24, 36

B
boundaryless careers, 125

C
career development
  traditional, 122
career management
  & HRM, 128
  boundaryless careers, 125
  cautionary issues, 127
  coaching, 130
  current perspectives, 125
  dual ladders, 131
  goals, 124
  integration of HRM, 134
  job change, 124
  job mobility, 127
  know-why, know-how, know-whom, 133
  lateral moves, 129
  mentoring, 131
  outplacements, 130
  performance management systems, 132
  protean careers, 125
  secondments, 129
  self-management, 133
  succession planning, 128
  the environment, 123
    casual labour, 124
    outsourcing, 124
    women in workforce, 123
  traditional, 125

D
drug testing, 238

E
ecommunication, 244
  monitoring software, 245
  privacy, 244
  surveillance, 245
eHRM, 71
  online recruitment, 72

Emotional Competency Inventory, 166
emotional dissonance, 162
  clear values and recruitment, 163
  coping strategies, 160
  core values, 163
  instrumental values, 162
  minimised, 163
  terminal values, 162
emotional labour
  coping strategies, 160
  defined, 157
  emotional dissonance, 158
  external conditions, 158
  external environment, 167
  internal conflict, 158
emotional quotient
  measuring, 166
Emotional Quotient Inventory, 166
e-unionism, 80
  benefits, 86
  challenges, 88, 89
  impacts, 87
  rationales, 83, 84, 85
  threats, 90
  uses, 81
  Web 2.0, 92

F
Fair Work Act 2009, 202

G
green skills
  definition, 286
  framework, 296
  Green electricians, 297
  historical, 288
  human capital, 293
  industry, 292
  NCS, 298
  policy, 290
  theory, 287
  Toyota Australia, 297
  Zoos Victoria, 297

H
health and well-being, 175
  definition, 175
  individual consequences, 179

individual predictors, 175
organisational consequences, 180
organisational predictors, 177
well-being interventions, 181
hotdesking, 3
hotelling, 3
hotracking, 3
HRD, 24, 28
human capital theory, 24

J
justice
context, 305
distributive justice, 303
interactional justice, 305
interpersonal justice, 304
organisational justice, 303
procedural justice, 304
theory, 302

K
Karpin Report, 29

L
Likert scale, 113

M
monitoring
and control, 246
Australian workplace survey, 248
emerging issues
genetic testing, 253
RFID, 252
Federal Privacy Commission, 249
guidelines, 250
policies, 249
monitoring employees, 245
MSCEIT, 167

N
near-shoring, 61

O
offshoring, 49
backlash, 58
benefits, 52
constraint, 59
costs, 53
hidden costs, 55
history, 50
IP issues, 56
management attitudes, 54
maturity, 54
security & legal, 55
online recruitment
benefits, 73
Online recruitment
costs, 73
pitfalls, 74, 76
onshoring, 61
Organising Works, 208
outsourcing, 50

P
protean careers, 125, 126
psychological contracts
and formal socialisation, 111
and HRM policies, 110
and job previews, 111
and organisational support, 112
and work status, 108
beliefs, 101
breached, 104
changes over time, 101
conceptually, 100
conscious loyalty, 114
employees' perceptions, 104
employees' perspective, 111
fulfilment, 107
line managers, 113
monitoring, 111
need, 101
paternalistic role, 102
performance management process, 112
relational, 102
rewards system, 113
terminations, 113
transactional, 103
types, 102
violation, 106

R
RBV, 24
risk
approaches, 266
crisis management, 269
crisis management team, 273
cultural theory, 267
economic approach, 267
event managers, 272
managing risk, 264
OH&S, 266
pandemics, 276
psychometric approach, 268
risk management process, 264
technical approach, 266
terrorism, 274

Index

S
service work
    agency workers, 147
    and stress, 148
    and violence, 150
    attributes, 143
    call centres, 150
    casual, 145
    challenges, 145
    emotional proletariat, 144
    flexibility, 145
    HRM practices, 147
    service organisations, 144
    trends, 142
    UN overview, 143
Social networking and HRM, 77
substance abuse, 238
    and culture, 240
    and performance, 239
    and privacy, 239
    fitness for duty, 243
    union view, 241
surveillance, 245

T
talent management, 25
teleworking, 1
    advantages, 3
    disadvantages, 6
    evidence, 2
    HRM implications, 9
    modes, 3
    personality traits, 7
    virtual teams, 10
TGA program, 29
trade union
    community unionism, 218
    corporate campaigning, 213
    creative compliance, 217
    decline, 196
        causes, 197
        climate, 198
        Howard govn, 200
        post 1990, 199
    future strategies, 211
    organising centre, 206
    organising model, 206, 208
    organising unionism, 211
    Organising Works, 206, 208
    outsourcing recruitment, 221
    renewal, 201
    strategies
        amalgamations, 205
        mergers, 205
        restructuring, 205
    Unions@Work, 208
trade unions
    & ICT, 81
training and development, 34

U
Unions@Work, 208

V
values and ethics, 31
virtual teams, 10
    advantages, 11
    disadvantages, 12
    HRM implications, 14

W
Work Choices, 200, 220
work/life balance, 35